Lecture Notes in Computer Science 15461

Founding Editors

Gerhard Goos
Juris Hartmanis

Editorial Board Members

Elisa Bertino, *Purdue University, West Lafayette, IN, USA*
Wen Gao, *Peking University, Beijing, China*
Bernhard Steffen, *TU Dortmund University, Dortmund, Germany*
Moti Yung, *Columbia University, New York, NY, USA*

The series Lecture Notes in Computer Science (LNCS), including its subseries Lecture Notes in Artificial Intelligence (LNAI) and Lecture Notes in Bioinformatics (LNBI), has established itself as a medium for the publication of new developments in computer science and information technology research, teaching, and education.

LNCS enjoys close cooperation with the computer science R & D community, the series counts many renowned academics among its volume editors and paper authors, and collaborates with prestigious societies. Its mission is to serve this international community by providing an invaluable service, mainly focused on the publication of conference and workshop proceedings and postproceedings. LNCS commenced publication in 1973.

Weitao Song · Frank Guan · Shuai Li ·
Guofeng Zhang

Editors

Extended Reality

First International Conference, ICXR 2024
Xiamen, China, November 14–17, 2024
Proceedings

 Springer

Editors
Weitao Song (ID)
Beijing Institute of Technology
Beijing, China

Frank Guan (ID)
Singapore Institute of Technology
Singapore, Singapore

Shuai Li (ID)
Beihang University
Beijing, China

Guofeng Zhang (ID)
Zhejiang University
Hangzhou, China

ISSN 0302-9743 ISSN 1611-3349 (electronic)
Lecture Notes in Computer Science
ISBN 978-981-96-3678-5 ISBN 978-981-96-3679-2 (eBook)
https://doi.org/10.1007/978-981-96-3679-2

© The Editor(s) (if applicable) and The Author(s), under exclusive license
to Springer Nature Singapore Pte Ltd. 2025

This work is subject to copyright. All rights are solely and exclusively licensed by the Publisher, whether
the whole or part of the material is concerned, specifically the rights of translation, reprinting, reuse of
illustrations, recitation, broadcasting, reproduction on microfilms or in any other physical way, and transmission
or information storage and retrieval, electronic adaptation, computer software, or by similar or dissimilar
methodology now known or hereafter developed.
The use of general descriptive names, registered names, trademarks, service marks, etc. in this publication
does not imply, even in the absence of a specific statement, that such names are exempt from the relevant
protective laws and regulations and therefore free for general use.
The publisher, the authors and the editors are safe to assume that the advice and information in this book
are believed to be true and accurate at the date of publication. Neither the publisher nor the authors or the
editors give a warranty, expressed or implied, with respect to the material contained herein or for any errors
or omissions that may have been made. The publisher remains neutral with regard to jurisdictional claims in
published maps and institutional affiliations.

This Springer imprint is published by the registered company Springer Nature Singapore Pte Ltd.
The registered company address is: 152 Beach Road, #21-01/04 Gateway East, Singapore 189721, Singapore

If disposing of this product, please recycle the paper.

Preface

In recent years, Extended Reality (XR) technology has advanced rapidly, becoming a key focus in the tech world. From immersive Virtual Reality (VR) in gaming, education, and training to Augmented Reality (AR) enhancing navigation, shopping, and remote collaboration, and Mixed Reality (MR) blending the virtual and real, XR is transforming how we perceive and interact with the world. Beyond driving enthusiasm in consumer entertainment, XR is revolutionizing industries and shaping a future of boundless potential.

The International Conference on Extended Reality (ICXR) 2024 was held from November 14 to 17 in the beautiful city of Xiamen, Fujian Province, China, and was co-located with China VR 2024. This event brought together leading experts, researchers, and practitioners in the field of XR to share and discuss the latest advancements and trends, providing an important platform for industry exchanges, knowledge sharing, and collaborations.

The peer-review process for ICXR 2024 was meticulously designed to ensure both high quality and objectivity. The conference employed a double-blind review process, wherein a total of 38 program committee (PC) members evaluated the submissions and potential conflicts of interest were diligently managed to maintain impartiality throughout the review process. In total, ICXR 2024 received 48 full paper submissions and acceptance decisions were based solely on scientific merit, originality, technical soundness, and alignment with the conference's themes. Following a rigorous and thorough review process, 21 papers were accepted for presentation, resulting in an acceptance rate of 43.75%.

The review process was conducted in a timely and transparent manner, with clear communication channels established between the editorial team, reviewers, and authors to address questions or concerns. This rigorous approach ensured that the accepted papers represented the most innovative and impactful contributions to the XR field, setting a high standard for ICXR 2024.

Looking ahead, we have high expectations for XR technology. With the continuous evolution of hardware devices, XR will bring more realistic and seamless immersive experiences to users. In terms of software and content creation, more diverse, personalized, and in-depth application scenarios will surely emerge. We expect to see XR achieve more interactive and effective teaching model transformations in the education field, help make breakthroughs in remote diagnosis and treatment technologies in the healthcare industry, promote the in-depth integration of virtual design and actual production in the industrial manufacturing field, and create unprecedented immersive experience forms in the cultural and artistic fields. We believe that through the exchanges and collaborations at this conference, XR technology will reach new heights and have a more profound impact on the development of human society.

December 2024

Weitao Song
Frank Guan
Shuai Li
Guofeng Zhang

Organization

General Chairs

Yongtian Wang   Beijing Institute of Technology, China
Henry Duh   Hong Kong Polytechnic University, China
Junfeng Yao   Xiamen University, China

Program Committee Chairs

Frank Guan   Singapore Institute of Technology, Singapore
Guofeng Zhang   Zhejiang University, China
Shuai Li   Beihang University, China
Weitao Song   Beijing Institute of Technology, China

Steering Committee

Qinping Zhao   Beihang University, China
Christian Sandor   Université Paris-Saclay, France

Local Organization Chair

Shihui Guo   Xiamen University, China

Publication Chair

Junjun Pan   Beihang University, China

Publicity Chair

Lin Lu   Shandong University, China

Contents

Motion Generation Review: Exploring Deep Learning for Lifelike Animation with Manifold

Jiayi Zhao[1]([✉])(iD), Dongdong Weng[1,2]([✉])(iD), Qiuxin Du[1](iD), and Zeyu Tian[1]

[1] Beijing Engineering Research Center of Mixed Reality and Advanced Display, School of Optics and Photonics, Beijing Institute of Technology, Beijing, China
3120230529@bit.edu.cn

[2] Zhengzhou Academy of Intelligent Technology, Beijing Institute of Technology, Beijing, China
crgj@bit.edu.cn

Abstract. Human motion generation involves creating natural sequences of human body poses, widely used in gaming, virtual reality, and human-computer interaction. It aims to produce lifelike virtual characters with realistic movements, enhancing virtual agents and immersive experiences. While previous work has focused on motion generation based on signals like movement, music, text, or scene background, the complexity of human motion and its relationships with these signals often results in unsatisfactory outputs. Manifold learning offers a solution by reducing data dimensionality and capturing subspaces of effective motion. In this review, we present a comprehensive overview of manifold applications in human motion generation—one of the first in this domain. We explore methods for extracting manifolds from unstructured data, their application in motion generation, and discuss their advantages and future directions. This survey aims to provide a broad perspective on the field and stimulate new approaches to ongoing challenges.

Keywords: Manifolds · Motion Generation · Virtual Human Motion · Literature Survey

1 Introduction

With the progression of computer technology, an increasing number of applications and media, such as virtual reality (VR), gaming, and film, are utilizing highly detailed digital human and animal characters. Films like "Avatar," "The Avengers," "The Lord of the Rings," and "Alita: Battle Angel," alongside the booming gaming industry, have showcased the potential of digital characters engaging in complex, lifelike motions. These interactive experiences have elevated the demand for generating high-fidelity and realistic virtual characters, crucial for immersive environments and interactive simulations.In particular, VR environments rely heavily on the seamless integration of virtual characters whose

© The Author(s), under exclusive license to Springer Nature Singapore Pte Ltd. 2025
W. Song et al. (Eds.): ICXR 2024, LNCS 15461, pp. 1–17, 2025.
https://doi.org/10.1007/978-981-96-3679-2_1

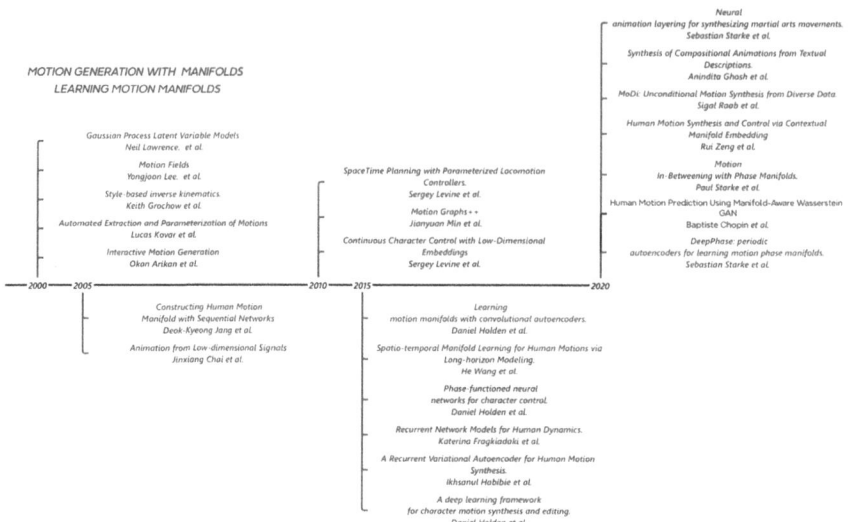

Fig. 1. The typical concept of learning manifold from motion and motion generating with manifold has been proposed in the recent twenty years.

motions mimic the fluidity and naturalness of real-world movements. This not only enhances the immersion but also elevates user interaction in these virtual worlds. Traditionally, Motion Capture (MOCAP) has been the dominant method for producing high-quality motion sequences. [41,77] However, MOCAP technologies are expensive and require specialized equipment, and they are restricted to capturing existing motions, offering limited flexibility when creating new or adaptive movements in real-time environments such as VR or interactive simulations. [9,46] In contrast, data-driven motion generation has gained momentum due to its flexibility, scalability, and reduced need for extensive motion capture setups. Unlike MOCAP, data-driven methods allow for generating novel and diverse movements with minimal input data, making them particularly suitable for real-time applications in immersive technologies like VR, where adaptability and automation are paramount. This method also integrates smoothly with traditional keyframe animation, making it a go-to solution in both film production and gaming environments.

Various techniques have been developed for data-driven motion generation, including Generative Adversarial Networks (GANs) [11], Variational Autoencoders (VAEs) [29], Motion Graphs [3,31,35], Reinforcement Learning [61], and Diffusion Models [16]. Each of these techniques brings unique advantages. For example, GANs [11] enable the generation of realistic and reasonable motions by using adversarial processes between a generator and a discriminator, such as PGGAN [26], Style-GAN [27,28], Manifold-Aware Wasserstein GAN [6], while VAEs [29] effectively represent motion data by encoding it into lower-dimensional spaces, facilitating easier manipulation of the motion output [56,66]. Reinforce-

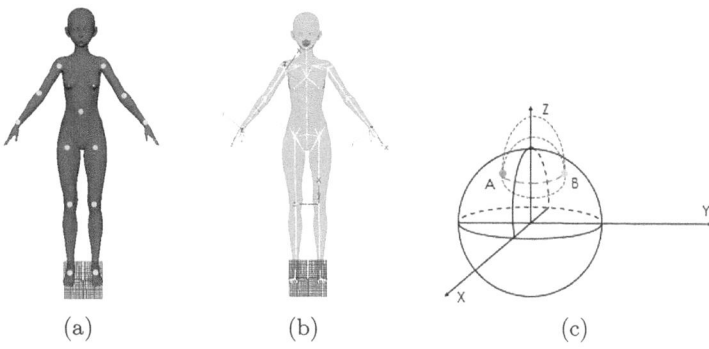

(a)　　　　　　　　(b)　　　　　　　　(c)

Fig. 2. Typical human pose and shape representations in (a) keypoint-based and (b) rotation-based (c) Find a valid motion in the entire motion space. A point and B point represent two statuses, there are many different motions between A and B like green lines, only the motion on the surface is valid like the red line. (Color figure online)

ment learning models such as DeepMimic, AMP [50], ASE [49], CALM [63], generate physically accurate and controllable motions, which are essential for VR interactions, where user immersion depends on the believability of the character's responses. Additionally, diffusion models [57], increasingly prominent in generative fields like image and audio synthesis, have recently been applied to motion generation [22,55,64,71,72], offering a novel approach to generating natural human motions for immersive environments. Previous research has focused on generating human motion based on fundamental conditional signals such as motion [7,43,51,69], music [33,39,62], text [1,2,25,52], video [75], and the scene backgrounds [15,22,73].

Many studies use unstructured motion data from Motion Capture (MOCAP) for generating motion sequences, representing digital character poses. Common databases include CMU [17], Human3.6 [23], NTU RGB+D [40], and HumanML3D [13], with data typically represented by joint angles and positions. However, challenges remain. First, validating the realism of generated motions is difficult due to the abstract and complex nature of motion sequences. Ensuring motions are realistic and executable by humans or quadrupeds is especially challenging for VR and immersive applications. Second, many methods require extensive manual pre-processing like segmentation, alignment, and labeling, where errors can lead to animation failures. This complicates full automation and often demands technical expertise.

Learning a manifold from MOCAP data and performing motion generation in this subspace can facilitate the discrimination between effective and ineffective motions, leading to enhanced automation. This is because this manifold is learning from the motion capture actor, which means constructing a valid motion subspace within the entire motion space. At the same time, this process is a kind of data dimensionality reduction that can reduce the required computing power. In immersive environments such as VR, where real-time performance is critical, reducing computational costs while maintaining motion quality is a significant advantage. Therefore, If we find good techniques for learning manifolds, it's easy for valid motion generating, interpolating, etc.

In this research review, we introduced the manifold in motion generation. And summarized methods for obtaining motion manifolds and the application of manifolds in motion generation, as shown in Fig. 1.

2   Preliminaries

2.1   Motion Data Representation

Motion data representations are generally categorized as keypoint-based or rotation-based [76], and they can be converted between forms. Keypoint-based data represent the human body using specific kinematic points (e.g., joints) in 2D or 3D space, as shown in Fig. 2(a). This data can be easily obtained from motion capture systems but is less suitable for animation or robotics due to difficulty in capturing relationships between keypoints. Each frame of a motion sequence records the position of these keypoints. Rotation-based data represent the human body through joint rotation angles in a hierarchical structure, as shown in Fig. 2(b). Formats for these angles include quaternions, euler angles, rotation vectors, and RT matrices. Certainly, there are other representations of human body posture [44, 74].

The Skinned Multi-Person Linear (SMPL) model [42] is a popular parametric 3D human model used in pose estimation, motion capture, and virtual character modeling. It uses Linear Blend Skinning (LBS) to realistically depict various poses and body shapes. Extensions of SMPL include SMPL-X [48], GHUM [68], and STAR [47].

2.2   Manifolds

Motion manifold is a new representation of animation data. In this section we introduce the definition of motion manifolds, the reason they can be used in the motion of digital humans and a kind of motion manifold like phase Manifold.

Motion Manifold. Strictly, manifold is a concept in mathematics and computer science that refers to a space that locally resembles Euclidean space. [4, 34] Manifold has a local space that is homomorphic to Euclidean space. The meaning of it is the local space has characteristics of Euclidean space that is the distance in this local space equivalent to Euclidean distance [65].

Motion manifold is a low-dimensional geometric structure used to represent and analyze motion data. [4] By embedding motion samples into a continuous manifold, it captures the intrinsic features and variations of motion. Each point on the manifold corresponds to a specific pose or motion state, and the geometric properties of the manifold make interpolation and generation between different poses feasible. Therefore, by performing interpolation or other operations on this manifold, new and smooth motion trajectories can be generated.

Compared to traditional motion sequences, the motion manifold is generally considered low-dimensional. Traditional motion sequences may contain a large amount of redundant data, while the motion manifold focuses on capturing the essential features of motion, eliminating unnecessary details and thus reducing dimensionality. Motion data often exhibits inherent geometric structures. Manifold learning can effectively identify and represent this structure, enabling motion state variations to be expressed in fewer dimensions.In summary, the motion manifold removes redundancies and emphasizes key features, allowing high-dimensional motion data to be efficiently represented as a low-dimensional manifold, thereby enhancing the efficiency of processing and generating motions. Thus, it provides us with a dimensionality reduction method. [18]

Animation data is typically represented as a time series of joint angles and positions, where each frame consists of high-dimensional vectors means the character's pose. This representation is suitable for data processing and computing. However, using this representation to compute may obtain unnatural results like the large differences between frames to make joints move too fast or unreasonable joint angles or positions resulting in physically impossible motion. Because all bones of the body are highly correlated in a motion, which should satisfy the constraint of bone lengths and joint rotations.

In space of motion, define the motion manifold as a subspace of valid motion. [18] It is of great interest for researchers to find motion manifolds in the whole space. In this subspace, it is very convenient to find a reasonable motion between two statuses. If we consider the entire three-dimensional space as motion space. Motion manifold is the surface of the ball in the space, as shown in Fig. 2(c). On the ball, A point and B point represent two digital human statuses. There are many different motions between A and B. Only the motion on the surface is valid. Other ways are not reasonable motions. Therefore, the motion manifold is a kind of dimensionality reduction, it describes the valid motion in whole space. It can provide more natural and smooth motion. At the same time, it still allows to reproduce complex movements of the human body.

Motion Phase Manifold. The motion manifold does not have a fixed data structure. [34] Motion phase manifold is a type of motion manifold. [20] About the data-driven method, MOCAP data of a single type of locomotion are dense, while transitions between different types of motions are very sparse. Thus, it causes a problem, which is modeling or learning the transitions between different motions is difficult, which requires attention to the phase of motion, and finding relationships of different types of motions in phase space. The phase manifold describes the manifold of the motion phase like fight, the position of the hands and legs change over time, and this alteration is the phase, like Fig. 2(b). Phase manifold refers to the manifold that describes alterations of phase. The features in the phase manifold describe the frame timing of the motion. It is great for aligning motions within the same category or between motions of different categories, whose meaning is the phase manifold can be an effective input feature for motion synthesis or motion matching. In the article of Holden. [20] delimit phase manifold can be computed by each frame of the motion sequence.

$$P_{2i-1}^{(t)} = A_i^{(t)} * \sin(2\pi * S_i^{(t)}), \tag{1}$$

$$P_{2i}^{(t)} = A_i^{(t)} * \cos(2\pi * S_i^{(t)}), \tag{2}$$

$$(s_x, s_y) = FC(L_i), S_i = atan2(s_x, s_y), \tag{3}$$

$$S_i = atan2(s_x, s_y), \tag{4}$$

where A is amplitude, F is frequency, B is offset, S is phase shift and $S \in R^M$. They are the periodic parameters. FC is a fully-connected layer. The phase features of phase should cluster the animations in both space and time, like Eq. 1–4. Features such as frequency and amplitude remain near-constant over time and do not help well for alignment purposes. After modeling the transition between motion and phase, which helps us to get smooth and coherent conversion between different motions. Thereby, we can obtain copious motions.

3   Learning Motion Manifolds

Manifold is a general term for general geometric objects, including curves and surfaces of various dimensions. Manifold learning is a type of dimensionality reduction method that re-represents a set of data in a high-dimensional space in a low-dimensional space. In motion, the motion manifold generalizes a high-dimensional vector to describe poses of character.

Generally, the original motion data we can get is from MOCAP. Thus, generating motion manifolds from human motion data is a great interest in machine learning and computer graphics. Firstly, use the principal component analysis (PCA) to get motion manifold from the original motion data. PCA is effective in modeling the manifold of human gait. Chai. [5] uses local PCA to obtain motion manifolds of various types of human motion data, which is used for motion synthesis. Lawrence. [32] introduces a new underlying probabilistic model for PCA, which is a particular Gaussian process before a mapping from a latent space to the observed data-space (GPLVM). And Grochow. [12] use GPLVM for motion synthesis. However, PCA often has a certain degree of ambiguity and is not as complete as the original data. In another way, Lee. [36] proposed a data structure that is motion fields. In this data structure, the user can effectively and interactively control the characters by using motion manifold. Although these methods can get manifold, they need a lot of pre-processing, including computing the distance of each frame. However, the shortcoming of these methods is only encode the temporal aspect of motion. They do not use deep learning that is unable to obtain manifolds for large amounts of data. Moreover, they exhibit poor robustness to different types of motions.

With the advancement of computing power and deep learning, more methods now leverage deep learning techniques. Holden et al. [21] proposed using Convolutional Autoencoders to learn a manifold of human motion data from time-series inputs. This method, which uses a three-layer convolutional autoencoder, is simple yet effective. Once the motion manifold is obtained, it can be applied to tasks such as fixing corrupt data, filling missing data, motion in-betweening, and comparison. It offers better scalability and handles large datasets more effectively than traditional methods, outperforming PCA-like techniques in nonlinear tasks.

Jang et al. [24] proposed a recurrent neural network-based method to construct a motion manifold capable of representing long sequences of diverse human motions. They introduced new regularization terms for the manifold and used two complementary decoders to predict joint rotations and velocities. A forward kinematics layer was added to account for both joint rotation and position errors. Their method uses an end-to-end unsupervised approach, minimizing the difference between the ground truth and reconstructed motion space distributions. The network consists of an RNN-based encoder with Gated Recurrent Units (GRU), a regularizer to align the encoded motion distribution with a prior distribution, and two decoders to map the latent space to joint angles and velocities.

Unlike images, human motion is represented on a graph structure, and the lack of spatial feature extraction can lead to convergence to a "mean posture," where spatial variation in movement disappears. Temporally, motion exhibits multi-modality and dynamic variations-different motions can share prefixes or endings, and identical postures may vary in timing. To address this, Wang et al. [67] proposed the Spatio-temporal Recurrent Neural Network (STRNN), which models both spatial and temporal variances to avoid generating "mean postures." STRNN comprises three sub-networks: a spatial network for hierarchical modeling of body parts, a temporal network for learning dependencies in long motion sequences, and a residual network to filter out high-frequency noise.

For phase manifold, Starke. [59] proposed a novel neural network architecture for character motion synthesis called the Periodic Autoencoder, which can learn periodic features from large unstructured motion datasets like phase. This method extracts multi-dimensional phases from whole body data, which validly clusters all kinds of motion animations and produces a phase manifold of them. In this measure, use convolutional autoencoders to transform the motion space into a phase manifold, whose structure is similar to Holden. [21] The periodic parameters for unstructured motion data can be computed for each frame by shifting the periodic autoencoder along the motion curves, like Eq. 1–2. After computing the phase manifold, it can be used to do many things like motion control, motion matching, stylistic movements, dance motion synthesis, etc.

4   Manifolds in Motion Generation

4.1   Motion Synthesis

Motion synthesis is a task using current MOCAP data to produce a series of new motions like blending motion of the same class to create new motion. For data-driven character motion synthesis, there are two ways to achieve, physical-based and data-based. Generally, approaches to motion synthesis are kernel-based methods, which synthesize motions via blending MOCAP data, and interactive character control, where user instructions to synthesize motions using a motion database and deep learning.

Kernel-based methods, Radial basis functions (RBF) is effective for blending motions of the same class. Rose. [54] defines motions of the same class as 'verbs' and applies RBF to motion interpolation based on the direction the character moves toward. To automate motion synthesis, Kovar. [30] computes the similarity of the movements and aligns them via dynamic time warping. But, RBF is dependent on data, if noise and variance of data are too many, it easily overfits the data. Therefore, Grochow. [12] uses GPLVM to map the motion to low-dimensional space to intuitively control the characters. Levine. [38]apply reinforcement learning to compute the optimal motion in the low-dimensional space, dimensionality reduced by GPLVM. Moreover, Kernel-based methods suffer from large memory costs, which cause motion can be blended is limited.

Interactive character control, a mechanism is applied to produce a series of consecutive motions via user-provided high-level commands. Motion graph [45] is an effective data structure for this purpose. Owing to Motion graphs are automatically computed from a large MOCAP data and only replay the MOCAP data. Arikan. [3] propose a technique to blend motion data of the same class to enrich the dataset. For automating this process and finding optimum motion, reinforcement learning is applied to motion synthesis. [37] However, reinforcement learning needs an amount of pre-computation, which will Increase exponentially with the number of characters. Thus, reinforcement learning requires a method to reduce the number of states and data dimensionality.

Deep learning methods, a technology that obtains consecutive and reasonable motions via applying deep neural networks to Learn unstructured motion data to produce new motion. Holden. [21] apply a convolutional autoencoder to the CMU MOCAP database and show the learned representation achieves good performance. Baptiste Chopin [6] employed a concise manifold-valued representation of human motion to address both the predicted motion's discontinuity and the performance decline over extended time horizons.

Most previous data-driven methods require extensive manual preprocessing, such as aligning, separating, and labeling motion data. Mistakes in preprocessing can lead to unreasonable results, making full automation challenging. To address this, Holden et al. [20] introduced a framework for synthesizing character movements based on high-level parameters instead of low-level details. This approach employs a convolutional autoencoder to learn the mapping between motion and the manifold represented by the network's hidden units, similar to Holden et al. [21]. High-level parameters, such as the root trajectory projected onto terrain or the end effector trajectories of hands and feet, are used as inputs. A feedforward network maps these parameters to the motion manifold, integrating current motion manifolds to create new ones. To ensure controllability, generated motions can be edited through optimization within the motion manifold space using an editing network, which maintains the naturalness and smoothness of the motion.

Previous approaches, apply one-dimensional convolutions along the timeline [20] or rely on Recurrent Neural Networks (RNN) to implement time series models with feedback structures. [8] However, these methods are difficult to predict frames of motion more than a little bit in the future, resulting in converging to a static pose. Therefore, Habibie. [14] proposes a novel approach to motion synthesis, which can accept user-provided control signals and encode the signals into a variational inference framework that learns the manifold of human motion. To predict the far future of the motion, they combine variational inference, the consideration of a control signal and several deep learning modules to produce high-quality long-term motion, which is VAE-LSTM architecture. This system is composed of an encoder and an autoregressive decoder. For the encoding, they encode the control signals and joint positions as manifolds, processing in manifolds.

To synthesize digital human motion from a given data distribution is a challenging task, especially when the dataset is highly diverse, unstructured, and unlabeled. And related works need priori conditions like root trajectory, trajectories of the end effectors [20], or focus on synthesizing specific types of motion with limited diversity [19]. Raab. [53] presents MoDi, an unconditional generative model that synthesizes diverse motions. The core of this method is a deep generative model trained in an unsupervised manner on an extremely diverse, unstructured and unlabeled motion dataset. Because many tasks in the motion domain are ill-posed. To be suitable for different tasks, present an encoder that inverts real motions into MoDi's natural motion manifold.

In addition to using the network to map the motion into the manifold, there is another way that is embedding the Gaussian Process Latent Variable Model(GPLVM) in deep learning framework to precisely model motion dynamics and rapid control [70]. Their model is encoder-decoder form. Their workflow is in two stages. Firstly, apply GPLVM to project motion poses to manifold, where motion states could be clearly recognized. Secondly, the Recurrent Neural Network (RNN) encoder makes temporal latent prediction via the manifold of previous motion and control states. An attention module is used to morph the prediction by calculating similarities between the control states and predicted states. In the end, the GP decoder reconstructs motion states back to motion frames. In this way, no need to train the encoder on the manifold in advance. GPLVM is a nonlinear, nonparametric probabilistic model that can better handle the randomness and uncertainty of motion.

Manifolds not only apply to ordinary motion blends but also used to achieve text-to-motion. Ghosh. [10] presents a new technique, a hierarchical two-stream model, for generating compositional motions, which can handle complex sentences as the input. The input sentence can not only describe a simple action but also can describe a human performing multiple actions either sequentially or simultaneously, like "a person is stretching his arms, taking them down, walking forwards for four steps and raising them again". the hierarchical two-stream model consists of a pose encoder, sentence encoder and pose decoder. The workflow is three steps. Firstly, use the pose encoder to hierarchical model motion, get features based on five major parts of the body and combine those features hierarchically. Secondly, use sentence encoder to represent the text, apply BERT as a contextualized language model, and at the same time apply Long-Short Term Memory units (LSTM) to capture the long-range dependencies of complex sentences. Besides, the motion modeled by the pose encoder and described by input text will map into manifold after processing. Finally, the pose decoder constructs the output motion and calculates loss to train the network.

In motion synthesis, traditional methods often rely on rule-driven or model-based algorithms, which, while capable of generating reasonable motions in specific scenarios, struggle to capture complex patterns in high-dimensional spaces. In contrast, motion manifolds embed high-dimensional motion data into a low-dimensional representation, better capturing the underlying structure and generating more natural, realistic movements. This data-driven approach ensures that generated motions maintain temporal and spatial continuity while preserving the characteristics of the original motion. Additionally, motion manifolds effectively mitigate artifacts resulting from insufficient motion modeling in traditional methods. However, their effectiveness depends heavily on the quality and diversity of the training data; insufficient or narrowly focused training data can significantly compromise the quality of the generated motions.

4.2 Motion Controller

Motion controller is a real-time data-driven controller for virtual characters that can allow humans via this real-time control of the movement of digital characters. They must be capable of learning from vast amounts of data, should not require extensive manual data pre-processing, and must execute extremely quickly at runtime with low memory requirements. The gap between changes in state and natural randomness becomes challenging to eliminate ambiguity. With the continuous development of deep learning and neural network technologies, there are more and more effective approaches.

Holden et al. [19] introduced a real-time character control mechanism using a Phase-Functioned Neural Network that learns motion capture data while considering environmental factors. This architecture allows characters to perform actions like walking, running, jumping, and climbing based on environmental conditions. The system comprises a prediction network that forecasts motions and a phase function that computes network weights each frame. The phase function predicts the next motion type using input parameters and motion data, applying cubic Catmull-Rom splines to assist in action prediction within a manifold space.

A key challenge in computer animation is the interactive synthesis of novel character actions. Starke et al. [60] proposed a deep learning framework to produce a wide variety of controllable movements from raw motion capture data. The framework consists of three modules: a motion generator, control modules, and a control interface. The motion generator learns the entire motion manifold from unstructured data using an expert-blended network. Control modules create future motion trajectories for various active behaviors, which are then processed through addition, overlay, or blending operations in the control interface before being used to generate novel full-body poses. These control modules can take various forms, including neural networks, physics-based simulations, and user-driven tools, allowing for flexible editing of trajectories. This deep learning framework is adaptable and requires minimal training data.

In motion controllers, motion manifolds improve efficiency and naturalness by simplifying the control of complex motions. Traditional controllers, often rule-based or physics-driven, struggle with flexibility and produce unnatural discontinuities. By mapping high-dimensional motion states into a low-dimensional space, motion manifolds allow for more efficient path planning and smoother transitions. They also enable controllers to handle diverse movements more flexibly. However, controlling within the manifold requires a higher learning demand, as the controller must adapt to the low-dimensional space. Additionally, since the manifold is constructed from existing data, it may struggle with new or unseen motion states, leading to poor performance in extreme or novel cases.

4.3   Motion In-betweening

Motion in-betweening uses computer algorithms to generate intermediate frames between keyframes, ensuring smooth transitions in animation. When keyframes have inconsistent durations, systems often rely on linear interpolation, which can produce unrealistic, overly smooth motion. Starke et al. [58] proposed a novel motion in-betweening framework that learns from a motion capture database using a phase manifold. The system includes a gating network that blends phase segments from a periodic autoencoder and a motion prediction network that takes the current pose, trajectory, contact, and control variables to predict the next frame.

Traditional linear interpolation methods can handle transitions but often result in unnatural artifacts, especially with complex motions. The motion manifold, by operating in a low-dimensional space, enables smoother and more natural transitions while preserving motion consistency and reducing artifacts. However, its effectiveness depends on the quality of training data. For complex or extreme motions not represented in the dataset, the manifold may fail to capture necessary patterns, leading to suboptimal interpolation results.

5   Conclusion and Future Work

Manifolds are widely used in synthesis, control, and motion in-betweening, offering superior performance in generating natural and smooth movements by encapsulating valid human motions. Compared to other methods, manifolds also reduce computational complexity. However, they struggle with interactions involving the environment and other elements because interactive features are not effectively mapped to the motion manifold. Existing methods [20] handle simple tasks like walking, jumping, and running but fail in complex environments with interactions, such as between multiple characters or with objects. This limitation arises because the interactive dynamics are not incorporated into the manifold, which affects motion generation in more challenging scenes, such as dancing, obstacle navigation, or object manipulation.

In future work, I believe the direction is about how to effectively encode external influencing factors into the manifold space, aiding in the discovery of movements that meet specified requirements. For instance, in text-to-motion scenarios, the challenge lies in encoding the objective constraints described in the text into the manifold. In the case of scene-to-motion scenarios, it involves encoding the objective constraints of the scene into the manifold. In complex interactive environments, the focus is on encoding the motion of other entities and objects into the manifold, ensuring effective influence on the predicted actions and thereby meeting diverse requirements.

Acknowledgement. This work was supported by the Strategic research and consulting project of Chinese Academy of Engineering (Grant No. 2023-HY-14).

References

1. Ahn, H., Ha, T., Choi, Y., Yoo, H., Oh, S.: Text2Action: Generative Adversarial Synthesis from Language to Action (2017). http://arxiv.org/abs/1710.05298. arXiv:1710.05298
2. Ahuja, C., Morency, L.P.: Language2Pose: Natural Language Grounded Pose Forecasting (2019). http://arxiv.org/abs/1907.01108. arXiv:1907.01108
3. Arikan, O., Forsyth, D.A.: Interactive motion generation from examples. ACM Trans. Graph. **21**(3), 483–490 (2002). https://doi.org/10.1145/566654.566606
4. Bishop, R.L., Crittenden, R.J.: Geometry of Manifolds: Geometry of Manifolds. Academic Press (2011)
5. Chai, J., Hodgins, J.K.: Performance animation from low-dimensional control signals. ACM Trans. Graph. **24**(3), 686–696 (2005). https://doi.org/10.1145/1073204.1073248
6. Chopin, B., Otberdout, N., Daoudi, M., Bartolo, A.: Human Motion Prediction Using Manifold-Aware Wasserstein GAN (2021). http://arxiv.org/abs/2105.08715. arXiv:2105.08715
7. Degardin, B., Neves, J., Lopes, V., Brito, J., Yaghoubi, E., Proença, H.: Generative adversarial graph convolutional networks for human action synthesis. In: Proceedings of the IEEE/CVF Winter Conference on Applications of Computer Vision, pp. 1150–1159 (2022)
8. Fragkiadaki, K., Levine, S., Felsen, P., Malik, J.: Recurrent network models for human dynamics. In: 2015 IEEE International Conference on Computer Vision (ICCV), pp. 4346–4354. IEEE, Santiago, Chile (2015). https://doi.org/10.1109/ICCV.2015.494. http://ieeexplore.ieee.org/document/7410851/
9. Gall, J., Stoll, C., De Aguiar, E., Theobalt, C., Rosenhahn, B., Seidel, H.P.: Motion capture using joint skeleton tracking and surface estimation. In: 2009 IEEE Conference on Computer Vision and Pattern Recognition, pp. 1746–1753. IEEE (2009)

10. Ghosh, A., Cheema, N., Oguz, C., Theobalt, C., Slusallek, P.: Synthesis of compositional animations from textual descriptions. In: Proceedings of the IEEE/CVF International Conference on Computer Vision, pp. 1396–1406 (2021)
11. Goodfellow, I., et al.: Generative adversarial networks. Commun. ACM **63**(11), 139–144 (2020). https://doi.org/10.1145/3422622
12. Grochow, K., Martin, S.L., Hertzmann, A., Popović, Z.: Style-based inverse kinematics. In: ACM SIGGRAPH 2004 Papers, pp. 522–531. ACM, Los Angeles California (2004). https://doi.org/10.1145/1186562.1015755. https://dl.acm.org/doi/10.1145/1186562.1015755
13. Guo, C., Zou, S., Zuo, X., Wang, S., Ji, W., Li, X., Cheng, L.: Generating diverse and natural 3D human motions from text. In: Proceedings of the IEEE/CVF Conference on Computer Vision and Pattern Recognition, pp. 5152–5161 (2022)
14. Habibie, I., Holden, D., Schwarz, J., Yearsley, J., Komura, T.: A recurrent variational autoencoder for human motion synthesis. In: Procedings of the British Machine Vision Conference 2017, p. 119. British Machine Vision Association, London, UK (2017). https://doi.org/10.5244/C.31.119. http://www.bmva.org/bmvc/2017/papers/paper119/index.html
15. Hassan, M., Ghosh, P., Tesch, J., Tzionas, D., Black, M.J.: Populating 3D scenes by learning human-scene interaction. In: Proceedings of the IEEE/CVF Conference on Computer Vision and Pattern Recognition, pp. 14708–14718 (2021)
16. Ho, J., Jain, A., Abbeel, P.: Denoising Diffusion Probabilistic Models (2020). http://arxiv.org/abs/2006.11239. arXiv:2006.11239
17. Hodgins, C.M.U.: CMU graphics lab motion capture database (2015). http://mocap.cs.cmu.edu/
18. Holden, D.: Reducing animator keyframes. Ph.D. thesis, The University of Edinburgh (2017)
19. Holden, D., Komura, T., Saito, J.: Phase-functioned neural networks for character control. ACM Trans. Graph. **36**(4), 1–13 (2017). https://doi.org/10.1145/3072959.3073663. https://dl.acm.org/doi/10.1145/3072959.3073663
20. Holden, D., Saito, J., Komura, T.: A deep learning framework for character motion synthesis and editing. ACM Trans. Graph. **35**(4), 1–11 (2016). https://doi.org/10.1145/2897824.2925975. https://dl.acm.org/doi/10.1145/2897824.2925975
21. Holden, D., Saito, J., Komura, T., Joyce, T.: Learning motion manifolds with convolutional autoencoders. In: SIGGRAPH Asia 2015 Technical Briefs, pp. 1–4. ACM, Kobe Japan (2015). https://doi.org/10.1145/2820903.2820918. https://dl.acm.org/doi/10.1145/2820903.2820918
22. Huang, S., et al.: Diffusion-based Generation, Optimization, and Planning in 3D Scenes (2023). http://arxiv.org/abs/2301.06015. arXiv:2301.06015
23. Ionescu, C., Papava, D., Olaru, V., Sminchisescu, C.: Human3.6m: large scale datasets and predictive methods for 3D human sensing in natural environments. IEEE Trans. Pattern Anal. Mach. Intell. **36**(7), 1325–1339 (2013)
24. Jang, D.K., Lee, S.H.: Constructing human motion manifold with sequential networks. Comput. Graph. Forum **39**(6), 314–324 (2020). https://doi.org/10.1111/cgf.14028. http://arxiv.org/abs/2005.14370. arXiv:2005.14370
25. Jiang, B., Chen, X., Liu, W., Yu, J., Yu, G., Chen, T.: MotionGPT: Human Motion as a Foreign Language (2023). http://arxiv.org/abs/2306.14795. arXiv:2306.14795
26. Karras, T., Aila, T., Laine, S., Lehtinen, J.: Progressive Growing of GANs for Improved Quality, Stability, and Variation (2018). http://arxiv.org/abs/1710.10196. arXiv:1710.10196

27. Karras, T., Laine, S., Aila, T.: A style-based generator architecture for generative adversarial networks. IEEE Trans. Pattern Anal. Mach. Intell. **43**(12), 4217–4228 (2021). https://doi.org/10.1109/TPAMI.2020.2970919
28. Karras, T., Laine, S., Aittala, M., Hellsten, J., Lehtinen, J., Aila, T.: Analyzing and improving the image quality of stylegan. In: Proceedings of the IEEE/CVF Conference on Computer Vision and Pattern Recognition, pp. 8110–8119 (2020)
29. Kingma, D.P., Welling, M.: Auto-encoding variational bayes. arXiv preprint arXiv:1312.6114 (2013)
30. Kovar, L., Gleicher, M.: Automated extraction and parameterization of motions in large data sets. ACM Trans. Graph. **23**(3), 559–568 (2004). https://doi.org/10.1145/1015706.1015760
31. Kovar, L., Gleicher, M., Pighin, F.: Motion graphs. ACM Trans. Graph. **21**(3), 473–482 (2002). https://doi.org/10.1145/566654.566605
32. Lawrence, N.: Gaussian process latent variable models for visualisation of high dimensional data. In: Advances in Neural Information Processing Systems, vol. 16. MIT Press (2003). https://proceedings.neurips.cc/paper_files/paper/2003/hash/9657c1fffd38824e5ab0472e022e577e-Abstract.html
33. Le, N., Pham, T., Do, T., Tjiputra, E., Tran, Q.D., Nguyen, A.: Music-driven group choreography. In: 2023 IEEE/CVF Conference on Computer Vision and Pattern Recognition (CVPR), pp. 8673–8682. IEEE, Vancouver, BC, Canada (2023). https://doi.org/10.1109/CVPR52729.2023.00838. https://ieeexplore.ieee.org/document/10205408/
34. Lee, J.M.: Manifolds and differential geometry, vol. 107. American Mathematical Society (2022)
35. Lee, J., Chai, J., Reitsma, P.S., Hodgins, J.K., Pollard, N.S.: Interactive control of avatars animated with human motion data. In: Proceedings of the 29th Annual Conference on Computer Graphics and Interactive Techniques, pp. 491–500 (2002). https://doi.org/10.1145/566570.566607
36. Lee, Y., Wampler, K., Bernstein, G., Popović, J., Popović, Z.: Motion fields for interactive character locomotion. ACM Trans. Graph. **29**(6) (2010). https://doi.org/10.1145/1882261.1866160
37. Levine, S., Lee, Y., Koltun, V., Popović, Z.: Space-time planning with parameterized locomotion controllers. ACM Trans. Graph. **30**(3), 1–11 (2011). https://doi.org/10.1145/1966394.1966402. https://dl.acm.org/doi/10.1145/1966394.1966402
38. Levine, S., Wang, J.M., Haraux, A., Popović, Z., Koltun, V.: Continuous character control with low-dimensional embeddings. ACM Trans. Graph. **31**(4), 1–10 (2012). https://doi.org/10.1145/2185520.2185524. https://dl.acm.org/doi/10.1145/2185520.2185524
39. Li, R., Yang, S., Ross, D.A., Kanazawa, A.: AI choreographer: music conditioned 3D dance generation with AIST++. In: Proceedings of the IEEE/CVF International Conference on Computer Vision, pp. 13401–13412 (2021)
40. Liu, J., Shahroudy, A., Perez, M., Wang, G., Duan, L.Y., Kot, A.C.: NTU RGB+D 120: a large-scale benchmark for 3D human activity understanding. IEEE Trans. Pattern Anal. Mach. Intell. **42**(10), 2684–2701 (2019)
41. Liu, Y., Stoll, C., Gall, J., Seidel, H.P., Theobalt, C.: Markerless motion capture of interacting characters using multi-view image segmentation. In: CVPR 2011, pp. 1249–1256. IEEE (2011)
42. Loper, M., Mahmood, N., Romero, J., Pons-Moll, G., Black, M.J.: SMPL: a skinned multi-person linear model. ACM Trans. Graph. **34**(6) (2015). https://doi.org/10.1145/2816795.2818013

43. Lucas, T., Baradel, F., Weinzaepfel, P., Rogez, G.: PoseGPT: Quantization-based 3D Human Motion Generation and Forecasting (2022). http://arxiv.org/abs/2210.10542. arXiv:2210.10542
44. Ma, X., Su, J., Wang, C., Zhu, W., Wang, Y.: 3D human mesh estimation from virtual markers. In: Proceedings of the IEEE/CVF Conference on Computer Vision and Pattern Recognition, pp. 534–543 (2023)
45. Min, J., Chai, J.: Motion graphs++: a compact generative model for semantic motion analysis and synthesis. ACM Trans. Graph. **31**(6), 1–12 (2012). https://doi.org/10.1145/2366145.2366172. https://dl.acm.org/doi/10.1145/2366145.2366172
46. Moeslund, T.B., Hilton, A., Krüger, V.: A survey of advances in vision-based human motion capture and analysis. Comput. Vis. Image Underst. **104**(2–3), 90–126 (2006)
47. Osman, A.A.A., Bolkart, T., Black, M.J.: STAR: Sparse Trained Articulated Human Body Regressor (2020). https://doi.org/10.1007/978-3-030-58539-6_36. http://arxiv.org/abs/2008.08535. arXiv:2008.08535
48. Pavlakos, G., et al.: Expressive body capture: 3D hands, face, and body from a single image. In: 2019 IEEE/CVF Conference on Computer Vision and Pattern Recognition (CVPR), pp. 10967–10977. IEEE, Long Beach, CA, USA (2019). https://doi.org/10.1109/CVPR.2019.01123. https://ieeexplore.ieee.org/document/8953319/
49. Peng, X.B., Guo, Y., Halper, L., Levine, S., Fidler, S.: ASE: large-scale reusable adversarial skill embeddings for physically simulated characters. ACM Trans. Graph. **41**(4), 1–17 (2022). https://doi.org/10.1145/3528223.3530110. https://dl.acm.org/doi/10.1145/3528223.3530110
50. Peng, X.B., Ma, Z., Abbeel, P., Levine, S., Kanazawa, A.: AMP: adversarial motion priors for stylized physics-based character control. ACM Trans. Graph. **40**(4), 1–20 (2021). https://doi.org/10.1145/3450626.3459670. https://dl.acm.org/doi/10.1145/3450626.3459670
51. Petrovich, M., Black, M.J., Varol, G.: Action-Conditioned 3D Human Motion Synthesis with Transformer VAE (2021). http://arxiv.org/abs/2104.05670. arXiv:2104.05670
52. Petrovich, M., Black, M.J., Varol, G.: TEMOS: Generating diverse human motions from textual descriptions (2022). http://arxiv.org/abs/2204.14109. arXiv:2204.14109
53. Raab, S., Leibovitch, I., Li, P., Aberman, K., Sorkine-Hornung, O., Cohen-Or, D.: Modi: unconditional motion synthesis from diverse data. In: Proceedings of the IEEE/CVF Conference on Computer Vision and Pattern Recognition, pp. 13873–13883 (2023)
54. Rose, C., Cohen, M., Bodenheimer, B.: Verbs and adverbs: multidimensional motion interpolation. IEEE Comput. Graphics Appl. **18**(5), 32–40 (1998). https://doi.org/10.1109/38.708559. http://ieeexplore.ieee.org/document/708559/
55. Shafir, Y., Tevet, G., Kapon, R., Bermano, A.H.: Human motion diffusion as a generative prior. arXiv preprint arXiv:2303.01418 (2023)
56. Sønderby, C.K., Raiko, T., Maaløe, L., Sønderby, S.K., Winther, O.: Ladder variational autoencoders. In: Proceedings of the 30th International Conference on Neural Information Processing Systems, NIPS 2016, pp. 3745–3753. Curran Associates Inc., Red Hook (2016)
57. Song, Y., Sohl-Dickstein, J., Kingma, D.P., Kumar, A., Ermon, S., Poole, B.: Score-based generative modeling through stochastic differential equations. arXiv preprint arXiv:2011.13456 (2020)

58. Starke, P., Starke, S., Komura, T., Steinicke, F.: Motion in-betweening with phase manifolds. Proc. ACM Comput. Graph. Interact. Tech. **6**(3), 1–17 (2023). https://doi.org/10.1145/3606921. https://dl.acm.org/doi/10.1145/3606921

59. Starke, S., Mason, I., Komura, T.: DeepPhase: periodic autoencoders for learning motion phase manifolds. ACM Trans. Graph. **41**(4), 1–13 (2022). https://doi.org/10.1145/3528223.3530178. https://dl.acm.org/doi/10.1145/3528223.3530178

60. Starke, S., Zhao, Y., Zinno, F., Komura, T.: Neural animation layering for synthesizing martial arts movements. ACM Trans. Graph. **40**(4), 1–16 (2021). https://doi.org/10.1145/3450626.3459881. https://dl.acm.org/doi/10.1145/3450626.3459881

61. Sutton, R.S., Barto, A.G.: The reinforcement learning problem. In: Reinforcement Learning: An Introduction, pp. 51–85 (1998)

62. Tang, T., Jia, J., Mao, H.: Dance with melody: an LSTM-autoencoder approach to music-oriented dance synthesis. In: Proceedings of the 26th ACM International Conference on Multimedia, pp. 1598–1606. ACM, Seoul Republic of Korea (2018). https://doi.org/10.1145/3240508.3240526. https://dl.acm.org/doi/10.1145/3240508.3240526

63. Tessler, C., Kasten, Y., Guo, Y., Mannor, S., Chechik, G., Peng, X.B.: CALM: conditional adversarial latent models for directable virtual characters. In: Special Interest Group on Computer Graphics and Interactive Techniques Conference Conference Proceedings, pp. 1–9. ACM, Los Angeles CA USA (2023). https://doi.org/10.1145/3588432.3591541. https://dl.acm.org/doi/10.1145/3588432.3591541

64. Tevet, G., Raab, S., Gordon, B., Shafir, Y., Cohen-Or, D., Bermano, A.H.: Human Motion Diffusion Model (2022). http://arxiv.org/abs/2209.14916. arXiv:2209.14916

65. Tu, L.W.: Manifolds. In: An Introduction to Manifolds, pp. 47–83. Springer (2011)

66. Van Den Oord, A., Vinyals, O., et al.: Neural discrete representation learning. In: Advances in Neural Information Processing Systems, vol. 30 (2017)

67. Wang, H., Ho, E.S.L., Shum, H.P.H., Zhu, Z.: Spatio-temporal Manifold Learning for Human Motions via Long-horizon Modeling (2019). http://arxiv.org/abs/1908.07214. arXiv:1908.07214

68. Xu, H., Bazavan, E.G., Zanfir, A., Freeman, W.T., Sukthankar, R., Sminchisescu, C.: GHUM & GHUML: generative 3D human shape and articulated pose models. In: 2020 IEEE/CVF Conference on Computer Vision and Pattern Recognition (CVPR), pp. 6183–6192. IEEE, Seattle, WA, USA (2020). https://doi.org/10.1109/CVPR42600.2020.00622. https://ieeexplore.ieee.org/document/9157563/

69. Yu, P., Zhao, Y., Li, C., Yuan, J., Chen, C.: Structure-Aware Human-Action Generation (2020). http://arxiv.org/abs/2007.01971. arXiv:2007.01971

70. Zeng, R., Dai, J., Bai, J., Pan, J., Qin, H.: Human motion synthesis and control via contextual manifold embedding. In: PG (Short Papers, Posters, and Work-in-Progress Papers), pp. 25–30 (2021)

71. Zhang, M., et al.: Motiondiffuse: text-driven human motion generation with diffusion model. IEEE Trans. Pattern Anal. Mach. Intell. **46**(6), 4115–4128 (2024). https://doi.org/10.1109/TPAMI.2024.3355414

72. Zhang, M., et al.: ReMoDiffuse: Retrieval-Augmented Motion Diffusion Model (2023). http://arxiv.org/abs/2304.01116. arXiv:2304.01116

73. Zhang, S., Zhang, Y., Ma, Q., Black, M.J., Tang, S.: PLACE: Proximity Learning of Articulation and Contact in 3D Environments (2020). http://arxiv.org/abs/2008.05570. arXiv:2008.05570

74. Zhang, Y., Black, M.J., Tang, S.: We are more than our joints: predicting how 3D bodies move. In: Proceedings of the IEEE/CVF Conference on Computer Vision and Pattern Recognition, pp. 3372–3382 (2021)
75. Zhu, W., Ma, X., Liu, Z., Liu, L., Wu, W., Wang, Y.: MotionBERT: A Unified Perspective on Learning Human Motion Representations (2023). http://arxiv.org/abs/2210.06551. arXiv:2210.06551
76. Zhu, W., et al.: Human Motion Generation: A Survey (2023). http://arxiv.org/abs/2307.10894. arXiv:2307.10894
77. Zuo, C., et al.: Loose inertial poser: motion capture with IMU-attached loose-wear jacket. In: Proceedings of the IEEE/CVF Conference on Computer Vision and Pattern Recognition, pp. 2209–2219 (2024)

Exploring XR Technologies for Lacquer Art: A Study on Virtual Simulations and the Digital Transformation of Traditional Craft

Heng Yu[1(✉)] 🆔 and Guobin Xia[2] 🆔

[1] School of Fine Arts, Harbin Normal University, Harbin 150080, China
hyart@hrbnu.edu.cn
[2] School of Engineering, The University of Liverpool, Liverpool L69 3GH, UK

Abstract. This study explores the potential of immersive Extended Reality (XR) technologies in lacquer arts education, focusing on how digital tools can enhance traditional, hands-on learning. Lacquer art is known for its specialised, tactile craftsmanship, presenting challenges for integration with digital education methods. This research aims to answer two key questions: 1) Which XR technologies are best suited to improve learning outcomes in lacquer art education? 2) How can immersive XR experiences engage learners and facilitate skill acquisition? The findings suggest that Virtual Reality (VR) stands out as the most effective XR tool for replicating the hands-on nature of lacquer art, allowing learners to practice techniques in a risk-free environment without material costs. Importantly, the study identifies the need for enhanced haptic feedback to simulate the tactile qualities critical to the craft. By bridging the gap between traditional craftsmanship and digital innovation, this research offers a novel framework for integrating XR in lacquer education, promoting cultural preservation while modernising educational practices. These insights provide new opportunities for reimagining how traditional crafts are taught in the digital era, with implications for expanding access and preserving artisana heritage.

Keywords: lacquer arts · Extended Reality (XR) · pedagogical application

1 Introduction

1.1 Research Background

Lacquer art, a significant component of traditional Chinese craftsmanship, represents not only a unique material technique but also a rich cultural heritage that spans thousands of years. The core material, lacquer, is derived from the sap of trees in the Anacardiaceae family [1]. This natural lacquer, rich in polymeric urushiol, laccase, and resins, forms a durable, resilient coating when dried under specific temperature and humidity conditions. These distinctive physical and chemical properties have historically made lacquer an ideal material for creating robust, water-resistant, and durable artefacts. In contemporary settings, lacquer art continues to thrive in the production and restoration of high-end

© The Author(s), under exclusive license to Springer Nature Singapore Pte Ltd. 2025
W. Song et al. (Eds.): ICXR 2024, LNCS 15461, pp. 18–30, 2025.
https://doi.org/10.1007/978-981-96-3679-2_2

furniture and art pieces, whilst also expanding into modern applications. From a crafts-manship perspective, lacquer art encompasses a variety of techniques, including painting, inlay, engraving, and layering, all of which demonstrate the artisan's deep understanding of both material and nature [2]. These intricate techniques, which take years to refine, showcase a continuous exploration of tradition and innovation. For example, lacquer painting involves not only decorative approaches but also abstract expressions of natural forms and colours. The evolution of lacquer exemplifies the sustained vitality of the craft, passed down through generations while adapting to innovations in each era. However, lacquer art education in modern society faces several critical challenges. Firstly, the long learning curve required to master lacquer techniques acts as a significant barrier. The sensitivity of the lacquer drying process, which requires precise environmental control, can take years of practice to fully understand. Secondly, high entry barriers, such as the need for specialised tools and materials, make it difficult for beginners to succeed, espe-cially in modern society, which often emphasises rapid production and consumption. As a result, traditional crafts such as lacquer art are marginalised, and the number of skilled artisans is steadily decreasing. In addition, the high cost of materials further deters potential learners. Precious metals, such as gold and silver, and delicate materials like abalone shells and natural minerals, make lacquer education an expensive endeavour, particularly during the early stages when mistakes are frequent. Despite technological advancements such as 3D printing, digital design, and virtual reality (VR), lacquer edu-cation has seen minimal integration of these innovations, limiting student exposure to modern tools that could enhance learning experiences. The lack of such integration, coupled with limited international exchange, stifles the development of lacquer art in the global context. These issues highlight two primary problems that this research aims to address: 1) the lack of research into how immersive XR technologies can be applied to lacquer art education, and 2) the practical challenges in lacquer art teaching, includ-ing long learning cycles, high material costs, and limited use of modern digital tools. Integrating XR (Extended Reality) technologies into lacquer education could provide innovative solutions that bridge the gap between traditional craft techniques and modern technological advancements.

1.2   What is XR and How Does It Work in Art Education?

XR, or Extended Reality, is a broad term that encompasses Virtual Reality (VR), Aug-mented Reality (AR), and Mixed Reality (MR). These immersive technologies merge the physical and digital worlds, creating interactive experiences that can transform the teaching and learning of art and crafts. Virtual Reality (VR) immerses users entirely in a digital environment, allowing them to interact with simulated objects and surroundings. In art education, VR is used to recreate historical art environments or simulate complex artistic processes that would otherwise be difficult or costly to replicate in the real world [3]. For instance, in lacquer art, VR could simulate the drying and application processes, enabling learners to practise without the associated material costs.

Augmented Reality (AR) overlays digital information or objects onto the real world, enhancing the user's interaction with their physical environment. AR has seen grow-ing use in museums and art education by providing additional layers of information, such as visual guides or historical context, to enhance the understanding of artworks or techniques [4]. In lacquer art, AR could offer real-time feedback on techniques, such as brushstroke quality or lacquer application, providing learners with a more interactive and guided learning experience.

Mixed Reality (MR) combines elements of both VR and AR, enabling users to manipulate and interact with both physical and virtual objects in real time. MR is particularly valuable in art education as it allows students to engage with physical tools and materials while receiving virtual guidance and feedback, thus bridging the gap between theoretical learning and hands-on practice [5]. This technology can help lacquer students experiment with different design approaches while receiving immediate virtual feedback on their work. The effectiveness of XR in art education has been well documented. According to [6] immersive technologies foster experiential learning, which is essential in art and craft education as it allows learners to engage with both the conceptual and practical aspects of artistic creation. Moreover, XR platforms enhance learner motivation and engagement through interactive simulations, offering a multisensory experience that deepens understanding. In lacquer art, this could involve using XR to simulate intricate processes like inlay or polishing, where students can experiment in a low-risk virtual environment before applying their skills to physical materials. Despite its growing use in other educational fields, the application of XR in traditional crafts like lacquer art remains underexplored. This research seeks to address this gap by investigating how XR technologies can be employed to enhance both the learning experience and skill acquisition in lacquer art education.

1.3 Research Aims and Significance

This research investigates the potential application of immersive XR technologies in lacquer art education to address both the lack of research in this area and the practical difficulties faced by the craft.

The study aims to:

Identify suitable XR technologies: Analyse which XR technologies are most appropriate for improving learning outcomes in lacquer art education, focusing on enhancing student engagement and skill acquisition.

Evaluate immersive learning experiences: Explore how immersive XR environments can provide interactive, hands-on experiences that enable learners to better understand complex lacquer techniques while fostering a deeper appreciation of traditional culture.

Promote innovation and modernisation: Examine how XR technologies can inspire creativity and innovation, contributing to the modernisation and sustainability of lacquer art. Expand cultural reach: Investigate how XR platforms can attract younger audiences and foster the preservation and transmission of traditional lacquer art.

1.4 Key Questions

The key questions this paper aims to address are: 1. What types of XR technologies are most suitable for enhancing lacquer art education, and how can they effectively support learning outcomes? 2. How can immersive XR experiences be designed engage learners and facilitate skill acquisition in lacquer arts? Through this investigation, the research will provide insights into how modern XR technologies can be effectively integrated into lacquer education, offering solutions to both the research gap and the practical challenges the craft faces in modern society.

2 Methodology

2.1 Research Design

This study adopts a quantitative research approach using a structured questionnaire to investigate how XR technologies can enhance lacquer art education. The questionnaire is designed to gather data on participants' perceptions regarding the suitability of XR technologies, their potential to support learning outcomes, and how immersive experiences can be designed to engage learners and facilitate skill acquisition. The questionnaire method allows for the collection of large-scale data across a variety of participants while maintaining consistency in responses. This approach will enable the study to quantify participants' attitudes and experiences regarding XR technology integration in lacquer art education.

2.2 Participants

The participants for this study were drawn from various institutions involved in lacquer arts education. A total of 72 individuals took part in the survey. The sample comprised a mix of students, educators, researchers, and practitioners, ensuring a broad representation of perspectives across different roles within the field. Participants were selected based on their involvement in lacquer arts education, with no restrictions on experience level, thus providing a diverse range of insights. The sample included individuals at varying stages of their experience, ranging from beginners with less than one year of practice to those with over five years of experience. Participants were invited via email and educational platforms to ensure wide outreach, and their participation was entirely voluntary. Each participant was provided with detailed information about the study, including the purpose and the option to withdraw at any time. All responses were anonymised to protect participants' privacy.

2.3 Questionnaire Design

The questionnaire is structured into five key sections to ensure comprehensive coverage of the research questions. It includes a mixture of single choice questions for quantitative analysis and open-ended questions for more detailed, qualitative insights.

Participant Background
This section collects demographic data such as age, education level, and experience with lacquer art and XR technologies. Understanding the background of participants will help contextualise their responses.

Perceptions of XR Technology Suitability

This section explores participants' perceptions of various XR technologies (VR, AR, MR) and their suitability for different aspects of lacquer art education. The questions will focus on the participants' understanding of how these technologies can enhance traditional methods.

Design of Immersive XR Experiences

This section will evaluate how well participants believe XR environments can be designed to effectively engage students in learning lacquer art techniques. The questions will ask participants to rate the importance of interactive features such as real-time feedback, visualisation of complex techniques, and multi-sensory engagement.

Impact on Learning Outcomes

This section investigates participants' beliefs about the impact XR technologies could have on learning outcomes in lacquer art education. Specifically, the questions will focus on whether XR can improve skill acquisition, engagement, and overall learning efficiency.

Challenges and Limitations

This section will explore potential challenges in integrating XR technologies into lacquer art education. Participants will be asked to identify obstacles such as cost, technical skills, and the difficulty of replicating the tactile nature of lacquer art in a digital environment. Each section of the questionnaire has been informed by literature on XR technology in education, particularly focusing on experiential and constructivist learning theories [7] The questions are designed to capture the participants' insights on both the advantages and limitations of using XR for practical, hands-on art education.

2.4 Data Collection Procedure

The questionnaire was distributed online via the secure survey platform Wenjuanxing to ensure ease of access for participants. The survey link was shared with potential participants through email and educational institution platforms. The data collection period lasted approximately four weeks, allowing sufficient time for participants to complete the survey. Participation was anonymous, and no personally identifiable information was collected to ensure privacy. All responses were stored securely in accordance with the data protection policies of the participating institutions.

2.5 Data Analysis

The data collected from the questionnaire underwent both quantitative and qualitative analysis. For the quantitative analysis, data from the closed-ended (single-choice) questions were analysed using descriptive statistics. This provided insights into trends and patterns in participants' perceptions of XR technology. The results were presented as mean scores and frequency distributions, and inferential statistics were employed to identify any significant differences between participant groups, such as beginners vs. advanced learners. For the qualitative analysis, open-ended responses were analysed using thematic analysis to identify recurring themes or concepts related to the challenges and benefits of integrating XR into lacquer art education. These qualitative insights provided depth to the quantitative findings and helped highlight specific concerns or recommendations from participants.

2.6   Ethical Considerations

The study adhered to the ethical standards outlined by the participating institutions. All participants provided informed consent before taking part in the study, and they were assured of their right to withdraw from the research at any time. Data were anonymised to protect participants' privacy, and all findings were reported in aggregate form to avoid the identification of individuals. The study ensured that all collected data were securely stored and were only accessible to authorised researchers.

3   Results

3.1   Participant Demographics and Background

A total of 72 participants completed the survey. The majority of respondents (75%) identified as students, followed by educators (15.28%), researchers (5.56%), and other roles (2.78%). Only one participant identified as a practitioner (1.39%). When asked about their experience in lacquer arts education or practice, nearly half of the participants (48.61%) reported having less than one year of experience, while 44.44% had between 1–3 years of experience. A small proportion of respondents (2.78%) had between 3–5 years, and only 4.17% had more than 5 years of experience.

In terms of previous experience with digital or XR technologies, 22.22% of participants had used such technologies in their teaching or learning, while the majority (77.78%) had not. This highlights a potential gap in exposure to XR technologies within lacquer arts education, which may influence perceptions of their applicability.

3.2   Suitability of XR Technologies in Lacquer Arts Education

When respondents were asked which XR technologies they believed would be most beneficial for lacquer arts education, Virtual Reality (VR) emerged as the most favoured technology, with 47.22% of participants selecting it. Augmented Reality (AR) was chosen by 15.28% of respondents, and Mixed Reality (MR) by 19.44%. A smaller proportion of participants identified potential in 360-degree video (9.72%), while 8.33% indicated that haptic feedback devices could play a valuable role in this context (as shown in Fig. 1). To examine whether these differences in preferences were statistically significant, a one-way analysis of variance (ANOVA) was conducted to compare the perceived effectiveness of the five XR technologies: VR, AR, MR, 360-degree video, and haptic feedback devices. The results of the ANOVA were statistically significant, $F(4,145) = 2352.58$, $p < .001$, indicating that participants perceived significant differences in the potential effectiveness of the different XR technologies for lacquer arts education.

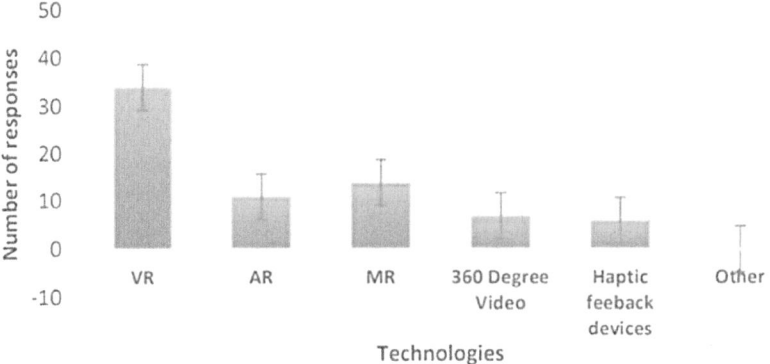

Fig. 1. Responses to the question "Which XR technologies do you believe would be most beneficial in Lacquer arts education?"

When respondents were asked which aspects of lacquer arts education could benefit most from XR technologies, 43.06% highlighted the visualisation of complex processes, while 40.28% believed that XR could support skill acquisition. Fewer respondents saw XR as beneficial for the preservation of traditional methods (6.94%) or collaborative learning (9.72%) (Fig. 2).

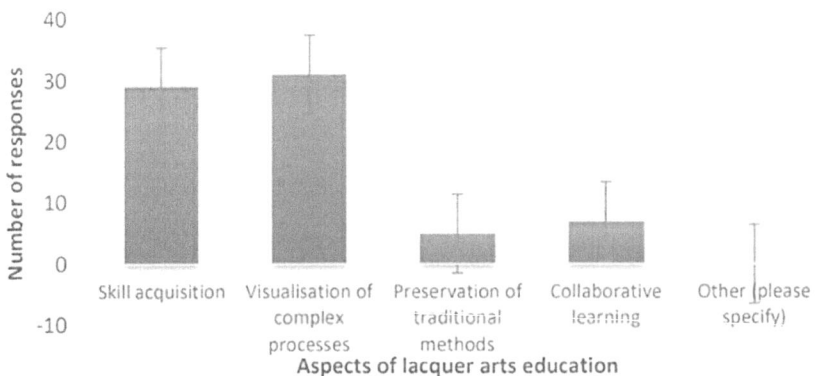

Fig. 2. Responses to the question "What aspects of Lacquer arts education do you think could benefit most from XR technologies?"

In terms of accessibility, 38.89% of participants agreed that XR technologies could enhance the accessibility of lacquer arts education by supporting remote learning or more flexible teaching approaches, with 25% strongly agreeing. However, 33.33% of respondents were neutral, and a small minority (2.78%) disagreed.

3.3 Design Features for Immersive XR Experiences

Respondents were asked which features of immersive XR experiences they believed would most effectively engage learners. Interactive simulations were considered the most engaging, selected by 37.5% of participants, followed by multi-sensory engagement (30.56%) and visual realism (13.89%). A smaller group (9.72%) expressed a preference for customisable learning environments (Fig. 3).

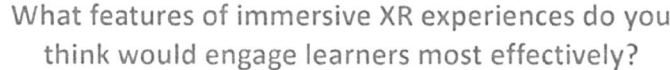

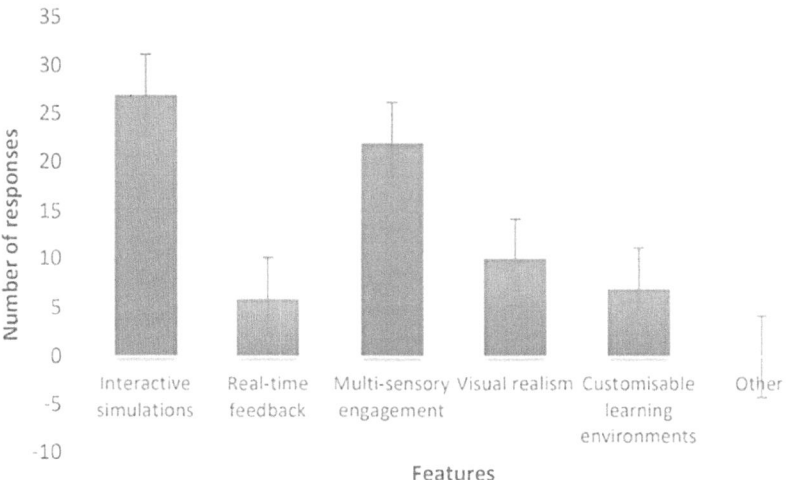

Fig. 3. Responses to the question "What features of immersive XR experiences do you think would engage learners most effectively?"

The ability of XR technologies to replicate the hands-on nature of lacquer arts education was viewed positively by most respondents. A majority (56.94%) believed that XR could somewhat replicate the hands-on experience, while 34.72% felt it could do so to a large extent. Only a small proportion (2.78%) believed XR could fully replicate the hands-on nature of lacquer practice (Fig. 4).

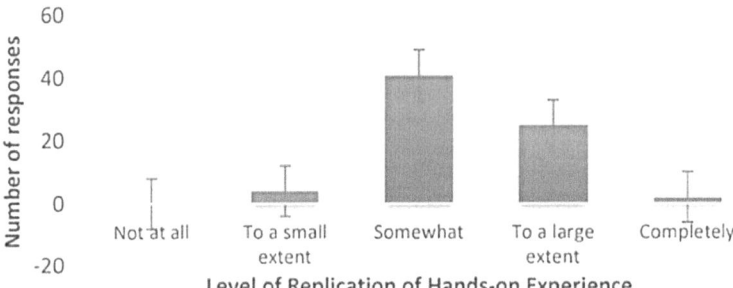

Fig. 4. Responses to the question "To what extent do you think immersive XR experiences can replicate the hands-on nature of Lacquer arts education?"

Simulating the tactile and sensory aspects of lacquer arts in XR environments was considered important by 48.61% of participants, with 20.83% indicating that this was very important, and 12.5% viewing it as essential. Only 1.39% of respondents felt that tactile simulation was not important (Fig. 5.).

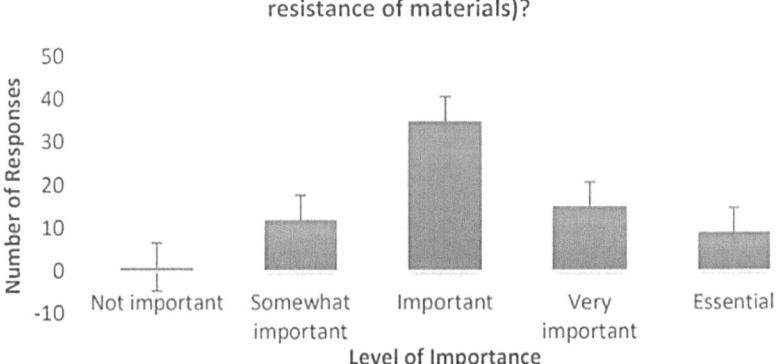

Fig. 5. Responses to the question "How important is it for XR environments to simulate the tactile and sensory aspects of Lacquer art practice (e.g., texture, resistance of materials)?"

3.4 Challenges and Barriers

Participants identified several challenges in integrating XR technologies into lacquer arts education. The most frequently cited challenge was cost and resource limitations (38.89%), followed closely by a lack of technical skills to use XR tools (30.56%) and difficulty in replicating traditional hands-on methods (29.17%) (Fig. 6).

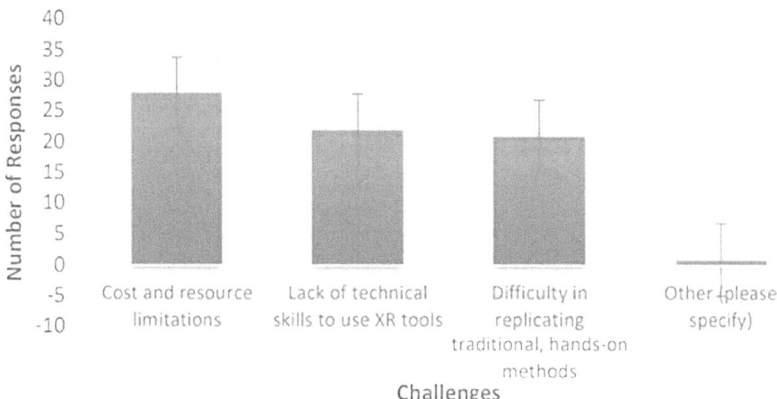

Fig. 6. Responses to the question "What challenges do you foresee in designing XR experiences for Lacquer arts education?"

3.5 Impact on Learning Outcomes

When asked about the potential impact of XR technologies on learning outcomes in lacquer arts education, 44.44% of respondents believed it was likely that XR would enhance outcomes, with 18.06% strongly agreeing (very likely). A further 31.94% were neutral on the matter. XR technologies were perceived to enhance various learning outcomes, particularly creativity and experimentation (27.78%), understanding of cultural and historical significance (29.17%), and engagement and motivation (22.22%) (Fig. 7).

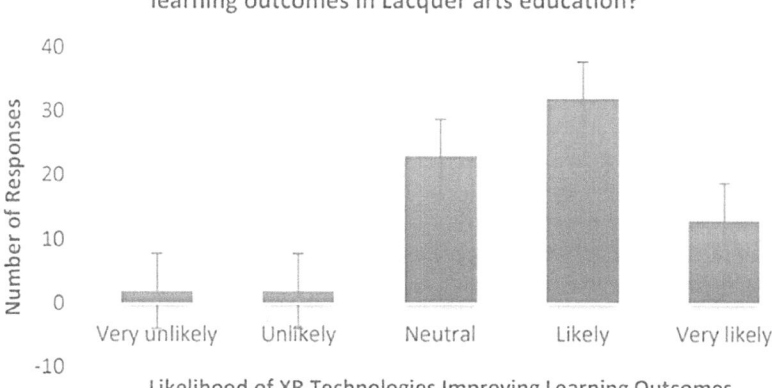

Fig. 7. Responses to the question "How likely do you think XR technologies are to improve learning outcomes in Lacquer arts education?"

In terms of preserving traditional lacquer techniques while integrating digital innovation, 52.78% of respondents believed that XR technologies would play a significant role, while 9.72% indicated that they would play an essential role. Only 1.39% felt that XR would play a minimal role in this regard (Fig. 8).

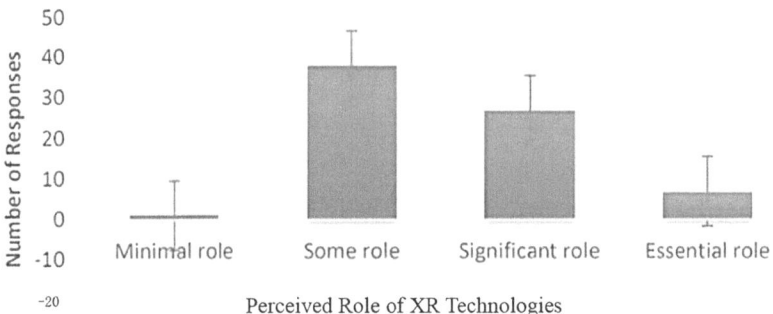

Fig. 8. Responses to the question "What role do you think XR technologies can play in preserving traditional Lacquer art methods while incorporating digital innovation?"

4 Discussion

The integration of XR technologies into lacquer arts education presents both exciting opportunities and notable challenges. As the findings of this study demonstrate, participants view Virtual Reality (VR) as the most beneficial XR tool for lacquer arts education. The ability of VR to visualise complex processes and simulate practice environments without material costs was highlighted as particularly useful, aligning with existing research on the effectiveness of VR in experiential learning contexts [6]. However, the results also reveal critical barriers, particularly around the cost of implementing XR systems and the challenge of replicating the tactile, hands-on aspects of lacquer art. The significant proportion of participants who had limited or no previous experience with XR technologies indicates a gap in the current integration of digital tools in lacquer arts education, which may further limit its potential impact. These findings suggest that while XR has the potential to address some of the issues associated with lacquer education, such as long learning cycles and material costs, additional development is needed to better replicate the sensory feedback essential to mastering the craft.

The importance of tactile simulation, as highlighted by almost half of the participants, underscores the need for XR experiences that go beyond visual and auditory engagement to incorporate haptic feedback. Although haptic technologies are still in the early stages of development and may be cost-prohibitive for educational institutions, advancements in this area could bridge the gap between traditional hands-on methods and digital learning environments. Moreover, while XR technologies were perceived to offer benefits for increasing accessibility, particularly through remote learning, there was a notable degree of neutrality on this topic among participants. This suggests that more research and development are necessary to fully realise the potential of XR in making lacquer arts education more widely accessible.

4.1 Implications for Lacquer Arts Education

This study provides several key implications for the future of lacquer arts education. Firstly, the results suggest a need for greater exposure to XR technologies among educators and students. Providing training and resources on the use of XR tools could help integrate these technologies more effectively into curricula. Secondly, there is a clear demand for XR experiences that can closely simulate hands-on practice, particularly in replicating the tactile elements of lacquer work. Lastly, given the concerns around cost and resource limitations, future implementations of XR technologies in lacquer arts education should be carefully planned to ensure they are accessible to a wide range of institutions. Collaborations between technology developers, educational institutions, and cultural organisations may help overcome these barriers, creating more sustainable solutions.

5 Conclusion

This study explored the untapped potential of immersive XR technologies in lacquer arts education, a field that has traditionally relied on hands-on, tactile learning experiences. The findings indicate that XR tools, particularly VR, can play a significant role in modernising lacquer education by offering cost-effective, flexible learning solutions. However, several challenges, including the high cost of XR technologies and the difficulty in replicating the tactile elements of lacquer art, must be addressed to fully realise their potential.

Despite these challenges, the study highlights the possibilities for XR technologies to enhance skill acquisition, visualise complex processes, and potentially preserve traditional methods in lacquer arts. Future research should focus on further developing XR systems that incorporate haptic feedback to simulate the tactile nature of the craft. Additionally, efforts should be made to provide more opportunities for educators and students to engage with these technologies, helping bridge the current gap in digital literacy within this field.

By addressing these issues, XR technologies could play a crucial role in both preserving the rich heritage of lacquer arts and promoting innovation in its educational practices. As the technology continues to evolve, its integration into traditional craft education may offer a pathway to sustaining these time-honoured techniques in a rapidly changing digital world.

Acknowledgments. A third level heading in 9-point font size at the end of the paper is used for general acknowledgments, for example: This study was funded by X (grant number Y).

Disclosure of Interests. The authors have no competing interests to declare that are relevant to the content of this article.

References

1. Zhu, T.: Digital protection and development of Yangjiang lacquer art pattern under the intangible heritage domain. China Raw Lacquer **12**(2), 35–39 (2024)

2. Li, M.: The relationship between the development status of lacquer art and the teaching mode of lacquer art in colleges and universities. J. Nanjing Univ. Arts (Fine Arts Des. Ed.) **12**(6), 201–203 (2013)

3. Dionisio, J.D., Burns III, W.G., Gilbert, R.: 3D virtual worlds and the metaverse: current status and future possibilities. ACM Comput. Surv. **45**(3), 1–38 (2013)

4. Fritz, F., Susperregui, A., Linaza, M.T.: Enhancing cultural heritage experiences with augmented reality technologies. J. Cult. Herit. **39**, 127–138 (2020)

5. Milgram, P., Kishino, F.: A taxonomy of mixed reality visual displays. IEICE Trans. Inf. Syst. **E77-D**(12), 1321–1329 (1994)

6. Davis, D., Moar, M., Wiedbusch, M.: Virtual immersive experiences for craft education: a new framework for learning. J. Arts Technol. **14**(4), 245–260 (2021)

7. Piaget, J.: The Origins of Intelligence in Children. International Universities Press, New York (1952)

8. Kolb, D.A.: Experiential Learning: Experience as the Source of Learning and Development. Prentice-Hall, New Jersey (1984)

TeleMotion: A Realtime Humanoid Teleoperation System with Motion Capture

Jiabao Gan[1]📷, Shihui Guo[1]📷, Zhijun Li[2], and Xiangren Shi[3(✉)]📷

[1] Xiamen University, Xiamen, China
ganjiabao@stu.xmu.edu.cn
[2] Harbin Institute of Technology, Harbin, China
[3] Bournemouth University, Bournemouth, UK
xshi@bournemouth.ac.uk

Abstract. Teleoperation serves as a vital means of interaction between humans and robots, aiming to enable robots to move in accordance with human intentions. An effective teleoperation system can facilitate seamless collaboration and communication between humans and robots, enhancing their cooperative capabilities. This paper presents a motion-capture-based upper-body teleoperation system for humanoid robots, called TeleMotion, which consists of two key modules. The first module is an inertial sensor-based motion capture subsystem that accurately tracks human motion while remaining unaffected by environmental factors such as lighting and occlusion. The second module is a learnable temporal neural network inverse kinematics algorithm (TNIK) that fully leverages the relationship between historical human motion data and robotic joint angles. This allows for the rapid and precise mapping of human motion to humanoid motion. By integrating these two modules, TeleMotion enables a highly natural and intuitive interaction method for real-time teleoperation of humanoid robot.

Keywords: Humanoid Teleoperation · Motion Capture · Motion Retargeting

1 Introduction

Humanoid robots have a body structure that is very similar to that of humans, and today's homes, factories, public facilities and other environments are designed for humans, which means that humanoid robots can directly work in our daily environment and provide help to humans. The huge application value of humanoid robots has attracted many scholars to promote its continuous development, and the research on humanoid robot teleoperation has been running through the entire development process of humanoid robots [6]. Humanoid robot teleoperation is an interaction pattern between humans and robots, the purpose is to achieve human control of robots. Traditional robot teleoperation technology is mainly used in industrial production, medical fields and dangerous

© The Author(s), under exclusive license to Springer Nature Singapore Pte Ltd. 2025
W. Song et al. (Eds.): ICXR 2024, LNCS 15461, pp. 31–45, 2025.
https://doi.org/10.1007/978-981-96-3679-2_3

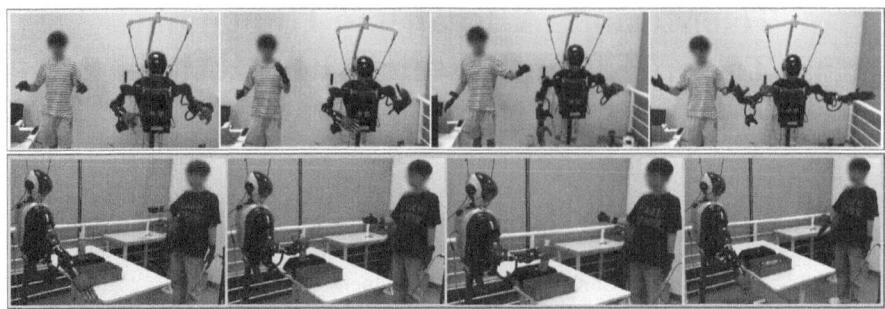

Fig. 1. TeleMotion. The upper section illustrates the operator uses TeleMotion to control the humanoid in real time. The lower section demonstrates the use of TeleMotion to manipulate a humanoid robot in grasping a water bottle.

operations [6], which can reduce the risk of worker injury and infection. In recent years, as imitation learning has shown great power in promoting the automation of humanoid robots [1,11,40,48], robotic teleoperation has gradually been used to collect the data required for imitation learning.

There are many different technical routes and solutions for robot teleoperation, but there is still no perfect solution that can have the advantages of low cost, accuracy, and ease of use at the same time. Customized teleoperation robotic arms or exoskeleton robotic arms [8,10,16,35,38,43,48] have the same joint structure as the robot itself. Using the advantages of mapping joints one by one, this scheme can achieve very accurate teleoperation, which is suitable for some scenarios that require a high degree of fineness, but it also has some shortcomings. First of all, the structure of robots produced by different manufacturers often has relatively large differences. A customized exoskeleton robotic arm can only be used for one type of robot, and the versatility is poor. At the same time, customized exoskeleton robotic arms cannot be operated by dexterous hands. The use of head-mounted VR devices [2,5,9,17,23,30,44] allows for immersive control of robots from the first perspective of the robot, especially recently Open-Television [2] has used VR to achieve real-time telecontrol over ultra-long distances across several states. But many VR devices are expensive and the discomfort of wearing them will gradually increase with the increase of wearing time. There are also some jobs [3,24] that use external end effectors to control the movement of the robot arm. Various motion capture-based methods [13,22,32–34,39] also have good results in teleoperation. For example, HumanPlus [11] use a RGB camera to achieve full-body control of the humanoid robot. The motion-capture-based method maps human motion into the humanoid robot, which is a very natural human-machine interaction method for the user. However, many motion capture methods have greater requirements for the working environment, such as the need to control lighting and reduce the impact of occlusion on the motion capture effect.

Considering that motion-capture-based methods can provide operators with a very natural interaction experience, in this paper, we implement a real-time half-body humanoid robot teleoperation system based on motion capture named TeleMotion, as show in Fig. 1. To solve the problem that optical motion capture or RGB visual motion capture is highly dependent on specific environments, this paper chooses to use eight wearable IMU sensors and a pair of commercial motion capture gloves to achieve accurate capture of human upper body motion and finger motion. And a learning-based temporal neural inverse kinematics algorithm is proposed to realize the retargeting of human motion to humanoid robot motion. Specifically, we first use the method proposed by [15] to synthesize a synthetic IMUs-motion paired dataset on the human motion dataset AMSASS [27], and then use this dataset to train an accurate inertial motion capture algorithm. The error of this algorithm on the validation set of the synthesized dataset is only 0.058 rad, ensuring the prerequisite for the realization of accurate teleoperation.

Although humanoid robots are relatively similar to the human body in appearance, there is still a big gap in joint structure between humans and humanoids. For humans, each joint is a spherical joint with three degrees of freedom. For humanoids, each joint is a single-axis joint with a single degree of freedom. At the same time, there is also a big difference between the range of motion of humanoid joints and that of human joints. Therefore, the retargeting of human body motion to humanoid motion is a relatively difficult problem. Inverse kinematics (IK) is currently the most commonly used method to achieve the retargeting of human body motion to humanoid motion. This method can work in most cases, but there will also be cases of calculation failure. Especially for redundant robots, more joint degrees of freedom and more complex structures make the probability of IK calculation failure even higher. To address this challenge, this paper proposes a learning-based temporal neural inverse kinematics algorithm (TNIK). Specifically, first, we use AMASS data to synthesize a paired data set of robot joint angle values and human wrist posture. Then, we design and train a temporal neural network model on this data set to achieve accurate inverse kinematics calculation and the retargeting of human body motion to humanoid motion. To the best of our knowledge, this paper is the first to use a temporal neural network to achieve the retargeting of human to humanoid motion in a real-time teleoperation system. The main contributions of this paper can be summarized as follows: 1. Accurate inertial motion capture using IMU sensors and its application in humanoid teleoperation. 2. Retargeting of human motion to humanoid motion using learnable temporal neural networks in a real-time teleoperation system for the first time. 3. A real-time humanoid teleoperation system based on motion capture.

2 Related Work

2.1 Inertial Motion Capture

Inertial motion capture refers to the use of inertial measurement units (IMU) tied to specific joints of the human body to capture human motion. Since inertial motion capture is not like visual motion capture, it is highly susceptible to factors such as lighting and occlusion, it can bring a more flexible motion capture experience. The xcense motion capture system [36] requires the user to wear 17 IMUs on the body and use a Kalman filter to filter and fuse the measured values. However, wearing too many sensors will bring poor user experience. The concept of sparse inertial motion capture was first proposed by [15], and the whole body motion capture is realized with only 6 IMUs. In recent years, the wide application scenarios of sparse inertial motion capture have attracted the attention of a large number of scholars, and a series of excellent work has appeared [18,29,42,45–47]. In [46], local motion capture and global displacement estimation are realized using 6 IMUs. Motion capture and vertical terrain reconstruction are realized using sparse inertial sensors. [42] proposed a unified motion capture algorithm under different sensor wearing positions is realized using Diffusion. And other works [29,45] is constantly improving the precision of the inertial motion capture algorithm. For the first time, the inertial sensor is integrated into a loose jacket for daily wear in [49], which brings a more comfortable use experience, and at the same time has not bad motion capture performance. Although the accuracy of sparse inertial motion capture is constantly improving, it still cannot achieve the precision required for accurate teleoperation. Therefore, this paper proposes a compromise plan, using 8 IMUs for upper body inertial motion capture. While greatly improving the precision of motion capture, it does not have a great impact on the wearing experience.

2.2 Motion Retargeting

In the early days, the retargeting of the full-body humanoid was achieved through model optimization [7,28]. In order to ensure the overall stability of the humanoid, it is necessary to determine the contact state [7] in advance, or measure and estimate the contact through sensors [28]. Recently, some works [11,13] has begun to use reinforcement learning algorithms trained on human motion datasets to realize the stability control of the full-body humanoid, which not only ensures the stability of the humanoid, but also reduces the complexity of the operation. When only the upper body of the humanoid is considered for teleoperation, the inverse kinematics (IK) algorithm can complete the retargeting of human-to-humanoid motion. Many works [2,13] have used the IK algorithm as their motion retargeting method for the upper body of their humanoid. However, traditional IK algorithms based on analytical and numerical solutions may encounter the possibility of computation failure, especially the humanoid arm generally has more than 6 degrees of freedom, and the complex joint structure brings greater challenges to the solution. Other works [14,19,26,37] try to use neural networks to solve the complex IK problem of the multi-degree-of-freedom robotic arm, and achieve good results. This paper also uses neural networks to solve the complex IK problem, but unlike previous work, we use temporal neural networks to take advantage of motion information of historical frames in the scene of real-time teleoperation, which can bring more accurate retargeting and smoother real-time control.

3   TeleMotion System

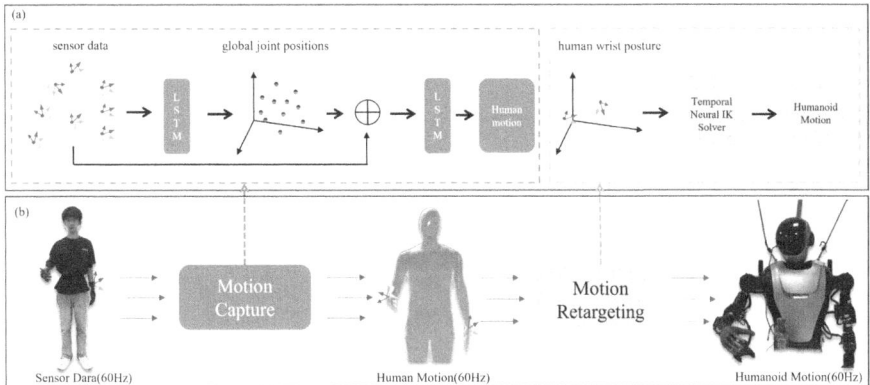

Fig. 2. Overall Structure of TeleMotion. In (a), the left side illustrates the specific implementation of the motion capture algorithm. The right side of (a) presents the implementation of the action redirection algorithm, TNIK. (b) Shows the workflow of TeleMotion, where the system receives 60 Hz sensor data as input, processes it through the motion capture algorithm to obtain human motion, and then applies the motion retargeting algorithm to derive the corresponding robotic motion.

The overall structure of our motion capture teleoperation system is shown in Fig. 2. The system uses IMUs and motion capture gloves to measure human movements at a rate of 60 Hz, and then uses the measured values of the sensors as the input of the inertial motion capture algorithm to capture human motion represented by the SMPL model [25]. After obtaining the real-time motion of the human body, the motion retargeting algorithm is used to obtain the real-time motion of the robot, that is, the angles of each joint of the humanoid robotic arm, and finally realizes the real-time teleoperation of the humanoid.

3.1   Hardware

The hardware used in the TeleMotion system is shown in the Fig. 3, mainly including the sensors used in the motion capture and the humanoid robot being remotely controlled. The IMU sensor is a 9-axis IMU that can measure 3-axis acceleration, 3-axis rotation and 3-axis magnetic force. Axis-lab contains a total of 6 IMUs, and their wearing positions are shown in Fig. 3, which are the upper and forearms of the left and right hands, as well as the head and waist. For more accurate teleoperation, we need to capture the rotation of the human wrist, so we also use the IMUs on the motion capture gloves, which are on the back of the left and right hands. These 8 IMUs are used to capture the movements of the human upper body. In order to control the dexterous hand, we chose to use a commercial product [41] to capture the motion of the human fingers. For the humanoid robot, we use Leju's Kuavo [21], equipped with dexterous hand as shown in Fig. 3. The Kuavo robot has 7 degrees of freedom on each of its left and right arms, and the arm length is 50 cm. The single dexterous hand has 6 degrees of freedom, of which the thumb has two degrees of freedom and the other fingers have one degree of freedom.

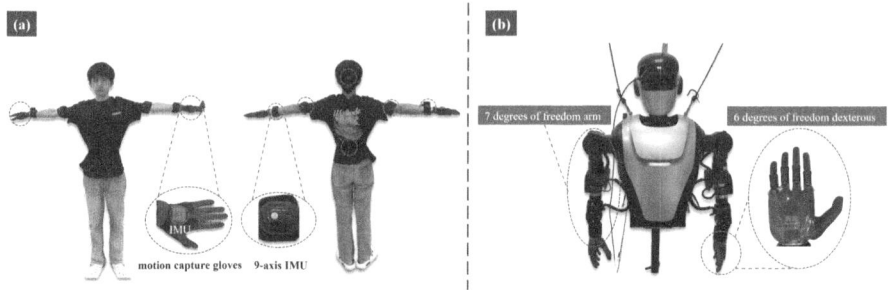

Fig. 3. This figure showcases the hardware used in TeleMotion. The left side displays the sensor hardware utilized in the system along with its wearing method, while the right side presents the humanoid robot and its dexterous hand used in this system.

3.2   Motion Capture Subsystem

Human Model. The human body model used in this paper is the SMPL model [25] with 24 body joints. The posture of each joint is represented by a three-dimensional vector $\theta_i \in R^3$. Therefore, the overall posture of this model is represented as $\theta \in R^{24 \times 3}$. The body shape of this model is represented by a 10-dimensional vector $\beta \in R^{10}$, representing the height, thinness, and fatness of the body shape. There is also a three-dimensional vector $p \in R^3$ representing the global displacement of the root node. Through the SMPL model function F, the parameters of 6890 triangular patches of this model can be obtained, that is, $F(\theta, \beta, p) \to R^{6890 \times 3}$.

Motion Capture. The goal of our upper body motion capture is to use a algorithm L to achieve accurate real-time mapping from IMU measurement value $x(t)$ to the upper body human posture $\theta(t)$ represented by the SMPL model, which can be expressed as: $L(x(t)) \to \theta(t)$. Inspired by [46,49], we also adopt a multi-stage pose estimation method, as shown in Fig. 2. Specifically, the first LSTM model realizes the mapping from IMU measurement value $x(t)$ to the spatial coordinates $p(t)$ of the upper body joint points of the SMPL model, that is:

$$p(t) = LSTM_1(x(t), H) \tag{1}$$

The H is the history information of the LSTM network. The second LSTM network uses the output $p(t)$ of the first LSTM network and the IMU measurement value to achieve the prediction of the final posture:

$$\theta(t) = LSTM_2(x(t), p(t), H) \tag{2}$$

Different from the previous method of using only one IMU on each arm, in order to achieve precise capture of arm movements, which is very important for accurate teleoperation, we wear three IMUs on each arm, including one IMU on the glove. This greatly improves the accuracy of motion capture and does not bring excessive discomfort to the user.

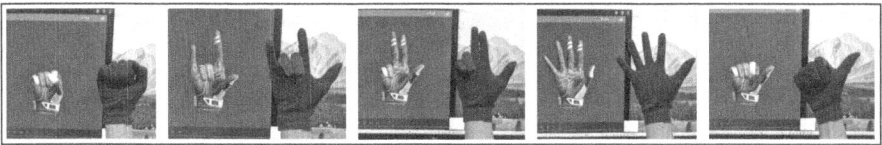

Fig. 4. Demonstration of the effectiveness of commercial motion capture gloves in capturing hand motion.

For hand motion capture, we directly use commercial motion capture gloves, which can capture hand motion up to 120 Hz, as shown in Fig. 4. The captured hand motion will be transmitted outward through the UDP protocol through the supporting driver software. Each finger has 5 degrees of freedom, including three degrees of freedom for the root joint, and one degree of freedom for the middle joint and the end joint, so there are 15 degrees of freedom in one hand.

3.3   Motion Retargeting and Robot Control

For teleoperation of a humanoid upper body, a crucial aspect is the control of the robotic arm's movements, which involves finding a method to convert human arm movements into humanoid arm actions. Due to the significant differences between human joint structures and humanoid joint structures, directly applying human joint angles to the humanoid often fails to achieve the intended movement to specific positions. As a compromise, many approaches focus on using the wrist posture $D = (p_x, p_y, p_z, r_x, r_y, r_z)$, as the posture of the robot's end effector, while the angles of the intermediate joints $Q = (q_1, q_2, q_3, \ldots, q_n)$, are computed using an inverse kinematics algorithm, f_{IK}. When the robotic joint structure is complex, the calculations of f_{IK} become increasingly complicated, leading to a higher probability of failure. This system adopts a data-driven approach, training a temporal neural network to solve the inverse kinematics problem, with a core network structure comprising a 2-layer LSTM [12]. Specifically, this solver takes the postures of the left and right human wrists $D_{human} = (D_{left}, D_{right})$ and historical movement information as inputs to the network, as illustrated in the Fig. 2, resulting in the joint angles of the robot's left and right arms $Q_{robot} = (Q_{left}, Q_{right})$:

$$Q_{robot} = f_{TNIK}(D_{human}, H) \tag{3}$$

Our dexterous hand's degrees of freedom are a subset of the finger degrees of freedom captured by the motion capture gloves. For the retargeting of finger motion, we opted for a relatively simple method: using the weighted average of the three joint angles of each finger from glove as the joint angles $Q_{finger} = (q_1, q_2, q_3, q_4, q_5, q_6)$ for the robot's fingers. Once we obtain the joint angles for the robot's arms and fingers, we send them at a rate of 60 Hz to a specific topic implemented in ROS [20], where the robot control program reads the target angle values from the topic at a fixed frequency and controls each joint to move to that target value.

4   Experiment

In this section, we first introduce the dataset used in this paper and the related evaluation metrics in Sect. 4.1. Subsequently, to validate the effectiveness of the core design of the proposed approach, we conducted a series of relevant experiments, including evaluating the impact of the number of IMUs used in the motion capture system on motion capture accuracy in Sect. 4.2, as well as verifying the effectiveness of TNIK in Sect. 4.3. Finally, in Sect. 4.4, we demonstrate the feasibility of using the TeleMotion system for robotic teleoperation tasks, and its potential for collecting data for imitation learning.

4.1   Data and Metrics

We primarily utilized two datasets. The first is the AMASS synthetic motion capture dataset, DS_{motion}, which is used for training our motion capture algorithms. We employed a data synthesis method similar to that described in [15]. This dataset contains over 8 million frames of synthetic IMU measurements paired with SMPL model pose parameters, sampled at 60 Hz. To train the TNIK algorithm, we synthesized another dataset, DS_{ik}, which pairs human wrist poses with robot joint angles, also exceeding 8 million frames. After obtaining DS_{motion} and DS_{ik}, we split them into training and testing sets in a 9:1 ratio for training and evaluation. For assessing the accuracy of the motion capture algorithm, we used evaluation metrics consistent with [46], which include: 1) SIP error, the average angular error of the upper body joints; 2) angular error, the average angular error of all upper body joints; 3) position error, the Euclidean distance error of upper body joints; and 4) mesh error, the Euclidean distance error of the mesh surface.

4.2   Number of IMUs

To validate that a more number of IMUs leads to more accurate motion capture, we configured three groups with different numbers of IMUs: 4, 6, and 8, which corresponds to the current number in the TeleMotion system. Specifically, with 4 IMUs, they are placed on the head, waist, and wrists. For 6 IMUs, an additional one is added to the forearm of the left and right arms. With 8 IMUs, one more is added to the upper arms of both the left and right arms. We trained a motion capture algorithm model for each configuration on the DS_{motion} training set and validated it on the test set of the same dataset, yielding the experimental results shown in Table 1. According to the results, we found that adding IMUs to the arms significantly improves motion capture accuracy, which is crucial for teleoperation systems based on motion capture.

Table 1. Accuracy of motion capture algorithm with different number of IMUs on the DS_{motion} dataset.

	SIP Err(deg)	Ang Err(deg)	Pos Err(cm)	Mesh Err(cm)
4 IMUs	7.28($\pm$3.53)	7.49($\pm$3.64)	3.51($\pm$1.68)	4.75($\pm$2.19)
6 IMUs	7.06($\pm$3.44)	6.21($\pm$3.30)	3.33($\pm$1.58)	4.22($\pm$1.99)
8 IMUs	**3.24($\pm$2.70)**	**4.54($\pm$2.97)**	**2.34($\pm$1.22)**	**3.01($\pm$1.52)**

4.3   The Effectiveness of TNIK

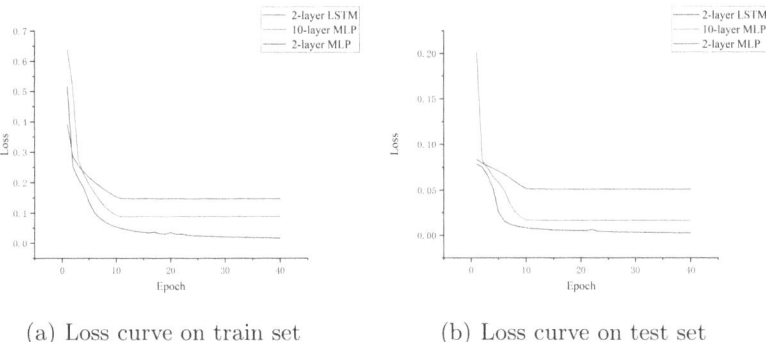

(a) Loss curve on train set   (b) Loss curve on test set

Fig. 5. Loss curves for the training and test sets of three different network structures on the DS_{ik} dataset.

TNIK is a key module in TeleMotion, enabling the rapid and accurate retargeting of human motion to humanoid motion. The algorithm is designed with the consideration that the historical motion data of a person's actions can be effectively utilized by a temporal network in real-time teleoperation scenarios. Thus, a two-layer LSTM was chosen as the core structure of TNIK. To validate whether this structure, leveraging temporal motion information, contributes to the inverse kinematics calculation, we replaced it with two-layer and ten-layer MLPs, train-ing and testing on the DS_{ik} dataset. During training, only the core network structure was modified while other parameters remained constant, using MSE as the loss function. We trained all three structures for 40 epochs and tested on the validation set at the end of each epoch, obtaining results as shown in Fig. 5. The two-layer LSTM structure achieved the lowest loss of 0.016 on the validation set, while the two-layer and ten-layer MLPs could only reduce the loss to 0.14 and 0.08, respectively. After training, we selected the weights corresponding to the lowest loss for each configuration and tested their performance on the test set, measuring the mean and standard deviation of the predicted robotic joint angle errors, as shown in Table 2, TNIK achieved the lowest angle error, with only $1.31°$.

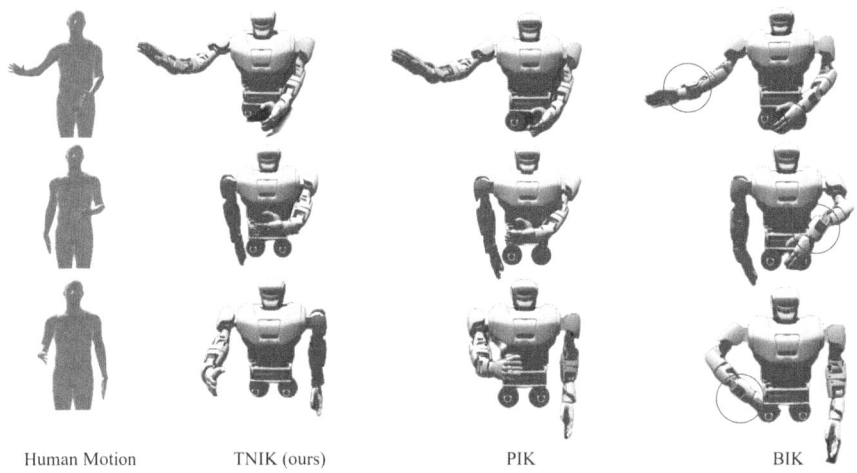

Human Motion   TNIK (ours)   PIK   BIK

Fig. 6. Visualization of the effectiveness of different IK solvers in retargeting human motion in a simulation environment.

After validating the effectiveness of the temporal structure in TNIK, we con-ducted a simple comparison between TNIK and two numerical IK algorithms. The first is the IK algorithm interface provided by the PyBullet [4] framework, referred to as BIK. The second is an IK algorithm implemented based on Pinoc-chio [31], referred to as NIK. We used these three algorithms to retarget 5000 frames of human motion in a simulation environment. Figure 6 displays some of the retargeting results, highlighting instances of calculation failure with BIK. Table 3 records the mean and standard deviation of the computation time for these three algorithms across the 5000 frames, showing that TNIK requires the least time, averaging just 0.139 milliseconds per calculation, which is less than one-tenth of the time taken by the NIK algorithm. These experimental results demonstrate that TNIK can achieve accurate and rapid motion retargeting by effectively utilizing temporal motion information.

Table 2. Joint angular error of different network structures on the DS_{ik} dataset.

Key Structure	Ang Err(deg)
2-layer MLP	5.75($\pm$1.72)
10-Layer MLP	3.66($\pm$1.03)
2-Layer LSTM	**1.31($\pm$0.25)**

Table 3. The execution time of different ik solvers.

IK Solver	Execution Time(ms)
PIK	3.090($\pm$0.695)
BIK	0.383($\pm$0.495)
TNIK	**0.139($\pm$0.346)**

4.4   The Application of TeleMotion in Specific Tasks

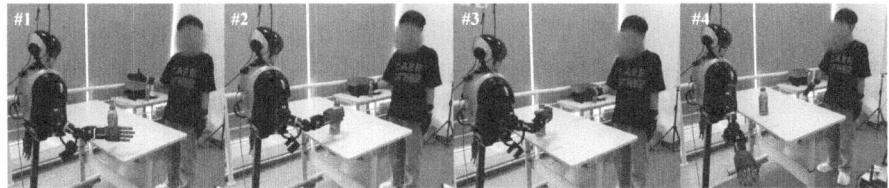

Fig. 7. Demonstration of TeleMotion smoothly controlling the robot to grasp the water bottle, move it in front of the robot, and then gently place it down.

To assess the applicability of TeleMotion for humanoid teleoperation and its potential for data collection in imitation learning, we employed TeleMotion to complete several specific tasks. One task involved using TeleMotion to control a robot to grasp a water bottle placed on a tabletop, move it in front of the robot, and then gently set it down, as shown in Fig. 7. Multiple attempts demonstrated that TeleMotion could successfully accomplish this task in a short amount of time. Another task required the robot to sequentially pick up several water bottles from the table and place them into a blue storage box positioned in front of it, as illustrated in Fig. 8. Similar to the first task, the operator was able to complete this task smoothly using TeleMotion. The successful execution of these tasks indicates that the system has significant potential for data collection in imitation learning, which is crucial for advancing the automation of humanoid robots.

5   Limitations and Future Work

The limitations of TeleMotion can be summarized as follows: First, we utilize IMUs as motion capture sensors; however, IMUs are susceptible to magnetic field interference, which can significantly affect motion capture accuracy in adverse magnetic environments, leading to unreliable teleoperation. Second, our system is currently limited to upper-body teleoperation of humanoid robots, greatly restricting its range of applications, as it can only focus on tasks performed on a stationary desktop. Lastly, we have not deeply explored the effectiveness of TeleMotion in imitation learning and data collection. In the future, we aim to

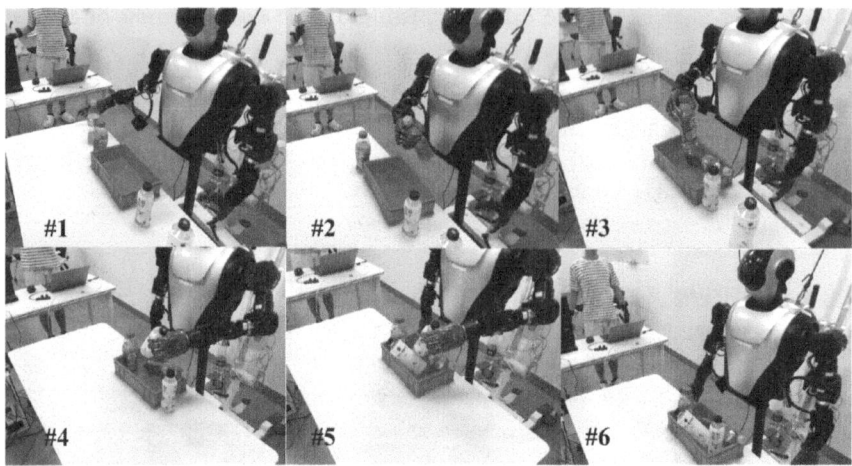

Fig. 8. Demonstration of TeleMotion controlling the robot to pick up the water bottles on both sides of the storage box directly in front and place them inside the box.

investigate full-body inertial motion capture and apply it to the teleoperation of full-body humanoid robots, enabling the manipulation of robots to perform a variety of complex tasks. Additionally, we plan to use this for data collection in imitation learning, thereby advancing the automation of humanoid robots. As we pursue this, it will be crucial to consider the overall stability of the robot during action retargeting across various movements, which presents greater challenges but also holds significant application value.

6   Conclusion

In this paper, we present a real-time upper-body teleoperation system for humanoid robots, called TeleMotion. This system features two key modules. The first is an inertial motion capture subsystem, which allows operators to interact with the robot in a very natural manner for real-time teleoperation. Unlike vision-based motion capture methods, which can be affected by lighting conditions and camera angles, this approach offers greater flexibility in teleoperation. The second key structure is a learnable temporal neural network IK algorithm, named TNIK, which effectively utilizes the temporal information of movements in real-time teleoperation scenarios, enabling accurate retargeting of human motion to robotic motion in a very short time. We conducted many experiments to demonstrate the effectiveness of these two key modules in TeleMotion, as well as its potential for data collection in imitation learning. We believe our TeleMotion system will further advance the development of humanoid robots in the future.

References

1. Brohan, A., et al.: RT-1: robotics transformer for real-world control at scale. arXiv preprint arXiv:2212.06817 (2022)
2. Cheng, X., et al.: Open-television: teleoperation with immersive active visual feedback. arXiv preprint arXiv:2407.01512 (2024)
3. Chi, C., et al.: Universal manipulation interface: In-the-wild robot teaching without in-the-wild robots. arXiv preprint arXiv:2402.10329 (2024)
4. Coumans, E., Bai, Y.: Pybullet quickstart guide (2021)
5. Dafarra, S., et al.: ICUB3 avatar system: enabling remote fully immersive embodiment of humanoid robots. Sci. Robot. **9**(86), eadh3834 (2024)
6. Darvish, K., et al.: Teleoperation of humanoid robots: a survey. IEEE Trans. Rob. **39**(3), 1706–1727 (2023)
7. Di Fava, A., et al.: Multi-contact motion retargeting from human to humanoid robot. In: 2016 IEEE-RAS 16th International Conference on Humanoid Robots (Humanoids), pp. 1081–1086. IEEE (2016)
8. Fang, H., et al.: Airexo: low-cost exoskeletons for learning whole-arm manipulation in the wild. In: 2024 IEEE International Conference on Robotics and Automation (ICRA), pp. 15031–15038. IEEE (2024)
9. Fritsche, L., et al.: First-person tele-operation of a humanoid robot. In: 2015 IEEE-RAS 15th International Conference on Humanoid Robots (Humanoids), pp. 997–1002. IEEE (2015)
10. Fu, Z., Zhao, T.Z., Finn, C.: Mobile aloha: Learning bimanual mobile manipulation with low-cost whole-body teleoperation. arXiv preprint arXiv:2401.02117 (2024)
11. Fu, Z., et al.: Humanplus: humanoid shadowing and imitation from humans. arXiv preprint arXiv:2406.10454 (2024)
12. Graves, A., Graves, A.: Long short-term memory. In: Supervised Sequence Labelling with Recurrent Neural Networks, pp. 37–45 (2012)
13. He, T., et al.: Learning human-to-humanoid real-time whole-body teleoperation. arXiv preprint arXiv:2403.04436 (2024)
14. Ho, C.-K., et al.: A deep learning approach to navigating the joint solution space of redundant inverse kinematics and its applications to numerical IK computations. IEEE Access **11**, 2274–2290 (2023)
15. Huang, Y., et al.: Deep inertial poser: learning to reconstruct human pose from sparse inertial measurements in real time. ACM Trans. Graph. (TOG) **37**(6), 1–15 (2018)
16. Ishiguro, Y., et al.: Bilateral humanoid teleoperation system using whole-body exoskeleton cockpit tablis. IEEE Robot. Autom. Lett. **5**(4), 6419–6426 (2020)
17. Iyer, A., et al.: Open teach: a versatile teleoperation system for robotic manipulation. arXiv preprint arXiv:2403.07870 (2024)
18. Jiang, Y., et al.: Transformer inertial poser: real-time human motion reconstruction from sparse IMUs with simultaneous terrain generation. In: SIGGRAPH Asia 2022 Conference Papers, pp. 1–9 (2022)
19. KöKer, R.I.: A genetic algorithm approach to a neural-network-based inverse kinematics solution of robotic manipulators based on error minimization. Inf. Sci. **222**, 528–543 (2013)
20. Koubaa, A., et al.: Robot Operating System (ROS), vol. 1. Springer (2017)
21. Lejurobot. Kuavo-my. Lejurobot (2024). https://www.lejurobot.com/application/kuavo-my

22. Li, S., et al.: A mobile robot hand-arm teleoperation system by vision and IMU. In: 2020 IEEE/RSJ International Conference on Intelligent Robots and Systems (IROS), pp. 10900–10906. IEEE (2020)
23. Lin, T., et al.: Learning visuotactile skills with two multifingered hands. arXiv preprint arXiv:2404.16823 (2024)
24. Liu, H., et al.: A glove-based system for studying hand-object manipulation via joint pose and force sensing. In: 2017 IEEE/RSJ International Conference on Intelligent Robots and Systems (IROS), pp. 6617–6624. IEEE (2017)
25. Loper, M., et al.: SMPL: a skinned multi-person linear model. In: Seminal Graphics Papers: Pushing the Boundaries, vol. 2, pp. 851–866 (2023)
26. Jiaoyang, L., Zou, T., Jiang, X.: A neural network based approach to inverse kinematics problem for general six-axis robots. Sensors **22**(22), 8909 (2022)
27. Mahmood, N., et al.: Amass: archive of motion capture as surface shapes. In: Proceedings of the IEEE/CVF International Conference on Computer Vision, pp. 5442–5451 (2019)
28. Otani, K., Bouyarmane, K.: Adaptive whole-body manipulation in human-to-humanoid multi-contact motion retargeting. In: 2017 IEEE-RAS 17th International Conference on Humanoid Robotics (Humanoids), pp. 446–453. IEEE (2017)
29. Pan, S., et al.: Fusing monocular images and sparse IMU signals for real-time human motion capture. In: SIGGRAPH Asia 2023 Conference Papers, pp. 1–11 (2023)
30. Park, Y., Agrawal, P.: Using apple vision pro to train and control robots (2024)
31. Parno, B., Howell, J., Gentry, C., Raykova, M.: Pinocchio: nearly practical verifiable computation. Commun. ACM **59**(2), 103–112 (2016)
32. Montecillo Puente, F.J., Sreenivasa, M., Laumond, J.P.: On real-time whole-body human to humanoid motion transfer. In: International Conference on Informatics in Control, Automation and Robotics (2010)
33. Qin, Y., et al.: Anyteleop: a general vision-based dexterous robot arm-hand teleoperation system. arXiv preprint arXiv:2307.04577 (2023)
34. Ramos, J., Kim, S.: Dynamic locomotion synchronization of bipedal robot and human operator via bilateral feedback teleoperation. Sci. Robot. **4**(35), eaav4282 (2019)
35. Ramos, J., Kim, S.: Humanoid dynamic synchronization through whole-body bilateral feedback teleoperation. IEEE Trans. Rob. **34**(4), 953–965 (2018)
36. Schepers, M., Giuberti, M., Bellusci, G., et al.: Xsens MVN: consistent tracking of human motion using inertial sensing. Xsens Technol. **1**(8), 1–8 (2018)
37. Shah, S.K., Mishra, R., Ray, L.S.: Solution and validation of inverse kinematics using deep artificial neural network. Mater. Today Proc. **26**, 1250–1254 (2020)
38. Shi, L.X., et al.: Yell at your robot: improving on-the-fly from language corrections. arXiv preprint arXiv:2403.12910 (2024)
39. Sivakumar, A., Shaw, K., Pathak, D.: Robotic telekinesis: learning a robotic hand imitator by watching humans on youtube. arXiv preprint arXiv:2202.10448 (2022)
40. Octo Model Team, et al.: Octo: an open-source generalist robot policy. arXiv preprint arXiv:2405.12213 (2024)
41. Udexreal. Udexreal. Udexreal (2024). http://www.udexreal.com/
42. Van Wouwe, T., et al.: Diffusionposer: real-time human motion reconstruction from arbitrary sparse sensors using autoregressive diffusion. In: Proceedings of the IEEE/CVF Conference on Computer Vision and Pattern Recognition, pp. 2513–2523 (2024)
43. Wu, P., et al.: Gello: a general, low-cost, and intuitive teleoperation framework for robot manipulators. arXiv preprint arXiv:2309.13037 (2023)

44. Yang, P.-C., Sasaki, K., Suzuki, K., Kase, K., Sugano, S., Ogata, T.: Repeatable folding task by humanoid robot worker using deep learning. IEEE Robot. Autom. Lett. **2**(2), 397–403 (2016)
45. Yi, X., Zhou, Y., Xu, F.: Physical non-inertial poser (PNP): modeling non-inertial effects in sparse-inertial human motion capture. In: ACM SIGGRAPH 2024 Conference Papers, pp. 1–11 (2024)
46. Yi, X., Zhou, Y., Feng, X.: Transpose: real-time 3D human translation and pose estimation with six inertial sensors. ACM Trans. Graph. (TOG) **40**(4), 1–13 (2021)
47. Yi, X., et al.: Physical inertial poser (PIP): physics-aware real-time human motion tracking from sparse inertial sensors. In: Proceedings of the IEEE/CVF Conference on Computer Vision and Pattern Recognition, pp. 13167–13178 (2022)
48. Zhao, T.Z., et al.: Learning fine-grained bimanual manipulation with low-cost hardware. arXiv preprint arXiv:2304.13705 (2023)
49. Zuo, C., et al.: Loose inertial poser: motion capture with IMU-attached loose-wear jacket. In: Proceedings of the IEEE/CVF Conference on Computer Vision and Pattern Recognition, pp. 2209–2219 (2024)

Detail Enhancement for Free Surface LBM Using Adaptive Sizing of Coupled Particles

Qingyue Qu[1,2], Huiwen Liu[2], Shaonan Zhu[2], Aimin Hao[1], Peng Yu[1],
and Yang Gao[1,2(✉)]

[1] State Key Laboratory of Virtual Reality Technology and Systems,
Beihang University, Beijing 100191, China
gaoyangvr@buaa.edu.cn
[2] Hubei Key Laboratory of Intelligent Yangtze and Hydroelectric Science,
Yangtze Power Co., Ltd., Yichang 443000, Hubei, China

Abstract. Physically based fluid simulation plays an important role in the immersion and realistic of VR and AR applications. However, efficiency is the bottleneck problem that restricts physical applications. Among those physics-related fluid models, the Lattice Boltzmann Method (LBM), with its localized algorithm, offers high efficiency. However, as a purely Eulerian grid-based approach, achieving rich detail necessitates high resolution. Conversely, Lagrange-based methods can capture intricate details but require substantial computational time to solve large-scale linear systems and manage numerous particle operations. To address these challenges, we propose a hybrid solver that couples the efficient LBM solver with an adaptive particle interpolation method for detail enhancement. Our innovative adaptive particle strategy further reduces particle count while preserving surface detail and improving temporal efficiency by dynamically adjusting particle size based on particle position, distance, and velocity. Experiments demonstrate that our method can display more surface details than LBM alone, delivering visual effects comparable to direct particle interpolation but with higher efficiency. Moreover, our method yields superior visual results compared to adaptive particle methods based on the FLIP approach. This approach is particularly well-suited for large-scale simulations, enhancing both visual quality and time efficiency, and shows great potential for real-time fluid simulations in VR applications.

Keywords: Fluid simulation · Lattice Boltzmann method · Virtual reality

1 Introduction

The computational efficiency demands of VR environments are extremely high to ensure that user interactions in the virtual world are smooth and without

© The Author(s), under exclusive license to Springer Nature Singapore Pte Ltd. 2025
W. Song et al. (Eds.): ICXR 2024, LNCS 15461, pp. 46–61, 2025.
https://doi.org/10.1007/978-981-96-3679-2_4

delay. Lag or low frame rates in fluid simulations can result in a poor user experience, or even cause motion sickness. The efficiency of the Lattice Boltzmann Method (LBM) aligns perfectly with VR's real-time requirements, making it a key advantage for VR-related fluid simulations. LBM excels in fluid simulation due to its inherent efficiency in parallelization, straightforward implementation, and natural management of complex boundary conditions [16,17,22]. However, as a purely Eulerian grid-based approach, LBM encounters significant limitations in representing fine fluid details. Unlike Lagrangian-particle-based methods, LBM does not employ particles to capture small-scale dynamics, resulting in a less detailed visualization of fluid phenomena. This grid-only structure results in smoother, more diffused fluid surfaces, making it challenging to accurately depict intricate features such as thin fluid sheets, splashes, and complex surface interactions. As a result, LBM's lack of particle representation limits its ability to achieve high-resolution detail and dynamic realism in fluid simulations, both of which are vital for numerous computer graphics applications.

Hybrid Eulerian/Lagrangian methods, such as Fluid Implicit Particle (FLIP) [5,6,27], Affine Particle-in-Cell (APIC) [7,12], and the Material Point Method (MPM) [3,11,13], offer superior detail preservation and reduced numerical dissipation, utilizing particles for a more dynamic and detailed representation of the fluid surface. These methods also benefit from adaptive sampling of the fluid domain, focusing computational resources where needed. However, they are more complex to implement, require handling both grid-based and particle-based data structures, and can be computationally expensive with large numbers of particles. Stability issues may also arise during particle-grid interactions.

To address these issues, combining the Eulerian-based LBM solver with FLIP-based particle interpolation would be an intriguing approach. This can leverage the high efficiency and good volume retention of the LBM solver while utilizing particles to represent the specific shape and details of the fluid. Thus, in this study, we develop an improved LBM model with adaptive interpolated sizing particles (AIPLBM), taking advantage of LBM's parallel efficiency and boundary robustness while integrating the detailed and adaptive capabilities of particle-based approaches. Additionally, we present an adaptive particle size adjustment method suitable for this hybrid solver, culminating in an efficient fluid simulation framework ideal for complex computer graphics applications. In conclusion, our contributions can be summarized as follows:

- We presented a new hybrid Eulerian-Lagrangian solver that couples Eulerian LBM with Lagrangian particles, delivering high temporal efficiency and rich surface details.
- We devised an adaptive particle strategy suitable for the new hybrid solver, considering factors such as particle position, distance, and velocity. This strategy further reduces the number of particles while preserving surface details and improving temporal efficiency.
- We conducted several experiments to demonstrate the efficiency of our proposed method and its ability to provide rich fluid surface details. Our findings introduce a new concept and potential for free surface fluid modeling.

2   Related Work

2.1   LBM in Computer Graphics

Fig. 1. IPLBM wall (top: IPLBM, bottom: AIPLBM). Water flowing out of a container with apertures in the shape of letters "IPLBM".

In the field of computer graphics, researchers led by Thürey et al. [20,22,24] have been exploring the use of LBM to simulate free surface fluids. They have made numerous improvements to the traditional LBM, enabling it to track interface movements and achieve realistic simulations of free surface fluid dynamics in graphics. During the past decade, researchers like Liu and Li et al. [15,18,19] have conducted extensive studies on the application of LBM in graphics.

Thürey et al. [22] introduced an interactive method for simulating free surface fluids based on LBM. By incorporating concepts like mass and volume fraction, this method tracks fluid surface changes. Then Thürey et al. [21] further extended their previous methods to simulate moving objects with varying surface roughness, bidirectional coupling interactions, and improved mass conservation. They demonstrated how to efficiently initialize boundary conditions for moving objects from arbitrary triangular meshes.

Liu et al. [18] developed an adaptive LBM model using viscosity correction to improve stability and accuracy, predicting multiple viscosities within a uniform grid. Guo et al. [9] created a unified LBM method for two-phase flows, enhancing stability and efficiency in simulating fluid dynamics like splashing and bubbles. Li et al. [15] introduced an adaptive relaxation method (ACM-MRT) to improve turbulence simulations at various resolutions. Li et al. [16] advanced LBM for multiphase flow by linking Navier-Stokes equations with a phase field equation, improving energy conservation and accuracy. Lyu et al. [19] developed a versatile

LBM for fluid-solid interactions, optimized for GPUs, improving performance over other solvers. Li et al. [17] optimized LBM for realistic water-air density ratios, improving stability in complex simulations.

2.2 Adaptive Acceleration Schemes for Fluid Simulation

Adaptive particles and adaptive time stepping play crucial roles in enhancing simulation time efficiency. Adaptive particles facilitate dynamic adjustments in particle size and quantity depending on their position within the fluid. In regions of lesser importance, larger particles are utilized to decrease computational demands, whereas smaller particles are employed in proximity to the fluid's surface to accurately capture intricate details [1]. This strategic deployment of particles effectively minimizes the overall particle count, substantially diminishing the computational time dedicated to particle operations, all while maintaining the precision of surface detail representation.

Building on the concept of spatial adaptivity in liquid simulations, Ando et al. [1] introduced a particle-based FLIP method to maintain thin fluid sheets in liquid simulations by adaptively splitting and merging particles, allowing for complex animations with efficient topology management. Ando et al. [2] later developed a more efficient liquid simulation using a tetrahedral mesh and an adaptive FLIP method, capturing detailed free-surface effects with fewer computational costs. Zhai et al. [25] improved fluid simulations with power particles, using adaptive sampling and GPU acceleration for better efficiency and visual quality. Ferstl et al. [4] reduced particle counts and simulation time by only using particles near the liquid surface, yielding results similar to traditional FLIP methods but more efficiently. Gao et al. [6] combined tetrahedral mesh discretization with the FLIP method, enhancing simulation robustness and reducing computational demands while capturing detailed fluid surfaces. Gao et al. [8] and Zheng et al. [26] improved SPH simulations by using k-means clustering to group particles by velocity and applying a two-scale time-step scheme, boosting efficiency and stability in high-speed fluid simulations.

Adaptive time-stepping adjusts the size of the time step in simulations based on stability and accuracy needs. Smaller steps are used during rapid changes for accuracy, while larger steps are used in stable regions to speed up the process. This method focuses computational power where it's needed most, making simulations more efficient. Thürey et al. [23] improved the speed and stability of free surface simulations using the Lattice Boltzmann Method (LBM) by changing the time step size adaptively, reducing the required steps and stabilizing gravity-driven simulations in 2D and 3D tests. Horstmann et al. [10] introduced another adaptive time-stepping method by increasing the speed of sound. This approach maintains mass and pressure continuity in simulations, like thermal plumes, minimizing errors and keeping convergence rates steady.

In conclusion, these methods create a more efficient simulation by intelligently managing computational resources, balancing the need for detail with the necessity of speed.

3   Free Surface LBM with Interpolated Particles

3.1   Improved Free Surface LBM

LBM is a second-order numerical scheme that provides an approximation to the Navier-Stokes equation in both time and space [14]. In LBM, fluid motion is simulated by evolving the distribution function f_i, which represents either the probability or the number density of the particles moving in the direction i with velocity c_i at position x_i and time t:

$$f_i(\mathbf{x} + \mathbf{c}_i \Delta t, t + \Delta t) = f_i(\mathbf{x}, t) + \Omega_i(\rho, \mathbf{u}), \tag{1}$$

where Δt denotes the time step, $\mathbf{u}$ denotes the velocity field, and Ω represents the function that describes particle collision, also known as the collision model. For our scheme, we utilize the single relaxation model, which is both simple and stable enough to simulate common free surface phenomena. The traditional LBM can be decomposed into two primary steps, as evident from Eq. (1): collision and streaming:

$$\begin{aligned} \text{Collision} \quad & f'_i(\mathbf{x}, t) = (1 - \tfrac{1}{\tau}) f_i(\mathbf{x}, t) + \tfrac{1}{\tau} f_i^{eq}(\mathbf{x}, t), \\ \text{Streaming} \quad & f_i(\mathbf{x} + \mathbf{c}_i \Delta t, t + \Delta t) = f'_i(\mathbf{x}, t), \end{aligned} \tag{2}$$

where c_i denotes the discrete direction of velocity, f'_i denotes the intermediate distribution function, τ denotes the relaxation time relating to the kinematic viscosity ν with $\tau = \nu/(c_s^2 \Delta t) + 0.5$ ($c_s = 1/\sqrt{3}$ is the speed of sound) and f_i^{eq} denotes the equilibrium distribution function computed as:

$$f_i^{eq} = \omega_i \rho \left[1 + \frac{\mathbf{c}_i \cdot \mathbf{u}}{c_s^2} + \frac{(\mathbf{c}_i \cdot \mathbf{u})^2}{2c_s^4} - \frac{\mathbf{u}^2}{2c_s^2} \right], \tag{3}$$

where ω_i denotes the weight, ρ denotes the density of a grid. The density and velocity can be computed with:

$$\rho = \sum_i f_i, \quad \rho \mathbf{u} = \sum_i \mathbf{c}_i f_i. \tag{4}$$

In order to track the interface of fluid, the free surface LBM [22] introduces two additional quantities, the mass m and the fluid fraction $\varepsilon = m/\rho$, stored in each node of the grid. The motion of the interface is tracked by calculating the mass change, which can be calculated by the distribution function f_i, since f_i denotes the number density of particles. Thus, the mass exchange between an interface grid at $\mathbf{x}$ and a fluid grid at $(\mathbf{x} + \mathbf{c}_i)$ can be computed with:

$$\Delta m_i(\mathbf{x}, t + \Delta t) = f_{\tilde{i}}(\mathbf{x} + \mathbf{c}_i, t) - f_i(\mathbf{x}, t) \tag{5}$$

where $\tilde{i}$ denotes the opposite direction of i. As for the exchange between two interface grids, the computation is a bit different. The interface grid is not full of fluid, so we need to take the fluid fraction ε into account:

$$\Delta m_i(\mathbf{x}, t + \Delta t) = (f_{\tilde{i}}(\mathbf{x} + \mathbf{c}_i, t) - f_i(\mathbf{x}, t)) \cdot \frac{(\varepsilon(\mathbf{x} + \mathbf{c}_i, t) + \varepsilon(\mathbf{x}, t))}{2}. \tag{6}$$

Thus, the total mass exchange for an interface grid can be computed by adding values for all directions:

$$m(\mathbf{x}, t + \Delta t) = m(\mathbf{x}, t) + \sum \Delta m_i(\mathbf{x}, t + \Delta t). \tag{7}$$

For the free surface LBM, the distribution function f_i is only streaming between fluid grids and the interface grids. However, the interface grid is probably near an empty grid, where the distribution function f_i is not valid. Thus, the distribution function f_i from the empty grid should be reconstructed with:

$$f_{\bar{i}}'(\mathbf{x}, t + \Delta t) = f_i^{eq}(\rho_A, \mathbf{u}) + f_{\bar{i}}^{eq}(\rho_A, \mathbf{u}) - f_i(\mathbf{x}, t), \tag{8}$$

where $\rho_A = 1$ is the density of air. For simplicity, we suppose ρ_A is constant. To balance the forces of each side of the interface, the distribution function f_i from the direction of interface normal should also be reconstructed with Eq. (8). The normal direction satisfies

$$\mathbf{n} \cdot \mathbf{c}_{\bar{i}} > 0 \quad \text{with} \quad \mathbf{n} = \frac{1}{2} \begin{pmatrix} \varepsilon\left(\mathbf{x}_{j-1,k,1}\right) - \varepsilon\left(\mathbf{x}_{j+1,k,1}\right) \\ \varepsilon\left(\mathbf{x}_{j,k-1,1}\right) - \varepsilon\left(\mathbf{x}_{j,k+1,1}\right) \\ \varepsilon\left(\mathbf{x}_{j,k,1-1}\right) - \varepsilon\left(\mathbf{x}_{j,k,1+1}\right) \end{pmatrix}. \tag{9}$$

After all distribution functions are filled, the intermediate interface type (filled or emptied), can be determined by the density and the mass with:

$$\begin{aligned} m(\mathbf{x}, t + \Delta t) > (1 + \kappa)\rho(\mathbf{x}, t + \Delta t) \rightarrow \text{cell filled} \\ m(\mathbf{x}, t + \Delta t) < (0 - \kappa)\rho(\mathbf{x}, t + \Delta t) \rightarrow \text{cell emptied} \end{aligned}, \tag{10}$$

where $\kappa = 10^{-3}$ is the threshold to prevent the frequent grid flag transform. Then, we should reinitialize the grid flag since the interface must be closed. Firstly, all neighboring empty grids of the filled grid are converted to the interface. For all these grids, the average density ρ^{avg} and velocity $\mathbf{v}^{avg}$ of their surrounding fluid and interface girds are calculated to initialize $f_i^{eq}(\rho^{avg}, \mathbf{v}^{avg})$. At the same time, the filled grid is converted to the fluid grid, and all empty grids around the fluid grids are converted to interface grids. Secondly, all neighboring fluid grids of the emptied gird are converted to the interface. There is no need to reconstruct f_i for these grids since all their distribution functions are valid.

According to Eq. (10), the filled and emptied grids have different density and mass values. We assume that $m = \rho$ for the fluid grid and $m = 0$ for the empty grid. Therefore, when the status of an intermediate grid cell transitions to either fluid or empty, a change in mass occurs. To ensure mass conservation, the excess mass should be redistributed in accordance with the direction of the normal vector $\mathbf{n}$:

$$m\left(\mathbf{x} + \mathbf{c}_i\right) = m\left(\mathbf{x} + \mathbf{c}_i\right) + m^{ex}\left(w_i / w_{\text{total}}\right), \tag{11}$$

where m^{ex} denotes the excessive mass, which is calculated from the difference between the mass and density in Eq. 10. w_{total} is the sum of w_i, which is computed with:

$$w_i = \begin{cases} \mathbf{n} \cdot \mathbf{c}_i & , \text{ if } \mathbf{n} \cdot \mathbf{c}_i > 0 \\ 0 & , \text{ otherwise} \end{cases} \quad \text{for filled grids,}$$

$$w_i = \begin{cases} -\mathbf{n} \cdot \mathbf{c}_i & , \text{ if } \mathbf{n} \cdot \mathbf{c}_i < 0 \\ 0 & , \text{ otherwise} \end{cases} \quad \text{for emptied grids.}$$

(12)

3.2 LBM Coupled Lagrangian Particles

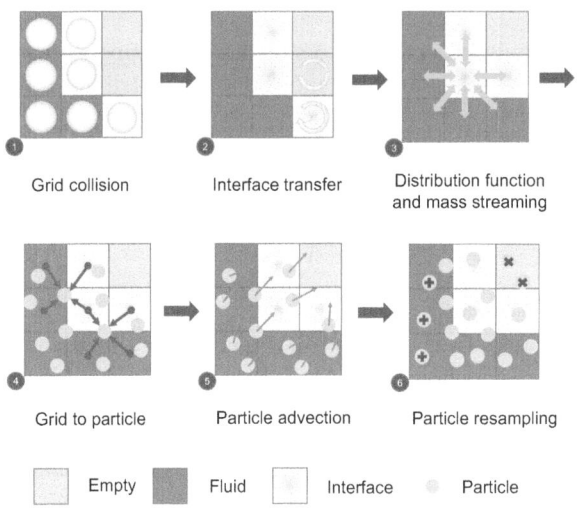

Fig. 2. Flow chart of IPLBM scheme. (1) Perform the collision step within the LBM framework. (2) Update the interface location by examining the density-mass relationship. (3) Stream both mass and the distribution function. (4) Transfer velocity and its increments from the grid to the particles, then update the particles' velocities. (5) Use the semi-Lagrangian method to update particle positions. (6) Remove particles outside the fluid domain and add particles to grids with insufficient numbers.

Similarly to FLIP-related methods, the particle velocity $\mathbf{u}_i$ in our coupled framework also comes from the LBM grid velocity field $\mathbf{u}$. The velocity field $\mathbf{u}$ is calculated before and after the LBM step, to calculate the increase in velocity for each time step.

As shown in Fig. 2, in the grid to particle step (G2P), the increase in velocity and the velocity itself are transferred to the particle with:

$$\mathbf{u}_i = \sum_v \mathbf{u}_v S(\mathbf{x}_v - \mathbf{x}_i),$$

$$\frac{d\mathbf{u}_i}{dt} = \sum_v \frac{d\mathbf{u}_v}{dt} S(\mathbf{x}_v - \mathbf{x}_i),$$

(13)

where $\mathbf{u}_v$ denotes the velocity of the grid computed by the LBM solver, and $\mathbf{x}_v$ denotes the position of the grid centre. The subscript v denotes variables stored in the centers of the grid, while the subscript i denotes variables stored in the particles. S is the interpolation function, and here we use the trilinear interpolation function. In LBM, the quantities are all cell-centered variants. After interpolation, the particles update their velocity with:

$$\mathbf{u}_i \leftarrow (1 - \alpha)\mathbf{u}_i^{\mathrm{PIC}} + \alpha\mathbf{u}_i^{\mathrm{FLIP}}, \tag{14}$$

where α is a parameter similar with classical FLIP, $\mathbf{u}_i^{\mathrm{PIC}}$ denotes the velocity interpolated from grids and $\mathbf{u}_i^{\mathrm{FLIP}}$ denotes the velocity increment interpolated from grids. Then, the particles advect through the semi-Lagrangian method.

At the end of each time step, a particle resampling is performed to control the number of particles and ensure that all fluid regions are sufficiently populated with particles. Initially, each grid is filled with particles n (in our approach, $n = 8$). Furthermore, the volume of each particle, ϵ_p, is set to $1/n$. In each time step, our method resamples the particles to fill the grid in a ratio of $\varepsilon/\varepsilon_p$, where ε represents the fluid fraction of the grid, instead of adding a fixed amount of particles as in conventional methods.

If the number of particles in a grid exceeds 1.5ε, we remove excess particles. However, particles in the interface grid are not removed to prevent artifacts. This approach helps maintain the accuracy of the simulation near the fluid interface while managing the overall number of particles in the fluid regions.

We refer to the aforementioned method as IPLBM, and the entire pipeline is illustrated in Fig. 2. Steps 1 to 3 are the traditional LBM steps, handling grid collision, interface transfer, and streaming. In step 4, we utilize the interpolation function to transfer grid information to the particles and update their velocities. Then, in step 5, we update the particle positions. Finally, in step 5 explained in detail in Sect. 3.3, we perform particle resampling, deleting, or adding particles in the fluid region.

3.3   Adaptive Particle Interpolating Scheme

In the method described above, the particles populate all the fluid regions. However, the considerable computational cost arises from the extensive operations on these particles, and employing a high volume of particles within the fluid does not markedly improve visual outcomes. To expedite the simulation process while maintaining the fidelity of surface detail, reducing the particle count within the fluid can effectively diminish the time dedicated to particle operations.

To attain a more realistic visual effect, larger particles are utilized within the fluid while smaller particles are used near the fluid's surface, as shown in Fig. 3. This approach is based on the principle that large particles consist of smaller particles, which implies that each large particle encompasses two or more smaller particles. The reason for using smaller particles at the fluid surface is that most of the fine details of the free surface are found in these areas. Employing large particles in these areas would compromise detail fidelity. To facilitate a seamless

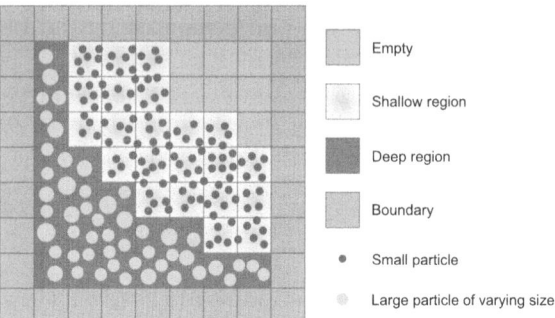

Fig. 3. Adaptive size particles. The entire fluid area is divided into shallow and deep water regions based on the distance from the surface. In the deep water region, particles that are too close to each other may be merged into larger particles. Once particles enter the shallow water region, they will be split into smaller particles.

transition between large and small particles, strategies have been developed to effectively manage the conversion between different particle sizes.

The fluid scene is divided into different regions, such as shallow, deep, and empty regions, as illustrated in Fig. 3, by computing the level set function $\phi(\mathbf{x})$. The value of $\phi(\mathbf{x})$ at a grid point indicates its distance from the interface. $\phi(\mathbf{x})$ is a signed distance field in which negative values indicate the interior of the fluid, and positive values represent the empty region. We define a positive parameter d; when a grid satisfies $-d < \phi(\mathbf{x}) < 0$, it is considered near the fluid surface, otherwise, it is located inside the fluid. In our experiments, we set $d = 3$.

Each particle needs to carry two additional variables, its radius r_i and the number of small particles it contains a_i. We define the smallest particle as having $r_i = 0.25\Delta x$ and $a_i = 1$. At the start of the simulation, each fluid grid is filled with small particles. The conversion between small and large particles is influenced by their position, distance, and velocity. When the distance between two particles is less than $0.5\Delta x$ and they are located inside the fluid, the two particles merge into a larger particle. The new particle is placed at the midpoint of the two original particles, its velocity being their average velocity, a_i being the sum of the two original values, and its radius set to $r_i = \sqrt{3}a_i \cdot 0.25\Delta x$. To prevent unlimited merging, we restrict the maximum a_i of a particle to 8. The merge will be skipped if the new particle's a_i exceeds 8. When a large particle enters the surface region, it splits into a_i small particles. The new particles' r_i and a_i are reset to their initial values, positioned around the original particle, and given the same velocity.

With the adaptive particle method, the particle resampling process also needs adjustment because the number and size of particles in each grid change significantly. When the sum of a_i values of all particles in a grid satisfies $\Sigma_i a_i > 1.5\varepsilon/\varepsilon_p$, some particles need to be removed until $\Sigma_i a_i <= 1.5\varepsilon/\varepsilon_p$. During deletion, particles are removed in ascending order of a_i, starting with the smallest. Conversely, when the sum of a_i values $\Sigma_i a_i < \varepsilon/\varepsilon_p$, the smallest particles are added until

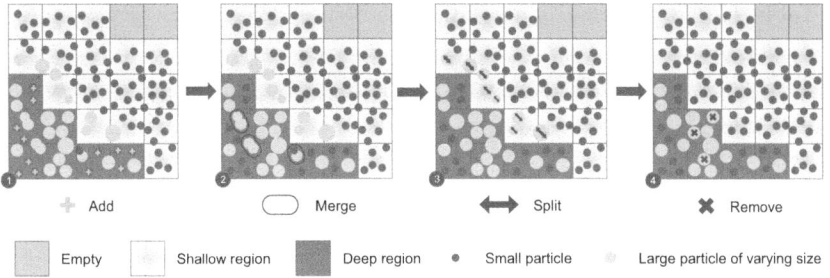

Fig. 4. Flow chart of adaptive size particles. (1) Add small particles to the grid that lack a sufficient total number of small particles. (2) Merge closely spaced particles into larger ones in deep regions. (3) Divide large particles entering shallow regions into smaller particles. (4) Remove redundant particles from the grid.

$\Sigma_i a_i >= \varepsilon/\varepsilon_p$. The whole process of our AIPLBM can be found in Fig. 4. In the deep region, new particles are added in areas with low particle density (step 1), and particles are merged if they are close to each other (step 2). In the shallow region, large particles are split into small particles (step 3). In the deep region, if the number of particles within a grid exceeds a certain threshold ($n = 8$), the particles will be deleted (step 4).

4   Experimental Results

4.1   Parameter Settings

We utilize the aforementioned algorithms to simulate various complex free surface scenarios. Our approach is implemented on a computer equipped with an Intel i7-7700k 4-Core CPU and 64 GB of system memory. For our experimental evaluations, we implement our method and all comparative methods using the CUDA framework and execute them on an NVIDIA RTX 3060 GPU with 12 GB of graphics memory.

To assess the efficiency of our solver, we conducted simulations encompassing diverse free surface scenarios. We compared our approach to other well-established solvers, namely IPLBM (Sect. 3.2), LBM [22], and FLIP [1]. Table 1 presents the number of particles used in each scenario and the corresponding temporal efficiency.

Table 1. Particle numbers, resolutions and temporal efficiency per scenario

Scene	Resolution	Avg. Particles (millions)		Avg. Time/Timestep (ms)		Speed up
		IPLBM	AIPLBM	IPLBM	AIPLBM	
IPLBM wall (Fig. 1)	$200 \times 200 \times 300$	19.84	3.98	313.98	193.67	1.62×
Three angels (Figs. 5 and 6)	$256 \times 64 \times 100$	3.42	0.71	52.86	36.09	1.46×
Water wheel (Fig. 7)	$250 \times 150 \times 200$	10.23	2.05	171.04	118.05	1.44×

Table 2. Efficient comparison of Fig. 6 between our AIPLBM and the FLIP with adaptive particle size.

Method	Resolution	Particles (million)	Avg. Time/Timestep (ms)
AIPLBM	$256 \times 64 \times 100$	3.422	118.05
FLIP [1]	$256 \times 64 \times 100$	3.421	486.36

4.2   Visual Effects

Comparison with Original LBM. Figure 5 shows the comparison between our method and LBM. The resolution of this scene is $256 \times 64 \times 100$, where the dam break on both sides impacts the angel model in the middle, creating a huge splash. As shown in the red box area, compared to LBM [22], our method can capture finer fluid details, such as small droplets and ripples on the water surface. In contrast, the LBM method is smoother or has noticeable jagged edges in detailed areas. This comparative analysis effectively underscores our decision to integrate particles into the LBM framework.

Comparison Between the Interpolated Particle LBM (IPLBM) and Our Adaptive Sizing Interpolated Particle LBM (AIPLBM). Figure 1 compares our AIPLBM, the adaptive particle sizing method, and the direct particle interpolated IPLBM. The scene resolution is $200 \times 200 \times 300$, which features a wall with a hole that displays the text "IPLBM", from which fluid flows out. The IPLBM uses 19.84 million particles, while our AIPLBM uses only 3.98 million particles, achieving comparable visual efficiency and demonstrating the stability of our algorithm in high-speed and relatively chaotic flows.

Interaction Scenario. Figure 7 illustrates a continuously rotating water wheel that agitates the surrounding fluid. As a result of the propeller's movement, water in the tank gushes out. Subsequently, the tank's bottom opens after some time, allowing the contained fluid to pour out. The terrain beneath the scene is composed of uneven soil. This entire scene encompasses a multitude of complex elements. Observing the particle view reveals that, despite highly complex boundary conditions and dynamic interactions with obstacles, the adaptive particle conversion process maintains stability, showcasing remarkable robustness.

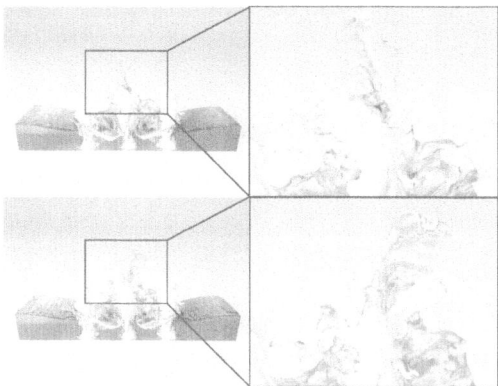

Fig. 5. Three angels (Mesh view) (top: AIPLBM, bottom: LBM [22]**).** When the dams on both sides burst, the surge of water crashes into the three angels in the middle, creating a massive splash. The AIPLBM can depict more detailed splashes and thinner fluid features. In comparison, the standard LBM [22] appears relatively coarse, losing details in particularly thin areas.

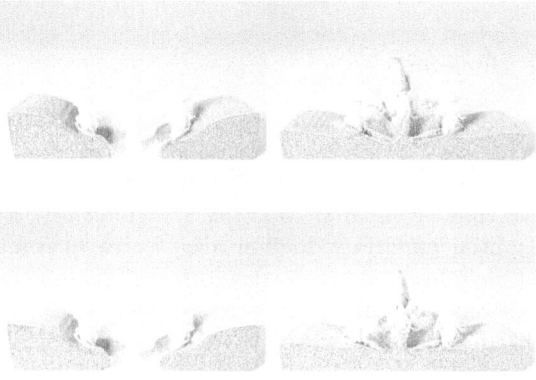

Fig. 6. Three angels (Particle view) (top: AIPLBM, bottom: FLIP [1]**).** Different colors represent particles of varying sizes. Compared to FLIP [1], AIPLBM considers velocity factors, allowing it to display a wider range of particle sizes near the fluid surface. This results in richer details in areas of the fluid that are of greater interest.

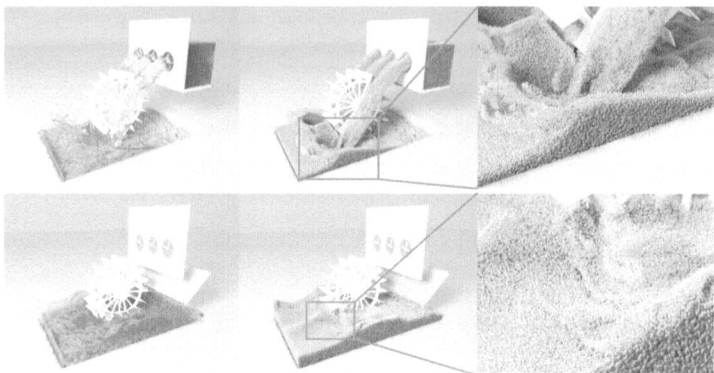

Fig. 7. Water wheel (AIPLBM, left: Mesh view; middle: Particle view; right: Zoom in particle view). The water from the tank and the left side rushes towards the central water wheel, which continuously stirs the incoming flow. In the particle view, different particle colors represent varying particle sizes. A zoomed-in view clearly shows that larger particles are used in deeper water areas, while smaller particles are utilized in shallow water regions.

4.3   Temporal Efficiency

We evaluate the scenarios depicted in Figs. 1, 5, and 7 regarding particle count and temporal efficiency. Each scenario uses different resolutions and initial particle numbers. During the simulations, AIPLBM reduces the particle count by approximately five times compared to IPLBM, significantly lowering memory usage. This substantial particle reduction also decreases computational overhead, improving time efficiency by about 1.5 times. These results demonstrate the effectiveness of our adaptive particle size algorithm in enhancing temporal efficiency and reducing memory usage. Additionally, as shown in Fig. 6 and Table 2, our method outperforms FLIP [1] in temporal efficiency, achieving 4.12 times faster performance while maintaining similar visual effects, due to the highly parallel LBM grid solver.

4.4   Discussion

Compared to pure LBM, our AIPLBM offers richer surface details and captures finer fluid phenomena. It also reduces the number of particles and improves time efficiency compared to the interpolated particle LBM (IPLBM) scheme. Additionally, our method outperforms FLIP-based adaptive particle methods due to a faster grid solver. Despite achieving visual effects similar to those of these pure-particle methods, our approach stands out with excellent efficiency performance, especially in large-scale fluid simulations.

However, there are some limitations. The acceleration effect is less significant when the fluid volume is low or the fluid is relatively shallow. Additionally, in scenarios where surface transformations are intense, frequent merging and splitting operations might impact computational efficiency.

5   Conclusion

This paper introduces an improved free surface liquid LBM model, AIPLBM, which combines the free surface LBM within interpolated particles using adaptive particles to capture fine details and is highly efficient in fluid dynamics. By combining Lagrangian interpolation particles with the LBM grid, our solver benefits from the high efficiency of LBM and the enhanced surface detail provided by particle representation. With an adaptive particle algorithm suitable for this hybrid solver, the number of particles is further reduced, thus improving time efficiency. Experiments show that our method achieves visual effects comparable to other pure particle methods while offering higher time efficiency, thanks to the computational efficiency of LBM and the reduced particle count from the adaptive particle algorithm. Our approach holds significant promise for simulating large-scale, computationally complex fluid scenarios that require detailed surface features. In particular, the efficiency of the method demonstrates its promising application in VR.

In the future, we plan to further refine the adaptive particle algorithm to reduce the number of particles and enhance time efficiency. Additionally, we aim to expand the algorithm for the grid solver to support a broader range of fluid phenomena. Given that our adaptive particles may not significantly accelerate simulations in scenarios with fewer particles or thinner surfaces, we will explore new methods to improve simulation speed in these cases. At the same time, we currently only focus on fluid computational efficiency to meet the real-time requirements of VR, but do not consider real-time rendering, which is one of the directions we will verify and improve on VR devices in the future.

Acknowledgement. This work was supported by the National Key R&D Program of China (2023YFC3604500), National Natural Science Foundation of China (L2324214, 62102036), Beijing Natural Science Foundation (L232102, 4222024), R&D Program of Beijing Municipal Education Commission (KM202211232003), Open Project Program of State Key Laboratory of Virtual Reality Technology and Systems, Beihang University (VRLAB2024A05).

References

1. Ando, R., Thurey, N., Tsuruno, R.: Preserving fluid sheets with adaptively sampled anisotropic particles. IEEE Trans. Visual Comput. Graphics **18**(8), 1202–1214 (2012)
2. Ando, R., Thürey, N., Wojtan, C.: Highly adaptive liquid simulations on tetrahedral meshes. ACM Trans. Graph. **32**(4), 1–10 (2013)
3. Deng, H., Li, J., Gao, Y., Liang, X., Wu, H., Hao, A.: Phyvr: physics-based multimaterial and free-hand interaction in VR. In: 2023 IEEE International Symposium on Mixed and Augmented Reality (ISMAR), pp. 454–462 (2023)

4. Ferstl, F., Ando, R., Wojtan, C., Westermann, R., Thuerey, N.: Narrow band flip for liquid simulations. Comput. Graph. Forum **35**(2), 225–232 (2016)

5. Fu, C., Guo, Q., Gast, T., Jiang, C., Teran, J.: A polynomial particle-in-cell method. ACM Trans. Graph. **36**(6), 1–12 (2017)

6. Gao, M., Tampubolon, A.P., Jiang, C., Sifakis, E.: An adaptive generalized interpolation material point method for simulating elastoplastic materials. ACM Trans. Graph. **36**(6), 1–12 (2017)

7. Gao, Y., Li, S., Hao, A., Qin, H.: Simulating multi-scale, granular materials and their transitions with a hybrid euler-lagrange solver. IEEE Trans. Visual Comput. Graphics **27**(12), 4483–4494 (2021)

8. Gao, Y., Zheng, Z., Li, J., Li, S., Hao, A., Qin, H.: Dynamic particle partitioning SPH model for high-speed fluids simulation. Graph. Models **109**, 101061 (2020)

9. Guo, Y., Liu, X., Xu, X.: A unified detail-preserving liquid simulation by two-phase lattice boltzmann modeling. IEEE Trans. Visual Comput. Graphics **23**(5), 1479–1491 (2016)

10. Horstmann, T., Touil, H., Vienne, L., Ricot, D., Lévêque, E.: Consistent time-step optimization in the lattice boltzmann method. J. Comput. Phys. **462**, 111224 (2022)

11. Hu, Y., et al.: A moving least squares material point method with displacement discontinuity and two-way rigid body coupling. ACM Trans. Graph. **37**(4), 1–14 (2018)

12. Jiang, C., Schroeder, C., Selle, A., Teran, J., Stomakhin, A.: The affine particle-in-cell method. ACM Trans. Graph. **34**(4), 1–10 (2015)

13. Jiang, C., Schroeder, C., Teran, J., Stomakhin, A., Selle, A.: The material point method for simulating continuum materials. In: ACM SIGGRAPH 2016 Courses, pp. 1–52 (2016)

14. Krüger, T., Kusumaatmaja, H., Kuzmin, A., Shardt, O., Silva, G., Viggen, E.M.: The Lattice Boltzmann Method. Springer (2017)

15. Li, W., Bai, K., Liu, X.: Continuous-scale kinetic fluid simulation. IEEE Trans. Visual Comput. Graphics **25**(9), 2694–2709 (2018)

16. Li, W., Liu, D., Desbrun, M., Huang, J., Liu, X.: Kinetic-based multiphase flow simulation. IEEE Trans. Visual Comput. Graphics **27**(7), 3318–3334 (2020)

17. Li, W., Ma, Y., Liu, X., Desbrun, M.: Efficient kinetic simulation of two-phase flows. ACM Trans. Graph. **41**(4), 1–17 (2022)

18. Liu, X., Pang, W.M., Qin, J., Fu, C.W.: Turbulence simulation by adaptive multi-relaxation lattice boltzmann modeling. IEEE Trans. Visual Comput. Graphics **20**(2), 289–302 (2012)

19. Lyu, C., Li, W., Desbrun, M., Liu, X.: Fast and versatile fluid-solid coupling for turbulent flow simulation. ACM Trans. Graph. **40**(6), 1–18 (2021)

20. Thurey, N.: Physically based animation of free surface flows with the lattice boltzmann method. Ph.D. thesis, University of Erlangen (2007)

21. Thürey, N., Iglberger, K., Rüde, U.: Free surface flows with moving and deforming objects for LBM. In: Proceedings of Vision, Modeling and Visualization, vol. 2006, pp. 193–200 (2006)

22. Thürey, N., Körner, C., Rüde, U.: Interactive free surface fluids with the lattice boltzmann method. Technical report 05-4. University of Erlangen-Nuremberg, Germany (2005)

23. Thürey, N., Pohl, T., Rüde, U., Oechsner, M., Körner, C.: Optimization and stabilization of LBM free surface flow simulations using adaptive parameterization. Comput. Fluids **35**(8–9), 934–939 (2006)

24. Thürey, N., Rüde, U.: Free surface lattice-boltzmann fluid simulations with and without level sets. In: VMV, pp. 199–207 (2004)
25. Zhai, X., Hou, F., Qin, H., Hao, A.: Fluid simulation with adaptive staggered power particles on GPUs. IEEE Trans. Visual Comput. Graphics **26**(6), 2234–2246 (2018)
26. Zheng, Z., Gao, Y., Li, S., Qin, H., Hao, A.: Robust and efficient SPH simulation for high-speed fluids with the dynamic particle partitioning method. In: Pacific Graphics Short Papers (2018)
27. Zhu, Y., Bridson, R.: Animating sand as a fluid. ACM Trans. Graph. **24**(3), 965–972 (2005)

Learning Dynamic Cloth Deformation for Virtual Try-on

Xianghui Chen[1], Huiyan Wang[2], Zhaopeng Cui[1],
and Guofeng Zhang[1(✉)]

[1] Zhejiang University, Hangzhou, China
{chenxianghui,zhpcui,zhangguofeng}@zju.edu.cn
[2] Zhejiang Gongshang University, Hangzhou, China
cederic@zjgsu.edu.cn

Abstract. This paper introduces an innovative approach for capturing data-driven cloth deformation in virtual try-on scenarios. The method involves aligning the garment to a T-posed avatar and generating a comprehensive dataset encompassing both dynamic and static cloth deformation. Leveraging the advancements of this dataset, we propose a novel pipeline to obtain dynamic cloth deformations and intricate cloth wrinkles. Evaluation results, obtained across various garments, highlight the superior performance of our proposed model compared to state-of-the-art methods. Our approach excels in terms of accuracy and speed while preserving a significant advancement in forecasting dynamic cloth wrinkles.

Keywords: Garment fitting · Cloth deformation · Virtual try-on

1 Introduction

Physics-based simulation (PBS) [2,4,9] has played a dominant role in various fields, spanning gaming, cloth simulation, fashion design, virtual try-on, and more. However, attaining high-quality results with PBS methods demands a substantial amount of computational resources, thereby restricting its applicative scope. This limitation becomes especially apparent in online virtual fitting rooms, where users often face challenges in achieving a seamless experience due to computational power constraints. The versatility of PBS is both its strength and limitation, affecting its effectiveness in specific application contexts. To tackle this effectiveness issue, various data-driven approaches have been proposed, resulting in plausible results.

To simulate cloth deformation, we encounter two primary challenges. The first one involves the shark contrast between the high complexity of clothing deformation and the low-dimensional representation of human body parameters, making predicting realistic wrinkles, which represent high-frequency signals, a challenging task. TailorNet [15] segregates deformation information into low-frequency and high-frequency signals. The summation of these components

© The Author(s), under exclusive license to Springer Nature Singapore Pte Ltd. 2025
W. Song et al. (Eds.): ICXR 2024, LNCS 15461, pp. 62–76, 2025.
https://doi.org/10.1007/978-981-96-3679-2_5

yields the un-posed deformation, processed using a standard skinning method to obtain the final deformation. However, this may introduce undesirable artifacts, such as volume loss or "candy-wrapper" effects, especially during extreme deformations like cloth deformation. Igor Santesteban et al. [20] proposed a two-level strategy to comprehend the intricate nonlinear deformations of clothing. On one level, their goal is to formulate a model for garment fitting as a function of body shape. On another level, their objective is to develop a model for local garment wrinkles as a function of body shape and motion. These methods addressed this challenge by employing the skinning method to provide speed advantages, resulting in significantly faster prediction speeds (even as fast as 1 to 2 milliseconds). However, skinning method tends to disrupt fine details and wrinkles in the predicted garment, ultimately yielding unsatisfactory results.

The second challenge entails predicting deformation dynamics resulting from body motion. DRAPE [7] addresses this challenge by learning a second-order dynamic model for pose-dependent wrinkle deformation, which can be a time-consuming process. On the other hand, [20,21] utilizes a Gated Recurrent Unit (GRU) to model deformation dynamics and pose-dependent deformation, limiting the accuracy in reproducing pose-dependent deformation.

In contrast to previous methods, we directly encode the Skinned Multi-Person Linear model (SMPL) parameters and generate cloth vertex displacement as the cloth deformation, eliminating the necessity for a skinning procedure. We addresses cloth deformation caused by body dynamics separately using a recursive mechanism, allowing for a more detailed representation of garment wrinkles. To extract intricate clothing deformation details, we leverage Graph Neural Networks (GNN) which introduces potent inductive biases by depicting intricate physical states as graphs composed of interacting particles. Utilizing learned message-passing techniques, these simulations approximate complex dynamics, enabling accurate modeling of realistic physical phenomena. Given the merits of Graph Network-based Simulation (GNS) [16,19], integrating GNS into our learning model can improve the accuracy and fidelity of our model's predictions and produce more realistic outcomes. Our method facilitates a more faithful representation of the complex dynamics inherent in the simulated system.

1. We have established a fitting and simulation pipeline to generate extensive datasets of fully dressed avatars. Different from previous work, our method provides the displacement of clothing mesh nodes induced by body movement, enhancing flexibility in predicting both dynamic and static simulations.
2. We introduce a recursive mechanism to analyze SMPL pose sequences, enabling us to predict vertex displacement due to motion, within which positional encoding approaches is utilized for shorter training time. Additionally, we integrate a residual GNN into our model instead of linear blend skinning to enhance the prediction of finer cloth wrinkle details.
3. Our method outperforms state-of-the-art techniques in predicting intricate cloth wrinkles, while achieving results ten times faster than traditional physics-based simulations.

2   Related Works

Physics-based cloth simulation is the predominant approach for investigating the interaction between clothing and the human body. Numerous studies are dedicated to cloth simulation, and for clarity, we categorize them into two classes: mass-spring system-based simulation [23] and particle-based system [11,24]. In a mass-spring system, fundamental components consist of a mass capable of movement along a single dimension and a spring exerting a restoring force when displaced from its equilibrium position. Within a cloth simulation using a mass-spring system [13,25], the cloth is represented as a grid or mesh of interconnected particles (masses). Each particle is assigned a mass, typically proportionate to the fabric's density. The interconnections between these particles emulate springs, akin to those found in a physical mass-spring system, forming a network of constraints that govern the cloth's deformation and response to external forces. Despite the power of the mass-spring system, accurately modeling shearing and bending behavior poses challenges. Real fabrics can undergo intricate deformations such as twitching and folding, which are challenging to reproduce using this system. Particle-based cloth simulations offer high flexibility; with the right configuration, they adeptly capture the dynamic motion of cloth in response to forces like wind and gravity. Additionally, developers can exert precise control over cloth behavior by adjusting parameters such as particle mass, damping, and stiffness. This level of control facilitates the creation of specific visual effects and allows for artistic choices in cloth animation.

Data-driven approaches in cloth simulation utilize data to enhance the realism and visual appeal of cloth animations. The pre-trained model effectively balances computational efficiency and realism in addressing PBS challenges, making it valuable for real-time applications like interactive experiences, games, and simulations. Extensive research, including notable works like DRAPE [7], has focused on virtual fitting. DRAPE streamlines realistic clothing animation on avatars across diverse shapes and poses without manual intervention. While data-driven, DRAPE's linear cloth deformation approach struggles to predict intricate wrinkle details accurately. GarNet [8] proposes a two-stream network for rapid and precise 3D cloth draping, combining body and cloth features to predict cloth deformation within a 1 cm margin. However, it lacks high-frequency detail. Igor et al. [20] separate cloth deformation into shape-dependent and pose-dependent components using two network modules. TailorNet [15] predicts 3D clothing deformation based on pose, shape, and style, separately handling low and high-frequency deformations. Both methods use a skinning technique for modeling outputs, impacting final accuracy. For increased realism and accuracy, Nuttapong Chentanez [5] proposes a novel convolutional neural network (CNN). This network incorporates newly designed convolution layers into an encoder-decoder framework, achieving high visual accuracy at small inference times. However, the network is expected to provide good quality inference only for data similar to the training set. Alvaro et al. [19] present a machine learning framework and model implementation capable of learning to simulate various challenging physical domains, including fluids, rigid solids, and deformable materials interacting with each other. Subsequently, several graph-based approaches were proposed. For example, Xiaoyu Pan et al. [14] present a learning algorithm utilizing bone-driven motion networks to predict the deformation of garment meshes, yielding plausible results. However, they solely modeled the deformation as a function of bone motion, disregarding human shapes.

Parameterized human body models such as MANO [18], BodyNet [22], Dyna [17], SMPL [10], and SCAPE [1] offer a flexible and efficient means to represent and manipulate human body geometry, facilitating a spectrum of applications in virtual environments, computer graphics, and related fields. MANO is specifically designed for hand geometry and articulation. It provides a concise representation of hand shape and pose, enabling realistic hand animation and interaction in virtual environments. BodyNet is a deep learning-based model utilizing convolutional neural networks. This approach directly predicts body shape and pose parameters from images and provides a data-driven methodology for deducing human body parameters from visual data, particularly beneficial for tasks like body tracking and virtual try-on. Dyna incorporates physics-based simulations to capture realistic body dynamics and soft tissue deformations. This feature enables more authentic and physically plausible animations and simulations of human movements. SMPL is a widely utilized parametric human body model, representing the human body as a deformable mesh. It employs a linear blend skinning approach to articulate how the mesh deforms with variations in body shape and pose. SCAPE is another model utilizing a linear blend skinning approach. It focuses on capturing body shape variations, particularly those arising from pose changes.

3   Pipeline

In this section, we describe our pipeline on predicting the animation of cloth deformation on an SMPL avatar of various shapes and poses.

3.1   Data Preparation

To train our model, we generated ground-truth data by creating diverse garments, including a t-shirt, male shirt, and two female dresses. Character motion sequences from the BioLrub data in the AMASS dataset [12]were selected. To simulate cloth deformation influenced by body shape and motion, we initially fit the garments to a template SMPL avatar with all parameters set to 0. Subsequently, simulation parameters such as cloth material and collision settings were configured, and character shape and motion parameter sequences were applied to the SMPL avatar. The final step involved generating deformed cloth for each combination of SMPL shape and pose parameters.

The primary challenge encountered in the data generation process is fitting garments to the template SMPL avatar. Building on the methodology proposed by Li [6], we adopt a key approach involving the extraction of vertex rings from both the 3D garment mesh and the SMPL template mesh. Through the

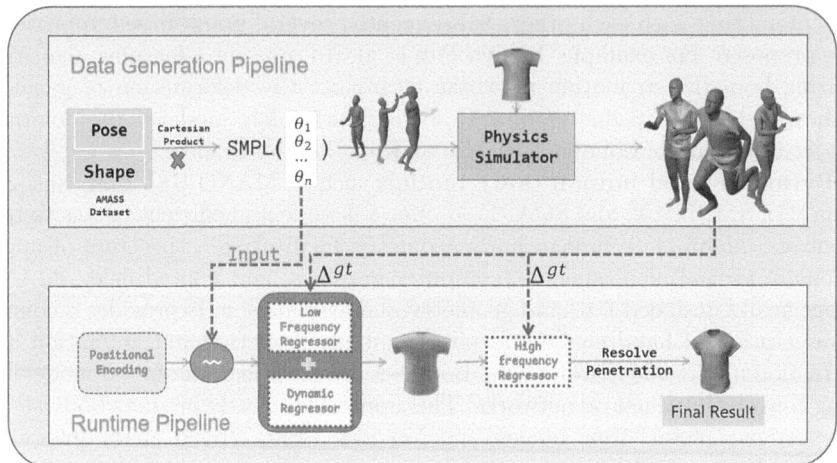

Fig. 1. Pipeline of our approach. In data generation pipeline, we generate dressed avatars with physics simulator from AMASS dataset [12] containing various SMPL parameters; In runtime process, our data-driven model regress coarse middle output with a low frequency regressor, human body motion caused cloth deformation is regressed with a dynamic regressor. To obtain detailed cloth wrinkles, we designed a high frequency regressor. After de-penetration process, we obtain the final result.

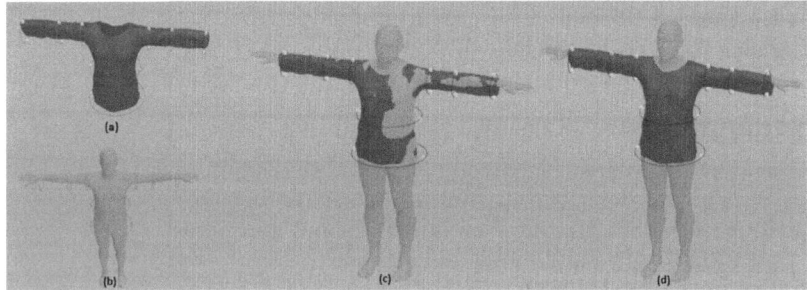

Fig. 2. Pipeline of fitting garment to SMPL template avatar.(a) Detect cut loops of garment from landmark pairs. (b) Detect cut loops from SMPL template avatar. (c) Align garment to avatar via least square optimization. (d) Final appearance after resolving penetration.

minimization of a least-squares optimization problem, we align the garment mesh with the template mesh. Furthermore, a de-penetration process is implemented to ensure a proper fit.

For convenience of explanation, we denote $\mathbf{H} = \mathbf{SMPL}(\beta, \theta)$, as 3D human body mesh modeled from SMPL parameters, where β, θ represents human shape and pose parameters respectively, $\mathbf{G} = \{(v, f) | v \in \mathcal{R}^3, f \in \mathcal{N}^3\}$ as 3D garment mesh. We manually select several pairs of key points $\mathbf{K} = \{(k_1, k_2), \cdots (k_{2n-1}, k_{2n})\}$ from template cloth $\mathbf{G}$. Key points can be automatically extracted by leveraging segmentation information derived from the SMPL template avatar with ease. Subsequently, cut loops, which encapsulate specific parts of a garment, such as sleeve openings and collarbands, are computed based on the identified landmarks. To determine the cutting direction, the cutting operation is applied within the orthogonal view. The process of our detection and cutting methodology is illustrated in Fig. 3. Given cut loops we align garment to SMPL template avatar with least square optimization method. After aligning the garment to SMPL template avatar, we operate a de-penetration algorithm following [7]. The detailed pipeline is shown in Fig. 2.

After fitting garment to template avatar, we can finally generate deformed clothes by feeding AMASS data set into simulation engine, as shown in data generation pipeline in Fig. 1. By employing parameters extracted from the AMASS dataset, we drive the SMPL model to produce a multitude of avatars exhibiting diverse shapes and poses. Leveraging the capabilities of a physics simulator, we are able to generate an extensive collection of well-fitted avatars, each characterized by distinct shapes and poses. To train our model, both static and dynamic ground truth deformation should be simulated. To simulate static deformed cloth, we perform parameter interpolation from 0 to the provided parameter value over a duration of 30 frames. Subsequently, we allow the cloth to rest, enabling us to obtain the static ground truth deformation. For simulating dynamic ground truth, we apply a sequence of body motions to the avatar, resulting in the generation of the dynamic ground truth deformation.

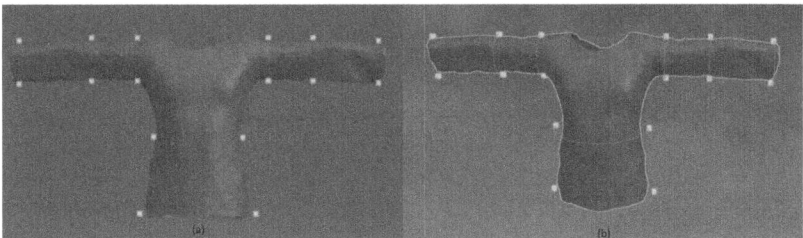

Fig. 3. Detect cut loops from landmark pairs in orthogonal view. (a) Manually selected landmark pairs. (b) Cut loops in orthogonal view.

3.2   Network Architecture

We decompose cloth deformation into two distinct components: static deformation and dynamic deformation. The static deformation is further decomposed into low-frequency deformation and high-frequency deformation. To obtain these three types of deformations, we design specific regressors: the Low-Frequency Regressor, the Dynamic Regressor, and the High-Frequency Regressor, respectively. As depicted in Fig. 1, we acquire the SMPL parameters generated from the AMASS dataset and utilize them as input for the Low-Frequency Regressor, thereby obtaining an all-encompassing deformation. Additionally, to capture dynamic deformation, we employ the Dynamic Regressor. In order to capture finer cloth wrinkles, we leverage the High-Frequency Regressor, utilizing the overall deformation as input. Note that our approach does not guarantee collision-free results, therefore post-processing steps are required to resolve penetration. By utilizing our data generation approaches discussed in Sect. 3.1, we generated dataset $\mathbf{D} = \{\beta \times \theta, \mathbf{G^s}, \mathbf{G^d}\}$, where $\beta \times \theta$ represents Cartesian product between SMPL shape set and pose set. $\mathbf{G^s}$ represents static garment mesh simulated from $\beta \times \theta$ in static pose, while $\mathbf{G^d}$ represents dynamic mesh simulated from pose sequences in $\beta \times \theta$. Thus, given $\mathbf{G^s}$ and $\mathbf{G^d}$, $\mathbf{\Delta_G^{d-s}} = \mathbf{G^d} - \mathbf{G^s}$ indicates the mesh displacement caused by temporal differences. One of our key contribution is the modeling of this aspect of deformation.

For a given garment, we start from a template garment mesh $\mathbf{T_G} \in \mathcal{R}^{3 \times V_G}$ with V_G vertices, and then deform it in three steps. Drawing inspiration from TailorNet, we adopt a similar approach, decomposing garment deformation into two components: low frequency and high frequency. For predicting the low-frequency component, we employ a MLP that operates based on the SMPL shape and pose parameters. In contrast, to predict the high-frequency components, we utilize a residual GNN. Notably, our method stands out as we explicitly model the garment deformation resulting from body dynamics as a separate component

$$\mathbf{R}(\beta, \theta) = R_L(\beta, \theta) + R_D(\beta, \theta) + R_H(\beta, \theta) \tag{1}$$

where R_L and R_H represent non-linear regressors for the low and high deformation components, respectively, our approach leverages these regressors to capture the intricate relationships between the input variables and the corresponding deformation components. Furthermore, to account for the temporal aspects of cloth motion, we introduce an additional regressor, R_D, which is specifically designed to predict dynamic deformation. The final deformation result, denoted by $\mathbf{R}(\beta, \theta)$, encompasses the combined effects of the regressors. By incorporating the template garment $\mathbf{T_G}$, we obtain the final garment mesh as the output. However, it is important to note that our regressor alone does not guarantee a collision-free output. Therefore, to address this issue, we apply a de-penetration approach to resolve any collisions or overlaps within the garment mesh, ensuring a physically plausible result. The pipeline of our approach is shown in Fig. 1. By decomposing cloth deformation into high and low frequency components, as well as dynamic cloth deformation, we distinguish between static and dynamic aspects of the deformation process. The high and low frequency components correspond to static deformations, which capture the overall shape and form of the cloth. On the other hand, the dynamic cloth deformation component accounts for the time-varying aspects of the cloth's motion and captures the wrinkles, folds, and other dynamic features. This decomposition allows us to separately model and predict the different types of deformations involved in cloth simulation.

3.3 Garment Regressor for Low Frequency

To capture the static low frequency garment deformation, we consider it as a function of the SMPL shape and pose parameters, denoted as $R_L(\beta, \theta) : \mathcal{R}^{(\beta,\theta)} \rightarrow \mathcal{R}^{|V_c|\times3}$. To train our regressor, we characterize static garment displacement as $\mathbf{\Delta_G} \in \mathcal{R}^{|\mathbf{V_c}|\times\mathbf{3}}$, The displacements represent the deviation between template garment mesh and static garment simulated from static human body shape and pose. Correspondingly, we define the ground-truth displacement as:

$$\mathbf{\Delta_{Gs}^{gt}} = \mathbf{S_{G_s}}(\beta, \theta) - \mathbf{T_G} \tag{2}$$

where $\mathbf{S_{Gs}}(\beta, \theta)$ represents simulation of garment on a static body characterized in β and θ.

As previously discussed, addressing the intricate complexity of clothing deformation while reconciling it with low-dimensional human body parameters is a challenging task for achieving realistic cloth appearance. To overcome this challenge, we employ an MLP encoder, a choice validated by its demonstrated capability to yield plausible results in experiments conducted in [TailorNet]. However, we also observed that the performance of a single MLP can be enhanced by incorporating a positional encoder to preprocess the SMPL parameters. This additional step helps to reduce training time as shown in Fig. 7c. We tested our finding on training our MLP module with and without Positional Encoding. The clear learning curves substantiated our claim that Positional Encoding reduces training time by over 40%. The test loss curve indicates that our network is not overfitted.

3.4 Garment Regressor for High Frequency

Graph-based simulators leverage the inherent advantages of graphs to incorporate strong inductive biases. These simulators represent rich physical states using graphs, where the nodes represent interacting particles and the edges capture their relationships. By employing learned message-passing mechanisms among the nodes, these simulators approximate the complex dynamics involved in the system. This approach allows for efficient and effective modeling of intricate physical phenomena, as the graph structure enables the representation of spatial and temporal dependencies, leading to accurate simulations and predictions. Recognizing that a single positional encoding combined with an MLP may not capture sufficient detail in cloth wrinkles, we incorporate Graph Neural Networks (GNNs) to enhance the generation of intricate cloth wrinkles. By leveraging the power of GNNs, we are able to effectively capture the spatial relationships and dependencies within the cloth mesh, facilitating the generation of fine-grained and realistic cloth wrinkles. This integration of GNNs complements the positional encoding and MLP, enabling our model to produce more detailed and visually compelling cloth deformation results.

As shown in Fig. 1, we stack graph convolution layer as residual blocks, the graph convolution act as a function of vertex features and edges:

$$H^{(l+1)} = \sigma(D^{-\frac{1}{2}}AD^{-\frac{1}{2}}H^{(l)}W^{(l)}) \tag{3}$$

where D is diagonal node degree matrix, A is the adjacency matrix, with $H^0 = V_G$ and l being the number layer.

3.5   Dynamic Garment Regressor

Unlike static garment fit, garment wrinkles display dynamic deformations that are dependent on the history of the system. To capture these dynamic effects, we introduce recursion within the regressor. By incorporating recursive mechanisms into our model, we enable the regressor to consider the temporal dependencies and history-dependent deformations inherent in garment wrinkles. This recursive approach ensures that our model effectively captures the dynamic nature of garment deformation, leading to more accurate and realistic predictions. Like regressor for predicting low frequency, we characterize dynamic garment regressor as function of SMPL shape and pose parameters denoted as $R_H(\beta, \theta) : \mathcal{R}^{(\beta,\theta)} \rightarrow \mathcal{R}^{|V_c| \times 3}$. To regress dynamic garment displacement caused by body motion, we simulate cloth deformation in sequences of SMPL parameters as:

$$\Delta_{\mathbf{Gd}}^{\mathbf{gt}} = \mathbf{S_{Gd}}(\beta, \theta) - \Delta_{\mathbf{Gs}}^{\mathbf{gt}} - \mathbf{T_G} \tag{4}$$

In our case, the objective of the dynamic garment regressor is to predict $\Delta_{\mathbf{Gd}}^{\mathbf{gt}}$, which represents the ground truth dynamic deformation. To achieve this, we leverage Gated Recurrent Units, which have demonstrated success in predicting dynamic systems, such as human pose direction. By employing GRU neural networks, we can effectively model the dynamic deformation of the garment. During training, we minimize the discrepancy between the predicted displacement R_H and the corresponding ground truth Δ_{Gd}^{gt}, ensuring that the model captures accurate and realistic dynamic deformations.

3.6   Network Implementation and Training

We implement the neural networks described in Fig. 1 using the PyTorch framework. Our MLP network consists of a single hidden layer with 128 neurons. Prior to feeding the SMPL parameters into the MLP, we apply positional cosine encoding to enhance the representation. Additionally, our GRU is constructed with two hidden layers, each having a dimension of 2048 for the hidden features. To mitigate overfitting, we incorporate a dropout layer with a dropout rate of 20%. Furthermore, we employ four graph convolution residual blocks, which have proven to be highly effective, to construct our graph neural network. These architectural decisions have resulted in a robust and reliable implementation of our method. Our training loss consists of three components: vertex L2 loss, mesh normal loss and laplace smoothing term:

$$\mathcal{L} = \|\mathbf{V^{pred}} - \mathbf{V^{gt}}\| + \lambda_1\|\mathbf{V_n^{pred}} - \mathbf{V_n^{gt}}\| + \lambda_2\|\mathbf{L}\|_F^2 \tag{5}$$

where $\|\mathbf{L}\|_F^2$ represents the F norm of the corresponding laplacian matrix, λ_1, λ_2, the loss ratios. In practice, we set the weight parameter λ_2 to a small value for the Laplacian smoothing term. This is because the Laplacian term has a tendency to smooth out high-frequency signals [3]. By assigning a small value to λ_2, we can control the extent of smoothing applied to the signals, striking a balance between preserving details and mitigating noise or fluctuations.

During the training process, we employ the Adam optimizer with an initial learning rate of 1.0e-5 for 200 epochs. Specifically, for the MLP network responsible for predicting low-frequency deformations, we train the module using simulated avatars with static poses and shapes. On the other hand, for the GRU network responsible for predicting dynamic deformations, we train the model using the ground truth data obtained from the procedure described in Eq. 4. To ensure efficient training, we set our batch size to 128, allowing for effective optimization and convergence.

4   Evaluation

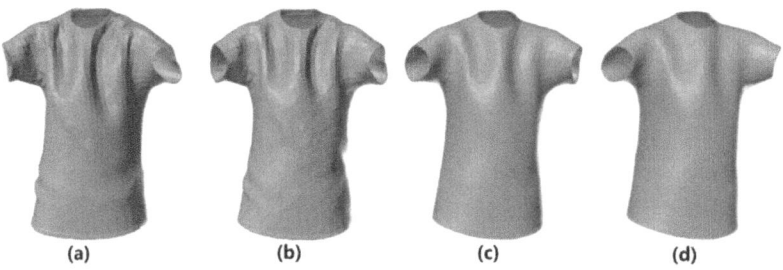

Fig. 4. Visual comparison with ground truth (a), Our method with GNN module (b), our method without GNN (c) and TailorNet [15](d)

In this section, we comprehensively evaluate our method for virtual try-on in terms of visual fidelity and runtime performance. We conduct quantitative and qualitative assessments, comparing our approach to state-of-the-art techniques.

Through these evaluations, we provide insights into the benefits and capabilities of our method for virtual try-on, including visual fidelity, runtime performance, positional encoding, dynamic deformation capture, and detailed cloth wrinkles.

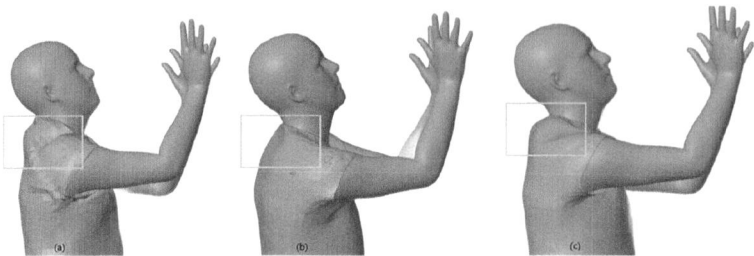

Fig. 5. Compare PBS (a) and TailorNet [15] (b) with our method(c). Garment predicted from TailorNet is tightly fitted to SMPL avatar while our work has the ability of modeling dynamic deforms.

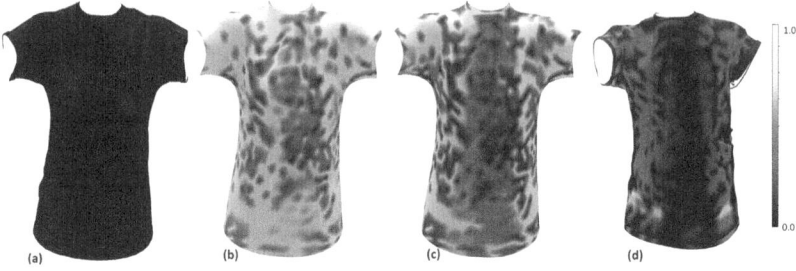

Fig. 6. Heat map result of our predicted garment with (a) or without GNN(b), TailorNet [15](c) and SNUG [21](d).

4.1 Evaluation on Model Accuracy

We thoroughly examine our model's capacity to capture intricate cloth wrinkles through quantitative and qualitative comparisons with PBS, TailorNet, and our method, both with and without the GNN module.

In Fig. 4, we present visual comparisons between our work with GNN, our work without GNN, and other approaches, alongside the ground truth generated from PBS. The visual differences are striking, highlighting that our work with GNN accurately predicts higher frequency information, resulting in a more detailed cloth representation. This is further supported by the error heat map depicted in Fig. 6, which solidifies our findings.

To confirm the efficacy of our penetration loss item, we performed an ablation study with and without this loss item, with results depicted in Fig. 8a.

In order to highlight the precision of our approach, we conduct a quantitative comparison with existing methods, as depicted in Fig. 7. Figure 7a presents the vertex displacement in relation to the ground truth, demonstrating that our method consistently outperforms state-of-the-art approaches in terms of accuracy. It achieves an impressive mean error of 0.3 cm in accurately predicting cloth deformation. Additionally, Fig. 7b provides a comprehensive comparison of the

Table 1. Execution time for each frame(in milliseconds) of our method for predicting deformed cloth with different number of mesh triangles

Triangle	Simulation		SNUG		Our	
	mean	std	mean	std	mean	std
5063	2608.2	1388.3	13.95	2.92	25.72	3.72
8055	4739.8	1580.7	14.37	3.17	34.86	5.65
17453	7654.5	2839.2	22.82	3.24	69.13	7.87
27207	12896.3	3987.1	26.66	3.90	138.67	12.39

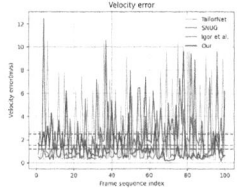 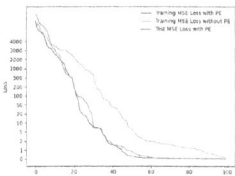

(a) Vertex displacement comparison with state-of-the-art works

(b) Vertex velocity comparison with state-of-the-art works

(c) Evaluation on positional encoding

Fig. 7. Quantitative comparison with state-of-the-art works proved that our work produced more accurate result

first-order (velocity) accuracy, further affirming the superiority and precision of our approach.

4.2 Evaluation on Positional Encoding

The advantages of positional encoding were examined by comparing our network's performance with and without it, assessing its impact on accuracy and convergence. As depicted in Fig. 7c, when training our model with positional encoding, the training loss demonstrated clear and faster convergence compared to training without positional encoding.

4.3 Runtime Performance

We conduct a comparison of the runtime performance of our method with PBS (Physics-Based Simulations) and SNUG [21] on a PC featuring an AMD 3700X processor, without the utilization of a GPU. As depicted in Table 1, our method achieves real-time performance when the number of triangles is less than 5000. Although our method is not as fast as SNUG, this outcome is highly promising for applications in digital fitting rooms, presenting it as a feasible solution for practical utilization.

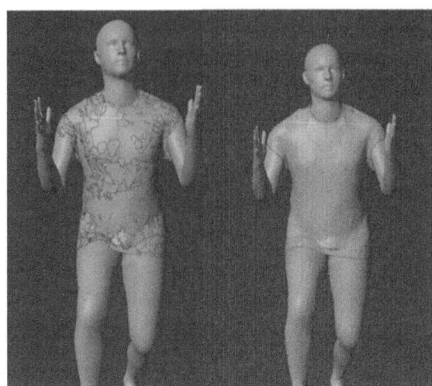 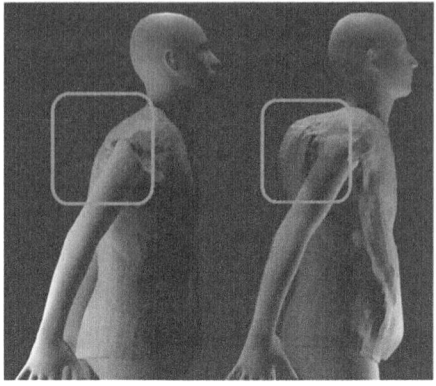

(a) Our prediction with or without pene-   (b) Our predictions, with and without the
tration loss item.   recursive module

Fig. 8. Ablation studies on the recursive module and penetration loss. Figure 8a show-cases the effect of our loss item: predictions without penetration loss on the left, and with it on the right. Figure 8b highlights the contrast in capturing dynamic details: the yellow cloth (recursive module) outperforms the green (non-recursive) method in representing dynamic elements. (Color figure online)

4.4   Evaluation on GRU Effectiveness

The effectiveness of our GRU module, capturing body dynamics and dynamic cloth deformations, is assessed by comparing it to TailorNet, a static cloth defor-mation method. By carefully examining the highlighted details within the yellow box in Fig. 5, it becomes apparent that the distance between the cloth and the neck of the avatar serves as an indication of the tendency for the avatar to fall after jumping. In contrast, TailorNet predicts that the garment mesh closely adheres to the avatar. This observation is consistent with the ablation study result shown in Fig. 8b.

5   Limitations and Discussion

We present a machine learning approach for predicting cloth deformation based on SMPL parameters. Our proposed method showcases superior performance, effectively and accurately forecasting dynamic cloth deformation. To capture intricate cloth wrinkles, we enhance our model by integrating a residual Graph Neural Network, allowing for the preservation of high-frequency details.

We believe our method represents a substantial advancement in the develop-ment of data-driven cloth simulation for virtual try-on. However, we acknowledge that there are still remaining limitations that need to be addressed in our work.

Initially, our model focused solely on body parameters, excluding cloth style and material. Further exploration is needed to incorporate these factors using graph neural networks.

Secondly, although our approach effectively predicts intricate deformations for specific garment styles, the process of retraining the network for newly designed garments remains labor-intensive.

Although our method exhibits higher accuracy than current state-of-the-art techniques, there is room for enhancing prediction speed. As the number of mesh triangles surpasses 30,000, a common occurrence in practical situations, computational time becomes a bottleneck. Thus, it is crucial to address this issue and minimize prediction time for future advancements.

References

1. Allen, B., Curless, B., Popović, Z.: The space of human body shapes: reconstruction and parameterization from range scans. ACM Trans. Graph. (TOG) **22**(3), 587–594 (2003)
2. Baraff, D., Witkin, A.: Large steps in cloth simulation. In: Proceedings of the 25th Annual Conference on Computer Graphics and Interactive Techniques, SIG-GRAPH 1998, p. 4354. Association for Computing Machinery, New York (1998). https://doi.org/10.1145/280814.280821
3. Bertiche, H., Madadi, M., Escalera, S.: Cloth3D: clothed 3D humans. In: Vedaldi, A., Bischof, H., Brox, T., Frahm, J.M. (eds.) Computer Vision - ECCV 2020, pp. 344–359. Springer, Cham (2020)
4. Breen, D.E., House, D.H., Getto, P.H.: A physically-based particle model of woven cloth. Vis. Comput. **8**, 264–277 (1992)
5. Chentanez, N., Macklin, M., Müller, M., Jeschke, S., Kim, T.Y.: Cloth and skin deformation with a triangle mesh based convolutional neural network. In: Computer Graphics Forum, vol. 39, pp. 123–134. Wiley Online Library (2020)
6. Duan, L., Yueqi, Z., Ge, W., Pengpeng, H.: Automatic three-dimensional-scanned garment fitting based on virtual tailoring and geometric sewing. J. Eng. Fibers Fabr. **14**, 1558925018825319 (2019)
7. Guan, P., Reiss, L., Hirshberg, D.A., Weiss, A., Black, M.J.: Drape: dressing any person. ACM Trans. Graph. (ToG) **31**(4), 1–10 (2012)
8. Gundogdu, E., Constantin, V., Seifoddini, A., Dang, M., Salzmann, M., Fua, P.: Garnet: a two-stream network for fast and accurate 3D cloth draping. In: Proceedings of the IEEE/CVF International Conference on Computer Vision, pp. 8739–8748 (2019)
9. Keckeisen, M., Stoev, S.L., Feurer, M., Straßer, W.: Interactive cloth simulation in virtual environments. In: Proceedings of the IEEE Virtual Reality, pp. 71–78. IEEE (2003)
10. Loper, M., Mahmood, N., Romero, J., Pons-Moll, G., Black, M.J.: SMPL: a skinned multi-person linear model. ACM Trans. Graph. **34**(6) (2015). https://doi.org/10.1145/2816795.2818013
11. Macklin, M., Müller, M., Chentanez, N., Kim, T.Y.: Unified particle physics for real-time applications. ACM Trans. Graph. (TOG) **33**(4), 1–12 (2014)
12. Mahmood, N., Ghorbani, N., Troje, N.F., Pons-Moll, G., Black, M.J.: Amass: archive of motion capture as surface shapes. In: Proceedings of the IEEE/CVF International Conference on Computer Vision, pp. 5442–5451 (2019)
13. Mozafary, V., Payvandy, P.: Study and comparison techniques in fabric simulation using mass spring model. Int. J. Clothing Sci. Technol. **28**(5), 634–689 (2016)

14. Pan, X., et al.: Predicting loose-fitting garment deformations using bone-driven motion networks. In: ACM SIGGRAPH 2022 Conference Proceedings, pp. 1–10 (2022)
15. Patel, C., Liao, Z., Pons-Moll, G.: Tailornet: predicting clothing in 3D as a function of human pose, shape and garment style. In: IEEE Conference on Computer Vision and Pattern Recognition (CVPR). IEEE (2020)
16. Peng, T., et al.: PGN-cloth: physics-based graph network model for 3D cloth animation. Displays **80**, 102534 (2023). https://doi.org/10.1016/j.displa.2023.102534. https://www.sciencedirect.com/science/article/pii/S0141938223001671
17. Pons-Moll, G., Romero, J., Mahmood, N., Black, M.J.: Dyna: a model of dynamic human shape in motion. ACM Trans. Graph. (TOG) **34**(4), 1–14 (2015)
18. Romero, J., Tzionas, D., Black, M.J.: Embodied hands: modeling and capturing hands and bodies together. arXiv preprint arXiv:2201.02610 (2022)
19. Sanchez-Gonzalez, A., Godwin, J., Pfaff, T., Ying, R., Leskovec, J., Battaglia, P.: Learning to simulate complex physics with graph networks. In: International Conference on Machine Learning, pp. 8459–8468. PMLR (2020)
20. Santesteban, I., Otaduy, M.A., Casas, D.: Learning-based animation of clothing for virtual try-on. CoRR abs/1903.07190 (2019). http://arxiv.org/abs/1903.07190
21. Santesteban, I., Otaduy, M.A., Casas, D.: SNUG: self-supervised neural dynamic garments. In: IEEE/CVF Conference on Computer Vision and Pattern Recognition (CVPR) (2022)
22. Varol, G., et al.: Bodynet: volumetric inference of 3D human body shapes. In: Proceedings of the European Conference on Computer Vision (ECCV), pp. 20–36 (2018)
23. Volino, P., Thalmann, N.M.: Developing simulation techniques for an interactive clothing system. In: Proceedings. International Conference on Virtual Systems and MultiMedia VSMM 1997 (Cat. No. 97TB100182), pp. 109–118. IEEE (1997)
24. Yao, W.M., et al.: Review of particle physics. J. Phys. G: Nucl. Part. Phys. **33**(1), 1 (2006)
25. Ying, D., et al.: A fast predictive-corrective mass spring method in cloth simulation. In: 2010 International Conference on Computer Application and System Modeling (ICCASM 2010), vol. 3, pp. V3–562. IEEE (2010)

Elderly Tourists' Acceptance of Augmented Reality for Promoting Leisure and Tourism

Lingyi Wu[1,2], Bolin Yu[3], Wending Xue[1], Le Li[1], Ameersing Luximon[4(✉)], and Riji Yu[1(✉)]

[1] School of Art, Hubei University, Wuhan, China
`Joe-yu@hubu.edu.cn`
[2] School of Design, Hong Kong Polytechnic University, Hung Hom, Hong Kong SAR, China
[3] Lynch School of Education and Human Development, Boston College, Boston, USA
[4] Industrial Design Department, Georgia Tech Shenzhen Institute, Tianjin University, Tianjin, China
`luximon@gtsi.edu.cn`

Abstract. The significance of digitalization in leisure & tourism is pronounced, particularly during an era of aging. Augmented reality has the potential to provide numerous advantages to the leisure & tourism industry. Nevertheless, there is still a significant amount of research to be conducted to fully understand the factors that influence the acceptance of augmented reality (AR) technology among older users in the context of leisure & tourism. Furthermore, limited research has been dedicated to investigating the influence of perceived enjoyment, perceived attractiveness, and self-efficacy on the acceptance of AR technology for elderly users in leisure & tourism. To fill in this gap, the study investigated the influence of perceived enjoyment, perceived attractiveness, and self-efficacy with the technology acceptance model (TAM), which is a highly influential theoretical framework in the field. A grand number of 342 replies were gathered. The findings indicated that among older users, perceived enjoyment, perceived attractiveness, and self-efficacy had a significant effect on the attitude of using AR for leisure & tourism. The findings assist AR application designers, developers, and practitioners in the leisure & tourism industry to enhance the efficiency of AR applications. Future research would improve the TAM by integrating psychological and technological factors specifically for senior users in the domain of leisure & tourism.

Keywords: Augmented reality · elderly users · leisure & tourism · technology acceptance model

Abbreviations

AR: augmented reality
TAM: technology acceptance model
APP: application

L. Wu and B. Yu—These authors contributed to the work equally and should be regarded as co-first authors.

© The Author(s), under exclusive license to Springer Nature Singapore Pte Ltd. 2025
W. Song et al. (Eds.): ICXR 2024, LNCS 15461, pp. 77–107, 2025.
https://doi.org/10.1007/978-981-96-3679-2_6

1 Introduction

1.1 An Introduction to Augmented Reality

Augmented reality (AR), according to Azuma (1997), is a type of computer visualization technique that "merges the real world and the virtual content, provides users with a real-time interactive environment, and registers in 3D" (Bekele, Pierdicca, Frontoni, Malinverni, & Gain, 2018). Recent studies on AR also describe it as a system that enhances users' perceptions of the natural environment using multimodal information, such as audio-visual information and olfactory information (Blanco-Pons, Carrion-Ruiz, & Lerma, 2019; Rodrigues, Ramos, Pereira, Sardo, & Cardoso, 2019; Schueffel, 2017).

Using a smartphone or tablet to access AR is one of the most common methods now. Due to their pervasiveness, affordability, and capacity, portable devices, such as smartphones and tablets, may be the best tools for augmented reality applications (Blanco-Pons et al., 2019; Morar, Balutoiu, Moldoveanu, Moldoveanu, & Butean, 2021; Scianna, Gaglio, & Guardia, 2019).

Nowadays, AR technology has rapidly advanced, as evidenced by the large number of AR applications available in a variety of fields, including medicine, education, entertainment, design, repair and maintenance, and even leisure & tourism (Blanco-Pons et al., 2019; Papakostas, Troussas, Krouska, & Sgouropoulou, 2022).

1.2 Benefits of AR for Promoting Leisure and Tourism

AR applications for tourism, especially leisure & tourism, have grown in popularity due to various benefits. The first benefit is to recreate lost historical buildings, cultural heritage, and historical ruins that no longer exist (Chiabrando, Sammartano, Spano, & Spreafico, 2019; K. Jung, Nguyen, Piscarac, & Yoo, 2020a; K. Jung, Nguyen, Yoo, et al., 2020b; Petrucco, 2016; Scianna et al., 2019). Without disturbing the actual environment or posing the risk of damage, cultural heritage preservation and presentation are well-balanced (Petrucco, 2016; tom Dieck & Jung, 2017).

The second benefit is to enhance the visitors' experience from a personalized perspective (K. Jung, Nguyen, Piscarac, et al., 2020; K. Jung, Nguyen, Yoo, et al., 2020; Scianna et al., 2019; Lingyi Wu, Yu, Su, & Ye, 2022; Yung & Khoo-Lattimore, 2017). On the one hand, AR applications provide tourists with navigation functions, which guide them to the relevant POI (point of interest) in the form of multimedia (Claudia, Jung, & Rauschnabel, 2018; Koo, Kim, Kim, Kim, & Cha, 2019; Rodrigues et al., 2019). This function considers various factors when designing a customized route, such as walking distance, accessibility, and so on (Koo et al., 2019). On the other hand, interactive AR games are incorporated so that tourists can review and reinforce what they saw and learned while intuitively having fun. (Koo et al., 2019; Nóbrega, Jacob, Coelho, Ribeiro, & Ferreira, 2018; Vassilakis, Charalampakos, Glykokokalos, Kontokalou, & Vidakis, 2018).

The third benefit is to create cultural and historical resources for learners (Petrucco, 2016). When used as a supporting tool, the AR application accomplishes instructional tasks for educational activities (Scianna et al., 2019). The AR approach could not only visualize scenes from challenging or practically unachievable angles (Petrucco, 2016) but also offer numerous opportunities for learners to practice at a low cost. As indicated by Shen et al., AR has great potential in tourism education (Shen, Xu, Sotiriadis, & Wang, 2022).

1.3 A Growing Aging Population

At the same time as ICT is becoming more widespread, the older people population is rapidly growing. In our study, we follow the World Health Organization's (WHO) standard that a person needs to be 60 years of age or older to be considered as "older" (World Health Organization - WHO, 2002) (Jovanović, De Angeli, McNeill, & Coventry, 2021). Compared to 2015, the number of individuals over 60 is predicted to more than double, while the number of persons over 80 is expected to triple (United Nations, 2015) (Vassli & Farshchian, 2017). The number of adults in this age group in the United States was over 70 million in 2017 (representing approximately 22% of the population). By 2050, it is anticipated to rise to 108 million (representing about 28%) (United Nations, 2017) (Werner, Huang, & Pitts, 2022). In China, the number of people over the age of 60 reached 260 million in 2020 (China National Bureau of Statistics, 2021), with a projected increase to 483 million by 2050 (World Health Organization, 2015) (Ma, Gao, & Yang, 2022).

Based on these figures, it is reasonable to expect that the number of elderly travelers is expanding. As a result, there is a growing interest in senior leisure & tourism (Ramos-Soler, Martínez-Sala, & Campillo-Alhama, 2019). In reality, recent research has revealed that a significant portion of senior tourists travel to personally enrich themselves, obtain novel experiences, interact with others, amuse themselves, and seek well-being (Mendes et al., 2022). The leisure & tourism industry faces a significant issue in figuring out how to help senior citizens enjoy their travels.

1.4 The Aim of This Study

Research has shown that due to a decline in physical, sensory, and cognitive capabilities, the needs and attitudes of older people towards technology usage could be different from those of young people (K. Chen & Chan, 2014; Tuena et al., 2020). Also, older people exhibit greater cognitive challenges in comprehension and learning and demonstrate a slower rate of skill acquisition compared to younger adults (K. Chen & Chan, 2014). In addition, the older population shows a higher level of caution and a stronger desire for certainty before acting compared to younger persons (Moraes & Meirelles, 2018). It has been shown that the older the user, the more negative their attitude towards technology is and the lower their usage of different technologies (Moraes & Meirelles, 2018; Venkatesh, Morris, Davis, & Davis, 2003). Furthermore, research confirmed that various factors make them less likely to use technology (K. Chen & Chan, 2014). In conclusion, older people may have different attitudes toward the usage of technology, and it is important to figure out the factors that impact their acceptance of technology, especially AR technology for leisure & tourism.

An issue arises regarding the experience of tourists, mainly elderly tourists, and their acceptance of augmented reality, considering its ongoing usage in leisure & tourism. There is plenty of potential for research in this field to identify the essential variables that influence the actual use of AR systems and ensure that tourists witness how AR can be utilized effectively in the leisure & tourism sector.

However, there are several limitations regarding the previous studies. First, specific constructs, such as perceived enjoyment, perceived attractiveness, and self-efficacy, especially the latter two, have yet to be examined in TAM for leisure & tourism. Second, according to Liang (Jingen Liang & Elliot, 2021), most of the AR leisure & tourism research was conducted in the United States, Australia, South Korea, and Europe. More research is needed that presents an established model with TAM in the acceptance of AR technology for leisure & tourism in China, and there is a gap in this area. In fact, AR technology is recently being utilized in China, and China is a fast-rising destination (Jingen Liang & Elliot, 2021). As a result, the acceptance of AR by tourists greatly benefits leisure & tourism policymakers and industry practitioners (Ronaghi & Ronaghi, 2022). Third, there is limited study on validating TAM in older adults in China. However, many older populations worldwide, particularly in China, still need more attention (K. Chen & Chan, 2014).

As a result, the current study expanded the TAM to investigate the role of perceived enjoyment, perceived attractiveness, and self-efficacy in influencing senior tourists' intentions to use AR technology for leisure & tourism. After that, the study will offer constructive recommendations to enhance tourists' acceptance of AR technology. Furthermore, Furthermore, utilizing the modified TAM to examine and assess users' adoption of various technologies is feasible.

2   Literature Review

2.1   Technology Acceptance Model (TAM)

A variety of adoption theories have been developed to study the intention to use systems, including Fishbein and Ajzen's Theory of Reasoned Action (TRA) (Fishbein & Ajzen, 1977), the Diffusion of Innovation Theory (DOI) (Rogers, 1983), the Technology Acceptance Model (TAM) by Davis (Fred D Davis, 1985), the Theory of Planned Behavior (TPB) by Ajzen (Ajzen, 1991), TAM2 by Venkatesh and Davis (Venkatesh & Davis, 2000), the Unified Theory of Acceptance and Use of Technology (UTAUT) by Venkatesh et al. (Venkatesh et al., 2003), TAM3 by Venkatesh and Bala (Venkatesh & Bala, 2010) and UTAUT2 by Venkatesh et al. (Venkatesh, Thong, & Xu, 2012). These theories have been employed in the literature to explain technology adoption and use (Senali et al., 2022).

TAM (Fig. 1) is one of the most important models that emphasize psychological factors to explain technology adoption, and it is beneficial in explaining the behavior of users of various computer technologies (Turan & Cetintas, 2019). TAM was first proposed by Davis (Fred D Davis, 1985), which integrates the Theory of Rational Behavior (Fishbein & Ajzen, 1977) and the Theory of Planned Behavior (Ajzen, 1991) as theoretical bases to explain and predict an individual's acceptance and adoption of specific information technology. (Rodrigues et al., 2019; Wang & Wang, 2022) Specifically, TAM includes four core constructs: perceived ease of use, perceived usefulness, attitude toward technology, and behavioral intention (Fred D. Davis, 1989). Perceived ease of use (PEU) and perceived usefulness (PU) have been shown to significantly influence a user's attitude towards using (ATU) a technology and behavioral intention (BI) to use the specific technology (Fussell & Truong, 2022). These four constructs have formed the basis of a large number of studies evaluating new technologies (Fussell & Truong, 2022).

Although TAM has been revised (e.g., TAM2, TAM3, UTAUT, and UTAUT2), the fundamental TAM was selected as a theoretical framework to clarify the intention to use AR for a variety of reasons. To begin, the TAM (Fred D. Davis, 1989) is the most widely acknowledged theory among these theories. TAM has previously been proven to be one of the most dependable models for exploring users' acceptance of diverse technologies (R. Wu & Yu, 2022).

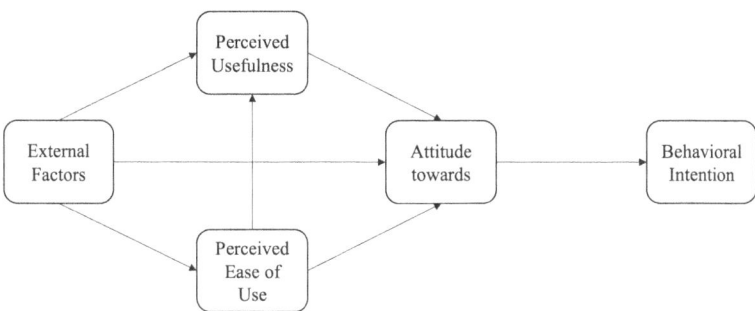

Fig. 1. Structure of the TAM model.

Secondly, several newly added constructs in revised versions (such as facilitating conditions, the price value of UTAUT, and UTAUT2) are inappropriate for AR in the leisure & tourism context. Facilitating conditions denote the availability of resources, including the internet and smartphone for AR. The penetration rates of mobile internet users (71%) and smartphone adoption (77%) are relatively high in China (GSMA, 2022). As a result, facilitating conditions are irrelevant and are unlikely to influence the decision to use AR for leisure & tourism. In addition, since AR for leisure & tourism in our study is an application free of charge, price value is insignificant in this context.

Third, TAM was selected since the research provides practical recommendations for leisure & tourism policymakers and industry practitioners. According to Davis (Fred D. Davis, 1989), the development of TAM was motivated by practical objectives. Finally, this research aims to clarify the factors influencing people's intention to utilize augmented reality for leisure & tourism. On the other hand, TAM2 and TAM3's primary concern is to discover the determinants of PEU and PU, which is outside the goal of this work.

The TAM's reliability, validity, and adaptability have been demonstrated as it has been extended with new constructs and tested in a range of domains (Fussell & Truong, 2022). This work has investigated the impact of perceived enjoyment, perceived attractiveness, and self-efficacy on a variety of users' acceptance of AR for leisure & tourism.

2.2 Perceived Enjoyment

In recent studies, the effect of perceived enjoyment has been investigated in various Information System sectors. Extensive study has shown that perceived enjoyment can impact the use of mobile services (Dickinger, Arami, & Meyer, 2017; Suki, 2011), mobile payment services (Winarno, Mas'Ud, & Palupi, 2021), educational technologies (Al-Sharafi, Mufadhal, Arshah, & Sahabudin, 2019; Alyoussef, 2021), mobile gaming (Nguyen, 2015), social networking (Ofori, Larbi-Siaw, Fianu, Gladjah, & Boateng, 2016; Ramírez-Correa, Grandón, Ramírez-Santana, & Rdenes, 2019), mobile video calling (Ronggang & Caihong, 2017), online commerce (Marza, Idris, & Abror, 2019), Internet of things (Hsu & Lin, 2016), instant messaging (Lu et al., 2009), and VR systems (Fussell & Truong, 2022).

The role of perceived enjoyment in the adoption of AR-related technology has also received considerable attention. For AR-supported mobile apps, it was determined by the research (Oyman, Bal, & Ozer, 2022) that perceived enjoyment has a positive and direct effect on the behavior intentions to use AR-supported mobile applications; In the field of AR for education, the research (Balog & Pribeanu, 2010) demonstrated that perceived enjoyment has a significant influence on the behavioral intention to use AR teaching platform. (Boboc, Chiriac, & Antonya, 2021) confirmed that perceived enjoyment plays an important role in students accepting the proposed AR system to learn the science of Mechanisms. In addition, the research supported the idea that perceived enjoyment significantly influences the intention to use the AR system. In the area of AR for tourism education, (Shen et al., 2022) argued that the factor relating students' enjoyment and playfulness with the efficiency and effectiveness of digital learning experiences are essential predicting factors for students' adoption and use of AR/VR applications within the context of current pandemic. As for AR for leisure & tourism, (Haugstvedt & Krogstie, 2012; Ronaghi & Ronaghi, 2022) indicated that perceived enjoyment directly impacts the intention to use mobile AR applications with historical pictures and information.

2.3   Perceived Attractiveness

Van der Heijden (Heijden, 2003) defines "perceived visual attractiveness" as the degree to which one individual believes the website is visually appealing from an aesthetic viewpoint. According to this definition, perceived attractiveness, related to visual appeal, might be generalized as the degree to which one perceives that a virtual environment/mediated environment is aesthetically acceptable to the eyes (Ghapanchi, 2017). Furthermore, "perceived attractiveness" refers to visual design, visual elements, and content quality, including colors, fonts, shapes, animations, and layouts (Heijden, 2003; Y. M. Li & Yeh, 2010).

Perceived attractiveness has also received increased attention. Van der Heijden (Heijden, 2003) introduced PA and extended TAM by suggesting that aesthetics play a role in the decision to use an IS and a crucial role in the decision to use a website (Ghapanchi, 2017). More specifically, aesthetics also plays an important role in AR applications (T. H. Jung, Lee, Chung, & tom Dieck, 2018). Researchers (Chung, Han, & Joun, 2015) have shown that perceived attractiveness has a significant influence on AR applications for promoting leisure & tourism. Obtaining helpful information could be the target of travelers seeking to satisfy functional and aesthetic needs. Furthermore, perceived attractiveness seems to be a significant factor in leisure & tourism experience results (Chung et al., 2015), which means that the aesthetic experience is likely a primary determinant of the leisure & tourism experience on the whole. As a result, perceived attractiveness is an essential factor in using AR to promote leisure & tourism.

2.4   Self-efficacy

Some research has provided various definitions of self-efficacy. Bandura (Bandura, 1977) was the first to propose the concept of self-efficacy. It refers to people's evaluation of their competence to plan and carry out an action required to attain a given objective. Self-efficacy is the ability to regulate the cognitive, social, emotional, and behavioral skills necessary to perform a task (Yesilyurt, Ulas, & Akan, 2016). Self-efficacy has been studied as a social cognitive theory in various academic fields. Moreover, computer self-efficacy is widely recognized as one aspect of the formed sense of self-efficacy. It defines people's assessment of their capacity to complete tasks when using specific computer technology (Higgins, 1995). It may also impact people's perception of the effectiveness and productivity of the technology (Teo & Zhou, 2014). In line with this definition, we propose a definition of SE of mobile AR technology rooted in the broader concept of self-efficacy. SE of AR denotes a user's perception of their ability to use mobile AR technology.

The precise effect of self-efficacy has received a great deal of scholarly attention. Scholars have identified that a variety of factors regarding behavior, cognition, attitude, and environment have an impact on computer self-efficacy, and they have proposed that computer self-efficacy is significantly related to computer anxiety, which is described as fears about the consequences of computer use, such as the loss of crucial data or other potential mistakes (Xie, Zheng, Liu, & Liu, 2022). That means people with a strong sense of computer self-efficacy are less likely to be discouraged by obstacles and will continue with their efforts, making them more likely to overcome whatever difficulties they face than those with a weak sense of computer self-efficacy (Xie et al., 2022).

Since utilizing AR applications sets a relatively high technical threshold for tourists, self-efficacy (of mobile AR technique) is a crucial factor influencing their use of AR applications to promote leisure & tourism. Based on the previous research, it is reasonable to assume that an individual with a weak sense of self-efficacy of mobile AR technique would have a low perception of one's own ability to use it in general (Gong, Xu, & Yu, 2004). The low perception of the ability to use mobile AR techniques would, in turn, throw a significant problem for he/she to use new technologies and new systems (Gong et al., 2004). The individual may feel that he/she will encounter various problems when using mobile AR techniques later, but he/she may be unable to solve these problems (Gong et al., 2004). Once the individual has encountered these problems, he/she is unlikely to persist in overcoming them (Gong et al., 2004). As a result, the individual would have a low intention to use such new technologies or systems in the future.

3   Research Model and Hypothesis Development

3.1   PU, PEOU, AT, BI

Figure 2 displays our proposed TAM model. Previous research has already validated the correlations of four important constructs of TAM in various contexts of AR use (Boboc et al., 2021; C. C. Chen, Liu, Chiu, Lee, & Wu, 2023; Shen et al., 2022), particularly in the context of using AR for leisure & tourism (Chung et al., 2015; Guo, Zhu, Li, Wang, & Shu, 2022; T. Jung & Kim; X. Z. Li, Chen, Kang, & Kang, 2022; S. T. Wu, Chiu, & Chen, 2020). Users were more likely to perceive AR systems as useful tools if they found them easy to use (Chung et al., 2015; T. H. Jung et al., 2018; Lee, Chung, & Jung, 2015). When visitors find the AR system useful and easy to use, their attitude will increase. If visitors have a positive attitude toward the AR system, their intention to use the AR system will increase, making them more likely to use it (Guo et al., 2022; X. Z. Li et al., 2022). We assume that if visitors master AR applications in the context of leisure & tourism and find them useful, they will have a positive attitude toward AR applications for leisure & tourism and a high intention to use them. As a result, we proposed the following hypotheses:

H1: Perceived ease of use of AR for leisure & tourism has a positive influence on the perceived usefulness of AR for leisure & tourism.
H2: Perceived ease of use of AR for leisure & tourism has a positive influence on a favorable attitude towards AR for leisure & tourism.
H3: Perceived usefulness of AR for leisure & tourism has a positive influence on a favorable attitude towards AR for leisure & tourism.
H4: A favorable attitude towards AR for leisure & tourism has a positive influence on behavioral intentions to use AR for leisure & tourism.

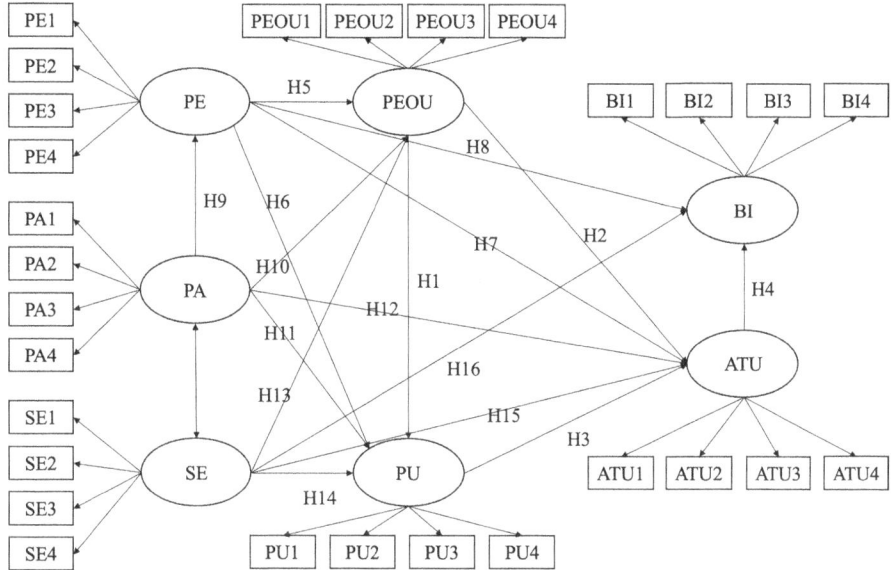

Fig. 2. Research Model. Note: PU: perceived usefulness; PEOU: perceived ease of use; ATU: attitude towards use; BI: behavioral intention; PE: perceived enjoyment; PA: perceived attractiveness; SE: self-efficacy.

3.2 Perceived Enjoyment

Perceived enjoyment was found to be an essential factor that could directly influence intentions to use technology ((Balog & Pribeanu, 2010; Oyman et al., 2022; Su & Chiu, 2020), especially in the context of using AR applications for leisure & tourism (Haugstvedt & Krogstie, 2012; T. H. Jung et al., 2018; Lee et al., 2015). Several studies have shown that perceived enjoyment has a significant impact on the perceived ease of use and perceived usefulness of the AR technology (Guo et al., 2022; Hammady, Ma, & Strathearn, 2020; X. Z. Li et al., 2022). It is suggested by (Guo et al., 2022) that perceived enjoyment is one of the most commonly used variables in the context of using AR/VR technologies, and perceived enjoyment has been shown as an important antecedent of perceived ease of use and perceived usefulness.

Therefore, we proposed the following hypotheses:

H5: Perceived enjoyment has a positive influence on perceived ease of use of AR for leisure & tourism.
H6: Perceived enjoyment has a positive influence on perceived usefulness of AR for leisure & tourism.
H7: Perceived enjoyment has a positive influence on a favorable attitude towards AR for leisure & tourism.
H8: Perceived enjoyment has a positive influence on behavioral intentions to use AR for leisure & tourism.

3.3 Perceived Attractiveness

Van der Heijden (Heijden, 2003) discovered that perceived visual appeal influences usefulness, enjoyment, and ease-of-use and then proposed that attractiveness be combined with enjoyment because attractiveness might better explain enjoyment (Su & Chiu, 2020). (Ha, Yoon, & Choi, 2007) showed that a game's visual and aural appeal gives users the perception of fun and encourages them to play more. This demonstrated a positive relationship between perceived attractiveness and perceived enjoyment. (Merhi, 2016) also discovered that visual appeal elements such as gorgeous colors, images, and layout might significantly impact users' enjoyment. The greater the quality of visual appearance, the more users are drawn to the game and the greater their level of enjoyment.

The study (Mihai, Mihaela, Cristian, Maria, & Stoica, 2021) found that the perceived enjoyment of wearable devices increases when the design, such as colors and user interface menus, is attractive. Furthermore, visual attractiveness positively impacts attitudes toward the use and perceived enjoyment of the field (Pengnate & Sarathy, 2017). Additionally, according to a study by Pengnate and Sarathy (Pengnate & Sarathy, 2017), two TAM constructs, perceived ease of use and usefulness, were influenced by the perceived visual attractiveness, which is the aesthetic impression of the website. As a result, the study considered visual attractiveness as a variable that should not be overlooked when investigating the impact of AR in promoting leisure & tourism.

Hence, we proposed the following hypotheses:

H9: Perceived attractiveness has a positive influence on perceived enjoyment.
H10: Perceived attractiveness has a positive influence on perceived ease of use of AR for leisure & tourism.
H11: Perceived attractiveness has a positive influence on perceived usefulness of AR for leisure & tourism.
H12: Perceived attractiveness has a positive influence on a favorable attitude towards AR for leisure & tourism.

3.4 Self-efficacy

Self-efficacy could play an essential role in the acceptance of technologies, as visitors' beliefs, a crucial element of self-efficacy, have a significant influence on their focus, involvement, and commitment in completing MAR activities, as well as their adoption of new technologies, their intentions and even the overall leisure & tourism experience. Previous studies (Fussell & Truong, 2022; Gong et al., 2004; Park, 2009; Xie et al., 2022) have empirically reported that the general perception of self-efficacy is the determinant of one's perception of how easy technologies or systems are easy to use, and that self-efficacy is a determinant that positively and significantly influences users' behavioral intention and perceived usefulness (Kang & Shin, 2015; Turan & Cetintas, 2019). (Fussell & Truong, 2022) has found that users more confident in their abilities to use VR technology are more likely to have a positive attitude towards utilizing VR.

Accordingly, we proposed the following hypotheses:

H13: Self-efficacy has a positive influence on perceived ease of use of AR for leisure & tourism.

H14: Self-efficacy has a positive influence on perceived usefulness of AR for leisure & tourism.

H15: Self-efficacy has a positive influence on a favourable attitude towards AR for leisure & tourism.

H16: Self-efficacy has a positive influence on behavioural intentions to use AR for leisure & tourism.

4 Methodology

4.1 Research Context and the AR System for Promoting Leisure and Tourism

China is one of the leading countries in leisure & tourism, and Wuhan is known as a popular destination in China. The Yellow Crane Tower, known as one of the "Four Great Towers of China," is located on Sheshan Mountain in Wuhan, Hubei Province. As one of Hubei's most popular tourist attractions, it is recognized as the icon of Wuhan City. The tower has existed in various forms for more than 1700 years. Over the centuries, many poets, writers, and artists have visited the Tower for inspiration, leaving behind unique cultural heritage resources, such as folklore stories of national intangible cultural heritage, collections of poetry, and artworks.

However, vanished historic buildings that cannot be rebuilt and ancient events that cannot be recreated make it difficult for tourists to imagine and experience them. As a result, the traditional form of exhibitions in tourist attractions, such as the Yellow Crane Tower, was unable to satisfy the needs of tourists (K. Jung, Nguyen, Yoo, et al., 2020). In response to this need and to promote cultural values, digital technology such as Augmented Reality has been explored as a way to enrich the experience of tourists (K. Jung, Nguyen, Yoo, et al., 2020; L. Wu, Su, Ye, & Yu, 2021; Lingyi Wu et al., 2022).

The presented AR system (developed with Unity) for promoting leisure & tourism allows tourists to explore cultural attractions in the Yellow Crane Tower Park intuitively. This application provides guidance, navigation, scanning, gaming, and entertainment. The guidance and navigation mode would inform tourists about the location of 19 points of interest and guide them to the relevant points of interest. For the virtual map, it describes the distribution and precise location of points of interest. For the virtual guide, she introduces the story of each end of interest. The scanning mode combines traditional sightseeing with interaction using mobile AR technology (Koo et al., 2019). In addition, AR games and entertainment will add more enjoyment to the Yellow Crane Tower Park tour and help tourists form a more lasting impression. As a result, this app is likely suitable for evaluating the use of AR and the perception of AR for leisure & tourism among tourists.

4.2 Sampling

Table 1. Descriptive statistics of participants.

Variables	Description	Frequency	Percentage (%)
Gender	Male	87	25.4
	Female	255	74.6
Age	60–64	226	66.1
	65–69	72	21.1
	70–74	24	7.0
	Above 74	20	5.8
Educational Level	High school	183	53.5
	University/junior college	44	12.9
	Master degree and above	24	7.0
	Others	91	26.6

Several researchers have proposed methods of selecting representative samples and estimating the quantity (Xie et al., 2022). According to Reinartz et al. (Reinartz, Haenlein, & Henseler, 2009), the minimum sample size for partial least squares (PLS) is 100. According to Kline et al. (Kline, 2016), sample sizes of less than 100, between 100 and 200, and greater than 200 are typically considered small, medium, and large, respectively. The rules proposed by Marsh (Marsh, Hau, Balla, & Grayson, 1998) have been widely used to estimate the minimum sample size. They found that the sample size is determined by a ratio r of indicators to latent variables; for example, if $r = 3$, a minimum sample size of 200 would be required. To calculate the minimum sample size, a mathematical formula has been proposed to consolidate and summarise the result (Westland, 2010):

$$N \geq 50 * r^2 - 450 * r + 1100$$

where r is the ratio of indicators to latent variables.

In this study, an on-site survey was conducted in the Yellow Crane Tower Park. Our participants were selected based on the following criteria: 1) aged 60 years or older; 2) were Chinese; 3) were able to use a smartphone; 4) were willing to participate in the survey. We surveyed 405 tourists. After eliminating 63 invalid samples due to missing or inconsistent responses, we ended up with 342 valid samples, which is sufficient to test the model of the study.

Table 1 shows the demographic statistics for the final samples. The respondents' gender ratio was 25.4% male to 74.6% female. Amongst them, 66.1% were 60–64 years old, 21.1% were 65–69 years old, 7% were 70–74 years old, and 5.8% were 75 years old and over. Regarding educational level, 53.5% had a high school education, 12.9% were educated at the university or junior college level, 7% had a master's degree or higher, and others (26.6%).

The users used our AR system to enrich their tour experience; examples of operations are illustrated in Figs. 3, 4 and 5.

(a) Operation of the virtual guide

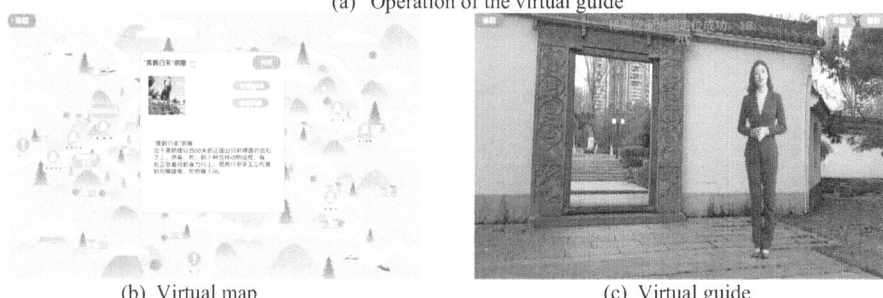

(b) Virtual map   (c) Virtual guide

Fig. 3. Augmented content of (a) Operation of virtual guide, (b) virtual map, and (c) virtual guide.

(a) Operation of the virtual model

(b) Virtual model

(c) Restoration

Fig. 4. Augmented content of (a)Operation of virtual model, (b) virtual model, and (c) restoration.

4.3   Research Instruments

This study employed a set of validated scales from previous research. A total of 7 scales determined seven constructs, e.g., perceived ease of use, perceived usefulness, attitude towards use, behavioral intention, perceived enjoyment, perceived attractiveness, and self-efficacy. In particular, scales of perceived ease of use and perceived usefulness were adapted from Fred D. Davis (1989) and T. H. Jung et al. (2018), respectively. We adopted valid scales to determine attitude toward use and behavioral intention from T. H. Jung et al. (2018), Venkatesh & Bala (2010), Xie et al. (2022), respectively. The scales of perceived enjoyment, perceived attractiveness, and self-efficacy were adapted from Iqbal & Sidhu (2022), T. H. Jung et al. (2018), Cyr, Head, & Ivanov (2006), Pengnate & Sarathy (2017), and Higgins (1995) respectively. Each scale was determined by four items, all of which were measured using a five-point Likert scale, ranging from "strongly disagree" to "strongly agree." The English language items were translated into Chinese and modified to investigate elderly tourists' perceptions toward the use of the AR app.

(a) Operation of the interactive game

(b) game scene   (c) game UI

Fig. 5. Augmented content of (a) Operation of interactive game, (b) game scene, and (c) game UI.

Three specialists in digital technology and English literature reconsidered and adjusted the translation and word usage to ensure that the original meanings were retained and that the translation was appropriate for elderly tourists. Items are provided in Table 2.

Table 2. Indicator questions.

Construct	Item Code	Item	Source
Perceived Ease of Use	PEOU1	Learning to use AR app would be easy for me	(Fred D. Davis, 1989)
	PEOU2	My interaction with AR app is clear and understandable	
	PEOU3	I find AR app to be flexible to interact with	
	PEOU4	It would be easy for me to become skilful at using AR app	
Perceived Usefulness	PU1	Using AR app can improve my travel information gathering performance	(Fred D. Davis, 1989; T. H. Jung et al., 2018)
	PU2	Using AR app can increase my travel information gathering productivity	
	PU3	Using AR app can enhance my travel information gathering effectiveness	
	PU4	I find AR useful for my travel	
Behavioural Intention	BI1	Assuming I had access to the AR app, I intend to use it	(T. H. Jung et al., 2018; Venkatesh & Bala, 2010; Xie et al., 2022)
	BI2	Given that I had access to the AR app, I predict that I would use it	
	BI3	I plan to use the AR app in the future	
	BI4	I would try to suggest others to use the AR app	
Attitude Towards Use	ATU1	I hold a positive evaluation of AR app	(T. Jung & Kim 2014)
	ATU2	Using the AR app in my travel is a good idea	(Chung et al., 2015)
	ATU3	I like using the AR app as part of the travel	

(*continued*)

Table 2. (*continued*)

Construct	Item Code	Item	Source
	ATU4	In my opinion, it would be very desirable to use AR app	
Perceived Enjoyment	PE1	Using the AR app brings me a lot of enjoyment	(Iqbal & Sidhu, 2022; T. H. Jung et al., 2018)
	PE2	I enjoy using the AR app	
	PE3	Using the AR app does not bore me	
	PE4	Traveling using the AR app is exciting	
Perceived Attractiveness	PA1	The AR app is visually attractive	(Cyr, Head, & Ivanov, 2006; Pengnate & Sarathy, 2017)
	PA2	The AR app looks professionally designed	
	PA3	The overall look and feel of the AR app are visually appealing	
	PA4	I like the way the AR app looks	
Self-Efficacy	SE1	I could use the AR app if there was no one around to tell me what to do as I go	(Higgins, 1995)
	SE2	I could use the AR app if I had never used a technology like it before	
	SE3	I could use the AR app if I had a lot of time to complete the job for which the AR app was provided	
	SE4	I could use the AR app if I had just the built-in help facility for assistance	

Note: PU: perceived usefulness; PEOU: perceived ease of use; ATU: attitude towards use; BI: behavioral intention; PE: perceived enjoyment; PA: perceived attractiveness; SE: self-efficacy.

4.4 Data Analysis

This study used AMOS 26.0 software to examine the relationships among the constructs within the proposed model through structural equation modeling (SEM), with maximum likelihood estimation as the way of estimation. SEM effectively evaluates the relationship between latent constructs (R. Wu & Yu, 2022). In addition, SEM can support the study of the model fits (R. Wu & Yu, 2022). As a result, SEM could help our investigation into the impact of perceived enjoyment, perceived attractiveness, and self-efficacy on elderly tourists' acceptance of AR technology.

The study was conducted with a two-stage analysis: assessing the measurement model for the convergent validity and discriminant validity and testing the hypotheses by evaluating the model fit using various fit indices and assessing the path model.

5 Results

5.1 Convergent Validity

Convergent validity is defined as the degree to which two measures of the same construct that should theoretically be correlated actually are (Kang & Shin, 2015; Xie et al., 2022). According to Fornell and Larcker (Fornell & Larcker, 1981), the convergent validity is assessed for the measurement model by measuring:1) the item reliability, (2) the composite reliability of each construct, and (3) the average variance extracted (AVE).

The item reliability could be measured using Cronbach's alpha value. Cronbach's alpha value should ideally be greater than 0.7 (Hair, Black, Babin, & Anderson, 2009). As shown in Table 3, Cronbach's alpha value of perceived enjoyment ($\alpha = 0.863$), perceived attractiveness ($\alpha = 0.880$), self-efficacy ($\alpha = 0.892$), perceived usefulness ($\alpha = 0.817$), perceived ease of use ($\alpha = 0.842$), attitude ($\alpha = 0.866$), and behavioral intention ($\alpha = 0.856$). Therefore, for all the constructs, Cronbach's alpha value reaches a satisfactory level in this study. As a second measure of reliability (Pal & Patra, 2020), the factor loading of each item was checked. According to Hair (Hair et al., 2009), the value of factor loading should be greater than 0.5 (Xie et al., 2022). As it is shown in Table 3, the factor loadings of all the items are greater than the required value of 0.5.

Composite reliability requires a value of 0.7 or greater, and the AVE value should be greater than 0.5 (Fornell & Larcker, 1981). Table 3 shows that the composite reliability of each construct and the AVE were ensured.

5.2 Discriminant Validity

Discriminant validity measures the extent to which two constructs are distinct (Xie et al., 2022). According to the Fornell Larcker criterion, which is an essential measure for determining the discriminant validity (R. Wu & Yu, 2022), it assesses whether the square root of AVE for each construct is over the correlation coefficients between constructs (Fornell & Larcker, 1981). In Table 4, the diagonal indices refer to the square root values of AVE, while other values are the correlation coefficients between constructs. Table 4 shows that the correlation coefficients between constructs are less than the square root values of AVE, which supports the discriminant validity.

Overall, all the scales are reliable, and the research instruments are valid.

Table 3. Results of the measurement model.

Construct	Item	Factor loading	CR	AVE	Cronbach's alpha
PEOU	PEOU1	0.803	0.842	0.573	0.847
	PEOU2	0.699			
	PEOU3	0.759			
	PEOU4	0.762			
PU	PU1	0.746	0.817	0.527	0.823
	PU2	0.713			
	PU3	0.731			
	PU4	0.714			
BI	BI1	0.785	0.856	0.599	0.861
	BI2	0.8			
	BI3	0.797			
	BI4	0.711			
ATU	ATU1	0.823	0.866	0.619	0.870
	ATU2	0.703			
	ATU3	0.77			
	ATU4	0.843			
PE	PE1	0.806	0.863	0.613	0.862
	PE2	0.739			
	PE3	0.752			
	PE4	0.83			
PA	PA1	0.809	0.880	0.647	0.879
	PA2	0.783			
	PA3	0.763			
	PA4	0.86			
SE	SE1	0.815	0.892	0.674	0.892
	SE2	0.844			
	SE3	0.83			
	SE4	0.795			

Note: PU: perceived usefulness; PEOU: perceived ease of use; ATU: attitude towards use; BI: behavioral intention; PE: perceived enjoyment; PA: perceived attractiveness; SE: self-efficacy.

5.3 Model Fit

The overall model's goodness-of-fit was assessed before evaluating the structural equation model. The criteria used to measure the goodness-of-fit for the model are the ratio of Chi-square to the degrees of freedom (CMIN/DF), the Root Mean Square Error of

Table 4. Inter-item correlation matrix (fornell larcker criterion of discriminant validity).

Construct	SE	PA	PE	PEOU	PU	ATU	BI
SE	**0.821**						
PA	0.25	**0.805**					
PE	0.088	0.351	**0.783**				
PEOU	0.31	0.272	0.395	**0.757**			
PU	0.37	0.303	0.336	0.399	**0.726**		
ATU	0.389	0.43	0.429	0.455	0.538	**0.787**	
BI	0.334	0.279	0.384	0.308	0.337	0.537	**0.774**

Note: PU: perceived usefulness; PEOU: perceived ease of use; ATU: attitude towards use; BI: behavioral intention; PE: perceived enjoyment; PA: perceived attractiveness; SE: self-efficacy.

Approximation (RMSEA), Comparative-Fit Index (CFI), Goodness-of-Fit Index (GFI), Normed-Fit Index (NFI) and Adjusted Goodness-of-Fit index (AGFI) (Hair et al., 2009). The results are shown in Table 5: CMIN/DF = 1.621; RMSEA = 0.043, GFI = 0.903, CFI = 0.959, AGFI = 0.881, TLI = 0.954 and NFI = 0.901. All indices are greater than the threshold recommended by Bentler and Bonett (Bentler & Bonett, 1980), and Hair et al. (Hair et al., 2009; Hair, Hult, Ringle, & Sarstedt, 2016), indicating that the goodness-of-fit of this study's overall model is acceptable.

Table 5. Model fit indices.

Fit indices	Model	Recommended Value	Source
CMIN/DF	1.621	<3	Bentler & Bonett, 1980; Hair et al., 2016; Hair et al., 2009
RMSEA	0.043	<0.08	
GFI	0.903	>0.80	
CFI	0.959	>0.90	
AGFI	0.881	>0.80	
TLI	0.954	>0.90	
NFI	0.901	>0.90	

5.4 Hypothesis Testing

Figure 6 and Table 6 show the results of the proposed hypotheses for the structural equation modeling. The analysis results are shown in Fig. 6, in which the path coefficients and the significant levels for each hypothesis are presented. Table 6 lists the result of the hypothesis testing, showing that fourteen of the sixteen hypotheses were supported.

Specifically, perceived ease of use was found to have a significant positive effect on perceived usefulness ($\beta = 0.213$, $p < 0.01$) and a favorable attitude ($\beta = 0.162$, $p <$

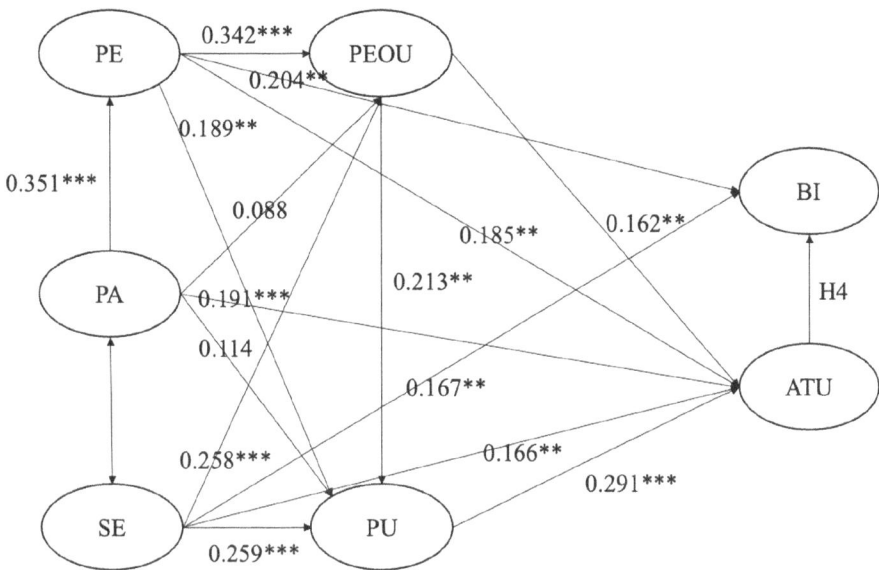

Fig. 6. Results of the structure model. Note: PU: perceived usefulness; PEOU: perceived ease of use; ATU: attitude towards use; BI: behavioral intention; PE: perceived enjoyment; PA: perceived attractiveness; SE: self-efficacy.

0.01), supporting Hypothesis 1 and Hypothesis 2. Further, perceived usefulness had a positive and direct impact on a favorable attitude ($\beta = 0.291$, $p < 0.001$), supporting Hypothesis 3; and a favorable attitude had a positive and direct impact on behavioral intentions ($\beta = 0.385$, $p < 0.001$), supporting Hypothesis 4. Therefore, we accepted H1, H2, H3, and H4.

In addition, perceived enjoyment was found to have a positive effect on perceived ease of use ($\beta = 0.342$, $p < 0.001$), perceived usefulness ($\beta = 0.189$, $p < 0.01$), a favorable attitude ($\beta = 0.185$, $p < 0.01$), and behavioral intentions ($\beta = 0.204$, $p < 0.01$), supporting H5, H6, H7, and H8.

Moreover, strong and positive relationships were identified between perceived attractiveness and perceived enjoyment ($\beta = 0.351$, $p < 0.001$), as well as perceived attractiveness and a favorable attitude ($\beta = 0.191$, $p < 0.001$), supporting H9 and H12. However, there were no significant relationships between perceived attractiveness and perceived ease of use ($\beta = 0.088$, $p > 0.05$), nor between perceived attractiveness and perceived usefulness ($\beta = 0.114$, $p > 0.05$), thus rejecting H10 and H11.

Furthermore, there were also significant and positive relationships between self-efficacy and perceived ease of use ($\beta = 0.258$, $p < 0.001$), self-efficacy and perceived usefulness ($\beta = 0.259$, $p < 0.001$), self-efficacy and a favorable attitude ($\beta = 0.166$, $p < 0.01$) and self-efficacy and behavioral intentions ($\beta = 0.167$, $p < 0.01$), supporting H13, H14, H15, and H16. As a result, we accepted H5, H6, H7, H8, H9, H12, H13, H14, H15, and H16, but rejected H10 and H11.

Table 6. Results of hypothesis testing.

Hypothesis	Path	β coefficient	p Value	Result
H1	PU ← PEOU	0.213	0.002	Supported
H2	ATU ← PEOU	0.162	0.009	Supported
H3	ATU ← PU	0.291	***	Supported
H4	BI ← ATU	0.385	***	Supported
H5	PEOU ← PE	0.342	***	Supported
H6	PU ← PE	0.189	0.006	Supported
H7	ATU ← PE	0.185	0.002	Supported
H8	BI ← PE	0.204	0.001	Supported
H9	PE ← PA	0.351	***	Supported
H10	PEOU ← PA	0.088	0.169	Rejected
H11	PU ← PA	0.114	0.077	Rejected
H12	ATU ← PA	0.191	***	Supported
H13	PEOU ← SE	0.258	***	Supported
H14	PU ← SE	0.259	***	Supported
H15	ATU ← SE	0.166	0.003	Supported
H16	BI ← SE	0.167	0.005	Supported

Note: PU: perceived usefulness; PEOU: perceived ease of use; ATU: attitude towards use; BI: behavioral intention; PE: perceived enjoyment; PA: perceived attractiveness; SE: self-efficacy

6 Discussion

6.1 Perceived Ease of Use, Perceived Usefulness, Attitude, and Behavioral Intention

The four core constructs of TAM were examined in the context of using AR for leisure & tourism. Visitors were more likely to utilize the AR technique for leisure & tourism if they felt it was easy to use, which facilitated the perception of the usefulness of AR technology for leisure & tourism. If visitors found AR technology for leisure & tourism easy, simple, and useful to use, they would have a favorable attitude towards AR technology for leisure & tourism use. People with a positive attitude towards AR technology for leisure & tourism would be more inclined to utilize it for longer. These results agree with the previous studies (Fred D. Davis, 1989; Papakostas et al., 2022; S. T. Wu et al., 2020).

6.2 Perceived Enjoyment

This study found positive and significant relationships between perceived enjoyment and perceived usefulness and between perceived enjoyment and perceived ease of use. This corroborates the ideas of Ramy Hammady (Hammady et al., 2020), Qiang Guo

(Guo et al., 2022), and Li (X. Z. Li et al., 2022). This finding could be explained by the study that users may find technology more useful if it provides more pleasure and less frustration (Vishwakarma, Mukherjee, & Datta, 2019) and by the fact that users may undermine the difficulty of utilizing the technology if they find it enjoyable and fun to use. (Angosto, García-Fernández, Valantine, & Grimaldi-Puyana, 2020).

Moreover, the findings in this study agree with studies that emphasized perceived enjoyment's significant influence on users' favorable attitude and intention to use AR technology. The result agrees with the previous studies involving perceived enjoyment, such as the study by Boboc et al. (Boboc et al., 2021) that has identified perceived enjoyment as having a positive effect on attitude and intention to use AR technology when they investigated university students' perceptions on the AR environments for learning the science of Mechanisms. In addition, Dickinger et al. pointed out that perceived enjoyment significantly influenced users' attitudes and intentions concerning the usage of technology with network externalities (Dickinger et al., 2017), whereas Su et al. (Su & Chiu, 2020) particularly emphasized perceived enjoyment as a powerful determinant that could influence users' attitudes and usage of interactive video learning. This implied that psychological factors play an important role in the decision to adopt AR technology. When delivering leisure & tourism with AR technology, it would be necessary to incorporate more fun and make the APP more interesting for senior tourists.

6.3 Perceived Attractiveness

Visual attractiveness had a significant and positive influence on perceived enjoyment. Also, it served as an important factor for senior tourists concerning favorable attitudes toward using AR technology for leisure & tourism. The finding could be explained by the fact that the good use of visual design, animation, and multimedia could create a sense of activity and fun, increase initial involvement, and inspire engagement for senior tourists (Ha et al., 2007). This is consistent with the findings of Soares et al. (Soares, Pinho, & Alves) that visual attractiveness had a positive impact on perceived enjoyment when they evaluated real customers' perception of a virtual customer service agent. In addition, Van der Heijden (Heijden, 2003) pointed out that visual attractiveness significantly influences users' acceptance and usage of a website, while Verhagen et al. (Meents, Verhagen, Feldberg, & Hooff, 2008) also found the positive influence of visual attractiveness on the attitudes towards virtual world usage.

It is not surprising that visual attractiveness did not posit a significant direct impact on perceived usefulness and perceived ease of use. The finding collaborates with the ideas of Su et al. (Su & Chiu, 2020) that visual attractiveness influences users' intentions to use interactive video learning indirectly through a favorable attitude.

6.4 Self-efficacy

The outcomes of the relationships between self-efficacy and perceived usefulness or between self-efficacy and perceived ease of use were also demonstrated to be positive and significant. The results are in line with the ideas of Chen et al. (K. Chen & Chan, 2014), which identified self-efficacy as having a positive influence on perceived usefulness and perceived ease of use as they evaluated the acceptance of gerontechnology by older Hong Kong Chinese people. Moreover, Teo et.al. (Teo, 2009)pointed out that self-efficacy significantly influenced perceived usefulness concerning technology usage by teachers in Singapore, while Fussell et al. (Fussell & Truong, 2022) validated that self-efficacy positively influenced perceived ease of use as they explored the factors that influence students' intention to use VR in a dynamic learning environment.

In addition, self-efficacy showed a significant positive effect on users' favorable attitudes and intention to use AR technology. This implies that if users' self-efficacy is improved, they may be more likely to adopt AR technology for leisure & tourism. This reasoning is consistent with the findings of Park (Sung Youl, 2009) and Kang et al. (Kang & Shin, 2015), where self-efficacy was found to play an important role in affecting attitude and behavioral intention to use e-learning.

7 Conclusion

7.1 Major Findings

This study employed an extended TAM model to test the influence of perceived enjoyment, visual attractiveness, and self-efficacy on AR technology for leisure & tourism. Our research findings indicate that users' perception of usefulness and easy-to-use AR technology has positively influenced users' favorable attitudes and intentions to use AR technology. This result agrees with the findings of a previous study, which suggested that perceived usefulness and ease of use significantly determined users' attitudes toward using AR technology in leisure & tourism and their intention to adopt new technologies (S. T. Wu et al., 2020).

Moreover, this study found that perceived enjoyment could positively influence users' favorable attitudes and intentions to use AR technology. The results are in line with those of qiang guo (Guo et al., 2022), who validated the positive and significant relationships between perceived enjoyment and perceived usefulness and between perceived enjoyment and perceived ease of use. Meanwhile, the study clearly indicated that users may have a positive attitude toward AR technology if it looks more visually attractive. This finding was also reported by Verhagen et al. (Meents et al., 2008), who stated that visual attractiveness could exert a positive influence on users' favorable attitude toward virtual world usage. In addition, the results of this research suggest that users with different levels of self-efficacy may have various degrees of acceptance of AR technology. Specifically, users with higher levels of self-efficacy might be more likely to have a high intention to use AR technology.

7.2 Major Contributions

First, the major theoretical contributions of this research are that it demonstrates that perceived enjoyment, visual attractiveness, and self-efficacy have a positive influence on perceived ease of use, perceived usefulness, a favorable attitude towards use, and behavioral intentions to use AR technology for leisure & tourism. Consequently, emphasizing these factors facilitates the acceptance of such applications among senior users in the tourism sector. Although these external constructs have previously been considered significant, they have not been evaluated for senior tourists in empirical research with TAM. Second, this work validates the reliability and validity of TAM in AR technology-based leisure & tourism settings. Third, this study serves as a foundation for future research that could consider psychological and technical factors in technology acceptance for senior users in the context of leisure & tourism.

7.3 Limitations

However, there are several limitations to this research.

Firstly, since we implemented the AR app in this study and used it to support leisure & tourism, caution should be taken when extending the findings to other applications of AR technology. Secondly, As the participants in our research are senior tourists to Wuhan, it is unclear whether our findings could be generalized to other age groups or tourists visiting different areas. It is also unclear whether the participants are representative of the entire population of older tourists at various destinations and from different cultures. Thirdly, other individual factors, such as gender, experience, and technostress, may influence tourists' favorable attitudes and intentions to use AR technology for leisure & tourism. Future research could further explore how these possibly moderating factors would affect the results. Fourthly, other factors may influence the results of the study that we may not neglect, such as the factors that are more related to AR (immersion) and the gender distribution in the participants. In addition, we may consider incorporating AR glasses in the study to explore the impact of different devices.

7.4 Implications and Future Work

(1) for AR application designers, developers, and leisure & tourism industry practitioners

To boost older tourists' favorable attitudes toward using AR technologies, designers and developers should stress the importance of evaluating the user experience to improve users' level of enjoyment, attractiveness, and interest (Guo et al., 2022; X. Z. Li et al., 2022). How to incorporate gamification elements with AR techniques to engage more tourists is also an important issue of leisure & tourism that industry practitioners could emphasize (Jingen Liang & Elliot, 2021), as we have found that perceived enjoyment has a significant impact on the acceptance of AR apps by older users. In addition, leisure & tourism industry practitioners might aim to deliver more user-friendly AR technologies to tourists to increase older tourists' perceptions of the usefulness and ease of use of the technologies (Guo et al., 2022).

(2) for future research

First, since users' acceptance of technologies may vary across different domains (R. Wu & Yu, 2022), it is important to focus on tourists in different leisure & tourism destinations or from different countries. Second, as previously observed in prior research (Chung et al., 2015), AR usage in the context of leisure & tourism would be better understood when other factors, such as cultural motivation, visitor knowledge, and value, are taken into account. As a result, future studies could also extend the TAM by incorporating these constructs stemming from leisure & tourism.

Acknowledgments. This research was supported by the Youth Project of Philosophy and Social Science in the Hubei Provincial Department of Education (22Q017- 202311401301004) and supported by the Research Center for Culture-Technology Integration Innovation, Key Research Base of Humanities and Social Sciences of Hubei Province (WK2022002, WK202105).

References

1. Lu, Y., Zhou, T., Wang, B.: Exploring Chinese users' acceptance of instant messaging using the theory of planned behavior, the technology acceptance model, and the flow theory. Comput. Hum. Behav. **25**(1), 29–39 (2009)
2. Ajzen, I.: The theory of planned behavior. Organizational Behavior and Human Decision Processes (1991)
3. Al-Sharafi, M.A., Mufadhal, M., Arshah, R.A., Sahabudin, N.A.: Acceptance of online social networks as technology-based education tools among higher institution students: Structural equation modeling approach. Scientia Iranica **26**(1), 136–144 (2019)
4. Alyoussef, I.Y.: Massive open online course (MOOCs) acceptance: the role of task-technology fit (TTF) for higher education sustainability. Sustainability **13** (2021)
5. Angosto, S., García-Fernández, J., Valantine, I., Grimaldi-Puyana, M.: The intention to use fitness and physical activity apps: a systematic review. Sustainability **12** (2020)
6. Balog, A., Pribeanu, C.: The role of perceived enjoyment in the students' acceptance of an augmented reality teaching platform: a structural equation modelling approach. Stud. Inform. Control **19**(3), 319–330 (2010)
7. Bandura, A.: Self-efficacy: toward a unifying theory of behavioral change. Psychol. Rev. **84**(2), 191–215 (1977)
8. Bekele, M.K., Pierdicca, R., Frontoni, E., Malinverni, E.S., Gain, J.: A survey of augmented, virtual, and mixed reality for cultural heritage. ACM J. Comput. Cultural Heritage **11**(2) (2018). https://doi.org/10.1145/3145534
9. Bentler, P.M., Bonett, D.G.: Significance tests and goodness of fit in the analysis of covariance structures. Psychol. Bull. **88**(3), 588–606 (1980). https://doi.org/10.1037/0033-2909.88.3.588
10. Blanco-Pons, S., Carrion-Ruiz, B., Lerma, J.L.: Augmented reality application assessment for disseminating rock art. Multimed. Tools Appl. **78**(8), 10265–10286 (2019). https://doi.org/10.1007/s11042-018-6609-x
11. Boboc, R.G., Chiriac, R.L., Antonya, C.: How augmented reality could improve the student's attraction to learn mechanisms. Electronics **10**(2), 175 (2021)
12. Chen, C.C., Liu, C.C., Chiu, T.H., Lee, Y.W., Wu, K.C.: Role of perceived ease of use for augmented reality app designed to help children navigate smart libraries. Int. J. Hum.-Comput. Interact. **39**(13), 2606–2623 (2023). https://doi.org/10.1080/10447318.2022.2082017
13. Chen, K., Chan, A.H.: Gerontechnology acceptance by elderly Hong Kong Chinese: a senior technology acceptance model (STAM). Ergonomics **57**(5), 635–652 (2014). https://doi.org/10.1080/00140139.2014.895855
14. Chiabrando, F., Sammartano, G., Spano, A., Spreafico, A.: Hybrid 3D models: when geomatics innovations meet extensive built heritage complexes. ISPRS Int. J. Geo-Inf. **8**(3) (2019). https://doi.org/10.3390/ijgi8030124
15. Chung, N., Han, H., Joun, Y.: Tourists' intention to visit a destination: the role of augmented reality (AR) application for a heritage site. Comput. Hum. Behav. **50**, 588–599 (2015). https://doi.org/10.1016/j.chb.2015.02.068

16. Claudia, D., Jung, T., Rauschnabel, P.A.: Determining visitor engagement through augmented reality at science festivals: an experience economy perspective. Comput. Hum. Behav. 44–53 (2018)
17. Cyr, D., Head, M., Ivanov, A.: Design aesthetics leading to m-loyalty in mobile commerce. Inf. Manag. **43**(8), 950–963 (2006)
18. Davis, F.D.: A technology acceptance model for empirically testing new end-user information systems: theory and results. Ph.D. dissertation Massachusetts Institute of Technology (1985)
19. Davis, F.D.: Perceived usefulness, perceived ease of use, and user acceptance of information technology. MIS Q. **13**(3), 319–340 (1989)
20. Dickinger, A., Arami, M., Meyer, D.: The role of perceived enjoyment and social norm in the adoption of technology with network externalities. Eur. J. Inf. Syst. **17**(1), 4–11 (2017). https://doi.org/10.1057/palgrave.ejis.3000726
21. Fishbein, M., Ajzen, I.: Belief, attitude, intention, and behavior: an introduction to theory and research. Philos. Rhetor. **10**(2), 130–132 (1977)
22. Fornell, C., Larcker, D.F.: Evaluating structural equation models with unobservable variables and measurement error. J. Mark. Res. **18**(1), 39–50 (1981). https://doi.org/10.2307/3151312
23. Fussell, S.G., Truong, D.: Using virtual reality for dynamic learning: an extended technology acceptance model. Virtual Reality **26**(1), 249–267 (2022). https://doi.org/10.1007/s10055-021-00554-x
24. Ghapanchi, A.: Investigating Antecedents and Consequences of User Acceptance of Three-Dimensional Virtual Worlds (2017)
25. Gong, M., Xu, Y., Yu, Y.: An enhanced technology acceptance model for web-based learning. J. Inf. Syst. Educ. **15**(4) (2004)
26. GSMA. The Mobile Economy China (2022). https://www.gsma.com/mobileeconomy/wp-content/uploads/2022/03/280322-The-Mobile-Economy-China-2022.pdf
27. Guo, Q., Zhu, D., Li, F.S., Wang, X., Shu, Y.: Tourists' adoption of extended reality technologies: a meta analytical structural equation modeling. J. Hosp. Tourism Res. 109634802211089 (2022). https://doi.org/10.1177/10963480221108906
28. Ha, I., Yoon, Y., Choi, M.: Determinants of adoption of mobile games under mobile broadband wireless access environment. Inf. Manag. **44**(3), 276–286 (2007)
29. Hair, J.F., Black, W.C., Babin, B.J., Anderson, R.E.: Multivariate Data Analysis, 7th edn. (2009)
30. Hair, J.F., Hult, G.T.M., Ringle, C.M., Sarstedt, M.: A Primer on Partial Least Squares Structural Equation Modeling (PLS-SEM), 2nd edn. (2016)
31. Hammady, R., Ma, M.H., Strathearn, C.: Ambient information visualisation and visitors' technology acceptance of mixed reality in museums. ACM J. Comput. Cultural Heritage **13**(2) (2020). https://doi.org/10.1145/3359590
32. Haugstvedt, A.-C., Krogstie, J.: Mobile augmented reality for cultural heritage: a technology acceptance study. Paper Presented at the 2012 IEEE International Symposium on Mixed and Augmented Reality (ISMAR) (2012)
33. Heijden, H.V.D.: Factors influencing the usage of websites: the case of a generic portal in The Netherlands. Inf. Manag. **40**(6), 541–549 (2003)
34. Higgins, C.C.A.: Computer self-efficacy: development of a measure and initial test. MIS Q. **19**(2), 189–211 (1995)
35. Hsu, C.L., Lin, C.C.: Exploring factors affecting the adoption of internet of things services. J. Comput. Inf. Syst. 1–9 (2016)
36. Iqbal, J., Sidhu, M.S.: Acceptance of dance training system based on augmented reality and technology acceptance model (TAM). Virtual Reality **26**(1), 33–54 (2022). https://doi.org/10.1007/s10055-021-00529-y

37. Jingen Liang, L., Elliot, S.: A systematic review of augmented reality tourism research: what is now and what is next? Tour. Hosp. Res. **21**(1), 15–30 (2021). https://doi.org/10.1177/146 7358420941913

38. Jovanović, M., De Angeli, A., McNeill, A., Coventry, L.: User requirements for inclusive technology for older adults. Int. J. Hum.-Comput. Interact. **37**(20), 1947–1965 (2021). https://doi.org/10.1080/10447318.2021.1921365

39. Jung, K., Nguyen, V.T., Piscarac, D., Yoo, S.C.: Meet the virtual Jeju Dol Harubang-the mixed VR/AR application for cultural immersion in Korea's main heritage. ISPRS Int. J. Geo-Inf. **9**(6) (2020a). https://doi.org/10.3390/ijgi9060367

40. Jung, K., Nguyen, V.T., Yoo, S.C., Kim, S., Park, S., Currie, M.: PalmitoAR: the last battle of the US civil war reenacted using augmented reality. ISPRS Int. J. Geo-Inf. **9**(2) (2020b). https://doi.org/10.3390/ijgi9020075

41. Jung, T., Kim, M.: Acceptance of GPS-Based Augmented Reality Tourism Applications **10** (2014)

42. Jung, T.H., Lee, H., Chung, N., tom Dieck, M.C.: Cross-cultural differences in adopting mobile augmented reality at cultural heritage tourism sites. Int. J. Contemp. Hospitality Manag. **30**(3), 1621–1645 (2018). https://doi.org/10.1108/IJCHM-02-2017-0084

43. Kang, M., Shin, W.S.: An empirical investigation of student acceptance of synchronous e-learning in an online university. J. Educ. Comput. Res. **52**(4), 475–495 (2015)

44. Kline, R.B.: Principles and Practice of Structural Equation Modeling, 4th edn. Guilford Press, New York (2016)

45. Koo, S., Kim, J., Kim, C., Kim, J., Cha, H.S.: Development of an augmented reality tour guide for a cultural heritage site. ACM J. Comput. Cultural Heritage **12**(4) (2019). https://doi.org/10.1145/3317552

46. Lee, H., Chung, N., Jung, T.: Examining the Cultural Differences in Acceptance of Mobile Augmented Reality: Comparison of South Korea and Ireland. Springer, Cham (2015)

47. Li, X.Z., Chen, C.C., Kang, X., Kang, J.: Research on relevant dimensions of tourism experience of intangible cultural heritage lantern festival: integrating generic learning outcomes with the technology acceptance model. Front. Psychol. **13**, 943277 (2022). https://doi.org/10.3389/fpsyg.2022.943277

48. Li, Y.M., Yeh, Y.S.: Increasing trust in mobile commerce through design aesthetics. Comput. Hum. Behav. **26**(4), 673–684 (2010)

49. Ma, Z., Gao, Q., Yang, M.: Adoption of wearable devices by older people: changes in use behaviors and user experiences. Int. J. Hum.-Comput. Interact. **39**, 964–987 (2022). https://doi.org/10.1080/10447318.2022.2083573

50. Marsh, H.W., Hau, K.T., Balla, J.R., Grayson, D.: Is more ever too much? The number of indicators per factor in confirmatory factor analysis. Multivar. Behav. Res. **33**(2), 181–220 (1998)

51. Marza, S., Idris, I., Abror, A.: The influence of convenience, enjoyment, perceived risk, and trust on the attitude toward online shopping. Paper Presented at the 2nd Padang International Conference on Education, Economics, Business and Accounting (PICEEBA-2 2018) (2019)

52. Meents, S., Verhagen, T., Feldberg, J.F.M., van den Hooff, B.: Explaining user adoption of virtual worlds: Towards a multipurpose motivational model. Res. Memorandum (2008)

53. Mendes, J., Medeiros, T., Silva, O., Tomás, L., Silva, L., Ferreira, J.A.: PERMA model of well-being applied to Portuguese senior tourists: a confirmatory factor analysis. Sustainability **14**(13) (2022). https://doi.org/10.3390/su14137538

54. Merhi, M.I.: Towards a framework for online game adoption. Comput. Hum. Behav. **60**(Jul.), 253–263 (2016)

55. Mihai, F., Mihaela, B., Cristian, N., Maria, N., Stoica, D.A.: Wearable technology adoption among romanian students: a structural model based on TAM. AMFITEATRU ECONOMIC J. (57) (2021)

56. Moraes, G.H., Meirelles, F.: The use of electronic government in the State of São Paulo by senior citizens. Revista Tecnologia e Sociedade - RTS **14**, 1 (2018). https://doi.org/10.3895/rts.v14n30.5598
57. Morar, A., Balutoiu, M.A., Moldoveanu, A., Moldoveanu, F., Butean, A.: CultReal-a rapid development platform for AR cultural spaces, with fused localization. Sensors **21**(19) (2021). https://doi.org/10.3390/s21196618
58. Nguyen, D.T.: Understanding perceived enjoyment and continuance intention in mobile games (2015)
59. Nóbrega, R., Jacob, J., Coelho, A., Ribeiro, J., Ferreira, S.: Leveraging pervasive games for tourism: an augmented reality perspective. Int. J. Creative Interfaces Comput. Graph. **9**(1), 1–14 (2018)
60. Ofori, K.S., Larbi-Siaw, O., Fianu, E., Gladjah, R.E., Boateng, E.O.Y.: Factors influencing the continuance use of mobile social media: the effect of privacy concerns. J. Cyber Secur. Mobility **4**(2), 105–124 (2016)
61. Oyman, M., Bal, D., Ozer, S.: Extending the technology acceptance model to explain how perceived augmented reality affects consumers' perceptions. Comput. Hum. Behav. **128** (2022)
62. Pal, D., Patra, S.: University students' perception of video-based learning in times of COVID-19: a TAM/TTF perspective. Int. J. Hum.-Comput. Interact. **37**(10), 903–921 (2020). https://doi.org/10.1080/10447318.2020.1848164
63. Papakostas, C., Troussas, C., Krouska, A., Sgouropoulou, C.: Exploring users' behavioral intention to adopt mobile augmented reality in education through an extended technology acceptance model. Int. J. Hum.-Comput. Interact. **39**, 1294–1302 (2022). https://doi.org/10.1080/10447318.2022.2062551
64. Park, S.Y.: An analysis of the technology acceptance model in understanding university students' behavioral intention to use e-learning. J. Educ. Technol. Soc. (2009)
65. Pengnate, S., Sarathy, R.: An experimental investigation of the influence of website emotional design features on trust in unfamiliar online vendors. Comput. Hum. Behav. **67**(FEB.), 49–60 (2017)
66. Petrucco, C.: Teaching Cultural Heritage using Mobile Augmented Reality (2016)
67. Ramírez-Correa, P., Grandón, E.E., Ramírez-Santana, M., Rdenes, L.B.: Explaining the use of social network sites as seen by older adults: the enjoyment component of a hedonic information system. Int. J. Environ. Res. Public Health **16**(10), 1673 (2019)
68. Ramos-Soler, I., Martínez-Sala, A.-M., Campillo-Alhama, C.: ICT and the sustainability of world heritage sites. Analysis of senior citizens' use of tourism apps. Sustainability **11**(11) (2019). https://doi.org/10.3390/su11113203
69. Reinartz, W., Haenlein, M., Henseler, J.: An empirical comparison of the efficacy of covariance-based and variance-based SEM. Int. J. Res. Mark. **26**(4), 332–344 (2009)
70. Rodrigues, J.M.F., Ramos, C.M.Q., Pereira, J.A.R., Sardo, J.D.P., Cardoso, P.J.S.: Mobile five senses augmented reality system: technology acceptance study. IEEE Access **7**, 163022–163033 (2019)
71. Rogers, E.M.: Diffusion of Innovations, 3rd edn. Free Press (1983)
72. Ronaghi, M.H., Ronaghi, M.: A contextualized study of the usage of the augmented reality technology in the tourism industry. Decis. Anal. J. **5**, 100136 (2022). https://doi.org/10.1016/j.dajour.2022.100136
73. Ronggang, Z., Caihong, F.: Difference between leisure and work contexts: the roles of perceived enjoyment and perceived usefulness in predicting mobile video calling use acceptance. Front. Psychol. **8**, 350 (2017)
74. Schueffel, P.: The concise fintech compendium. Fribourg, Switzerland (2017)

75. Scianna, A., Gaglio, G.F., Guardia, M.L.: Augmented reality for cultural heritage: the rebirth of a historical square. ISPRS – Int. Arch. Photogrammetry Remote Sens. Spatial Inf. Sci. **XLII-2/W17**, 303–308 (2019)

76. Senali, M.G., Iranmanesh, M., Ismail, F.N., Rahim, N.F.A., Khoshkam, M., Mirzaei, M.: Determinants of intention to use e-wallet: personal innovativeness and propensity to trust as moderators. Int. J. Hum.-Comput. Interact. **39**, 2361–2373 (2022). https://doi.org/10.1080/10447318.2022.2076309

77. Shen, S., Xu, K., Sotiriadis, M., Wang, Y.: Exploring the factors influencing the adoption and usage of Augmented Reality and Virtual Reality applications in tourism education within the context of COVID-19 pandemic. J. Hosp. Leis. Sport Tour. Educ. **30**, 100373 (2022)

78. Soares, A.M., Pinho, J.C., Alves, A.: Understanding the navigation experience: do virtual customer service agents make a difference? J. Creative Commun. 09732586221084137. https://doi.org/10.1177/09732586221084137

79. Su, C.-Y., Chiu, C.-H.: Perceived enjoyment and attractiveness influence Taiwanese elementary school students' intention to use interactive video learning. Int. J. Hum.-Comput. Interact. **37**(6), 574–583 (2020). https://doi.org/10.1080/10447318.2020.1841423

80. Suki, N.M.: Exploring the relationship between perceived usefulness, perceived ease of use, perceived enjoyment, attitude and subscribers' intention towards using 3G mobile services. J. Inf. Technol. Manag. (2011)

81. Sung Youl, P.: An analysis of the technology acceptance model in understanding university students' behavioral intention to use e-learning. J. Educ. Technol. Soc. **12**(3), 150–162 (2009). http://www.jstor.org/stable/jeductechsoci.12.3.150

82. Teo, T.: Modelling technology acceptance in education: a study of pre-service teachers. Comput. Educ. **52**(2), 302–312 (2009). https://doi.org/10.1016/j.compedu.2008.08.006

83. Teo, T., Zhou, M.: Explaining the intention to use technology among university students: a structural equation modeling approach. J. Comput. High. Educ. **26**(2), 124–142 (2014)

84. tom Dieck, M.C., Jung, T.H.: Value of augmented reality at cultural heritage sites: a stakeholder approach. J. Destination Mark. Manag. **6**(2), 110–117 (2017). https://doi.org/10.1016/j.jdmm.2017.03.002

85. Tuena, C., et al.: Usability issues of clinical and research applications of virtual reality in older people: a systematic review. Front. Hum. Neurosci. **14**, 93 (2020). https://doi.org/10.3389/fnhum.2020.00093

86. Turan, Z., Cetintas, H.B.: Investigating university students' adoption of video lessons. Open Learn. J. Open Distance e-Learn. **35**(2), 122–139 (2019). https://doi.org/10.1080/02680513.2019.1691518

87. Vassilakis, K., Charalampakos, O., Glykokokalos, G., Kontokalou, P., Vidakis, N.: Learning by playing: an LBG for the Fortification Gates of the Venetian walls of the city of Heraklion. EAI Endorsed Trans. Creative Technol. **5**(16), 156773 (2018)

88. Vassli, L.T., Farshchian, B.A.: Acceptance of health-related ICT among elderly people living in the community: a systematic review of qualitative evidence. Int. J. Hum.-Comput. Interact. **34**(2), 99–116 (2017). https://doi.org/10.1080/10447318.2017.1328024

89. Venkatesh, V., Bala, H.: Technology acceptance model 3 and a research agenda on interventions. Decis. Sci. **39**(2), 273–315 (2010)

90. Venkatesh, V., Davis, F.D.: A theoretical extension of the technology acceptance model: four longitudinal field studies: a theoretical extension of the technology acceptance model: four longitudinal field studies (2000)

91. Venkatesh, V., Morris, M.G., Davis, G.B., Davis, F.D.: User acceptance of information technology: toward a unified view. MIS Q. **27**(3), 425–478 (2003)

92. Venkatesh, V., Thong, J.Y.L., Xu, X.: Consumer acceptance and use of information technology: extending the unified theory of acceptance and use of technology. MIS Q. **36**(1), 157–178 (2012)

93. Vishwakarma, P., Mukherjee, S., Datta, B.: Antecedents of adoption of virtual reality in experiencing destination: a study on the Indian consumers. Tour. Recreat. Res. **45**(2), 1–15 (2019)
94. Wang, Y.H., Wang, H.R.: Measuring perceived usability in Chinese questionnaires: mTAM, SUS, and UMUX. Int. J. Hum.-Comput. Interact. **38**(11), 1052–1063 (2022). https://doi.org/10.1080/10447318.2021.1979291
95. Werner, L., Huang, G., Pitts, B.J.: Smart speech systems: a focus group study on older adult user and non-user perceptions of speech interfaces. Int. J. Hum.-Comput. Interact. **39**, 1149–1161 (2022). https://doi.org/10.1080/10447318.2022.2050541
96. Westland, J.C.: Lower bounds on sample size in structural equation modeling. Electron. Commer. Res. Appl. (2010)
97. Winarno, W.A., Mas'Ud, I., Palupi, T.W.: Perceived enjoyment, application self-efficacy, and subjective norms as determinants of behavior intention in using OVO applications. Korea Distrib. Sci. Assoc. (2) (2021)
98. Wu, L., Su, W., Ye, S., Yu, R.: Digital museum for traditional culture showcase and interactive experience based on virtual reality. Paper Presented at the 2021 IEEE International Conference on Advances in Electrical Engineering and Computer Applications (AEECA) (2021)
99. Wu, L., Yu, R., Su, W., Ye, S.: Design and implementation of a metaverse platform for traditional culture: the chime bells of Marquis Yi of Zeng. Heritage Sci. **10**(1), 1–13 (2022)
100. Wu, R., Yu, Z.: The influence of social isolation, technostress, and personality on the acceptance of online meeting platforms during the COVID-19 pandemic. Int. J. Hum.-Comput. Interact. **39**, 3388–3405 (2022). https://doi.org/10.1080/10447318.2022.2097779
101. Wu, S.T., Chiu, C.H., Chen, Y.S.: The influences of innovative technological introduction on interpretive experiences of exhibition: a discussion on the intention to use augmented reality. Asia Pac. J. Tourism Res. **25**(6), 652–667 (2020)
102. Xie, T., Zheng, L., Liu, G.P., Liu, L.P.: Exploring structural relations among computer self-efficacy, perceived immersion, and intention to use virtual reality training systems. Virtual Reality **26**(4), 1725–1744 (2022). https://doi.org/10.1007/s10055-022-00656-0
103. Yesilyurt, E., Ulas, A.H., Akan, D.: Teacher self-efficacy, academic self-efficacy, and computer self-efficacy as predictors of attitude toward applying computer-supported education. Comput. Hum. Behav. **64**(Nov.), 591–601 (2016)
104. Yung, R., Khoo-Lattimore, C.: New realities: a systematic literature review on virtual reality and augmented reality in tourism research. Curr. Issue Tour. **22**(1), 1–26 (2017)

Enhancing Real-Time Fluid Simulations with Lagrangian Methods and GPU-Based Techniques in Unity

Yanrui Sun[1], Feng Zhou[1(✉)], and Ju Dai[2]

[1] North China University of Technology, Beijing, China
syr@mail.ncut.edu.cn, zhoufeng@ncut.edu.cn
[2] Peng Cheng Laboratory, Shenzhen, China
daij@pcl.ac.cn

Abstract. Fluid simulation remains a core challenge in computer graphics, with ongoing progress in achieving realistic modeling, rendering, and dynamic behavior. This paper introduces a novel real-time fluid simulation framework grounded in the Lagrangian approach, leveraging Smoothed Particle Hydrodynamics (SPH) for flexible and efficient boundary condition handling. Our primary innovation lies in integrating GPU acceleration to address performance bottlenecks commonly seen in high-resolution simulations. By utilizing multi-texture operations and spatial hashing, we streamline neighbor searches and boost computation efficiency. This implementation, developed within the Unity engine, enhances real-time interactions through custom interactive components—such as collision handling, fluid collectors, and visual effects—enabled by Signed Distance Fields (SDF). Additionally, we improve upon conventional Position-Based Fluids (PBF) techniques by optimizing the algorithm for interactive applications. The paper details the theoretical foundations, data structures, and algorithmic processes, along with GPU-specific optimizations employed. We conclude by discussing potential future research directions, such as exploring alternative GPU acceleration techniques, introducing color blending for visual variety, and creating more advanced SDF-based interactions.

Keywords: Fluid simulation · SPH · GPU acceleration

1 Introduction

The accurate simulation of fluid dynamics in computer graphics is essential for applications across entertainment, engineering, and scientific fields. Traditional Eulerian methods, which use a fixed grid to simulate fluid, have been the backbone of fluid simulation but face limitations with complex boundaries and free surfaces, often resulting in artificial constraints and reduced accuracy. To address these challenges, the field has increasingly shifted towards Lagrangian methods,

© The Author(s), under exclusive license to Springer Nature Singapore Pte Ltd. 2025
W. Song et al. (Eds.): ICXR 2024, LNCS 15461, pp. 108–119, 2025.
https://doi.org/10.1007/978-981-96-3679-2_7

which offer a particle-based perspective better suited to handling free surfaces and dynamic interactions.

Smoothed Particle Hydrodynamics (SPH) is a prominent Lagrangian method, excelling in simulations with complex boundaries and dynamic free surfaces without the need for a grid. However, achieving real-time performance with SPH, particularly in high-resolution simulations, is computationally demanding. To overcome this, we adopt a GPU-accelerated framework that leverages the Position-Based Fluids (PBF) approach, enhancing fluid realism by applying position constraints directly to particles. This allows for the simulation of realistic fluid behaviors, such as maintaining particle separation and preventing interpenetration, within an interactive environment.

Our approach addresses key limitations in existing real-time SPH implementations by integrating advanced GPU programming techniques, such as multitexture operations and spatial hashing, to expedite neighbor search processes and improve computational efficiency. Implemented within the Unity engine, our system facilitates real-time interaction with the fluid, including custom effects like collision response, fluid collectors, and special SDF-based interactions. These innovations are designed to support high-fidelity visual outcomes, making our framework a valuable tool for both developers and researchers seeking practical and visually compelling fluid simulation solutions.

The paper is organized as follows: Sect. 2 provides an overview of the existing literature, with a focus on the progression of Lagrangian methods and the contributions of GPU acceleration to real-time fluid simulation. Section 3 discusses our theoretical framework and the formulation of the PBF algorithm tailored for real-time performance. Section 4 covers practical implementation details, including data preparation, collision handling, and the SDF-based interactive elements. Section 5 analyzes our results, highlights limitations, and suggests areas for future work.

Through this work, we aim to advance real-time fluid simulation by presenting a scalable, high-performance framework that addresses the challenges of real-time interactions and computational efficiency in modern graphics applications.

2   Related Work

Fluid simulation [1] has been a prominent area of focus in computer graphics for years, with numerous approaches targeting modeling, rendering, and dynamic simulation [7]. Lagrangian methods, particularly particle-based techniques like Smooth Particle Hydrodynamics (SPH) [16], are widely used due to their ability to simplify boundary condition handling. Variants such as Weakly Compressible SPH (WSPH) and the Moving Particle Semi-Implicit Method (MPS) enhance the accuracy and stability of incompressible fluid simulations [3]. Additionally, iterative schemes like Predictive-Corrective Incompressible SPH (PCISPH) [4, 5,8,9,11,13,27] and Divergence-Free SPH (DFSPH) further improve simulation stability under larger time steps.

Recent advancements in machine learning have introduced data-driven models for fluid simulation, using neural networks to either replace or augment traditional solvers. For instance, deep neural networks can learn complex dynamics from data or approximate computationally intensive steps, enhancing the efficiency and accuracy of simulations [31]. Graph Neural Networks (GNNs) have also become popular for learning interactions in particle-based systems due to their ability to handle unstructured data and capture the locality of particle interactions.

In addition to traditional CPU-based methods, the advent of GPU programmability has enabled significant performance improvements in fluid simulations. GPUs have been employed to solve partial differential equations (PDEs) and perform linear algebra operations for real-time simulations. Techniques like multi-texture operations and texture shaders have been utilized to solve complex fluid equations, offering interactive fluid effects and accelerating computations through parallelism [32].

3   Method

3.1   Theoretical Foundations in Fluid Simulation

Fluid simulation has long been a central issue in computer graphics, requiring both theoretical rigor and computational efficiency to achieve realistic results [20]. The simulation of fluid dynamics in real-time settings presents significant complexity, as it demands accurate modeling of physical interactions and stability over numerous particles or elements. Two widely recognized approaches in this domain are Smoothed Particle Hydrodynamics (SPH) and Position-Based Fluids (PBF), each offering distinct advantages for fluid simulation tasks.

The Smoothed Particle Hydrodynamics (SPH) method, originally developed for astrophysical simulations, is a particle-based approach that uses kernel functions to interpolate physical properties, such as density and pressure, across neighboring particles. By estimating fluid density and pressure through kernel-based weighting, SPH achieves smooth fluid interactions and is commonly used for highly viscous or compressible fluids. However, the computational cost associated with SPH grows with particle count, particularly due to the repeated density and pressure calculations across neighbors.

The Position-Based Dynamics (PBD) method simplifies fluid simulation by bypassing direct acceleration computations and instead focusing on constraint enforcement to regulate particle interactions. Constraints, denoted as C, enforce physical properties such as maintaining fixed distances or collision avoidance, enabling efficient simulation of a variety of behaviors. For example, the stretching constraint for simulating elasticity in cloth or fluids is represented as:

$$C(x) = |\mathbf{x}_i - \mathbf{x}_j| - L = 0 \tag{3.1}$$

where L represents the rest length, ensuring a consistent distance between particles. By iteratively solving these constraints, PBD maintains simulation stability with lower computational requirements, making it highly suitable for real-time applications.

The Position-Based Fluids (PBF) algorithm builds on PBD principles but emphasizes the need for efficient neighbor searching—a key aspect of SPH. By employing spatial data structures, such as hash grids, PBF enhances computational performance, ensuring that the local density of each particle meets a predefined threshold. This is critical for achieving realistic incompressibility, which is vital in applications like gaming and interactive simulations.

3.2   Pressure Factor in Fluid Dynamics

A central component of PBF is the **pressure factor** ϕ_k, which ensures incompressibility by adjusting particle positions based on local density fluctuations. This factor is computed for each particle by comparing its density to a target value and adjusting positions to converge towards a stable state, preventing excessive compression and preserving realistic fluid behavior. The iterative updates of ϕ_k maintain fluid volume stability across time steps, achieving a balance between accuracy and computational efficiency.

3.3   Basic Data Preparation for Fluid Simulation

In our simulation, fluid particles are represented as instances of the PBFParticle class, where each particle has essential properties such as position, predicted position, and velocity, which are crucial for Position-Based Fluids (PBF) simulation [24]. Additional attributes like color and mass [25] provide flexibility for customized simulation elements.

Particle generation can be achieved using two primary methods [12]: cubic and spherical distributions [10]. For cubic particles, a three-dimensional grid along the x, y, and z axes is used, iterating over the specified dimensions to initialize particles within a cube, as shown in Fig. 1(b). In contrast, spherical particles are generated by first creating a cubic volume [17], then retaining only particles within a certain radius from the center, effectively forming a sphere, as shown in Fig. 1(a). Additionally, the spatial distribution of initialized particles can exhibit a gradient or density variation, as illustrated in Fig. 1(c), where a density gradient from the bottom to the top is evident. Throughout the particle initialization process, all core attributes are assigned to each particle [6].

Algorithm 1. Modified Fluid Dynamics Algorithm

1: Initialize particles with initial positions and velocities
2: **for** each time step **do**
3:     **for** each particle k **do**
4:         apply forces: $v_k \leftarrow v_k + F\Delta t$
5:         predict next position: $x_k^{pred} \leftarrow x_k + v_k\Delta t$
6:     **end for**
7:     determine neighboring particles for all particles
8:     **while** currentIteration ¡ maxIterations **do**
9:         **for** each particle k **do**
10:             compute pressure factor: ϕ_k ▷ Adjusts for local density
11:             compute position correction: Δp_k
12:             perform collision detection and apply corrections
13:             update predicted position: $x_k^{pred} \leftarrow x_k^{pred} + \Delta p_k$
14:         **end for**
15:         increment currentIteration
16:     **end while**
17:     **for** each particle k **do**
18:         update velocity: $v_k \leftarrow \frac{x_k^{pred} - x_k}{\Delta t}$
19:         apply damping and viscosity effects
20:         finalize position: $x_k \leftarrow x_k^{pred}$
21:     **end for**
22: **end for**

3.4   Spatial Hash Algorithm

To optimize particle distribution and neighbor searches, a spatial hashing algorithm replaces fixed grids. Spatial hashing allows particles to freely move within the simulation space without confinement, achieving significant performance gains. This approach enables efficient particle interactions, as illustrated in Fig. 2(a), where particles interact dynamically within the simulation space.

In implementation, a GlobalHashCounter buffer [7] stores particle counts for each spatial cell. The first kernel, ResetCounter, initializes this buffer, while InsertToBucket assigns particles to grid cells based on spatial hash values [2]. The resulting buffer enables efficient access to particles within the same grid, as demonstrated in Fig. 2(b), which highlights the structured particle distribution achieved through spatial hashing.

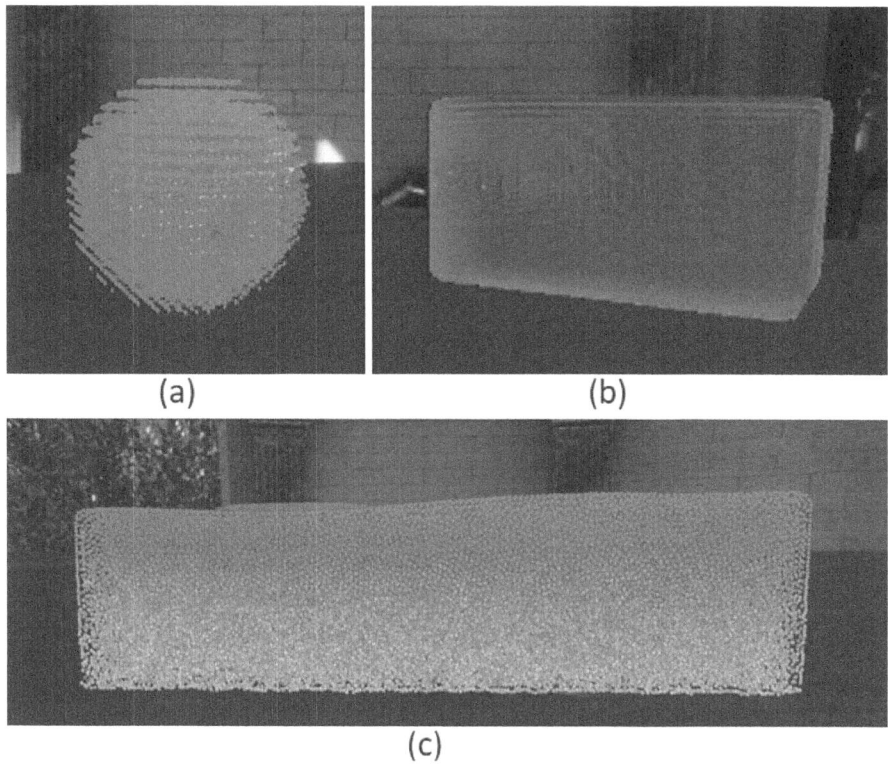

Fig. 1. Generated spherical and cubic particles

3.5   GPU Radix Sort Algorithm

Radix sort is adapted for GPU implementation using Compute Shaders [21,30], capitalizing on shared memory for inter-thread communication. Shared memory, with a capacity of 2048 in each thread group, facilitates sorting operations efficiently [14,15]. Prefix sums are used in radix sort to calculate particle indices within each grid, ensuring accurate neighbor relationships for all particles in each frame of the simulation [19]. The integration of spatial hashing with GPU-based radix sorting enables efficient particle neighbor searches, which is crucial for real-time particle interaction and dynamic behavior within the simulation.

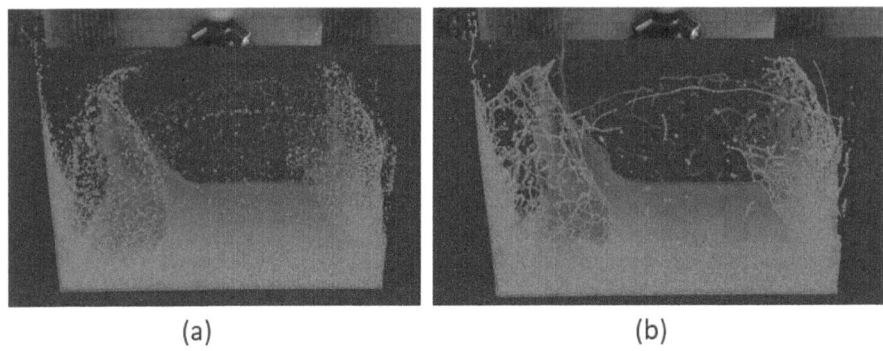

(a)   (b)

Fig. 2. Particle Interaction and Distribution

4   Experiment

4.1   Collision Implementation

Collision detection is performed by calculating the difference between the particle's position and the plane's center to produce a directional vector. This vector is dotted with the plane's normal vector to check if the particle is below the plane. A particle is considered to have penetrated the plane if the dot product is less than 0 but greater than negative SizeZ (the plane's thickness), taking the particle's radius into account.

Once the boundaries are determined, a collision is calculated if conditions are met [22,23]. The collision logic applies an offset to the particle's position in the opposite direction of the plane's normal after penetration [18]. This offset is determined by the dot product of the distance difference and the normal vector, ensuring that the particle is fixed to the plane.

Next, the particle's velocity is checked to see if it is directed opposite to the plane's normal. If so, a reverse velocity is applied to achieve a bouncing effect, with a coefficient added to control the bounce. These calculations are executed after handling boundary collisions.

Here is the actual collision effect, as shown in Fig. 3:

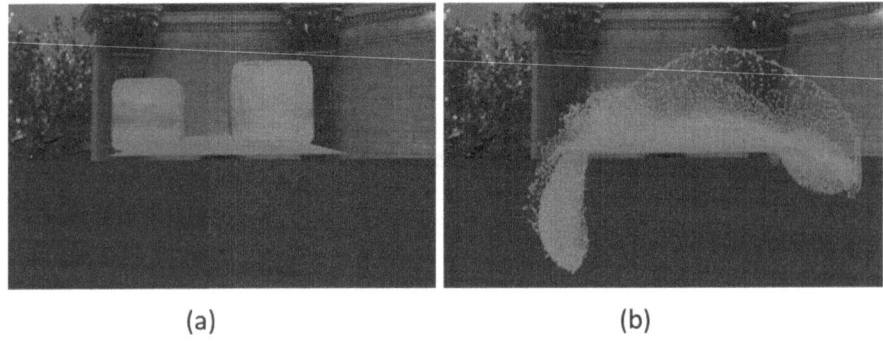

(a)   (b)

Fig. 3. Fluid particle collision before and after

The Fluid Particle Collector and Emitter are designed for collecting and emitting fluid particles. Two components, FluidSource and FluidCollector, inherit from a common class called FluidObject [28]. Both are box-shaped, with a UI drawing function in the parent class to facilitate rendering. FluidCollector records the coordinates of its bottom-left and top-right corners [29], while FluidSource includes an emission speed and UI display for the emission direction. A kernel named FluidCollector is added for interaction.

In the Compute Shader, two constants, NEEDTOEMIT (1) and NORMAL-STATE (0), are defined. Upon initializing particles, the State is set to NORMAL-STATE. The system checks if particles have entered the Collector's volume using the IsInsideVolume function, which compares corner coordinates with particle coordinates. Once inside, the State changes to NEEDTOEMIT.

When the State is NEEDTOEMIT, particles are emitted by updating their positions to random locations within the emitter box using the RandomInArea function, which generates a random coordinate based on the box size. The particles' velocity is then set to the specified emission speed, and the State is reset to NORMALSTATE.

4.2   Implementation of Special Effect Interactions

In Unity, a Signed Distance Field (SDF) is a 3D texture where each texel represents the distance to the nearest surface: positive values are outside, negative values are inside, and zero is on the surface. SDFs can be generated using external tools like Houdini or Unity's SDF baking tool. The texture resolution affects the accuracy; in this project, SDFs for a duck model were baked at resolutions of 64 and 32, with 32 chosen for a balance between memory efficiency and sufficient surface detail.

An SDF Object script stores the SDF texture and manages transformations between world and local coordinates. Particle coordinates are normalized to the 0–1 range for sampling the SDF texture. For particle adhesion, an enclosing box around the SDF Object determines whether calculations occur inside or outside the bounding box.

Outside the bounding box, fluid particles are attracted to the surface, and once they enter, they adhere to it. This adhesion is achieved by using the stored distance values as target velocities. The particle velocity decreases as particles approach the surface, with the dot product of the normal and velocity serving as an attenuation factor to prevent excessive speed.

In Unity, the SDF's stored distance values are linked to the model's actual size. If the mesh used for baking is smaller than 1 m, a scaling factor must be applied to avoid distortion.

For fluid simulation, the original neighbor search algorithms inefficiency reduces frame rates, especially with particle counts exceeding 60,000, which may cause simulation failure. To address this, a GPU-accelerated neighbor search algorithm using a hash grid and prefix sum sorting is implemented. The updated algorithm, utilizing seven new kernels, maintains its goal of listing neighboring particles efficiently. Each thread group is set to 1024, with a hash grid size of 2^{20} (numHashes).

We present a series of sub-images illustrating fluid simulation in Unity, as shown in Fig. 4.

- Figure 4(a): At the initial stage of the simulation, fluid particles are dispersed randomly in space.
- Figure 4(b): As time progresses, the particles start to flow, gradually forming more defined shapes and contours.
- Figure 4(c): The fluid moves further, beginning to interact with surfaces and objects within the environment.
- Figure 4(d): At the final stage, the particles have settled, displaying the fluid's distribution and state in its final form.

These images capture the fluids distribution and behavior at various points in time, highlighting interactions between fluid particles and geometric objects in the scene.

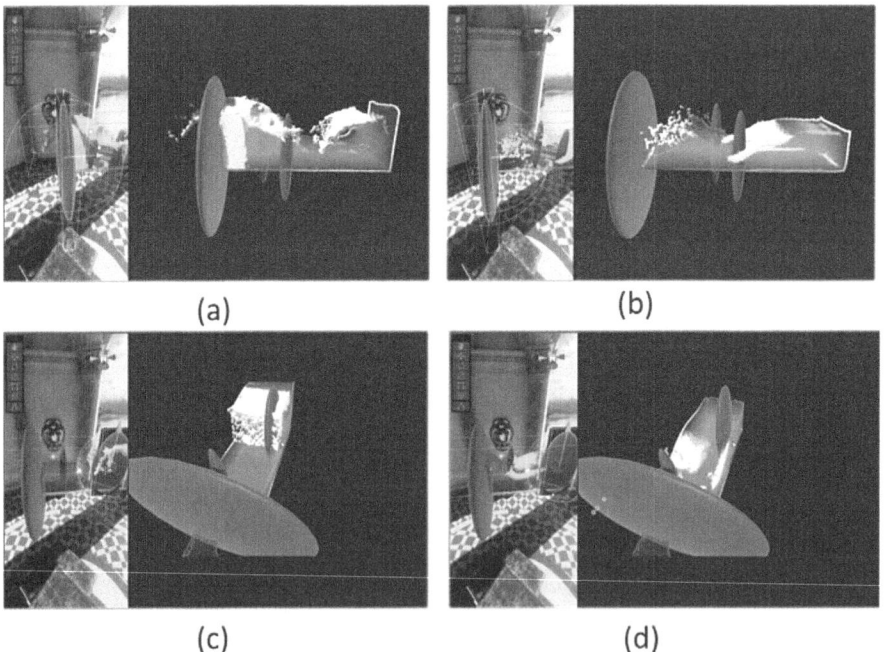

(a)   (b)

(c)   (d)

Fig. 4. Unity Fluid Simulation

4.3 Sorting

Before sorting, we will create a Compute Buffer, called SortedBuffer, with the same size as the previous particle size. This buffer will be used to store the information of the sorted particles, and the actual sorting operation will take place in the Kernel Sort. In the previous section, we obtained the actual prefix sum for each grid, which allows us to read the hash values of each particle from the Hashes Buffer. By subtracting 1 from the current hash value, we can get the prefix sum of the previous grid. By adding this value to the local index of the particle in its current grid, we can obtain the actual index of the sorted particle.

In the final kernel, a Compute Buffer named HashRange will be created to store the starting and ending indices of particles in each grid, noting that these are the sorted particle indices. Once this table is obtained, we can proceed with the actual lookup.

4.4 Searching

The actual lookup operation involves calculating the hash values of the 27 grids surrounding the current particle, including itself, based on the particle's actual position. Using these hash values, we can refer to the HashRange list obtained in the previous section. By using the head of the HashRange as the starting point for a for loop and iterating until it is less than the tail of the HashRange, we can accumulate the current index. With the accumulated index combined with the SortedBuffer, we can retrieve the neighboring particles of the current particle.

5 Conclusion

This paper studies the theory related to fluid simulation, prepares the essential data required, clarifies the fundamental concepts of fluid simulation methods, and finally derives the formulas and algorithmic processes of the Position-Based Fluids (PBF) simulation algorithm.

The implementation successfully achieves basic fluid simulation functionalities within the Unity engine, employing a PBF-based approach. It integrates custom interactive features such as collision handling, fluid collection, and special effect interaction components. By incorporating GPU-based spatial hashing and sorting algorithms, the simulation is notably accelerated, achieving high frame rates in fluid simulation.

To assess the effectiveness of our approach, we compared our simulation with other common fluid simulation methods, focusing on algorithm execution time and detail level. Our method, leveraging advanced GPU programming techniques, including multi-texturing and custom shaders, demonstrated significantly reduced computation times in comparison to traditional CPU-based methods and other GPU-accelerated techniques lacking spatial hashing optimizations.

While this study demonstrates the potential of our approach, several areas remain for future research: 1. Exploration of alternative GPU acceleration algorithms and data structures to further refine simulation efficiency and performance. 2. Implementation of fluid color blending features to enhance visual realism. 3. Development of additional custom effect components using Signed Distance Fields (SDF) to broaden interactive capabilities. 4. Integration of our methods into practical applications to address real-world fluid simulation needs.

Acknowledgements. This work is supported by the R&D Program of the Beijing Municipal Education Commission (KM202310009002), the Yuxiu Innovation Project of NCUT (2024NCUTYXCX202), and in part by the Beijing Natural Science Foundation (4232023).

References

1. Müller, M., Charypar, D., Gross, M.: Particle-based fluid simulation for interactive applications. In: ACM SIGGRAPH/Eurographics Symposium on Computer Animation, pp. 154–159 (2003)
2. Macklin, M., Müller, M.: Position-based fluids. ACM Trans. Graph. (TOG) **32**(4), 104 (2013)
3. Bridson, R.: Fluid Simulation for Computer Graphics, 2nd edn. CRC Press, Boca Raton (2015)
4. Ihmsen, M., Akinci, G., Gissler, M., Teschner, M.: Boundary handling and adaptive time-stepping for PCISPH. In: VRIPHYS 2010, pp. 79–88 (2010)
5. Solenthaler, B., Pajarola, R.: Predictive-corrective incompressible SPH. ACM Trans. Graph. (TOG) **28**(3), 40 (2009)
6. Zhu, Y., Bridson, R.: Animating sand as a fluid. ACM Trans. Graph. (TOG) **24**(3), 965–972 (2005)
7. Akinci, N., Ihmsen, M., Akinci, G., Solenthaler, B., Teschner, M.: Versatile rigid-fluid coupling for incompressible SPH. ACM Trans. Graph. (TOG) **31**(4), 62 (2012)
8. Schechter, H., Bridson, R.: Ghost SPH for animating water. ACM Trans. Graph. (TOG) **31**(4), 61 (2012)
9. Bender, J., Koschier, D.: Divergence-free smoothed particle hydrodynamics. In: ACM SIGGRAPH/Eurographics Symposium on Computer Animation, pp. 147–155 (2015)
10. Narain, R., Golas, A., Lin, M.: Free-flowing granular materials with two-way solid coupling. ACM Trans. Graph. (TOG) **29**(6), 173 (2010)
11. He, X., Wang, G., Tong, Y., Shi, X., Bao, H., Desbrun, M.: Robust simulation of sparsely sampled thin features in SPH-based free surfaces. In: ACM SIGGRAPH 2014, Article no. 79 (2014)
12. Müller, M., Teschner, M., Gross, M.: Physically-based simulation of objects represented by surface meshes. In: Proceedings of Computer Graphics International, pp. 26–33 (2004)
13. Becker, M., Teschner, M.: Weakly compressible SPH for free surface flows. In: Proceedings of ACM SIGGRAPH/Eurographics Symposium on Computer Animation, pp. 209–217 (2007)
14. Lentine, M., Zheng, W., Fedkiw, R.: A novel algorithm for incompressible flow using the FFT. ACM Trans. Graph. (TOG) **29**(4), 29 (2010)
15. Harada, T., Koshizuka, S., Kawaguchi, Y.: Smoothed particle hydrodynamics on GPUs. In: Computer Graphics International, pp. 63–70 (2007)
16. Ihmsen, M., Orthmann, J., Solenthaler, B., Kolb, A., Teschner, M.: SPH fluids in computer graphics. In: Eurographics, pp. 21–42 (2014)

17. Adams, B., Pauly, M., Keiser, R., Guibas, L.J.: Adaptively sampled particle fluids. ACM Trans. Graph. (TOG) **26**(3), 48 (2007)
18. Raveendran, K., Thuerey, N., Wojtan, C., Turk, G.: Controlling liquids using meshes. In: ACM SIGGRAPH 2012, p. 4 (2012)
19. Goswami, P., Weiler, M., Tejada, E., Gobron, S., Groß, H., Ertl, T.: Interactive SPH simulation and rendering on the GPU. In: Eurographics Symposium on Point-Based Graphics, pp. 1–10 (2010)
20. Keiser, R., Adams, B., Gasser, D., Bazzi, P., Dutré, P., Gross, M.: A unified Lagrangian approach to solid-fluid animation. In: Eurographics Symposium on Point-Based Graphics, pp. 125–133 (2005)
21. Ren, B., Jiang, Z., Jiang, F., Zhang, M., Yuan, Y., Zhan, Y.: GPU-accelerated particle-based simulation of fluid dynamics. J. Supercomput. **72**(4), 1621–1641 (2016)
22. Fan, W., Yao, Z., Deng, Y., Bao, H.: A robust SPH-based method for simulating continuous material under extreme deformation. In: ACM SIGGRAPH Asia 2016, Article no. 190 (2016)
23. Tiwari, M., Mahesh, K.: Simulation of hydrodynamic instabilities using smoothed particle hydrodynamics. J. Comput. Phys. **273**, 483–499 (2014)
24. Yu, T., Thürey, N., Xu, W., Rüegg, C., Macklin, M., Li, H.: 3D modeling of liquids interacting with dynamic objects. ACM Trans. Graph. (TOG) **36**(4), 16 (2017)
25. Cornelis, J., Keck, T., Thürey, N., Weinkauf, T.: Heat maps for SPH simulations. IEEE Trans. Visual Comput. Graph. **22**(10), 2395–2407 (2016)
26. Zhang, Q., Zhang, Y., Hu, H., Yang, X.: Hybrid SPH simulation with anisotropic XSPH correction. Vis. Comput. **30**(6), 751–759 (2014)
27. Jiang, G., Li, S., Bao, H., Wei, L.Y.: Anisotropic blue noise for SPH fluids. In: ACM SIGGRAPH Asia 2017 Technical Briefs, Article no. 9 (2017)
28. Zehnder, J., Narain, R.: Rigid-fluid coupling with surface tension and viscosity. ACM Trans. Graph. (TOG) **38**(4), 47 (2019)
29. Tessendorf, J.: Simulating ocean water. ACM SIGGRAPH Courses (2004)
30. Zhu, H., Pan, M., Xu, K., Bao, H., Wu, E.: Efficient neighbor search for particle-based fluid simulation on GPUs. Comput. Graph. **82**, 233–242 (2019)
31. Ladický, Ľ., Jeong, S., Solenthaler, B., Pollefeys, M., Gross, M.: Data-driven fluid simulations using regression forests. ACM Trans. Graph. **34**(6), 199:1–199:9 (2015)
32. Yang, C., Zhang, W., Bao, H.: Data-driven projection method in fluid simulation. Comput. Animat. Virtual Worlds **27**(3-4), 415–424 (2016)

Enhancing Text Entry in Mixed Reality with Tangible Feedback

Haofei Wang[1] , Yawen Zhang[1] , and Feng Lu[1,2](✉)

[1] Peng Cheng Laboratory, Shenzhen, China
lufeng@buaa.edu.cn
[2] Beihang University, Beijing, China

Abstract. Text entry stands as a fundamental interaction modality in mixed reality systems. Existing systems usually require users to type on a virtual keyboard displayed in air using their index fingers, i.e., in-air typing (IAT) system. However, this approach diverges from traditional physical keyboards on personal computers in that it lacks haptic feedback and entails substantial arm movements during typing, potentially inducing fatigue over extended periods of use. In this paper, we explore the possibilities of on-hand typing (OHT) in a head-mounted mixed reality system. A virtual keyboard materializes upon the user's palm, affording the user the ability to input text upon their own hand with tangible feedback. Both OHT and IAT systems were both instantiated on the Microsoft HoloLens 2, and their performance was assessed utilizing the standardized MacKenzie phrase set. Furthermore, subjective feedback was garnered via the NASA-Task Load Index Questionnaire and the User Experience Questionnaire. Experimental results reveal that while the OHT system exhibits a slower typing velocity, it entails a notably reduced physical exertion in comparison to the IAT system. This work opens a new pathway for merging virtual and real environments for text input in future mixed reality systems.

Keywords: text entry · mixed reality · human-computer interaction · augmented reality · gesture recognition

1 Introduction

Augmented/Mixed Reality (AR/MR) directly overlays the virtual content on top of the real environment [30]. To interact with virtual content, various input modalities have been proposed, such as hand gesture, speech, and gaze [36]. Text entry is one of the important components of AR systems and the in-air typing (IAT) technique is the most widely adopted. For example, Microsoft Hololens displays the virtual QWERTY keyboard in mid-air, and the user presses the

This work was supported in part by the National Natural Science Foundation of China under Grant 62202248 and in part by the China Postdoctoral Science Foundation under Grant 2024M751556.

© The Author(s), under exclusive license to Springer Nature Singapore Pte Ltd. 2025
W. Song et al. (Eds.): ICXR 2024, LNCS 15461, pp. 120–135, 2025.
https://doi.org/10.1007/978-981-96-3679-2_8

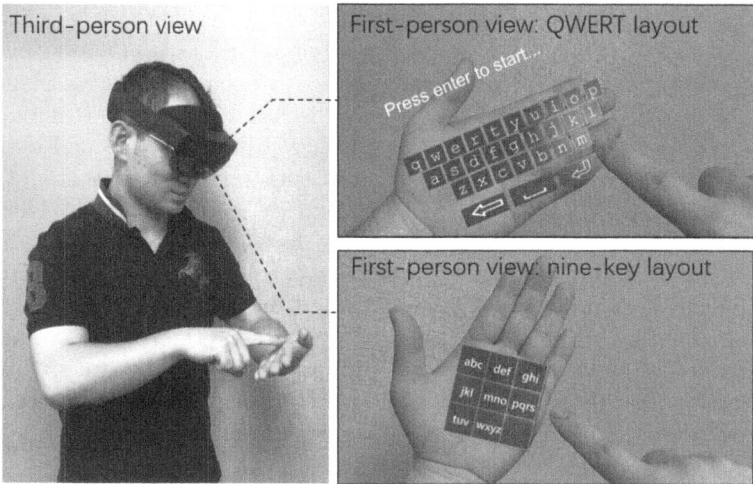

Fig. 1. The proposed on-hand typing (OHT) system for mixed reality devices. The left part shows the third-person view of the OHT system, and the right part shows the first-person view of two keyboard layouts: the QWERT layout and the nine-key layout. The virtual keyboard is overlaid on the user's palm. The user enters text by pressing the virtual button on his/her hand, just like inputting text with a physical keyboard on personal computers.

virtual button using his/her index fingers. However, the in-air text entry system has several drawbacks. Firstly, it provides no physical feedback to the user. Although the system could offer audio and visual feedback, the user does not have the sense of touch as they type on the physical keyboard. Secondly, the virtual keyboard in the IAT system often occupies a relatively large space of the display, which may interfere with the other content. This issue could be partly solved by reducing the size of the keyboard, however, reducing the size may lead to performance degradation as there is a trade-off between the keyboard size and the typing speed. Thirdly, users have to perform a large arm movement to enter the text, which may lead to arm fatigue and privacy disclosure. In particular, when the user types sensitive words such as account name or password, the observer can predict the typed words based on the arm movement pattern. Such systems cannot be used on the subway or bus, since the user can not perform large arm movement in a crowded environment.

To provide users with physical feedback when typing in virtual reality (VR) systems, several solutions have been proposed. The most straightforward way is to use a physical keyboard [20]. Typing on a physical keyboard is highly efficient and an experienced typist can type in an eye-free way. Although the physical keyboard provides haptic feedback, it is impossible to carry an additional keyboard anytime and anywhere. Other studies investigate the in-air text entry with haptic feedback, which can be divided into three categories: hand-held devices [4,6–8,19,34], non-contact devices [5,15,31] and wearable devices [13,14,28,42]. Hand-held devices bring extra burden to users, which limits the diversity of interaction. Non-contact devices, such as laser and ultrasound, introduce additional costs. The wearable device is a compromise, for example, a smartwatch provides simple yet effective feedback for free-hand VR interaction.

However, text entry in AR/MR differs from VR in many aspects. Firstly, the AR/MR system overlays the virtual content with physical surroundings while the VR system can only render the content in a virtual environment. Therefore, we should exploit the advantage of merging the virtual content with the real environment. Secondly, the AR systems only have head-mounted displays but have no controllers. Unlike VR systems which the user can interact with the virtual environment using a controller, in AR systems, the user has to perform the hand/gesture movement in a real environment, so the keyboard size can not be arbitrarily determined. Therefore, the ideal text entry system in AR should require no additional device and combine the virtual keyboard with the real environment.

When entering text in the public or mobile environment, the user's privacy is likely to be disclosed. There are two possible solutions to preserve user privacy in text entry systems. One solution is to use eye gaze [32], since gaze is an implicit cue for communication. However, eye-tracking systems are not always available and reliable. The typical gaze-based text entry system uses the dwell time [27], which requires rapid eye movements coupled with a certain period of time (dwell time) for the eye to be fixed and gazing at a specific position. The other solution is to use the micro finger gesture [39]. The user enters the text by tapping on the index finger using the thumb tip. However, this requires wearable sensors and the recognition is not always accurate.

To address the drawbacks of the aforementioned approaches, we explore the possibility of an on-hand typing (OHT) system in a head-mounted mixed reality system, as shown in Fig. 1. The system tracks the user's hand and overlays a virtual keyboard on the user's hand, which enables the user to type on his/her own palm. The user can switch off the keyboard as well as the typed words anytime when s/he feels the surroundings unsecured by closing his/her palm. Furthermore, we conducted comparative experiments with the existing IAT system and evaluated the system performance both objectively and subjectively. In summary, the primary contributions of this paper are as follows:

– We present a novel on-hand typing system (OHT) in a head-mounted mixed reality system. Unlike the existing in-air typing (IAT) system, the proposed on-hand typing system provides users tangible feedback that conforms to user habits as using the physical keyboard. Since the system only requires a small range of arm movement, it has the potential to be used in mobile or crowded environments.
– We conducted a user study to compare the system performance of the OHT system with the existing IAT system in terms of both objective evaluation and subjective feedback. Experimental results demonstrate that although the typing speed of the OHT system is slower than that of the IAT system, the OHT system requires significantly less physical effort.

2   Related Work

Different kinds of typing systems have been proposed for AR/VR [10]. In this section, we summarize the existing works of in-air typing, on-hand typing, typing with physical feedback as well as privacy protection in AR systems.

2.1   In-Air Text Entry Systems

In-air text entry, also known as mid-air text entry, is the most commonly used text entry modality in both AR and VR systems. Such text entry systems require users to press the virtual keys in the air [11]. A variety of interaction modalities have been explored, such as head pointing, hand pointing, eye gaze, and controllers. Xu et al. [38] compared the system performance and user preference using different pointing and selection methods. Yi et al. [41] proposed an in-air typing system that tracks the hand pose by Leap Motion [37]. Lee et al. [23] proposed the HIBEY, a keyboard-less interface for Hololens, which enables the users to pick characters through hand movements from the preparation zone to the fast-forward zone. Multimodal text entry systems have also been investigated. Adhikary et al. [1] combined hand tracking with speech recognition to allow typing on an auto-correcting in-air keyboard in a VR system, which achieves a significantly faster typing speed.

Although in-air text entry systems are fast, it has two disadvantages: 1) they provide no physical feedback, which is different from the user behavior of typing on a physical keyboard; 2) to maintain accuracy, the keyboard size is usually large. As a result, the users have to perform a large arm movement, which may lead to arm fatigue after prolonged usage.

2.2   Text Entry Systems with Physical Feedback

The somatosensory system in the human body consists of a huge network of nerve endings and touch receptors in the skin, which enables us to sense the touch [21]. Many on-hand interaction systems have been investigated, however, most of them are not developed for AR systems. PalmRC [9] is the first work that uses the palm surface as a remote controller for television interaction. Harrison et al. proposed the Skinput [17] appropriating the human body as an input surface. They designed an armband to detect the finger tapping on the arm and equipped it with a pico-projector which allows the rendering of interactive elements on the skin. OmniTouch [16] is a shoulder-worn system, which detects the hand pose by a RGB-D camera and projects the keyboard onto any moving surfaces using a pico-projector.

To provide physical feedback, the most ideal channel is to directly type on our body, such as the palm or the arm. However, on-hand typing in AR systems has been rarely investigated. Wang et al. [35] used wrist-worn sensors to detect the finger position when using Google Glass. Commercial AR devices usually use a controller or real keyboard to provide physical feedback during typing. Pham et al. [29] introduce a new keyboard, worn on a hawker's tray in front

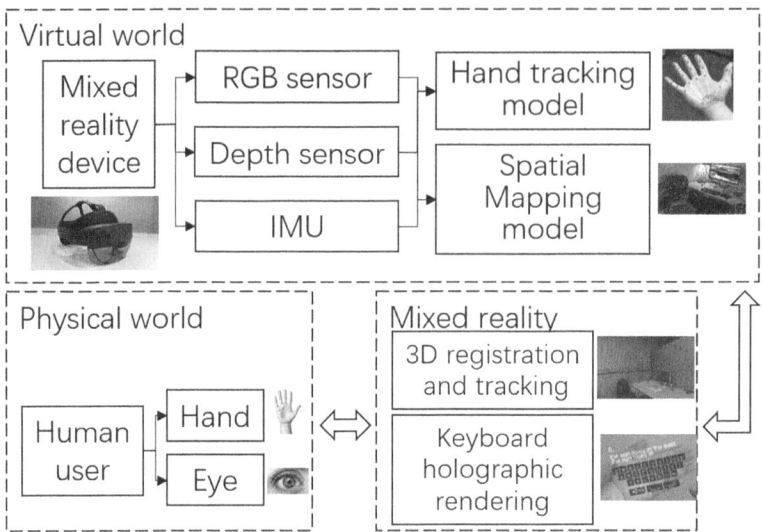

Fig. 2. System architecture of the proposed OHT system. This diagram demonstrates the transition workflow between the virtual world, the physical world, and the mixed reality devices.

of the user, which provides physical feedback for typing in a VR system. This method is faster than typing on virtual keyboards. Ahn et al. [2] propose to use the touchpad on Google glasses to assist the gaze-typing, which is faster than the typing using eye alone.

The above-mentioned systems cannot provide natural physical feedback during text entry. They either require additional devices or are not designed for AR systems.

3   Methodology

3.1   System Architecture

Figure 2 shows the system architecture of merging the virtual world with the physical world. In the virtual world, the mixed reality device captures the RGB image and depth image of the environment. The inertial measurement unit (IMU) records the acceleration, orientation, angular rates, and other gravitational forces. The RGBD images and the IMU measurements are fed into a hand-tracking model and an environment-understanding model. The hand-tracking model constructs a two-handed fully articulated model. The environment understanding model provides real-time 6-degree-of-freedom tracking as well as spatial mapping of the environment. Through the 3D registration and tracking model and the holographic rendering model, the user in the physical world is able to see the keyboard and type on his/her own hand.

3.2   Evaluation Metrics

Based on the chronological order, the texts during typing can be categorized into three groups: the presented text, the input stream, and the transcribed text. Assuming that the task is to transcribe the sentence *'the book is mine'*. The *presented text* is the ground-truth text that we need to follow, *i.e.*, *'the book is mine'*. The *input stream* is the all keystrokes that we pressed during typing, including the delete keystrokes. For example, $thw \leftarrow e\ bo\mathbf{a}k\ is\ minn \leftarrow e$. The *transcribed text* is the final text after correction, *i.e.*, *the boak is mine*.

Words per Minute. We use the words per minute (WPM) to evaluate the typing speed [3]. WPM is defined as the number of words of the *transcribed text* per minute. WPM is calculated as the following equation,

$$WPM = \frac{|T| - 1}{S} \times 60 \times \frac{1}{5}, \tag{1}$$

where $|T|$ denotes the number of characters in the *transcribed text*, S denotes the total time in seconds used for typing. The constant 60 is the number of seconds per minute, and the constant 5 is the average length of a word in characters including spaces, numbers, and other printable characters [40].

Error Rates. We followed the method in [33] to compute the error rate. For the completeness of the paper, we briefly introduce this method here. We define four basic components in the input stream: *Correct (C)*, *Incorrect Not Fixed (INF)*, *Incorrect Fixed (IF)* and *Fixes (F)*, as shown in Fig. 3. The C is the part of the *input stream* that matches the *presented text*, the INF is the part of the *input stream* that does not match the *presented text*. The IF and F only appear in the *input stream*, not in the *transcribed text*. In our system, IF refers to the keystrokes that are mistyped and deleted later; F refers to the delete keystrokes, which are represented in the *Input Stream* as '$\leftarrow$'. The total number of IF is equal to F and only C and INF appear in the final *transcribed text*. An example of these four components is shown in Fig. 4.

In the following, we use C, INF, IF and F to denote the total number of characters in the *Input Stream* for each of the above four basic components. The definition of the *Total Error Rate (TER)* is as follows,

$$TER = \frac{INF + IF}{C + INF + IF} \times 100\%. \tag{2}$$

It can be seen that IF (the errors corrected during typing) and INF (the errors uncorrected during typing) have the same contribution to the final *Total Error Rate*. If all errors are corrected during typing, then INF will be 0, but IF will compensate for the decrease in INF, and $IF + INF$ will remain the same. The TER will not change. The *Not Corrected Error Rate (NCER)* and *Corrected Error Rate (CER)* can be calculated as follows:

$$NCER = \frac{INF}{C + INF + IF} \times 100\%, \tag{3}$$

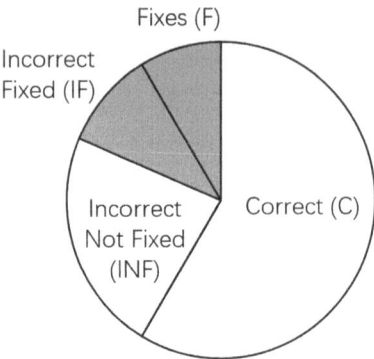

Fig. 3. The basic compositions of *input stream*. The shaded part does not appear in the transcribed text since F is the number of the delete keystrokes used to eliminate IF in typing. C indicates the correct part in transcribed text and *INF* indicates the incorrect part in transcribed text.

$$\underset{C}{\underbrace{\text{th}\overset{\overset{IF\;\;F}{\frown}}{\text{w}\leftarrow\text{e}}}} \; \underset{C}{\underbrace{\text{bo}\overset{INF}{\frown}\text{ak}}} \; \underset{C}{\underbrace{\text{is minn}}}\overset{\overset{IF\;\;F}{\frown}}{\underset{C}{\leftarrow\text{e}}}$$

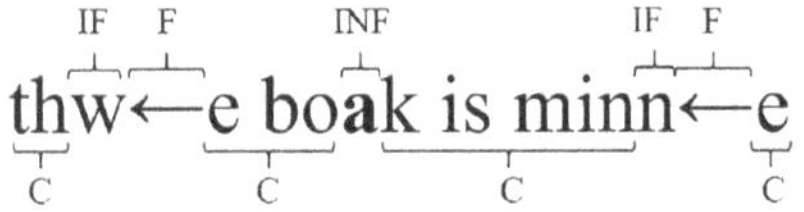

Fig. 4. An example of the *Correct (C)*, the *Incorrect Not Fixed (INF)*, the *Incorrect Fixed (IF)*, and the *Fixes (F)*.

$$CER = \frac{IF}{C + INF + IF} \times 100\%. \tag{4}$$

4   Experimental Results

We conducted a user study to compare the in-air typing system and the on-hand typing system. We evaluated the system performance based on objective performance and subjective feedback.

4.1   Participants and Apparatus

Eight subjects (6 male, 2 female) were recruited on campus to conduct the experiment, the average age is 25.6 ± 1.6. Two subjects had previously used the head-mounted AR/MR system while the remaining six had no prior experience using an AR/MR device. All the subjects were fluent in English and they are frequent keyboard users. They all had normal or corrected-to-normal vision.

We implemented both the in-air typing system and the on-hand typing system in Microsoft Hololens 2. The project was developed on a desktop computer running Windows 10, which had an i7 CPU, 16 GB RAM, and a Nvidia GeForce GTX 2080 super GPU.

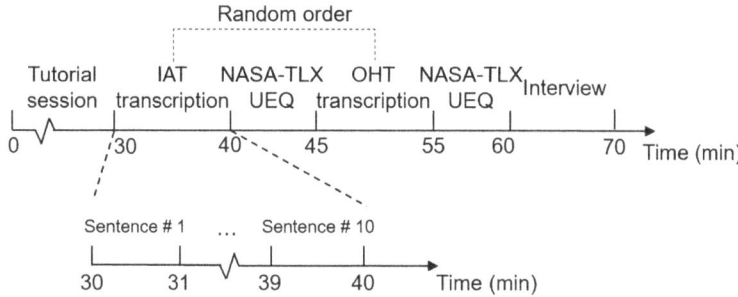

Fig. 5. Experimental procedure.

4.2   Experimental Procedure

The subjects were asked to conduct two transcription tasks using IAT and OHT systems. The experimental procedure is shown in Fig. 5. The illustration of the transcription task is shown in Fig. 6. The order of two experiments was random. There is a short break between the two experiments. Before the experiment, the experimenter first introduced the experiment to the subjects. Then, the subjects were first asked to fill in a consent form for participating in the experiments. Next, they were required to try the HoloLens device and practice typing several phrases until they mastered the typing system. In each experiment, subjects were instructed to transcribe ten sentences, which were randomly selected from the standard MacKenzie phrase set [25] with a list of 500 phrases. Note that this phrase set is commonly used for evaluating text entry systems [12,24,26]. The timestamps and the typed characters were recorded during typing.

After each experiment, the subjects were asked to fill out the NASA Task Load Index questionnaire (NASA-TLX) [18] and the User Experience Questionnaire (UEQ) [22]. The NASA-TLX questionnaire evaluates the cognitive load from six perspectives: mental, physical, temporal, performance, effort, and frustration. The UEQ evaluates subjective feedback from six perspectives: attractiveness, efficiency, perspicuity, dependability, stimulation, and novelty. After the experiment, we interviewed the subjects and collected their comments/suggestions for the system. The whole experiment lasted approximately one hour for each subject.

4.3   Performance Evaluation

Figure 7 shows the boxplots comparing the *WPM*, *TER*, *NCER*, and *CER* of the OHT system and the IAT system. The boxplot shows five metrics: minimum, first quartile (Q1), median, third quartile (Q3), and maximum, and ° represents the outliers. We observe that the *WPM* of IAT is significantly higher than OHT (IAT: 8.00 ± 1.08, OHT: 4.82 ± 1.15). The *TER* of IAT is significantly lower than OHT (IAT: $1.92\% \pm 1.02$, OHT: $7.48\% \pm 2.99$), which indicates that OHT was more prone to mistyping. The difference of *NCER* between IAT and OHT

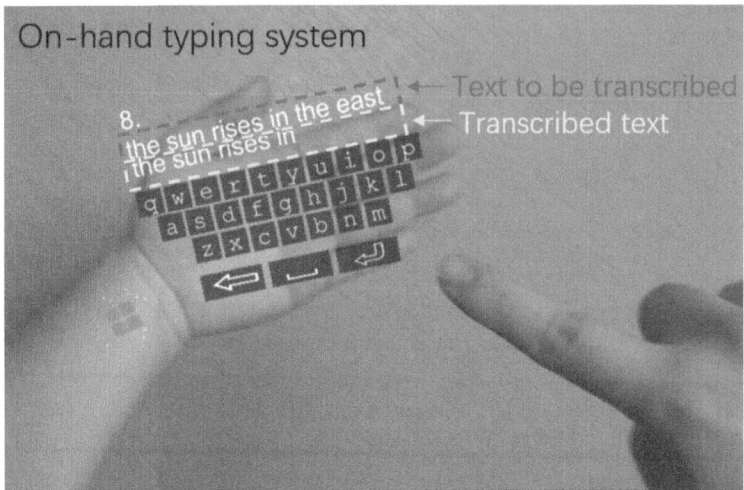

Fig. 6. Illustration of the transcription task. The upper figure shows the user's view of the OHT system while the bottom figure shows the user's view of the IAT system. As shown in the upper figure, the text above the keyboard shows the text that is to be transcribed(*'the sun rises in the east'*) and the transcribed text(*'the sun rises in'*).

is not significant (IAT: $0.22\% \pm 0.39$, OHT: $0.48\% \pm 0.31$). It suggests that the uncorrected parts in two typing tasks were approximately the same. The *CER* of IAT is significantly smaller than OHT (IAT: $1.71\% \pm 1.10$, OHT: $7.01\% \pm 2.88$). The *CER* contributes most to the *TER*. This indicates that most of the typing errors were corrected for both of these two techniques. In other words, the subjects were responsible and cooperative in the experiment. The one-way *ANOVA* test results are shown in Table 1. We found that the *WPM, TER, CER* of two typing systems show significance ($p < 0.01$).

We also investigated the performance changes over sentences, the results are shown in Fig. 8. It can be seen that the WPMs in both typing methods generally

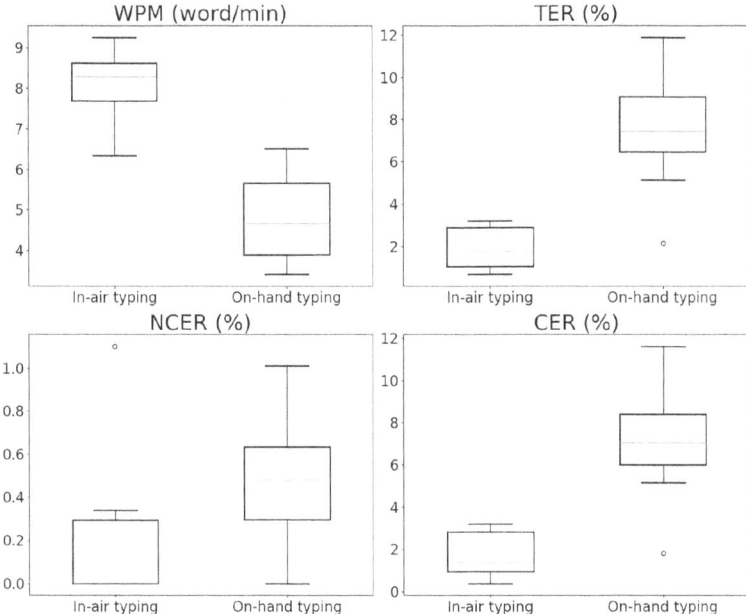

Fig. 7. Performance comparison of the OHT system and the IAT system using boxplots. Top left: average Word Per Minute (WPM) (words/min), top right: Total Error Rate (TER) (%), bottom left: Not Corrected Error Rate (NCER) (%) and bottom right: Corrected Error Rate (CER) (%).

Table 1. ANOVA test results of system performance.

	WPM	TER	NCER	CER
$F_{1,6}$	32.49	24.82	2.30	23.66
p	<0.01	<0.01	>0.05	<0.01

show an increasing trend over the sentence index. This indicates the learning effect of the subjects on the typing task. In contrast, the error rates fluctuate over the sentence index for both tasks, meaning that the subject's mental state and engagement level are relatively consistent during the experiment.

4.4   Subjective Results

NASA-TLX Results. Figure 9 shows the details of six indicators of NASA-TLX comparing two typing approaches. The scales for NASA-TLX were normalized between 0 (excellent) to 7 (very bad). The one-way ANOVA test results are shown in Table 2. We found that there is no significance between the two approaches overall. However, the OHT approach achieves significantly lower physical effort than the IAT approach ($F_{1,6} = 7.13, p = 0.018$). This is due

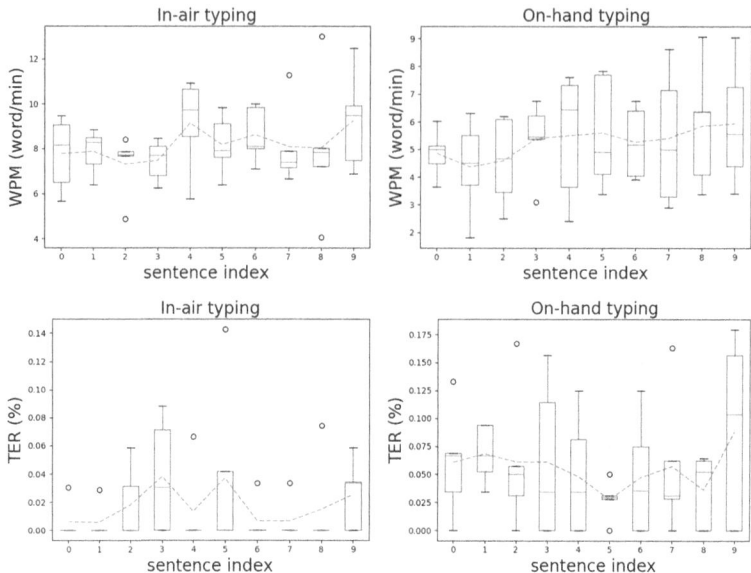

Fig. 8. Boxplots of performance change over sentence index. The red dashed lines are the mean values. The first row shows the WPM change of the two typing systems. The second row shows the TER change of the two typing systems. (Color figure online)

Table 2. ANOVA test results of NASA-TLX.

Item	$F_{1,6}$	$p-value$
Mental	0.07	>0.05
Physical	7.13	<0.01
Temporal	0.05	>0.05
Performance	0.01	>0.05
Effort	1.07	>0.05
Frustration	0.91	>0.05
Overall	0.15	>0.05

to the fact that users have to perform a relatively large arm movement during typing, which leads to arm fatigue after prolonged usage.

UEQ Results. Figure 10 shows the UEQ results of two typing approaches. The scales were normalized between 0 (very bad) to 7 (excellent). The ANOVA results show that there is no significance between the two approaches. However, we found that the perceived novelty of OHT is slightly higher than IAT ($F_{1,6} = 2.82, p = 0.11$). This is interesting that users show a preference for the OHT system. More details will be discussed in Sect. 5.

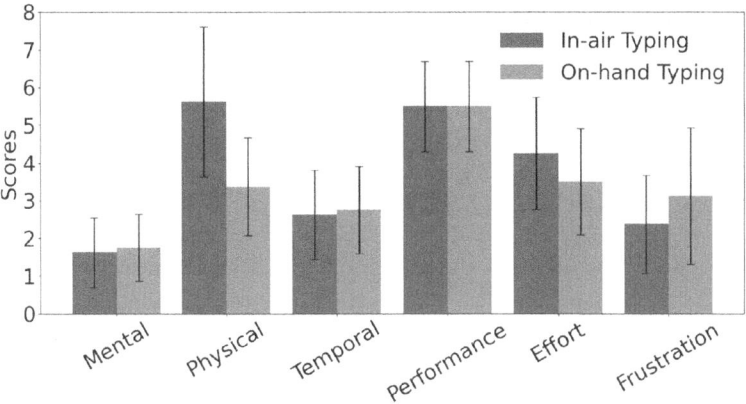

Fig. 9. Results of NASA-TLX.

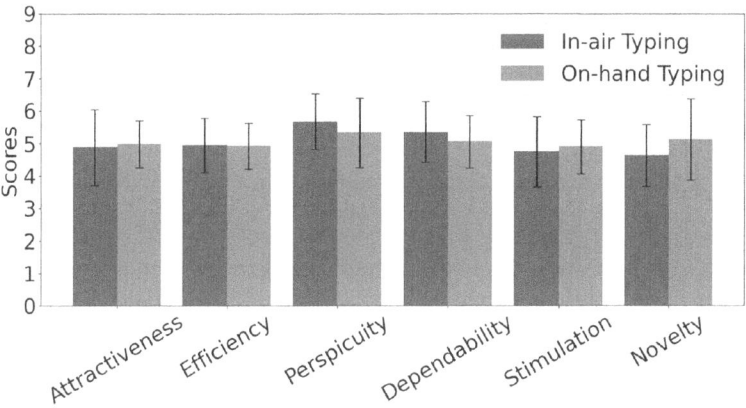

Fig. 10. Results of UEQ.

5   Discussion

5.1   User Preference

We interviewed all eight subjects after the experiments and asked them their experience of using two typing systems. For the IAT system, more than half of them reported that it was tiring and not suitable for long-time typing (S3, S4, S5, S6, S7). This is consistent with the significantly higher physical efforts in NASA-TLX, as shown in Fig. 9. In addition, two participants thought that it was inaccurate for hand gesture recognition (S1, S8). S2 complained that the field of view is small and sometimes he cannot see the full keyboard. S1 suggested introducing the auto-correction function and incorporating the language model. For the OHT system, most participants favored the physical feedback (S1, S3, S5, S6, S8). However, due to the keyboard size is small, it is easy to type the neighboring keys (S1, S5, S6). Two subjects said that the depth of the press was difficult to control (S7, S8).

5.2   System Limitations

The system limitation lies in two aspects.

Firstly, the hand tracking accuracy is not satisfactory especially when one hand occludes the other. During the experiments, we also observed some latency of hand tracking. This issue is also listed on Hololens official documents that *"While this sometimes works, quickly doing hand gestures may result in highly inaccurate destinations."* Moreover, since the OHT system involves simultaneous tracking of two hands and two hands are coupled, while the IAT system only tracks one hand with a simpler structure, this may explain the higher error rate of OHT over IAT.

Secondly, since the hand sizes of the subjects are different, the size and position of the keyboard should be automatically adjusted for each subject to achieve an optimized performance. Although reducing the keyboard size is beneficial to privacy protection, typing on a small palm is more challenging than typing in a large space. For one subject (S3), we observed that the system often mistakenly detected the fingertip of the left index finger of pressing character p. This is due to the hand size of this subject being too small, so the character p is placed on the fingertip of the left index finger.

6   Conclusion

In this paper, we explored the possibility of an on-hand typing technique in a head-mounted mixed reality system and compared the system performance over the existing in-air typing technique. By overlapping the virtual keyboard onto the user's real hand, the OHT system enables the user to type in mixed reality with tangible feedback. Experimental results show that the physical feedback provided by the OHT system is favored by most of the users. Compared with the IAT system, the physical effort of OHT is significantly lower. This research demonstrates the potential of integrating virtual and physical environments for future text input systems.

In the future, we plan to extend the system in several directions: 1) incorporating the language model into the system to improve the typing speed, 2) combining eye gaze with hand gestures to improve the robustness of the system, and 3) conducting a quantitative evaluation of privacy protection in a crowded environment.

References

1. Adhikary, J., Vertanen, K.: Text entry in virtual environments using speech and a midair keyboard. IEEE Trans. Visual Comput. Graph. **27**(5), 2648–2658 (2021). https://doi.org/10.1109/TVCG.2021.3067776
2. Ahn, S., Lee, G.: Gaze-assisted typing for smart glasses. In: Proceedings of the 32nd Annual ACM Symposium on User Interface Software and Technology, UIST 2019, pp. 857–869. Association for Computing Machinery, New York (2019). https://doi.org/10.1145/3332165.3347883

3. Arif, A.S., Stuerzlinger, W.: Analysis of text entry performance metrics. In: 2009 IEEE Toronto International Conference Science and Technology for Humanity (TIC-STH), pp. 100–105. IEEE (2009)
4. Benko, H., Holz, C., Sinclair, M., Ofek, E.: Normaltouch and texturetouch: high-fidelity 3D haptic shape rendering on handheld virtual reality controllers. In: Proceedings of the 29th Annual Symposium on User Interface Software and Technology, UIST 2016, pp. 717–728. Association for Computing Machinery, New York (2016). https://doi.org/10.1145/2984511.2984526
5. Carter, T., Seah, S.A., Long, B., Drinkwater, B., Subramanian, S.: Ultrahaptics: multi-point mid-air haptic feedback for touch surfaces. In: Proceedings of the 26th Annual ACM Symposium on User Interface Software and Technology, UIST 2013, pp. 505–514. Association for Computing Machinery, New York (2013). https://doi.org/10.1145/2501988.2502018
6. Chen, D.K., Chossat, J.-B., Shull, P.B.: HaptiVec: Presenting Haptic Feedback Vectors in Handheld Controllers Using Embedded Tactile Pin Arrays, pp. 1–11. Association for Computing Machinery, New York (2019)
7. Choi, I., Culbertson, H., Miller, M.R., Olwal, A., Follmer, S.: Grabity: a wearable haptic interface for simulating weight and grasping in virtual reality. In: Proceedings of the 30th Annual ACM Symposium on User Interface Software and Technology, UIST 2017, pp. 119–130. Association for Computing Machinery, New York (2017). https://doi.org/10.1145/3126594.3126599
8. Choi, I., Ofek, E., Benko, H., Sinclair, M., Holz, C.: Claw: a multifunctional handheld haptic controller for grasping, touching, and triggering in virtual reality. In: Proceedings of the 2018 CHI Conference on Human Factors in Computing Systems, CHI 2018, pp. 1–13. Association for Computing Machinery, New York (2018). https://doi.org/10.1145/3173574.3174228
9. Dezfuli, N., Khalilbeigi, M., Huber, J., Müller, F., Mühlhäuser, M.: PalmRC: imaginary palm-based remote control for eyes-free television interaction. In: Proceedings of the 10th European Conference on Interactive TV and Video, EuroITV 2012, pp. 27–34. Association for Computing Machinery, New York (2012). https://doi.org/10.1145/2325616.2325623
10. Dube, T.J., Arif, A.S.: Text entry in virtual reality: a comprehensive review of the literature. In: Kurosu, M. (ed.) Human-Computer Interaction. Recognition and Interaction Technologies, pp. 419–437. Springer, Cham (2019)
11. Dudley, J.J., Vertanen, K., Kristensson, P.O.: Fast and precise touch-based text entry for head-mounted augmented reality with variable occlusion. ACM Trans. Comput.-Hum. Interact. 25(6) (2018). https://doi.org/10.1145/3232163
12. Goel, M., Findlater, L., Wobbrock, J.: Walktype: using accelerometer data to accomodate situational impairments in mobile touch screen text entry. In: Proceedings of the SIGCHI Conference on Human Factors in Computing Systems, pp. 2687–2696 (2012)
13. Gupta, A., Irudayaraj, A.A.R., Balakrishnan, R.: HapticClench: investigating squeeze sensations using memory alloys. In: Proceedings of the 30th Annual ACM Symposium on User Interface Software and Technology, UIST 2017, pp. 109–117. Association for Computing Machinery, New York (2017). https://doi.org/10.1145/3126594.3126598
14. Gupta, A., Ji, C., Yeo, H.-S., Quigley, A., Vogel, D.: RotoSwype: Word-Gesture Typing Using a Ring, pp. 1–12. Association for Computing Machinery, New York (2019)

15. Gupta, S., Morris, D., Patel, S.N., Tan, D.: Airwave: non-contact haptic feedback using air vortex rings. In: Proceedings of the 2013 ACM International Joint Conference on Pervasive and Ubiquitous Computing, UbiComp 2013, pp. 419–428. Association for Computing Machinery, New York (2013). https://doi.org/10.1145/2493432.2493463

16. Harrison, C., Benko, H., Wilson, A.D.: Omnitouch: wearable multitouch interaction everywhere. In: Proceedings of the 24th Annual ACM Symposium on User Interface Software and Technology, UIST 2011, pp. 441–450. Association for Computing Machinery, New York (2011). https://doi.org/10.1145/2047196.2047255

17. Harrison, C., Tan, D., Morris, D.: Skinput: appropriating the body as an input surface. In: Proceedings of the SIGCHI Conference on Human Factors in Computing Systems, CHI 2010, pp. 453–462. Association for Computing Machinery, New York (2010). https://doi.org/10.1145/1753326.1753394

18. Hart, S.G., Staveland, L.E.: Development of NASA-TLX (task load index): results of empirical and theoretical research. Adv. Psychol. **52**, 139–183 (1988)

19. Heo, S., Chung, C., Lee, G., Wigdor, D.: Thor's hammer: an ungrounded force feedback device utilizing propeller-induced propulsive force. In: Extended Abstracts of the 2018 CHI Conference on Human Factors in Computing Systems, CHI EA 2018, pp. 1–4. Association for Computing Machinery, New York (2018). https://doi.org/10.1145/3170427.3186544

20. Jeong, H., Singh, A., Kim, M., Johnson, A.: Using augmented reality to assist seated office workers' data entry tasks. In: 2020 IEEE Conference on Virtual Reality and 3D User Interfaces Abstracts and Workshops (VRW), pp. 293–294. IEEE (2020)

21. Kaas, J.H.: Somatosensory system. Hum. Nervous Syst. 1059–1092 (2004)

22. Laugwitz, B., Held, T., Schrepp, M.: Construction and evaluation of a user experience questionnaire. In: Symposium of the Austrian HCI and Usability Engineering Group, pp. 63–76. Springer, Cham (2008)

23. Lee, L.H., Lam, K.Y., Yau, Y.P., Braud, T., Hui, P.: Hibey: hide the keyboard in augmented reality. In: 2019 IEEE International Conference on Pervasive Computing and Communications (PerCom), pp. 1–10. IEEE (2019)

24. Lyons, K., et al.: Twiddler typing: one-handed chording text entry for mobile phones. In: Proceedings of the SIGCHI Conference on Human Factors in Computing Systems, pp. 671–678 (2004)

25. MacKenzie, I.S., Soukoreff, R.W.: Phrase sets for evaluating text entry techniques. In: CHI 2003 Extended Abstracts on Human Factors in Computing Systems, pp. 754–755 (2003)

26. Majaranta, P., Ahola, U.-K., Špakov, O.: Fast gaze typing with an adjustable dwell time. In: Proceedings of the SIGCHI Conference on Human Factors in Computing Systems, pp. 357–360 (2009)

27. Majaranta, P., MacKenzie, I.S., Aula, A., Räihä, K.-J.: Effects of feedback and dwell time on eye typing speed and accuracy. Univ. Access Inf. Soc. **5**(2), 199–208 (2006)

28. Pezent, E., et al.: Tasbi: multisensory squeeze and vibrotactile wrist haptics for augmented and virtual reality. In: 2019 IEEE World Haptics Conference (WHC), pp. 1–6 (2019). https://doi.org/10.1109/WHC.2019.8816098

29. Pham, D.-M., Stuerzlinger, W.: Hawkey: efficient and versatile text entry for virtual reality. In: 25th ACM Symposium on Virtual Reality Software and Technology, VRST 2019. Association for Computing Machinery, New York (2019). https://doi.org/10.1145/3359996.3364265

30. Poupyrev, I., Tan, D., Billinghurst, M., Kato, H., Regenbrecht, H., Tetsutani, N.: Developing a generic augmented-reality interface. Computer **35**(3), 44–50 (2002). https://doi.org/10.1109/2.989929

31. Rakkolainen, I., Sand, A., Raisamo, R.: A survey of mid-air ultrasonic tactile feedback. In: 2019 IEEE International Symposium on Multimedia (ISM), pp. 94–944 (2019). https://doi.org/10.1109/ISM46123.2019.00022

32. Sarcar, S., Panwar, P., Chakraborty, T.: Eyek: an efficient dwell-free eye gaze-based text entry system. In: Proceedings of the 11th Asia Pacific Conference on Computer Human Interaction, APCHI 2013, pp. 215–220. Association for Computing Machinery, New York (2013). https://doi.org/10.1145/2525194.2525288

33. Soukoreff, R.W., MacKenzie, I.S.: Metrics for text entry research: an evaluation of MSD and KSPC, and a new unified error metric. In: Proceedings of the SIGCHI Conference on Human Factors in Computing Systems, pp. 113–120 (2003)

34. Strasnick, E., Holz, C., Ofek, E., Sinclair, M., Benko, H.: Haptic links: bimanual haptics for virtual reality using variable stiffness actuation. In: Proceedings of the 2018 CHI Conference on Human Factors in Computing Systems, CHI 2018, pp. 1–12. Association for Computing Machinery, New York (2018). https://doi.org/10.1145/3173574.3174218

35. Wang, C.-Y., Chu, W.-C., Chiu, P.-T., Hsiu, M.-C., Chiang, Y.-H., Chen, M.Y.: Palmtype: using palms as keyboards for smart glasses. In: Proceedings of the 17th International Conference on Human-Computer Interaction with Mobile Devices and Services, MobileHCI 2015, pp. 153–160. Association for Computing Machinery, New York (2015). https://doi.org/10.1145/2785830.2785886

36. Wang, Z., Wang, H., Yu, H., Lu, F.: Interaction with gaze, gesture, and speech in a flexibly configurable augmented reality system. IEEE Trans. Hum.-Mach. Syst. **51**(5), 524–534 (2021)

37. Weichert, F., Bachmann, D., Rudak, B., Fisseler, D.: Analysis of the accuracy and robustness of the leap motion controller. Sensors **13**(5), 6380–6393 (2013)

38. Xu, W., Liang, H.-N., He, A., Wang, Z.: Pointing and selection methods for text entry in augmented reality head mounted displays. In: 2019 IEEE International Symposium on Mixed and Augmented Reality (ISMAR), pp. 279–288 (2019). https://doi.org/10.1109/ISMAR.2019.00026

39. Xu, Z., et al.: Tiptext: eyes-free text entry on a fingertip keyboard. In: Proceedings of the 32nd Annual ACM Symposium on User Interface Software and Technology, UIST 2019, pp. 883–899. Association for Computing Machinery, New York (2019). https://doi.org/10.1145/3332165.3347865

40. Yamada, H.: A historical study of typewriters and typing methods, from the position of planning Japanese parallels. J. Inf. Process. (1980)

41. Yi, X., Yu, C., Zhang, M., Gao, S., Sun, K., Shi, Y.: ATK: enabling ten-finger freehand typing in air based on 3D hand tracking data. In: UIST 2015, pp. 539–548. Association for Computing Machinery, New York (2015). https://doi.org/10.1145/2807442.2807504

42. Zhu, M., et al.: Pneusleeve: in-fabric multimodal actuation and sensing in a soft, compact, and expressive haptic sleeve. In: Proceedings of the 2020 CHI Conference on Human Factors in Computing Systems, CHI 2020, pp. 1–12. Association for Computing Machinery, New York (2020). https://doi.org/10.1145/3313831.3376333

N-Gram Swin Transformer for CT Image Super-Resolution

Zhenghao Gao[1], Danni Ai[1(✉)], Wentao Li[2], Hong Song[2], and Jian Yang[1]

[1] School of Optics and Photonics, Beijing Institute of Technology, Beijing 100081, China
danni@bit.edu.cn
[2] School of Computer Science and Technology, Beijing Institute of Technology, Beijing 100081, China

Abstract. The insufficient resolution of medical images, especially the low spatial resolution in the depth direction, may lead to the loss of critical information, thereby affecting the accuracy of medical diagnosis. Super-resolution (SR) technology plays a crucial role in medical imaging by enhancing image resolution to provide more detailed structural information. However, traditional single-image super-resolution (SISR) methods struggle to fully exploit 3D spatial information, resulting in insufficient spatial consistency between slices, which leads to artifacts and discontinuous textures, limiting their applicability in 3D medical image reconstruction. To address these challenges, this paper proposes the N-gram Swin Transformer Network (NGSWN) for super-resolution of CT images, specifically aiming to address the issue of insufficient resolution in the depth direction. The proposed model adopts an asymmetric encoder-decoder structure and integrates an N-gram-based mechanism to enhance feature extraction and reconstruction capabilities. By leveraging spatial relationships between slices, the NGSWN generates high-resolution CT images with better continuity and fewer artifacts. Experimental results demonstrate that the NGSWN outperforms both traditional and state-of-the-art methods in terms of PSNR and SSIM metrics, highlighting its significant potential for enhancing medical imaging quality and improving diagnostic accuracy.

Keywords: Super-Resolution · N-gram · Swin Transformer

1 Introduction

Image super-resolution (SR) reconstruction aims to reconstruct high-resolution (HR) images from low-resolution (LR) images. In recent years, numerous deep learning-based methods have made significant progress in this field. Since the introduction of SRCNN [5], deep neural network-based methods have driven the development of SR. Super-resolution has also been increasingly applied in medical imaging. Studies have shown that SR is particularly important in medical imaging, such as low-dose computed

This work was supported by the National Science Foundation Program of China [grant numbers 62331005, U22A2052].

© The Author(s), under exclusive license to Springer Nature Singapore Pte Ltd. 2025
W. Song et al. (Eds.): ICXR 2024, LNCS 15461, pp. 136–148, 2025.
https://doi.org/10.1007/978-981-96-3679-2_9

tomography (CT), which aims to acquire high-quality images under limited radiation exposure. For medical images, higher resolution is crucial for obtaining key diagnostic details. However, the practical acquisition of CT images involves challenges such as prolonged acquisition times, high storage costs, and excessive radiation exposure. For example, CT images are usually obtained via helical scanning, which offers high resolution in the axial plane but limited resolution between slices due to slice thickness. This discrepancy may lead to insufficient resolution in the depth direction during image reconstruction, resulting in anisotropy [13]. It is relatively easy to improve in-plane resolution by using high-resolution detectors or increasing image sampling density (i.e., reducing pixel size) without significantly increasing scan time or radiation dose [14]. However, improving resolution between slices requires reducing slice thickness to collect more slice data, which results in longer scan times and higher radiation doses [15]. Therefore, SR reconstruction techniques can be used to improve image quality for medical images with insufficient resolution.

Furthermore, medical images such as CT consist of continuous slices. If only single-image super-resolution (SISR) models are used, the lack of utilization of 3D spatial information results in insufficient spatial continuity, and coherent texture information between slices is not fully exploited. These issues can lead to artifacts or the loss of important features in the depth dimension of SR images, affecting the accuracy of 3D images in sagittal and coronal planes. The loss of lesion details may hinder physicians from accurately identifying and evaluating structural abnormalities such as tumors or inflammation. Additionally, the robustness of images and the accuracy of subsequent processing algorithms may also be reduced.

To address the aforementioned challenges, researchers have begun exploring models that can effectively utilize 3D spatial information and inter-slice correlations. Among them, deep learning-based models have become a research hotspot due to their powerful feature extraction and representation capabilities. Traditional convolutional neural networks (CNNs) have achieved significant success in medical image processing, but the limited receptive fields of CNNs make it challenging to capture long-range dependencies and global information. To better handle complex structures and texture details in medical images, researchers have introduced Transformer models. Compared to traditional CNN models, various methods utilizing the self-attention mechanism of the Swin Transformer (Window Self-Attention, WSA) [6–10] have made new advances, combining the long-range dependencies of Vision Transformer with the local features of convolution. Despite these advancements, a key issue persists: the receptive field of local window self-attention is limited to a small local area [11, 12], hindering the model's ability to leverage adjacent window textures to restore degraded pixels, resulting in unrealistic images.

To obtain clearer reconstructed images, we propose the N-gram Swin Transformer Network (NGSWN), which combines the Swin Transformer with an N-gram-based network structure to enhance feature extraction and reconstruction capabilities. Firstly, our network incorporates the N-gram approach into both the encoder and decoder sections of the Swin Transformer, extending the receptive field of WSA, enhancing contextual understanding and modeling of local windows, and thus addressing the issue of incomplete recovery of degraded pixels [16]. Subsequently, in the Mask Interpolation section, masks are inserted to determine the locations of new SR blocks in the reconstructed SR images. In the decoder section, spatial positions in the sagittal and coronal planes are combined for 3D reassembly, increasing consistency between continuous slices. Finally, the Reconstruction module convolves the output features of the decoder to reconstruct the SR image. These approaches allow the network to more effectively capture texture information between slices, reduce artifacts, and significantly improve the restoration of important features in the depth dimension.

In summary, our contributions are as follows:

1) We propose a 3D anisotropic CT image model called the N-gram Swin Trans-former Network, specifically aimed at addressing the issue of insufficient slices in the depth direction. The model includes an asymmetric encoder-decoder structure with enhanced detail reconstruction capabilities, incorporating further N-gram contextual feature integration within each Swin Transformer block. This model addresses the shortcomings of traditional CT image processing methods in handling depth information, thereby improving image quality and accuracy.

2) We adopt an asymmetric encoder-decoder structure combined with the Swin Trans-former network and a cross-slice attention module to focus on the positional relationships between different blocks in the 3D image. This enables the learning of texture details from different dimensions, resulting in fused CT images with greater continuity in depth space.

3) We introduce the N-gram contextual mechanism in both the encoder and decoder to allow the integration of contextual information before processing by the Swin Transformer, thereby expanding the receptive field and contributing to the reconstruction of degraded image details.

2   Related Work

Traditional image super-resolution methods include interpolation methods, reconstruction-based methods, and example-based methods. Interpolation methods, such as bilinear and bicubic interpolation, are computationally efficient but often fail to generate sharp high-resolution images when dealing with complex textures and details [2]. Due to their linear characteristics, these methods exhibit significant limitations in handling edges and high-frequency details, resulting in images that lack realism and structural fidelity. Reconstruction-based methods leverage prior information about the image to constrain the generation of high-resolution images, often using regularization techniques [3]. These methods build mathematical models to fully exploit the statistical properties of the images and the priors of the imaging system in order to restore high-frequency details and structural information. However, these methods face computational complexity issues, especially when dealing with large-scale data. Example-based methods perform super-resolution by finding and matching low-resolution and high-resolution image patches, such as the sparse coding method proposed by Yang et al. [4]. However, the performance of these methods heavily depends on the quality and diversity of the sample library. When processing images that differ significantly from those in the sample library, their effectiveness is limited. Consequently, despite some initial success, these traditional approaches still face significant challenges in handling diverse and complex real-world scenarios.

With the rise of deep learning, convolutional neural networks (CNNs) have been introduced into the field of image super-resolution. The SRCNN model proposed by Dong et al. [5] was the first to apply deep CNN to super-resolution tasks, achieving a significant breakthrough. Subsequently, models such as VDSR [19], EDSR [20], and RCAN [21] improved image reconstruction quality through deeper network structures, residual learning, and attention mechanisms. These models made significant progress in high-frequency information recovery, edge sharpening, and detail enhancement. However, CNN-based methods are inherently limited in capturing long-range dependencies and processing global information due to their local receptive fields, which may hinder the full reconstruction of an image's holistic structure.

The success of Transformer models in natural language processing has led to their application in computer vision. The IPT model proposed by Chen et al. [22] was the first to apply Transformers to image restoration tasks, demonstrating their ability to capture long-range dependencies. Swin Transformer [23] made significant progress by introducing the local window self-attention mechanism (WSA), and SwinIR [6] applied it to super-resolution tasks, showing superior performance. However, the limited receptive field of the local window mechanism remains a challenge [24]. To address this, Zhou et al. proposed a permuted self-attention mechanism, expanding the attention window by introducing permutation operations along the channel dimension [12]. Yang et al. proposed the DAT method, which introduced the Dual Aggregation Transformer Block (DATB) to achieve more efficient feature aggregation by fusing multi-scale information [25].

In the field of medical imaging, super-resolution technology has been widely used to enhance the resolution of CT and MRI images. Due to the anisotropic nature of medical images, traditional single-image super-resolution methods are insufficient for processing 3D medical images. Shan et al. proposed a model based on three-dimensional convolutional neural networks (3D CNN) to improve MRI image resolution [26]. By employing 3D convolutional kernels, 3D CNNs can better capture local and global information in 3D space, improving spatial consistency and detail preservation. However, challenges remain in capturing global information and detailed features in 3D space. In particular, balancing resolution and noise remains a challenge when dealing with low-dose or low-field-strength images. Additionally, the integration of biosignals and artificial intelligence (AI) in healthcare has been increasingly explored to achieve more comprehensive health monitoring and diagnostics. For example, a systematic review on the use of commercial wearable activity trackers for monitoring recovery in individuals undergoing total hip replacement surgery highlights the role of biosignals in post-surgery recovery monitoring [27]. Similarly, AI's capability to analyze and understand the body's signals has been emphasized as a growing trend [28]. These studies that combine biosignals and AI provide valuable insights for advancing super-resolution reconstruction, particularly in fusing multidimensional information and improving precise diagnosis in medical imaging.

3 Methodology

3.1 Network Overall Architecture

The process of converting a 3DCT image from low resolution to high resolution aims to reconstruct the slices between the low-resolution CT layers so that the restored SRCT slices are as close as possible to the Ground Truth slices. We designed an asymmetric encoder-decoder structure consisting of four parts: Encoder, Mask Interpolation, Decoder, and Reconstruction. First, the encoder, equipped with N-gram Swin Transformer blocks, is responsible for capturing multi-scale texture, edge, and structural features from the input low-resolution image. Next, Mask Interpolation is used after the encoder to interpolate between low-resolution image layers, focusing on the target reconstruction region, enhancing reconstruction accuracy, and improving model stability. Then, to enable the decoder to learn more inter-slice reconstruction details, an asymmetric structure is used, making the decoder more complex than the encoder. The decoder includes a Cross-Slice Attention Block (CSAB) that focuses on the spatial relationships within the CT, generating more coherent high-resolution slices. Finally, the Reconstruction module maps the features output by the decoder back to image space, producing a high-quality super-resolved image. The overall framework is illustrated in Fig. 1.

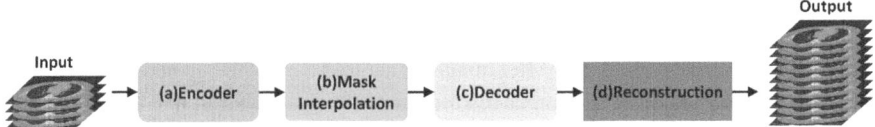

Fig. 1. N-gram Swin Transformer Network Overall Architecture

Encoder. The low-resolution image is mapped to a latent feature map. The input LRCT $I_{enc}^{LR} \in \mathbb{R}^{D \times H \times W}$ where D, H and W denote the number of slices, the height, and the width of a single slice, respectively. First, I_{enc}^{LR} passes through a Linear Embedding layer to obtain shallow features, resulting in the output $F_{enc}^s \in \mathbb{R}^{C \times D \times H \times W}$, where C is the number of feature channels. Then, a Reshape operation is performed to adapt the input for the Swin Transformer, resulting in $F_{enc}^0 \in \mathbb{R}^{CD \times H \times W}$. Subsequently, the data passes through four N-gram Swin Transformer Blocks sequentially, with a patch merging operation between every two blocks to progressively reduce the feature map size and expand the receptive field, extracting deeper and more abstract information. The resolution $H \times W$ is halved at each step, while the depth increases twofold. Each of the four N-gram Swin Transformer Blocks contains {4,4, 6,4} basic layers of N-gram Swin Transformers by default, and the input and output of each N-gram Swin Transformer Block are connected via residual connections, as shown in Fig. 2. In the encoder, the mapping function of the $k - th$ ($1 \leq k \leq 4$) N-gram Swin Transformer Block is denoted as $\mathcal{G}_k$:

$$F_{enc}^k = Trans_k\left(\mathcal{G}_k\left(F_{enc}^{k-1}\right) + F_{enc}^{k-1}\right)$$

where $Trans_k$ denotes patch merging ($k = 1, 2, 3$) and merging reverse ($k = 4$). After patch merging, $F_{enc}^k \in \mathbb{R}^{(2)^k CD \times H/(2)^k \times W/(2)^k}$, After merging reverse, the output is $F_{enc}^4 \in \mathbb{R}^{CD \times H \times W}$. Finally, a Reshape operation is performed to restore the dimensions to the input size, and the encoder output is $F_{enc}^{out} \in \mathbb{R}^{D \times H \times W}$.

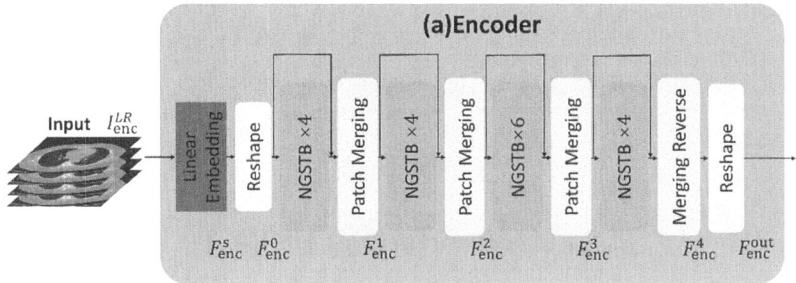

Fig. 2. Encoder structure diagram.

Mask Interpolation. The SRCT reconstruction region is preset. The encoder output feature map F_{enc}^{out} is input to the Mask Interpolation module, where mask slices are inserted into the feature map slices. The values of these mask slices are initialized to 0, as shown in Fig. 3. These mask slices represent the parts of the SR image that the decoder needs to learn to reconstruct. The mask, together with the encoder output features F_{enc}^{out} is rearranged into the module output feature map $F_{mask} \in \mathbb{R}^{C \times D_{GT} \times H \times W}$, which serves as the input to the decoder. Here, D_{GT} is equal to the number of slices in the HRCT. The insertion of mask slices helps guide the model's learning objective, enabling more accurate reconstruction of specific regions when generating high-resolution images. This helps to reduce artifacts and blurring, improving the realism of the generated images.

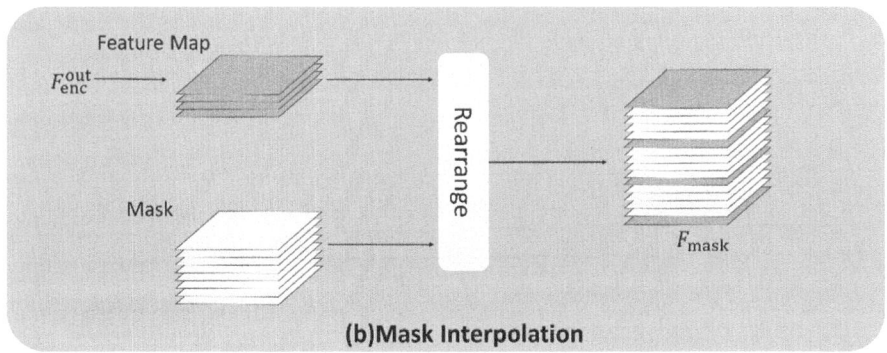

Fig. 3. Mask Interpolation structure diagram.

Decoder. F_{mask} Is fed into the decoder, which primarily includes two stages: the Cross-slice Attention Block (CSAB) and the N-gram Swin Transformer, as shown in Fig. 4. The Cross-slice Attention Block receives the output of Mask Interpolation F_{mask}, and transforms it into sagittal and coronal views, $F_{dec}^{sag(0)} \in \mathbb{R}^{\frac{W}{4} \times 4C \times D \times H}$ and $F_{dec}^{cor(0)} \in \mathbb{R}^{\frac{H}{4} \times 4C \times D \times W}$, respectively. Then, it passes through the N-gram Swin Transformer Block and undergoes a Reshape operation. The output of the CSAB module is $F_{dec}^{out} \in \mathbb{R}^{C \times D_{GT} \times H \times W}$. Finally, residual connections are introduced between the input and output of the decoder within the network. The overall workflow of the decoder is as follows:

$$F_{dec}^{sag(in)} = \mathcal{R}_{sag}(F_{mask}), F_{dec}^{cor(in)} = \mathcal{R}_{cor}(F_{mask})$$

$$F_{dec}^0 = Re\left(F_{dec}^{CSAB}\right)$$

$$F_{dec}^{sag(k)} = Trans_k\left(\mathcal{G}_k\left(F_{dec}^{k-1}\right) + F_{dec}^{k-1}\right)$$

$$F_{dec}^{out} = Re\left(F_{dec}^4\right) + F_{mask}$$

where $\mathcal{R}_{sag}$ and $\mathcal{R}_{cor}$ are dimension transformation operations on the input feature map, used to convert the horizontal plane view into sagittal and coronal views. Re represents the Reshape operation for dimensional transformation. $\mathcal{G}_k$ is the mapping function of the N-gram Swin Transformer Block. $Trans_k$ denotes patch merging (k = 1, 2, 3) or merging reverse (k = 4), which is the same as in the encoder.

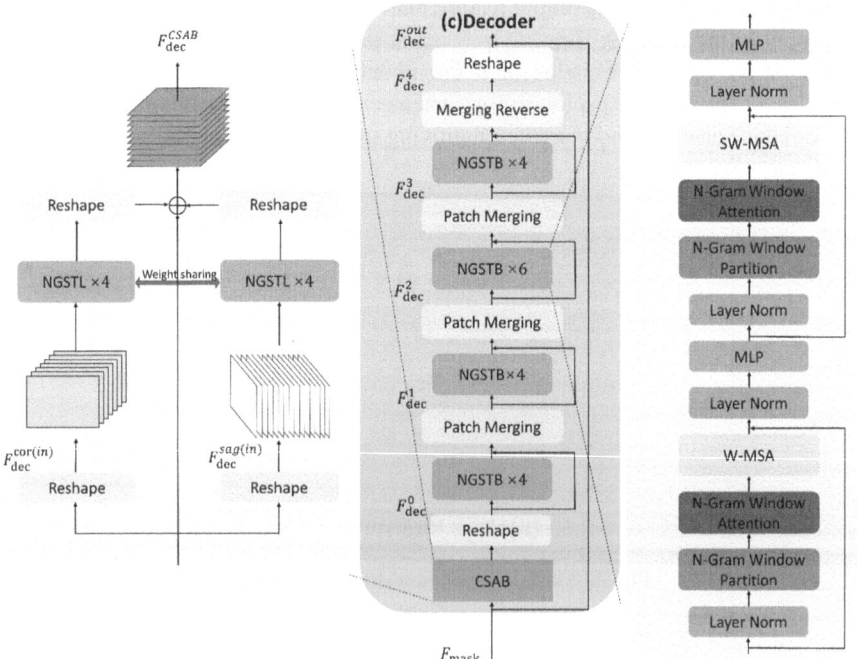

Fig. 4. Decoder structure diagram.

Reconstruction. The output features of the decoder are mapped to the final high-resolution image. The feature map processed by the decoder is passed through a sequence of convolutional layers. This sequence includes a 3D convolutional layer followed by a Leaky ReLU activation function, and then another 3D convolutional layer. Finally, edge slices are cropped along the depth direction to remove image edge artifacts, resulting in the final SR image output $I_{rec}^{SR} \in \mathbb{R}^{D_{GT} \times H \times W}$.

3.2 Cross-Slice Attention Block

The Cross-slice Attention Block (CSAB) is a module within the decoder and differs from the encoder. The encoder's output enters the CSAB, where it is transformed into sagittal and coronal view features. Unlike attention operations on a single image from a single viewpoint, the CSAB performs self-attention on both views, treating the depth dimension as the width of the attention window and sharing parameters between the two branches. This approach incorporates the spatial relationships between slices into the network, resulting in more continuous and realistic slices during training, thereby preventing the layering effect between sagittal and coronal slices.

3.3 N-gram Swin Transformer Block

The N-gram Swin Transformer Block (NGSTB) has the same primary structure as the Swin Transformer Block (STB) [10], but it incorporates N-gram contextual associations before the (S)W-MSA to enhance the receptive field, strengthen connections between windows, and address the limitations of the Swin Transformer.

This paper applies Bi-gram (N = 2) to CT image data. The Bi-gram large window consists of four Uni-gram small windows, including one target Uni-gram window and three neighboring Uni-gram windows. Each Uni-gram small window contains 2×2 pixels, as shown in Fig. 5. The green window represents the target Uni-gram window, while the red area represents the neighboring Uni-gram windows. The two Figures illustrate the window division methods and window position relationships during the Forward N-gram sliding-WSA and backward N-gram sliding-WSA operations.

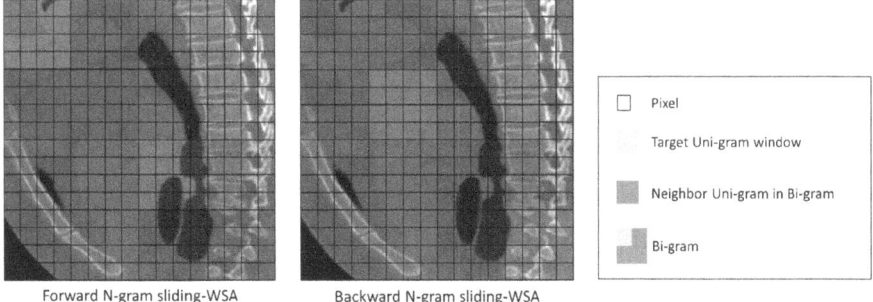

Forward N-gram sliding-WSA   Backward N-gram sliding-WSA

Fig. 5. Forward N-gram sliding-WSA and Backward N-gram sliding-WSA.

The Bi-Gram model captures dependencies and contextual information between pixels in the image through forward and backward window associations. This approach effectively enhances the performance of image processing tasks. The N-gram Swin Transformer Block involves two main steps: N-gram Window Partition and N-gram Window Attention.

In the N-gram Window Partition, the input $F_{in} \in \mathbb{R}^{D \times H \times W}$ passes through an $M \times M$ convolution to map the input feature map to the N-gram space, which corresponds to the partitioning of Uni-gram windows, resulting in the Uni-gram Embedding $F_{uni} \in \mathbb{R}^{\frac{D}{2} \times wH \times wW}$. Here, wH and wW represent the number of Uni-gram windows that can be divided along the H and W directions of the input feature map, respectively. This step reduces the channels and resolution of the feature map, decreases computational parameters, and prepares for the subsequent association of N-gram window position features.

In the N-gram Window Attention, the Uni-gram windows in the N-gram window are treated as tokens for sliding-WSA attention feature extraction, resulting in the forward N-gram attention feature F_{for} and the backward N-gram attention feature F_{back}. These two are shared in terms of weights and concatenated to form the N-gram contextual feature $F_{ng} \in \mathbb{R}^{D \times wH \times wW}$. The N-gram contextual feature F_{ng} is then added to the original input F_{in}, so that each window of size $M \times M$ in the original input contains contextual information. This bidirectional N-gram attention learning facilitates better semantic association across contexts. The overall process is shown in Fig. 6.

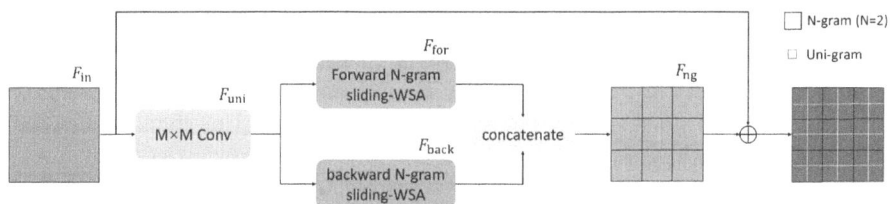

Fig. 6. Basic operational workflow of the N-gram Swin Transformer Block.

4 Experiments

4.1 Experiments Setup

We used 250 LH-HR (low-resolution and high-resolution) image pairs from the RPLHR-CT dataset. The ratio of the training set, validation set, and test set was 3:1:1. During training, a cube of size $4 \times 256 \times 256$ was randomly cropped from the LRCT images as input, where 4 represents the length in the depth direction. The corresponding cube of size $16 \times 256 \times 256$ from the HRCT images was used as the Ground Truth. For a scaling factor of 5, excluding the bottommost slice of LRCT, each remaining slice in LRCT corresponds to 4 newly generated slices. In the N-gram Window Partition, the convolution kernel size $M \times M$ is set to 7×7 by default. During inference, LRCT is divided into four parts—top-left, top-right, bottom-left, and bottom-right—in the horizontal plane, with a depth length of 4, and each part is of size $4 \times 256 \times 256$, which is fed into the model as input. The strategy for generating HR from LR involves moving the input cube only in the depth direction with a stride of 2. The overlapping 2 slices before and after the movement are our focus region, and the network generates 10 CT slices. We used the Adam optimizer to train and optimize the L1 loss function, with a learning rate of 0.0001 and a batch size of 1. All frameworks were implemented in Pytorch and the experiments were conducted on NVIDIA GeForce RTX 4090 GPUs.

4.2 Comparison with State-of-the-Art Methods

Table 1 summarizes the quantitative comparison between traditional and advanced 3DCT SR methods: Bicubic, Saint [17], and TVSRN [18]. Compared with these methods, our proposed method achieved superior PSNR and SSIM metrics on the same public dataset.

Table 1. PSNR and SSIM of different methods.

Method	PSNR	SSIM
Bicubic	28.3918	0.8358
Saint	37.5881	0.9263
TVSRN	38.8301	0.9378
NGSWN	39.4997	0.9421

We displayed the SRCT results obtained by different methods in three directions: axial, sagittal, and coronal views. As shown in Fig. 7, it can be clearly observed that our results restore richer details and fewer structural artifacts, making them closer to the HR images across different views.

4.3 Ablation Studies

The ablation experiments verified the impact of two components on the super-resolution results. First, the effect of adding N-gram Window Attention and N-gram Window Partition to NGSWN on model performance. Second, the effect of the number of NGSWB blocks and the corresponding number of self-attention heads on model performance after adding the N-gram mechanism (Table 2).

From the data in the table, it can be seen that replacing the standard Swin Transformer Block with NGSWB improves model performance. Additionally, incorporating Patch Merging and adjusting parameter settings (as per [8]) can further enhance the super-resolution effect. This indicates that the N-gram mechanism effectively extracts neighborhood information, and its combination with the Swin Transformer enables dependency on both long- and short-range sequences, making it effective for super-resolution modeling.

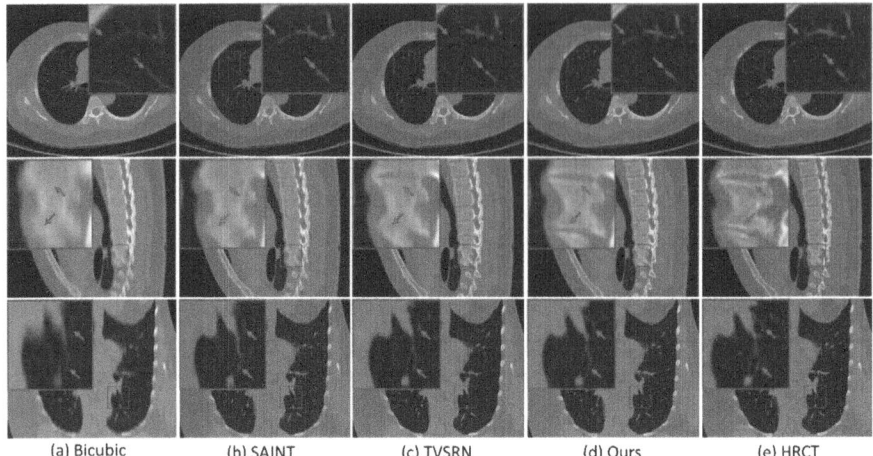

(a) Bicubic   (b) SAINT   (c) TVSRN   (d) Ours   (e) HRCT

Fig. 7. Experimental performance of different methods in axial, sagittal, and coronal views.

Table 2. The quantitative results of the ablation experiments are presented. Block nums represents the number of NGSWB blocks, Head nums represents the number of self-attention heads, (w/o) indicates without N-gram, and (w) indicates with N-gram.

Method	Block nums	Head nums	PSNR	SSIM
NGSwinir(w/o)	(4, 4, 4, 4)	(8, 8, 8, 8)	38.8341	0.9378
NGSwinir(w)	(4, 4, 4, 4)	(8, 8, 8, 8)	39.0023	0.9389
NGSWN(w)	(2, 2, 6, 2)	(4, 4, 4, 4)	38.9855	0.9385
NGSWN(w)	(2, 2, 6, 2)	(8, 8, 16, 32)	39.2137	0.9402
NGSWN(w)	(4, 4, 6, 4)	(8, 8, 16, 32)	39.4997	0.9421

5   Conclusion

We proposed applying the N-gram technique, which is commonly used in text data processing, to the synthesis of 3D medical image slices. This approach takes into account the informational relationships between different positions within 3D images. By incorporating the Swin Transformer to enhance long-range dependencies, and using N-gram to supplement short-range neighborhood information, we effectively improved performance. We evaluated our method on a publicly available real CT dataset, and found that NGSWN outperformed other methods in terms of both visual quality and quantitative results.

References

1. Diao, S., Bai, J., Song, Y., et al.: ZEN: pre-training Chinese text encoder enhanced by n-gram representations. arXiv preprint arXiv:1911.00720 (2019)

2. Azam, N., Yazid, H., Rahim, S.A.: Super resolution with interpolation-based method: A review. IJRAR-Int. J. Res. Anal. Rev. (IJRAR) **9**(2), 168–174 (2022)
3. Yang, J., Wright, J., Huang, T.S., et al.: Image super-resolution via sparse representation. IEEE Trans. Image Process. **19**(11), 2861–2873 (2010)
4. Tang, Y., Yuan, Y., Yan, P., et al.: Single-image super-resolution via sparse coding regression. In: 2011 Sixth International Conference on Image and Graphics, pp. 267–272 (2011)
5. Dong, C., Loy, C.C., He, K., et al.: Learning a deep convolutional network for image super-resolution. In: Computer Vision–ECCV 2014: 13th European Conference, Zurich, Switzerland, 6–12 September 2014, Part IV 13, pp. 184–199. Springer (2014)
6. Liang, J., Cao, J., Sun, G., et al.: SwinIR: image restoration using swin transformer. In: Proceedings of the IEEE/CVF International Conference on Computer Vision, pp. 1833–1844 (2021)
7. Conde, M.V., Choi, U.J., Burchi, M., et al.: Swin2SR: swinV2 transformer for compressed image super-resolution and restoration. In: European Conference on Computer Vision, pp. 669–687 (2022)
8. Liu, J., Gui, Z., Yuan, C., et al.: Residual dense swin transformer for continuous-scale super-resolution algorithm. Appl. Sci. **14**(9), 3678 (2024)
9. Lu, W., Jiang, J., Tian, H., et al.: Asymmetric convolution swin transformer for medical image super-resolution. Alex. Eng. J. **85**, 177–184 (2023)
10. Li, B., Li, X., Lu, Y., et al.: HST: hierarchical swin transformer for compressed image super-resolution. In: European Conference on Computer Vision, pp. 651–668. Springer, Cham (2022)
11. Zhang, L., Li, Y., Zhou, X., et al.: Transcending the limit of local window: advanced super-resolution transformer with adaptive token dictionary. In: Proceedings of the IEEE/CVF Conference on Computer Vision and Pattern Recognition, pp. 2856–2865 (2024)
12. Chen, Z., Zhang, Y., Gu, J., et al.: Dual aggregation transformer for image super-resolution. In: Proceedings of the IEEE/CVF International Conference on Computer Vision, pp. 12312–12321 (2023)
13. Bae, K.T.: Intravenous contrast medium administration and scan timing at CT: considerations and approaches. Radiology **256**(1), 32–61 (2010)
14. Boas, F.E., Fleischmann, D.: CT artifacts: causes and reduction techniques. Imaging Med. **4**(2), 229–240 (2012)
15. McCollough, C.H., Primak, A.N., Braun, N., et al.: Strategies for reducing radiation dose in CT. Radiol. Clin. **47**(1), 27–40 (2009)
16. Mikolov, T., Sutskever, I., Chen, K., et al.: Distributed representations of words and phrases and their compositionality. In: Advances in Neural Information Processing Systems, vol. 26 (2013)
17. Peng, C., Lin, W.A., Liao, H., et al.: SAINT: spatially aware interpolation network for medical slice synthesis. In: Proceedings of the IEEE/CVF Conference on Computer Vision and Pattern Recognition, pp. 7750–7759 (2020)
18. Yu, P., Zhang, H., Kang, H., et al.: RPLHR-CT dataset and transformer baseline for volumetric super-resolution from CT scans. In: International Conference on Medical Image Computing and Computer-Assisted Intervention. Cham: Springer Nature Switzerland, pp. 344–353 (2022)
19. Kim, J., Lee, J.K., Lee, K.M.: Accurate image super-resolution using very deep convolutional networks. In: Proceedings of the IEEE Conference on Computer Vision and Pattern Recognition, pp. 1646–1654 (2016)
20. Lim, B., Son, S., Kim, H., et al.: Enhanced deep residual networks for single image super-resolution. In: Proceedings of the IEEE Conference on Computer Vision and Pattern Recognition Workshops, pp. 136–144 (2017)

21. Zhang, Y., Li, K., Li, K., et al.: Image super-resolution using very deep residual channel attention networks. In: Proceedings of the European Conference on Computer Vision (ECCV), pp. 286–301 (2018)
22. Chen, H., Wang, Y., Guo, T., et al.: Pre-trained image processing transformer. In: Proceedings of the IEEE/CVF Conference on Computer Vision and Pattern Recognition, pp. 12299–12310 (2021)
23. Liu, Z., Lin, Y., Cao, Y., et al.: Swin transformer: hierarchical vision transformer using shifted windows. In: Proceedings of the IEEE/CVF International Conference on Computer Vision, pp. 10012–10022 (2021)
24. Zhang, L., Li, Y., Zhou, X., et al.: Transcending the limit of local window: advanced super-resolution transformer with adaptive token dictionary. arXiv preprint arXiv:2401.08209 (2024)
25. Zhou, Y., Li, Z., Guo, C.L., et al.: SRFormer: permuted self-attention for single image super-resolution. In: Proceedings of the IEEE/CVF International Conference on Computer Vision, pp. 12780–12791 (2023)
26. Li, J., Zhu, S.: Channel-spatial transformer for efficient image super-resolution. In: ICASSP 2024–2024 IEEE International Conference on Acoustics, Speech and Signal Processing (ICASSP), pp. 2685–2689. IEEE (2024)
27. Babaei, N., Hannani, N., Dabanloo, N.J., et al.: A systematic review of the use of commercial wearable activity trackers for monitoring recovery in individuals undergoing total hip replacement surgery. Cyborg Bionic Syst. (2022)
28. Björn, K.Q.B.H.Y.Y., Schuller, W.: The voice of the body: why ai should listen to it and an archive. Cyborg Bionic Syst. **4**, 0005 (2023)

Cluster-Detection-Based Local Super-Resolution Network for Remote Sensing Image Enhancement

Lu Li[1], Xia Zhu[2], Shaofeng Ni[1(✉)], Fan Gao[3], Dinglun Cao[3], Ziyi Pei[3], and Shuai Li[3]

[1] State Grid Location based Service Co., Ltd, Beijing, China
{lilu,nishaofeng}@sgitg.sgcc.com.cn
[2] State Grid Information & Telecommunication Group Co., Ltd., Beijing, China
[3] State Key Laboratory of Virtual Reality Technology and Systems, Beihang University, Beijing, China
lishuai@buaa.edu.cn

Abstract. Remote sensing images are essential for various applications such as environmental monitoring and urban planning. However, the spatial resolution of these images often hinders the accurate detection of small-scale or densely packed targets. In this work, we advocate a novel method that introduces clustering into local super-resolution networks to enhance image resolution and improve the detectability of small-scale and dense regions. First, K-means clustering is applied to identify dense areas based on both the color and spatial properties of image pixels, efficiently pinpointing regions where small objects are concentrated. Next, a lightweight cross-attention-based super-resolution network is employed to enhance the resolution of these key regions, which improves object detection accuracy. The proposed method is computationally efficient, incorporating depthwise separable convolutions and focusing the cross-attention mechanism on regions of interest, thereby minimizing overhead. Extensive experiments on the WV-3 and DOTA datasets demonstrate that our method significantly improves image quality, outperforming existing methods in terms of both PSNR and SSIM.

Keywords: Remote Sensing · Image Enhancement · Cluster Detection · Super-resolution GANs

1 Introduction

Remote sensing image has become an invaluable resource for a wide range of applications, including environmental monitoring, urban planning, and disaster management. However, the effectiveness of these applications often hinges on the quality and resolution of the available imagery [19]. In many cases, the spatial resolution of remote sensing images is insufficient for detecting and analyzing small-scale objects or densely packed features, which are common in urban landscapes, agricultural fields, and natural environments.

© The Author(s), under exclusive license to Springer Nature Singapore Pte Ltd. 2025
W. Song et al. (Eds.): ICXR 2024, LNCS 15461, pp. 149–161, 2025.
https://doi.org/10.1007/978-981-96-3679-2_10

Traditional super-resolution methods and object detection algorithms often struggle to provide high efficiency and accuracy when applied to remote sensing image, particularly when dealing with small-scale objects and densely packed targets [21]. This limitation significantly impacts the utility of remote sensing data in various critical applications. Our work addresses these challenges by proposing a novel approach: remote sensing image enhancement using cluster-detection-based local super-resolution network. The innovative method integrates clustering algorithms with local super-resolution techniques, specifically tailored for remote sensing image. By combining these approaches, we aim to enhance the resolution and detectability of small-scale and densely packed objects in satellite and aerial imagery.

The use of clustering algorithms in our method helps to effectively distinguish between closely spaced objects in remote sensing scenes, reducing false positives and improving overall detection precision. Concurrently, the local super-resolution network selectively enhances image regions likely to contain small or densely packed objects, providing richer feature information without incurring prohibitive computational costs. This synergistic combination allows for more efficient and accurate super-resolution of remote sensing images, particularly in areas with complex, small-scale features. In summary, our work makes the following contributions:

- **K-means clustering for dense region detection.** We introduce the use of K-means clustering to accurately identify densely packed areas in remote sensing images, improving the detection of small objects in complex scenes.
- **Lightweight cross attention super-resolution network.** A novel, computationally efficient cross-attention-based super-resolution network is developed to enhance the resolution of key regions without significant overhead.
- **Superior image quality enhancement.** Combining the above content and the Generative Adversarial Networks (GAN)-based super-resolution method outperforms existing techniques in PSNR and SSIM metrics, providing higher resolution and better detection accuracy for remote sensing applications, as demonstrated on the WV-3 and DOTA datasets.

In the following, Sect. 2 presents a review of related work in the field of super-resolution for remote sensing imagery. Section 3 details the proposed method, including its architecture and loss function. Section 4 provides a comprehensive demonstration of the results obtained using our proposed method across various datasets, along with relevant analyses. Finally, Sect. 5 summarizes the main findings of the paper. Through this research, we aim to enhance the utility of remote sensing data by improving the resolution and detectability of small-scale and densely packed objects, thereby advancing the capabilities of remote sensing applications across various domains.

2   Related Work

2.1   Clustered-Based Object Detection

Clustering algorithms play a crucial role in dense object detection by optimizing feature aggregation and anchor generation. K-means partitions data into clusters by minimizing the variance within each cluster [14]. It iteratively assigns data points to the nearest centroid and updates centroids based on the mean of the assigned points. This method is efficient for generating anchor boxes, as demonstrated in YOLOv2; however, it assumes clusters are spherical and of similar size [20]. Agglomerative clustering builds a hierarchy by initially treating each data point as an individual cluster and merging them based on similarity [1]. This hierarchical approach captures multi-level relationships but is computationally expensive.

Gaussian Mixture Models (GMM) assume that data is generated from a mixture of Gaussian distributions, employing the Expectation-maximization algorithm to estimate parameters [22]. GMM models clusters probabilistically, effectively capturing complex, overlapping regions, but it is sensitive to initialization and computationally demanding. Spectral clustering utilizes eigenvectors of a similarity matrix to partition data, effectively handling non-convex clusters [25]. By transforming data into a lower-dimensional space, this method simplifies the clustering process. However, it requires careful tuning of the similarity matrix and can be computationally intensive. Each of these methods can enhance object detection results [7, 24].

2.2   Super-Resolution Generative Adversarial Network

The field of deep learning-based super-resolution (SR) has seen significant advancements, primarily driven by the development of various convolutional neural network (CNN) architectures and attention mechanisms [9].

In terms of Deep CNN Structures, Dong et al. introduced the Super-resolution Convolutional Neural Network (SRCNN), which outperformed traditional methods like bicubic interpolation. However, its shallow architecture limited its ability to learn deep features [5]. Following this, Hara and Tanaka proposed the Very Deep Super-resolution (VDSR) network with 20 convolutional layers, leveraging residual learning to speed up training [16]. Shi et al. developed the Efficient Sub-Pixel Convolutional Neural Network (ESPCN), which improved reconstruction speed by upscaling low-resolution (LR) feature maps within the network [23]. Additionally, Dong et al. introduced the Fast Super-resolution Convolutional Neural Network (FSRCNN), which also trained directly on LR images and used deconvolutional layers for up-sampling [6].

Regarding Attention Mechanisms, Hu et al. focused on learning 1D vector feature maps to enhance channel interdependencies [12]. Woo et al. aimed to learn 2D attention feature maps to capture spatial dependencies [29]. Zhao et al. proposed generating 3D attention maps for pixel-level feature enhancement [32]. Furthermore, Zhang et al. introduced the Residual Channel Attention Network (RCAN) to focus on high-frequency information [31].

In the area of Cascading Networks, Ahn et al. designed the Cascading Residual Network (CARN) to implement a cascading mechanism on a residual network for improved SR performance [3]. Similarly, Lan et al. proposed the Cascading Residual Network (CRN) with local wider residual blocks for single-image super-resolution (SISR) [17].

Finally, in the realm of Generative Adversarial Networks (GANs), Ledig et al. presented the Super-resolution Generative Adversarial Network (SRGAN), which used a deep residual network and perceptual loss to generate photo-realistic images [8,18]. Wang et al. enhanced SRGAN by introducing Residual-in-Residual Dense Blocks (RRDB) and training with relativistic GAN, achieving better visual quality [28]. These advancements highlight the continuous evolution of deep learning techniques in enhancing image super-resolution, addressing challenges related to model complexity, computational cost, and feature extraction.

3　Method

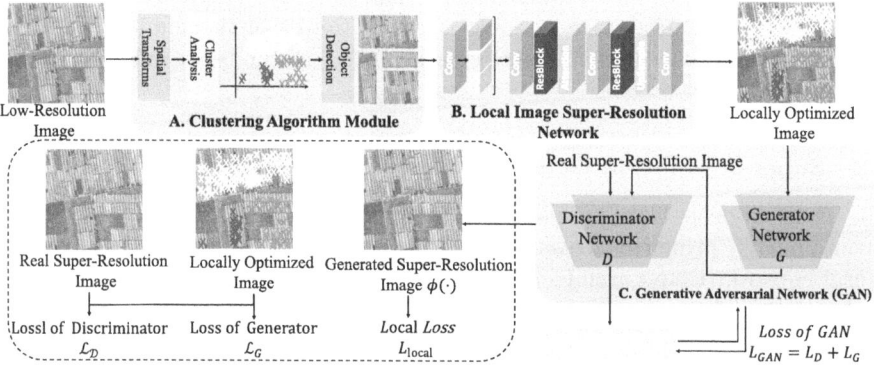

Fig. 1. The pipeline of our method. Figure A represents the clustering algorithm module, Figure B shows a schematic diagram of the local super-resolution network structure, and Figure C depicts super-resolution network based on GAN. The dotted part in the figure explains the composition of the Loss function.

This section presents a novel approach to remote sensing image super-resolution, combining dense region detection, local image enhancement, and generative adversarial networks (GANs). The pipeline of the above content is shown in Fig. 1.

Our method addresses the challenges of processing large-scale remote sensing imagery by first identifying areas of high pixel concentration using K-Means clustering. These dense regions are then processed by a local image super-resolution network that incorporates a lightweight cross-attention mechanism to capture spatial and contextual information. Finally, the overall framework is based on a GAN architecture, which ensures the generation of high-quality, detailed images through adversarial learning. This multi-stage approach allows for efficient and effective super-resolution of remote sensing images, with particular emphasis on enhancing critical areas while maintaining computational efficiency.

3.1   K-Means for Dense Region Detection

The dense areas of remote sensing images have a great interference on the overall image super-resolution. Therefore, we first need to detect the local areas of the image where small targets are concentrated.

We choose K-Means algorithm for clustering analysis to achieve dense area detection [2, 4, 26].

By leveraging both the color and spatial properties of image pixels, K-Means clustering efficiently partitions the image into distinct clusters, identifying areas with high pixel concentration.

In the context of image analysis, each pixel can be treated as a data point, characterized by both its color and spatial information. The clustering process iteratively assigns each pixel to one of K clusters, and the centroids of these clusters represent the dense regions in the image.

The specific algorithm steps are as follows:

1. Problem Formulation
Let the input image be $I \in \mathbb{R}^{m \times n \times 3}$, where m and n are image dimensions and 3 represents RGB channels. Each pixel is described by $p = [r, g, b, x, y]$, where r, g, b are color values and x, y are spatial coordinates. K-Means partitions the pixels $\{p_1, p_2, \ldots, p_N\}$, where $N = m \times n$, into K clusters $\{C_1, C_2, \ldots, C_K\}$ by minimizing:

$$J = \sum_{i=1}^{K} \sum_{p \in C_i} \|p - \mu_i\|^2 \tag{1}$$

where μ_i is the centroid of cluster C_i and $\|p - \mu_i\|$ is the Euclidean distance between pixel p and centroid μ_i.

2. Algorithmic Processing Flow
Feature Extraction: Each pixel is represented by a 5D vector $p = [r, g, b, x, y]$, combining color and spatial information. Centroid Initialization: Randomly select K pixels as initial centroids $\mu_1, \ldots, \mu_K$.

Cluster Assignment: For each pixel p_i, assign it to the nearest centroid μ_k by calculating the Euclidean distance:

$$d(p_i, \mu_k) = \sqrt{(r_i - r_k)^2 + (g_i - g_k)^2 + (b_i - b_k)^2 + (x_i - x_k)^2 + (y_i - y_k)^2} \tag{2}$$

Centroid Update: Recompute each centroid μ_k as the mean of its assigned pixels:

$$\mu_k = \frac{1}{|C_k|} \sum_{p_i \in C_k} p_i \tag{3}$$

Convergence Check: Repeat the assignment and update steps until centroids stabilize or a maximum number of iterations is reached.

3. Dense Region Detection

After convergence, the clusters $\{C_1, C_2, \ldots, C_K\}$ represent different regions. Dense regions are identified by cluster size and pixel concentration. Then morphological operations are applied to refine these regions and remove noise.

The flowchart of the above process is shown in Fig. 2.

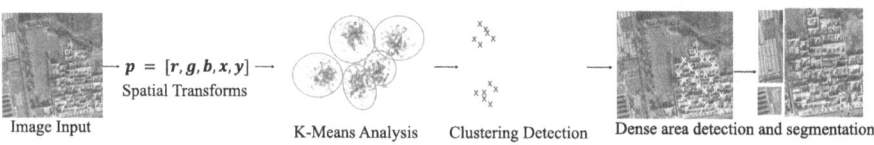

Fig. 2. K-Means clustering algorithm for dense target detection process diagram.

3.2 Local Image Super-Resolution Fused with Lightweight Cross-Attention

To enhance the details of key areas in remote sensing images, thereby optimizing the overall image processing and analysis, we propose to exploit a cross attention mechanism [11,13] to capture spatial and contextual information from multiple feature maps to more accurately reconstruct a high-resolution image from a low-resolution input. The schematic diagram of local image super-resolution network fused with lightweight cross-attention is shown in Fig. 3.

The network operates in the following stages:

1. Feature Extraction: First, we extract multi-scale feature maps from the low-resolution input using a series of convolutional layers. These features serve as the foundation for the subsequent cross-attention process.

2. Cross-Attention Module: In this module, we introduce a cross-attention mechanism. The attention mechanism helps the network focus on key contextual information relevant to the ROI, such as neighboring objects or background texture, enabling more precise reconstruction of the high-resolution image. This cross-attention not only improves spatial details but also allows the network to utilize information from different channels or time steps in the remote sensing data.

3. Upsampling and Reconstruction: Once the ROI feature maps are enhanced through cross-attention, the method applies an efficient upsampling method - sub-pixel convolution, to scale the feature maps to higher resolutions. The reconstructed high-resolution image for each ROI is then merged with the original low-resolution image to produce the final output.

Besides, given the size of remote sensing image, our method is designed with efficiency in mind. We employ depthwise separable convolutions and residual

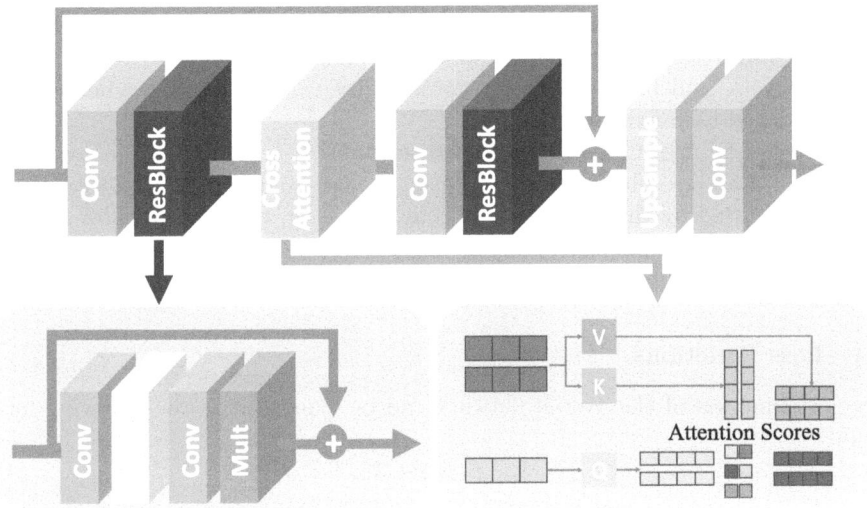

Fig. 3. Structure diagram of Local Image Super-resolution Network Fused with Lightweight Cross-Attention.

connections to reduce the computational complexity without sacrificing accuracy. The cross-attention module is restricted to the ROI regions, further minimizing the computational burden by focusing on key areas rather than the entire image.

3.3   Overall Framework of Remote Sensing Image Enhancement

In order to ensure the quality of super-resolution image generation, this paper refering to [8,15] uses the Generative Adversarial Network (GAN) as the basic framework of the overall method. Its basic principle is to generate high-quality images through mutual adversarial learning between two neural networks, the generator and the discriminator. For the super-resolution task of remote sensing images, the unique advantage of GAN is that it can generate high-resolution images with rich details and natural textures through this adversarial learning mechanism. The GAN network consists of two parts, the generator and the discriminator. Its sample structure is shown in the Fig. 1(C), and its basic principle is as follows.

Generator: The generator receives low-resolution remote sensing images and gradually generates images with high-resolution features through operations such as convolutional layers, activation functions, and upsampling.

   In order to ensure that the details and textures of high-resolution images are restored as realistically as possible, our generator uses ResNet [10], which can alleviate the gradient vanishing problem during deep network training through residual connections, thereby retaining more high-frequency information in the original image, such as edges and texture details.

Discriminator: As a binary classification network, the discriminator receives the input image, extracts the features of the image through a series of convolutional layers, and finally outputs a probability value indicating whether the image is a real high-resolution image.

This method uses CNN as the structure of the discriminator, and the input includes real high-resolution remote sensing images and pseudo high-resolution images generated by the generator. Through training, the discriminator gradually learns to distinguish the subtle differences between these images, including textures, edges, and other high-frequency details.

3.4 Loss Functions

The loss function of the overall network can be expressed as the following formula.

$$\mathcal{L}_G = \lambda_{\mathrm{adv}}\mathcal{L}_{\mathrm{GAN}} + \lambda_{\mathrm{loc}}\mathcal{L}_{\mathrm{local}} \tag{4}$$

where λ_{adv} and λ_{loc} are the weight parameters of adversarial loss, local super-resolution network loss respectively.

The $\mathcal{L}_{\mathrm{GAN}}$ is the overall loss function of the GAN network, which consists of the generator loss function $\mathcal{L}_G$ and the discriminator loss function $\mathcal{L}_D$.

$$\mathcal{L}_{\mathrm{GAN}} = \min_G \max_D \mathbb{E}_{\mathbf{x} \sim p_{\mathrm{data}}(\mathbf{x})}[\log D(\mathbf{x})] + \mathbb{E}_{\mathbf{z} \sim p_{\mathbf{z}}(\mathbf{z})}[\log(1 - D(G(\mathbf{z})))] \tag{5}$$

The specific calculation methods of $\mathcal{L}_G$ and $\mathcal{L}_D$ are as follows

$$L_G = -\mathbb{E}_{\mathbf{z} \sim p_{\mathbf{z}}(\mathbf{z})}[\log D(G(\mathbf{z}))] \tag{6}$$

$$\mathcal{L}_D = -\mathbb{E}_{\mathbf{x} \sim p_{\mathrm{data}}(\mathbf{x})}[\log D(\mathbf{x})] - \mathbb{E}_{\mathbf{z} \sim p_{\mathbf{z}}(\mathbf{z})}[\log(1 - D(G(\mathbf{z})))] \tag{7}$$

where $D(\mathbf{x})$ is the discriminant probability of the real image $\mathbf{x}$, $G(\mathbf{z})$ is the fake image generated by the generator with random noise $\mathbf{z}$ as input; $D(G(\mathbf{z}))$ is the discriminant probability of the generated image $G(\mathbf{z})$; $\mathbb{E}_{\mathbf{x} \sim p_{\mathrm{data}}(\mathbf{x})}$ is the expectation of the real data; $\mathbb{E}_{\mathbf{z} \sim p_{\mathbf{z}}(\mathbf{z})}$ is the expectation of the generator input noise.

The $\mathcal{L}_{\mathrm{local}}$ adopts perceptual loss. Based on the feature extraction layer of the pre-trained local super-resolution neural network with fused cross attention, the difference between high-resolution and low-resolution images in feature space is calculated.

$$\mathcal{L}_{\mathrm{local}} = \mathbb{E}_{\mathbf{x} \sim p_{\mathrm{data}}(\mathbf{x})}[\|\phi(\mathbf{x}) - \phi(G(\mathbf{z}))\|_2^2] \tag{8}$$

where $\phi(\cdot)$ represents the high-level features extracted from the pre-trained network.

4 Experiments

4.1 Evaluation Metrics

(1) **Peak Signal-to-Noise Ratio (PSNR):** PSNR is a widely used metric for evaluating image and video quality, especially in the context of compression or

reconstruction.Given a super-resolved image I_{SR} and a target high-resolution image I_{HR} with same pixels, PSNR first calculates the mean squared error (MSE) between the images:

$$MSE = \frac{1}{N}\Sigma(I_{HR}(i) - I_{SR}(i))^2 \tag{9}$$

$$PSNR = 10 \cdot log_{10}(\frac{M^2}{MSE}) \tag{10}$$

where M represents the maximum possible pixel value. The PSNR is expressed in decibels (dB), and a higher PSNR value indicates better visual quality and less distortion.

(2) **Structural Similarity Index Measure (SSIM):** Unlike PSNR, SSIM measures structural information between two images, taking into account luminance, contrast, and texture. This makes SSIM more aligned with human visual perception.Given a super-resolved image I_{SR} and a target high-resolution image I_{HR}, SSIM is calculated by:

$$SSIM = l(I_{SR}, I_{HR}) \times c(I_{SR}, I_{HR}) \times s(I_{SR}, I_{HR}) \tag{11}$$

where $l(I_{SR}, I_{HR})$, $c(I_{SR}, I_{HR})$, and $s(I_{SR}, I_{HR})$ represent the similarity of the luminance, contrast, and structure.

4.2   Experiment Setting

The model is trained using a combined dataset that includes the training sets from both the WV-3 (Data Fusion Contest 2019) and DOTA [30] datasets. During the training process, the batch size is set to 32, and the Adam optimizer is employed to ensure efficient and stable convergence. To improve the model's performance, the training incorporates a combination of two loss functions: GAN loss and local super-resolution loss. These two losses are balanced with a weight ratio of 0.5:1, where more emphasis is placed on the local super-resolution loss. This approach allows the model to better capture both global structural patterns and finer local details, enhancing overall translation quality.

4.3   Results and Analysis

We conducted a comprehensive comparison between our proposed model and several well-established remote sensing super-resolution methods, including SRCNN [5], SRGAN [18], ESRGAN [28], and CARS [27].

Specifically, SR-CNN [5] is an early deep learning method for super-resolution that uses a simple CNN to convert low-resolution images into high-resolution ones. SRGAN [18] improves super-resolution by generating photo-realistic images using a perceptual loss for better textures. ESRGAN [28] enhances SRGAN with Residual-in-Residual Dense Blocks and relativistic GANs for sharper results. CARS [27] employs channel attention to improve feature focus and image quality in remote sensing super-resolution.

The quantitative experiments were carried out using the test set of the WV-3 dataset, and the performance of each method was evaluated based on two widely-used image quality metrics: PSNR and SSIM. The detailed results of these experiments are presented in Table 1.

Table 1. Results on WV-3 images

Method	Our Method	SRCNN [5]	SRGAN [18]	ESRGAN [28]	CARS [27]
PSNR	**32.8359**	32.5257	32.6259	31.3952	32.7794
SSIM	**0.9681**	0.9612	0.9659	0.9624	0.9670

From the results in Table 1, it is evident that our method consistently surpasses the traditional approaches in both PSNR and SSIM scores. This superior performance highlights the effectiveness of our clustering-local super-resolution algorithm, which is capable of accurately identifying dense regions within the images and performing high-quality super-resolution reconstruction. The results demonstrate that our approach not only preserves global image structure but also excels in recovering fine local details, making it particularly well-suited for the complex patterns commonly found in remote sensing image.

In addition to the quantitative analysis presented in Figs. 4 and 5, we selected images from both the WV-3 and DOTA test sets to visually demonstrate the effectiveness of our super-resolution model. The results for the WV-3 dataset are shown in Figs. 4, while those for the DOTA dataset are in Figs. 5. To ensure

Fig. 4. Quantitative results on the WV-3 dataset, the top row represents the original images, and the bottom row shows the images after super-resolution reconstruction.

a fair comparison, the visualized outputs display the target regions scaled to the same dimensions, as the super-resolution process involves upsampling the images.

These visualizations clearly indicate that our proposed model excels in handling densely packed objects, effectively completing the super-resolution task while preserving critical details. The model not only enlarges the images but also maintains a high level of sharpness and clarity. This underscores the model's capability to enhance both resolution and visual quality, making it particularly suitable for remote sensing applications that require precise object identification and detail preservation.

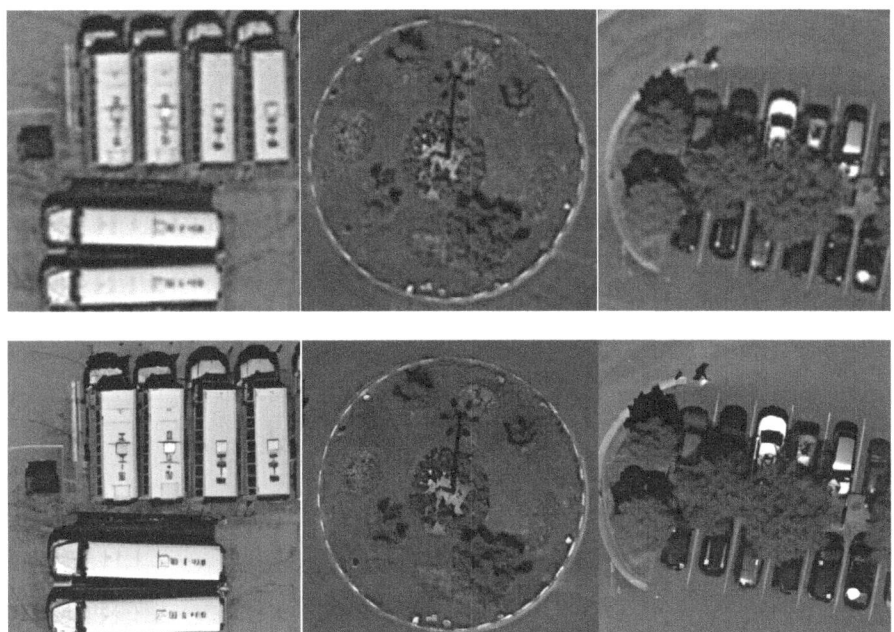

Fig. 5. Quantitative results on the DOTA dataset, the top row represents the original images, and the bottom row shows the images after super-resolution reconstruction.

5 Conclusion

This paper introduces a novel method for remote sensing image enhancement, combining clustering algorithms with a local super-resolution network. Our approach effectively identifies dense regions using K-Means clustering and employs a lightweight cross-attention-based network to enhance these key areas. By integrating these techniques with a GAN-based framework, we achieve superior image quality and object detection capabilities, as demonstrated through experiments on the WV-3 and DOTA datasets. Our method enhances remote sensing image quality by focusing super-resolution on key areas, improving both image fidelity and utility for object detection and efficient processing. This approach shows potential for environmental monitoring, urban planning, and disaster management applications.

References

1. Ackermann, M.R., Blömer, J., Kuntze, D., Sohler, C.: Analysis of agglomerative clustering. Algorithmica **69**, 184–215 (2014)
2. Agarwal, R., Hariharan, S., Rao, M.N., Agarwal, A.: Weed identification using k-means clustering with color spaces features in multi-spectral images taken by UAV. In: 2021 IEEE International Geoscience and Remote Sensing Symposium IGARSS, pp. 7047–7050. IEEE (2021)
3. Ahn, N., Kang, B., Sohn, K.A.: Fast, accurate, and lightweight super-resolution with cascading residual network. In: Proceedings of the European Conference on Computer Vision (ECCV), pp. 252–268 (2018)
4. Ali, I., Rehman, A.U., Khan, D.M., Khan, Z., Shafiq, M., Choi, J.G.: Model selection using k-means clustering algorithm for the symmetrical segmentation of remote sensing datasets. Symmetry **14**(6), 1149 (2022)
5. Dong, C., Loy, C.C., He, K., Tang, X.: Learning a deep convolutional network for image super-resolution. In: Computer Vision–ECCV 2014: 13th European Conference, Zurich, Switzerland, 6–12 September 2014, Part IV 13, pp. 184–199. Springer (2014)
6. Dong, C., Loy, C.C., Tang, X.: Accelerating the super-resolution convolutional neural network. In: Computer Vision–ECCV 2016: 14th European Conference, Amsterdam, The Netherlands, 11–14 October 2016, Part II 14, pp. 391–407. Springer (2016)
7. Fatemi, N., Sajedi, H., Shiri, M.E.: Salient object detection with segment features using mean shift algorithm. In: 2018 8th International Conference on Computer and Knowledge Engineering (ICCKE), pp. 20–26. IEEE (2018)
8. Goodfellow, I., et al.: Generative adversarial networks. Commun. ACM **63**(11), 139–144 (2020)
9. Gu, J., et al.: Recent advances in convolutional neural networks. Pattern Recogn. **77**, 354–377 (2018)
10. He, K., Zhang, X., Ren, S., Sun, J.: Deep residual learning for image recognition. In: Proceedings of the IEEE Conference on Computer Vision and Pattern Recognition, pp. 770–778 (2016)
11. Hou, R., Chang, H., Ma, B., Shan, S., Chen, X.: Cross attention network for few-shot classification. Adv. Neural Inf. Process. Syst. **32** (2019)
12. Hu, J., Shen, L., Albanie, S., Sun, G., Wu, E.: Squeeze-and-excitation networks. IEEE Trans. Pattern Anal. Mach. Intell. **42**(08), 2011–2023 (2020)
13. Huang, Z., Wang, X., Huang, L., Huang, C., Wei, Y., Liu, W.: CCNet: criss-cross attention for semantic segmentation. In: Proceedings of the IEEE/CVF International Conference on Computer Vision, pp. 603–612 (2019)
14. Ikotun, A.M., Ezugwu, A.E., Abualigah, L., Abuhaija, B., Heming, J.: K-means clustering algorithms: a comprehensive review, variants analysis, and advances in the era of big data. Inf. Sci. **622**, 178–210 (2023). https://doi.org/10.1016/j.ins.2022.11.139

15. Jia, S., Wang, Z., Li, Q., Jia, X., Xu, M.: Multiattention generative adversarial network for remote sensing image super-resolution. IEEE Trans. Geosci. Remote Sens. **60**, 1–15 (2022)
16. Kim, J., Lee, J.K., Lee, K.M.: Accurate image super-resolution using very deep convolutional networks. In: Proceedings of the IEEE Conference on Computer Vision and Pattern Recognition, pp. 1646–1654 (2016)
17. Lan, R., et al.: Cascading and enhanced residual networks for accurate single-image super-resolution. IEEE Trans. Cybern. **51**(1), 115–125 (2020)
18. Ledig, C., et al.: Photo-realistic single image super-resolution using a generative adversarial network. In: Proceedings of the IEEE Conference on Computer Vision and Pattern Recognition, pp. 4681–4690 (2017)
19. Navalgund, R.R., Jayaraman, V., Roy, P.: Remote sensing applications: an overview. Curr. Sci. 1747–1766 (2007)
20. Redmon, J., Farhadi, A.: YOLO9000: better, faster, stronger. In: Proceedings of the IEEE Conference on Computer Vision and Pattern Recognition, pp. 7263–7271 (2017)
21. Ren, Y., Zhu, C., Xiao, S.: Small object detection in optical remote sensing images via modified faster R-CNN. Appl. Sci. **8**(5), 813 (2018)
22. Reynolds, D.A., et al.: Gaussian mixture models. Encycl. Biomet. **741**, 659–663 (2009)
23. Shi, W., et al.: Real-time single image and video super-resolution using an efficient sub-pixel convolutional neural network. In: Proceedings of the IEEE Conference on Computer Vision and Pattern Recognition, pp. 1874–1883 (2016)
24. Shin, G., Albanie, S., Xie, W.: Unsupervised salient object detection with spectral cluster voting. In: Proceedings of the IEEE/CVF Conference on Computer Vision and Pattern Recognition, pp. 3971–3980 (2022)
25. Von Luxburg, U.: A tutorial on spectral clustering. Stat. Comput. **17**, 395–416 (2007)
26. Waleed, M., Um, T.W., Khan, A., Khan, U.: Automatic detection system of olive trees using improved k-means algorithm. Remote Sens. **12**(5), 760 (2020)
27. Wang, P., Bayram, B., Sertel, E.: Super-resolution of remotely sensed data using channel attention based deep learning approach. Int. J. Remote Sens. **42**(16), 6048–6065 (2021)
28. Wang, X., et al.: ESRGAN: enhanced super-resolution generative adversarial networks. In: Proceedings of the European Conference on Computer Vision (ECCV) Workshops (2018)
29. Woo, S., Park, J., Lee, J.Y., Kweon, I.S.: CBAM: convolutional block attention module. In: Proceedings of the European Conference on Computer Vision (ECCV), pp. 3–19 (2018)
30. Xia, G.S., et al.: DOTA: a large-scale dataset for object detection in aerial images. In: Proceedings of the IEEE Conference on Computer Vision and Pattern Recognition, pp. 3974–3983 (2018)
31. Zhang, Y., Li, K., Li, K., Wang, L., Zhong, B., Fu, Y.: Image super-resolution using very deep residual channel attention networks. In: Proceedings of the European Conference on Computer Vision (ECCV), pp. 286–301 (2018)
32. Zhao, H., Kong, X., He, J., Qiao, Y., Dong, C.: Efficient image super-resolution using pixel attention. In: Computer Vision–ECCV 2020 Workshops: Glasgow, UK, 23–28 August 2020, Part III 16, pp. 56–72. Springer (2020)

LipText: Lip Tracking Based Text Entry in VR

Jiaye Leng[1], Zijun Wang[2], Jian Wu[2(✉)], and Lili Wang[2]

[1] School of Creative Media, City University of Hong Kong, Kowloon Tong, Hong Kong
jiayeleng2-c@my.cityu.edu.hk
[2] State Key Laboratory of Virtual Reality Technology and Systems, School of Computer Science and Engineering, Beihang University, Beijing 100191, China
{lanayawj,wanglily}@buaa.edu.cn

Abstract. Text entry is an important task in virtual reality (VR), and most existing methods require hand involvement, while hands-free typing has great potential for applications in mobile scenarios. Existing hands-free text entry methods are usually implemented by combining the head and eyes with techniques such as Dwell, Blink and Gesture, which can easily fatigue the user. In this paper, we propose LipText, a lip-tracking-based text entry method in VR. We use a neural network to perform letter-level prediction on the lip data captured by the facial tracker and use head-based selection as an auxiliary to improve the accuracy. We conduct a user study to evaluate our method, the results show a typing speed of 8.63 WPM for the novice group, 9.81 WPM for the potential expert group, and the highest recorded typing speed is 11.13 WPM achieved by a potential expert. Our method is also novice-friendly, and their typing speed increased by 64.38% over a six-day practice.

Keywords: Virtual reality · Text entry · Hands-free

1 Introduction

Text entry is a common application in virtual reality (VR), where users need to communicate with each other and record information. Existing text entry methods usually require hand involvement and use devices such as physical keyboards, touch screens, sensors, and handles for input. While in mobile scenarios, these devices impose an additional burden, and the user's hands may be occupied, so it makes sense to explore hand-free text entry techniques. It is also beneficial for those users with hand motion deficits.

Several existing works have explored hands-free input. RingText [23] allows the user to use head motions to control a cursor for selection, eliminating the need for the user to hold a specialized input device to select letters. iText [11] is a technique for text entry in augmented reality (AR) systems based on an imaginary keyboard, and the keyboard area is transparent. Although both methods

© The Author(s), under exclusive license to Springer Nature Singapore Pte Ltd. 2025
W. Song et al. (Eds.): ICXR 2024, LNCS 15461, pp. 162–178, 2025.
https://doi.org/10.1007/978-981-96-3679-2_11

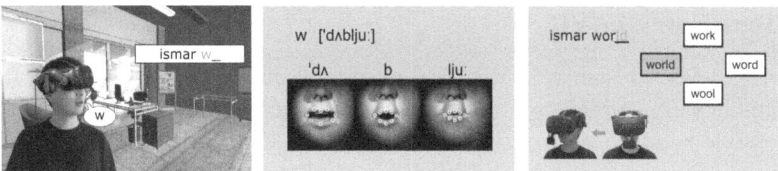

Fig. 1. When the user enters a word, he reads the letter silently (left), and the facial tracker captures the lip shape in a sequence (middle). The head motion of the user captured by VR HMDs is used for the auxiliary selection of a word from the four predicted candidates (right).

achieve efficient typing speeds (13.24 WPM for RingText and 13.76 WPM for iText), they both require the user to focus on the keyboard interface, which tends to make the user feel fatigued, and it is also not easy to select a target letter from the 26 letters. We think that introducing new interaction methods may provide a new solution for hands-free typing and provide a more natural interaction experience, and narrowing the range of letters to select when typing can also reduce the user's fatigue.

In this paper, we propose LipText, a lip tracking-based text entry method in VR. Firstly, we set up a facial tracker on the VR HMDs to capture the user's lip shapes. After that, the lip shape sequences with 37 feature points are obtained, which we segment and denoise to generate the lip shape features of the input letters. Secondly, we use a neural network to classify the lip shape features to recognize the input letters. Thirdly, we adopt a head motion-based auxiliary selection method to improve the correctness of the text entry. We design a user study to evaluate our LipText. The results show that the typing speed is about 9.8 WPM, and a potential expert can type at 11.13 WPM. The average NCER and TER are 2.43% and 6.66% respectively. Our method also has good learnability, for the novices, the typing speed can be raised by 64.38% through a six-day practice. Figure 1 shows the diagram of inputting the letter 'W' using our lip tracking-based text entry method.

In summary, the contributions of this paper are as follows:

- We propose a lip tracking-based text entry pipeline in VR. We introduce a new interaction method of silent reading into the hands-free text entry techniques for the first time.
- We introduce a neural network-based letter recognition method for the lip tracking data captured by the facial tracker.
- We design a user study to evaluate the performance of our LipText.

2   Related Work

In this section, we review the existing text entry methods in VR and hands-free text entry techniques.

2.1 Text Entry in VR

Unlike input text in reality, in VR users need to wear HMDs and type in a virtual environment (VE), which creates visual and interactive differences to text entry. One possible solution is to integrate the physical keyboard directly to the VR system, which can achieve typing efficiency similar to that in the real world [9]. The above methods requires the user to sit down and type, while Pham et al. [16] proposed the HawKey application for mobile scenarios, where the user wore a tray in front of him to place the keyboard on it.

Speech-based techniques are also capable of efficient typing, but due to it being difficult to correct errors [20], it is usually presented in a multimodal form. Adhikary et al. [1] combined hand tracking and speech in VR, allowing the user to speak a sentence and then correct the errors on a mid-air keyboard by avatar hands. Touch screen-based techniques introduces a touch screen, such as tablets and smartphones, to perform text entry. Gugenheimer et al. [6] mounted a multi-touch surface on the back of a VR HMD, which allowed for precise interaction and thus performed text entry in mobile scenarios. Mid-air typing techniques are also solutions for mobile scenarios, mostly requiring sensors to detect the user's typing behavior. Whitmire et al. [21] proposed DigiTouch, which enabled thumb-to-finger touch interaction for text entry through a glove with continuous touch tracking, and similar techniques were available in [10,24].

Head-based techniques focus on the user using head movements to control the cursor for selections on a virtual keyboard. Yu et al. [25] explored three head-based text entry techniques: Tap, Dwell, and Gesture, with Gesture outperforming the other two. Xu et al. [23] proposed RingText, where the user used dwell-free technique on a circular layout with two concentric circles for input. The handle-based techniques mainly use the handle controllers provided in the existing VR systems for input. Yu et al. [26] proposed PizzaText, which chunked 26 letters and used a handle with two joysticks for two-step selection. Jiang et al. [8] proposed HiPad, which used a handle with a circular touchpad, and a circular virtual keyboard to support single-hand input.

The existing techniques in VR usually use people's hands, heads, voices, and eyes to perform text input, while the mouth has not been explored as a potential input source. Silent reading avoids to some extent the problems associated with speech-based techniques and, similar to speech techniques, it may be able to support letter-level, word-level, and sentence-level input as well.

2.2 Hands-Free Text Entry Techniques

Hands-free text entry techniques are being explored due to the possible limitations of devices, or people's hands being occupied. Speech-based techniques are possible to achieve this, transcribing people's speech into text through speech recognition. Ruan et al. [17] used a deep learning-based speech recognition system and compared it to a smartphone's default keyboard, showing that transcribing text using speech was nearly three times faster than on a touchscreen keyboard and that it had a higher uncorrected error rate. Although speech-based techniques are fast to type, their effectiveness suffers in noisy environments [18], and people avoid using them in public for the security of privacy. Some techniques that utilize the head and eyes are also capable of hands-free input, Dwell [25], Dwell-free, Gesture, and Blink are common solutions. E. Mott et al. [15] proposed cascaded gaze typing, which dynamically adjusted the dwell time of keys in the on-screen keyboard based on the likelihood of the next key being selected and the position of the key on the keyboard.

Compared with the dwell techniques, the dwell-free techniques eliminate the cost of dwell time and improve the selection efficiency. RingText [23] adopted hands-free technique where the user used head movements to control the cursor to type on a circular keyboard. Typing with blink was also a dwell-free technique, and the findings of [12] showed it was superior to the dwell technique. Gesture was also a hands-free technique that used head movements to draw a path on the keyboard through letters of a word in order, it had been found to work well on both visible [25] and invisible [11] keyboards.

The above methods usually require the user to focus on the virtual keyboard (the invisible keyboard still has an input area) and control the cursor for selection, which can lead to user fatigue, and it is attractive to free the user's attention from the virtual keyboard.

3   Method

Our lip tracking-based text entry method takes the lip shape data stream captured by the facial tracker and head motion captured by VR HMDs as inputs. The output is the letter or word the user intends to enter. Our method has three main steps: lip shape sequences generation, letter recognition, and auxiliary selection. The pipeline is shown in Fig. 2.

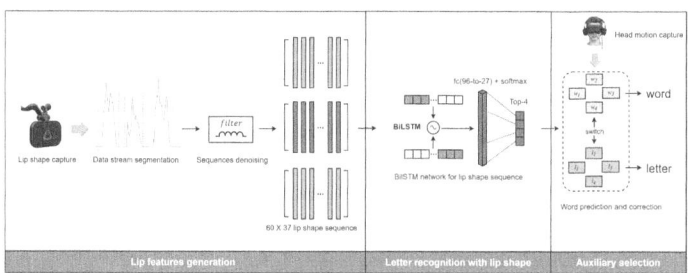

Fig. 2. The pipeline of our lip tracking-based text entry method.

3.1   Lip Shape Sequences Generation

In this section, we capture lip shape with the facial tracker, segment the data stream into the sequences of a single letter with a normalized length, and denoise the sequences.

Lip Shape Feature Capture. We use the HTC VIVE facial tracker to capture lip shape features when users read the letters silently. It tracks 37 blend shapes related to the lip shape, including the points on the lip, jaw, teeth, tongue, chin, and cheeks. Its tracking refresh rate is 60 Hz, and latency is less than 10ms. The device is also able to access the VR HMDs quickly. Therefore, our method can easily be integrated into the existing VR HMDs-based systems. Our method can achieve high accuracy and low latency lip shape tracking even in low light environments since the device uses an infrared camera. Figure 1 left shows the user wearing the VR HMD with a facial tracker mounted on the bottom of it. When the user reads a letter of words, the device outputs the 37-dimension vector stream that presents the changes of lip shapes.

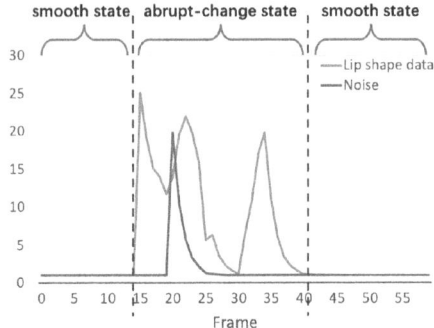

Fig. 3. The one-dimensional data in the lip shape 37-dimensional data when the user reads a is given by the orange line, which can be divided into smooth and abrupt-change states. The blue line represents the noise data. (Color figure online)

Data Stream Segmentation. The 37-dimensional vector stream captured is continuous and must be segmented into normalized sequences for each letter before letter recognition. The orange line in Fig. 3 shows the change in one of the 37 dimensions as the user reads the letter 'a', where the lips move from closed to open and then closed again. Our approach to segmenting the continuous data stream is based on detecting abrupt-change points. The state where the lips remain closed is referred to as the "smooth state" (frames 0–14), and the point where the data sharply fluctuates from this smooth state is called the "abrupt-change point" (frame 15). We designed a segmentation algorithm 1 to capture the sequence of fluctuating data as the lip shape data for each letter, starting from the abrupt-change point until the smooth state is restored (frames 15–40, abrupt-change state). The details of the algorithm are as follows.

The algorithm inputs three consecutive frames of lip features: LF_{i-2}, LF_{i-1}, LF_i; the current state S_i, which can be "smooth state" (S) or "abrupt-change state" (AC), initialized as "S"; and the current frame count Cnt for the "AC" state. The output is the segmentation flag F_i, indicating a segmented frame.

Algorithm 1: Data Stream Segmentation

Input   : previous lip features LF_{i-2}, LF_{i-1}, current lip feature LF_i, current
state S_i, current written frames Cnt

Output : segmentation flag F_i

1   $SumStd = 0$
2   $F_i = $ **False**
3   **for** $j = 0 \rightarrow 37$ **do**
4       $m = (LF_{i-2}[j] + LF_{i-1}[j] + LF_i[j])/3$
5       $std = (LF_{i-2}[j] - m)^2 + (LF_{i-1}[j] - m)^2 + (LF_i[j] - m)^2$
6       $SumStd = SumStd + \sqrt{std/3}$
7   **end for**
8   **if** $(S_i == S$ && $SumStd > MINSTD)$
9   **then**
10   $S_i = AC$
11   $F_i = $ **True**
12   **if** $(S_i == AC$ && $\text{Check}(SumStd, Cnt) == $ **True**$)$
13   **then**
14   $S_i = S$
15   $F_i = $ **True**

First, we initialize $SumStd$ (the sum of the standard deviations of the three frames) to 0 and F_i to False (lines 1–2). We then compute $SumStd$ as the sum of the standard deviations in each dimension across LF_{i-2}, LF_{i-1}, and LF_i (lines 3–7).

If S_i is "S" and $SumStd$ exceeds a predefined threshold $MINSTD$, this indicates an "abrupt-change point", so S_i switches to "AC" and F_i is set to True (lines 8–11). During silent reading, the lips remain active, so the standard deviation stays above the threshold until the user finishes reading and closes their mouth.

If S_i is "AC" and it ends at this frame, we reset S_i to "S" and set F_i to True (lines 12–15). The function Check determines if the "AC" state should end: if $SumStd$ falls below $MINSTD$, S_i switches to "S". Two special cases may occur: 1) Subtle lip movements may cause $SumStd$ to drop prematurely, exiting "AC" too early. 2) Fast reading may result in consecutive letters being treated as one sequence since the "S" state is not detected. To address this, we set $MINACFRAME$ to 15 and $MAXACFRAME$ to 60, based on the observations of 26 letters' temporal data. The function Check returns True if Cnt exceeds $MINACFRAME$ and $SumStd$ is below $MINSTD$, or if Cnt exceeds $MAXACFRAME$. Otherwise, it returns False. This prevents exiting "AC" too early or recording noisy data. However, we advise users to ensure clear lip movements and avoid reading too quickly.

Sequences Denoising. Noise significantly impacts the performance of our method, as the segmentation algorithm relies on detecting "abrupt-change points" for mode switching, making it sensitive to noise. In the "S" state, even slight facial jitters can trigger an abrupt change, causing the algorithm to switch to the "AC" state and record noisy data. Since itâĂŹs unrealistic to expect users to keep their lips perfectly still when not reading letters, an effective denoising algorithm is necessary. As shown in Fig. 3, noise data typically exhibit low frequency and short duration, with jitter lasting less than ten frames. Based on this, our denoising algorithm calculates the sum of standard deviations for each dimension from the 10th frame onward. If this sum falls below a threshold, the data is considered noisy and discarded. We then normalize sequences shorter than 60 frames by padding them with zeros.

3.2   Letter Recognition

We use a neural network-based method to recognize the letters according to the normalized lip shape sequences when the user reads silently.

Dataset. We recruited ten participants (five males, five females, aged 22–30) from our university to collect training data. Six had prior experience with VR headsets. Each participant completed 30 phrases, including randomly generated phrases from the Mackenzie phrase set [14] and semantic-free phrases to ensure balanced data for each letter. For the 26 letters, we used the standard lip shapes from the International Phonetic Alphabet [22]. The space key was represented by a distinct "pouting" lip shape, designed to be easily distinguishable from the letters. Participants were instructed to enter text naturally while ensuring clear and complete lip shapes. In total, we collected 300 phrases (10 participants × 30 phrases), resulting in 8100 sequences (27 characters × 300).

Neural Network. Lip tracking generates a 37-dimensional data sequence, requiring neural networks capable of processing multivariate time series data. We consider three options: Long Short-Term Memory (LSTM) [4], Gated Recurrent Unit (GRU) [5], and Bidirectional LSTM (BiLSTM) [2]. LSTM excels at handling time-series data by using gates (Input, Output, Forget) to manage long-term dependencies and address vanishing gradients. GRU, with two gates (Update and Reset), is simpler and has fewer parameters than LSTM. BiLSTM combines forward and backward LSTMs, allowing the model to capture bidirectional patterns in the sequence. We incorporate a Leaky ReLU activation function to increase sparsity and mitigate overfitting. A fully-connected layer follows, outputting a 1×27 vector, with 27 representing the classification categories. The input to the network is a 60×37 matrix.

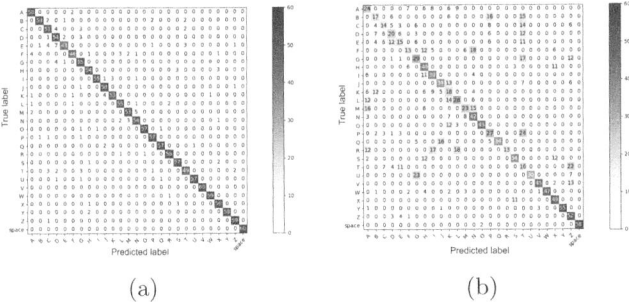

(a)   (b)

Fig. 4. The confusion matrices for 27 labels (26 letters + space key) on the validation (a) and test (b) sets. The horizontal axis represents the predicted labels, and the vertical axis represents the true labels. Each element of the matrices represents the number of times a given true label was predicted as different labels. The diagonal of the matrix shows the number of correct predictions for each letter, and each row sums to 60.

We used the 8100 collected lip shape sequences, split into a 3:1:1 ratio for training, validating, and testing, to evaluate the classification accuracy of the LSTM, GRU, and BiLSTM models. All three models achieved notable results, with BiLSTM, LSTM, and GRU achieving accuracies of 92.72%, 86.30%, and 78.65%, respectively. We further optimized the BiLSTM model by adjusting training parameters, including learning rate, loss function, batch size, optimizer, and hidden unit dimensions. The best BiLSTM model had a hidden size of 96. Figure 4(a) shows the confusion matrix for BiLSTM on the validation set, where letters like 'B', 'C', 'F', 'K', 'M', and 'T' had accuracies between 80% and 90%, with 'E' being the lowest at 71.67%, and the rest above 90%. On the test set (Fig. 4(b)), accuracy dropped for some letters except 'X', 'Y', 'Z', and 'space'. We then calculated the top-4 prediction accuracy (Fig. 5), which improved compared to the top-1. Except for 'B', 'C', 'D', and 'E', the accuracy for all other letters exceeded 80%, suggesting that a multi-choice auxiliary selection method may enhance usability.

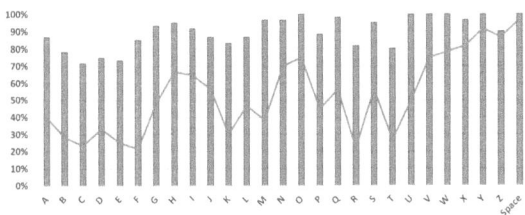

Fig. 5. The probability of the correct predicted results of 27 letters appearing in the top-4 (blue) versus the top-1 (orange). (Color figure online)

3.3   Auxiliary Selection

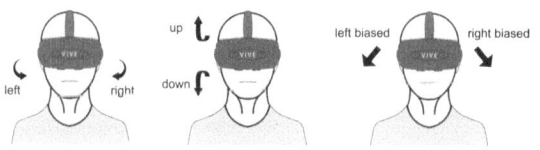

Fig. 6. Head-motion for auxiliary selection.

Head-Based Selection Method. To improve text entry accuracy, we allow users to select from the recognition results. Since our approach is hands-free, we consider integrating head-based selection methods to minimize user learning effort. To further enhance accuracy and speed, we integrate a word correction technique using SymSpell [3], combined with the head-based selection approach, following similar methods from previous works [8,23]. Common head selection methods, such as Dwell and Dwell-free [23], often lead to misselection. Therefore, we propose a head motion-based selection method to choose between the top four predictions. As shown in Fig. 6, this method detects six head movements: up, down, left, right, left bias (for Switch), and right bias (for Backspace). The first four are used to select from the top-4 predictions, while Switch toggles between letter and word selection.

4   Pilot User Study

Referring to the now popular approach of head selection, we considered adding the auxiliary selection strategies mentioned in Sect. 3.3 to our method. In this pilot user study, we evaluated three potential head-based selection methods: Dwell, Dwell-free, and ours. There are top-4 candidates of the prediction as well as the Switch and Backspace keys in the dwell layout.

4.1   Pilot User Study Design

Participants and Hardware Setup. Eighteen participants (thirteen males and five females, aged between 22–30) from our university participated in this study. We used a VIVE Pro 2 headset to provide an immersive experience and a VIVE facial tracker to capture lip shapes. Our computer configuration was the Intel Core i7 processor with an NVIDIA GeForce RTX 1060 graphics card. The system was developed with Unity 2021.2.

Task and Procedure. This study used a within-subject design with one independent variable. Session 1–3 represented Dwell (CC1), Dwell-free (CC2) and our selection method (EC) respectively, where the dwell time for Dwell was set to 400ms. Each session required participants to input ten randomly generated phrases from the Mackenzie phrase set [14], and the order of the sessions was also randomly assigned. Before starting the experiment, we gave participants approximately 3 min to familiarize themselves with these methods. The two metrics for this experiment are typing speed and single letter selection time, where single-letter selection time is the time between the model predicting a candidate letter and the participant completing the selection. We kept correctly selected data and excluded incorrectly selected data (the target letter was not in top-4). Participants were required to fill out a NASA-TLX questionnaire [7] at the end of each session. A total of 3 (methods) × 10 (phrases) × 18 (participants) = 540 phrases were collected. The Words Per Minute (WPM) was calculated following the equation in [13].

4.2 Results

We used a one-way repeated ANOVA to analyze the results of the experiment and used Bonferroni correction in pair-wise comparisons.

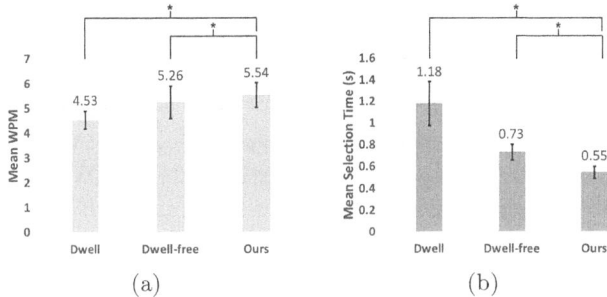

Fig. 7. Mean typing speed (a) and selection time (b) for three head-based selection methods. Error bars indicate standard deviation. Asterisks denote statistical significance (same for all figures below).

Typing Speed and Selection Time. Figure 7 shows the average typing speed and the average selection time of a single letter for the three methods, with details of pair-wise comparisons given in Table 1 and 2. The results of the ANOVA showed that the different methods had a significant effect on both typing speed $(F_{1.39,23.63} = 94.06, p < 0.001, \eta_p^2 = .85)$ and selection time $(F_{1.01,22.24} = 312.01,$

Table 1. The typing speed, in seconds.

Condition	Avg ± std. dev.	$(EC\text{-}CC_i)/\ CC_i$	p	Cohen's d	Effect size
CC_1	4.53 ± 0.36	22.30%	$<0.001^*$	2.56	Huge
CC_2	5.26 ± 0.66	5.32%	$= 0.009^*$	0.47	Small
EC	5.54 ± 0.52				

$p < 0.001$, $\eta_p^2 = .93$). For typing speed, pair-wise comparisons showed that our selection method had a significant improvement compared to Dwell ($p < 0.001$) and Dwell-free ($p = .009$), and there was also a significant difference between Dwell and Dwell-free ($p = .009$). The effect size of our selection method compared with Dwell and Dwell-free were 'Huge' and 'Small', respectively. For selection time, pair-wise comparisons showed that our selection method had a significant reduction compared to Dwell ($p < 0.001$) and Dwell-free ($p < 0.001$), and there was also a significant difference between Dwell and Dwell-free ($p < 0.001$). The effect size of our selection method compared with other two were 'Huge'.

Table 2. The selection time, in seconds.

Condition	Avg $\pm$ std. dev.	$(CC_i\text{-}EC)/\ CC_i$	p	Cohen's d	Effect size
CC_1	1.18 ± 0.20	53.39%	$<0.001^*$	4.24	Huge
CC_2	0.73 ± 0.07	24.66%	$<0.001^*$	2.86	Huge
EC	0.55 ± 0.05				

Workload. The average scores for the six questions of the NASA-TLX questionnaire are shown in Fig. 8. Over all six questions, the ANOVA results showed significantly different workloads between the three methods ($F_{2,44} = 77.95$, $p < 0.001$, $\eta_p^2 = .780$). The pair-wise comparisons on overall score showed that our selection method had less workload on the user, compared to Dwell ($p < 0.001$) and Dwell-free ($p < 0.001$), and there was also a significant difference between Dwell and Dwell-free ($p < 0.001$).

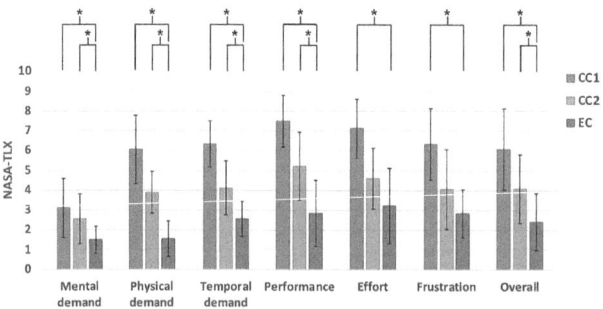

Fig. 8. Mean scores for the six individual questions and overall in NASA-TLX for three head-based selection methods (smaller value is better, from 0 to 10).

4.3   Discussion

The experimental results support our two hypotheses. Firstly, our head selection method has a faster typing speed and less selection time for a single letter. The Dwell and Dwell-free method require the user to control a cursor with the head and use the head motion to select keys on the layout. This is an unnatural way of selection because the user cannot freely deflect the head as they are used to. When using the two methods, we observed that participants moved their heads slowly at first when making a selection and then sped up as the cursor approached the target key, while this process was usually absent when using our head selection method. In addition, the Dwell method requires an additional period of dwell for selection determination, which results in a longer selection process. As reflected by the experimental results, the Dwell method had the slowest typing speed and the longest selection time.

Secondly, our head selection method has a lower workload. The Dwell and Dwell-free methods require the user to focus on a layout and use the head control a cursor to make the selection. Some participants reported that this kind of selection method made them tired quickly, while the orientation-based selection was simpler and easier, and they could make the right choice without hesitation. We decided to use our head motion-based selection method as the auxiliary selection method based on the above analysis.

5   User Study

A six-day user study was conducted to evaluate the performance of LipText, including typing speed and error rates. We divided the participants into a novice group and a potential expert group to explore how their performance would improve with the increased use of LipText. The hardware setup for this user study was the same as the previous pilot user study.

5.1   User Study Design

Participants. We recruited ten participants (eight males and two females, aged between 22–28) to participate in the user study, who formed a potential expert group and a novice group. The potential expert group participants were the top five performers from the previous pilot user study. The novice group was five participants who had not used our LipText, but had previous experience with VR head-mounted display devices.

Task and Procedure. The entire experiment was divided into six sessions, with each user required to complete one session per day, and in each session the user was required to complete ten randomly generated phrases from the Mackenzie phrase set [14]. In each session, participants were asked to complete each session as 'quickly and accurately' as possible. In total, we collected 5 (participants) × 2 (groups) × 6 (sessions) × 10 (phrases) = 600 phrases. The error rates were calculated according to [19], Total Error Rate (TER) = Not Corrected Error Rate (NCER) + Corrected Error Rate (CER).

5.2   Results

We conducted a mixed-design ANOVA on the experimental results, where 'session' (session 1–6) was the within-subject factors and 'group' (novice group and potential expert group) was the between-subject factors.

Typing Speed. We found that both 'session' ($F_{1.81,14.44} = 202.26$, $p < 0.001$, $\eta_p^2 - .96$) and 'session' $\times$ 'group' ($F_{1.81,14.44} = 4.870$, $p = .027$, $\eta_p^2 = .38$) had a significant effect on typing speed. This indicated that after a period of practice, participants in both groups experienced a significant increase in typing speed. And 'group' ($F_{1,8} = 24.71$, $p = .001$, $\eta_p^2 = .76$) was also found to have a significant effect on typing speed. In the pair-wise comparisons, significant differences were found between all session pairs (all $p < .01$) except for pair 3vs4. These results indicated that there was still an upward trend in the typing speed of the participants after six days of practice.

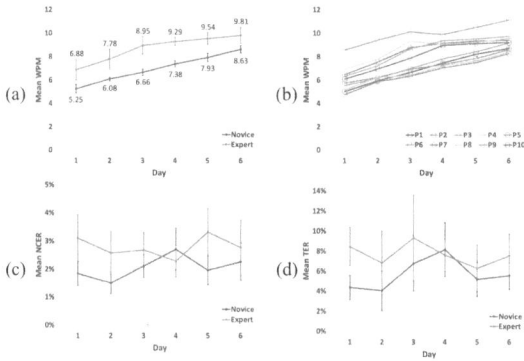

Fig. 9. Mean typing speed of novice group and potential expert group (a), mean typing speed of 10 participants (b), mean NCER (c) and TER (d) of novice group and potential expert group of 6 sessions.

Figure 9(a) shows the daily mean typing speed of two groups. The mean typing speed of the novice group was 6.99 WPM (s.e. = 0.25), and their typing speed increased from 5.25 WPM (s.e. = 0.34) on the first day to 8.63 WPM (s.e. = 0.26) on the last day, raising by 64.38%. The mean typing speed of the potential expert group was 8.71 WPM (s.e. = 0.25), and their typing speed increased from 6.88 WPM (s.e. = 0.34) on the first day to 9.81 WPM (s.e. = 0.26) on the last day, raising by 42.59%. Figure 9 (b) shows the daily mean typing speed of all ten participants, where the fastest typing speed was recorded as 11.13 WPM achieved by one potential expert participant on the last day.

Error Rates. For NCER, the results of ANOVA showed that 'session' ($F_{5,40} = .92$, $p = .48$, $\eta_p^2 = .103$) and 'session' $\times$ 'group' ($F_{5,40} = 2.35$, $p = .058$, $\eta_p^2 = .227$)

had no significant effects on it, while 'group' ($F_{1,8} = 7.62$, $p = .025$, $\eta_p^2 = .488$) had a significant effect on it, and the novice group had a significantly lower NCER than the potential expert group ($p = .025$) in the pair-wise comparisons. For TER, no significant effects were found on 'session' ($F_{1.96,15.69} = 2.36$, $p = .128$, $\eta_p^2 = .228$), 'session' × 'group' ($F_{1.96,15.69} = 1.25$, $p = .312$, $\eta_p^2 = .135$), and 'group' ($F_{1,8} = 3.20$, $p = .112$, $\eta_p^2 = .286$), and no significant differences were found in the pair-wise comparisons. The results indicated that multi-day training did not sacrifice accuracy. Figure 9(c) and (d) show the mean NCER and TER for ten participants over six days. The mean NCER and TER of the novice group for six days were 2.06% (s.e. = 0.19%) and 5.66% (s.e. = 0.79%) respectively. The mean NCER and TER of the potential expert group for six days were 2.79% (s.e. = 0.19%) and 7.66% (s.e. = 0.79%).

5.3   Discussion

In term of efficiency, our LipText can reach 11.13 WPM, which is comparable to the state-of-the-art hands-free methods, such as RingText (13.24 WPM) [23] and iText (13.76 WPM) [11]. And as we can see in Fig. 9(a) and (b), the learning curve of the participants is still on an upward trend, and we believe that the typing speed can still be improved after more time of practice. In terms of accuracy, the six-day average NCER and TER for the novice group and the potential expert group are 2.06%, 5.66% and 2.79%, 7.66%, respectively. It can be found that the TER is higher relative to NCER, and the error rates of the novice group are lower than that of the expert group. The statistical analysis results show that the NCER of the novice group is significantly smaller than that of the potential expert group. We find that the reason why TER is higher than NCER is that the model is still not accurate enough to predict the letters, such as 'B', 'C', 'D', 'E'. The reason for the lower error rates of the novice group than the potential expert group may be that reading silently at a slower speed gives a more complete lip shape and thus a more accurate prediction. In terms of learnability, after six days of practice, the average typing speed of all ten participants improved by 52.15%, with the novice group improving by 64.38% and the potential expert group improving by 42.59%. This shows that our LipText is very novice-friendly and users can master it after a short period of practice.

6   Conclusions, Limitations and Future Work

We have proposed LipText, a lip tracking-based text entry method in VR. Lip shape features are captured using a facial tracker and analyzed by a neural network to obtain the letters that the user reads silently. We also used the user's head motion to execute auxiliary selection to improve the correctness of text entry. Our method achieves 8.63 WPM for the novice group and 9.81 WPM for the potential expert group in typing speed and has the highest typing speed of 11.13 WPM. The error rates are 2.43% and 6.66% for NCER and TER respectively. Our method also has good learnability.

However, our method still has some limitations: 1) Limited dataset: We were unable to recruit enough participants, resulting in a smaller dataset, which prevented us from training a robust model. Additionally, the task is complex: users' speech rates are difficult to standardize, and several letters have similar lip shapes. These issues lead to limited model accuracy and a relatively high TER. 2) Model selection: We tested only three neural network models, which may not be the most suitable options for our task. 3) Inefficient selection process: Our method uses a two-step selection process, which is not the most efficient. 4) Letter-level input only: Our method currently supports only letter-level input, and the typing speed is constrained by the time overhead of the user's silent reading.

In future work, we plan to improve our method in the following areas: 1) Build a more comprehensive and generalizable dataset. Additionally, we will refine the design of the neural network to achieve more accurate and robust results, enabling single-step selection or reducing the need for two-step selections. 2) Redesign letters with similar lip shapes. As observed in the experimental results, 'space' achieved high accuracy both in the validation and test sets due to its distinct lip shape. Therefore, we may redesign letters with similar lip shapes to make them more distinguishable, improving model accuracy. 3) Incorporate word lip shape data into the dataset for word-level input, which could significantly increase the typing speed of our method.

Acknowledgments. This work was supported by the National Natural Science Foundation of China through Projects 61932003 and 62372026, by Beijing Science and Technology Plan Project Z221100007722004, and by NationalKey R&D plan 2019YFC1521102.

References

1. Adhikary, J., Vertanen, K.: Text entry in virtual environments using speech and a midair keyboard. IEEE Trans. Visual Comput. Graphics **27**(5), 2648–2658 (2021)
2. Fu, R., Zhang, Z., Li, L.: Using LSTM and GRU neural network methods for traffic flow prediction. In: 2016 31st Youth Academic Annual Conference of Chinese Association of Automation (YAC), pp. 324–328. IEEE (2016)
3. Garbe, W.: SymSpell (2012). https://github.com/wolfgarbe/SymSpell
4. Gers, F.A., Schraudolph, N.N., Schmidhuber, J.: Learning precise timing with LSTM recurrent networks. J. Mach. Learn. Res. **3**(Aug), 115–143 (2002)
5. Graves, A., Schmidhuber, J.: Framewise phoneme classification with bidirectional LSTM and other neural network architectures. Neural Netw. **18**(5–6), 602–610 (2005)
6. Gugenheimer, J., Dobbelstein, D., Winkler, C., Haas, G., Rukzio, E.: FaceTouch: enabling touch interaction in display fixed uis for mobile virtual reality. In: Proceedings of the 29th Annual Symposium on User Interface Software and Technology, pp. 49–60 (2016)
7. Hart, S.G.: Nasa-task load index (NASA-TLX); 20 years later. In: Proceedings of the Human Factors and Ergonomics Society Annual Meeting, vol. 50, pp. 904–908. Sage Publications, Los Angeles (2006)

8. Jiang, H., Weng, D.: HiPad: text entry for head-mounted displays using circular touchpad. In: 2020 IEEE Conference on Virtual Reality and 3D User Interfaces (VR), pp. 692–703 (2020). https://doi.org/10.1109/VR46266.2020.00092

9. Jiang, H., Weng, D., Zhang, Z., Bao, Y., Jia, Y., Nie, M.: HiKeyb: high-efficiency mixed reality system for text entry. In: 2018 IEEE International Symposium on Mixed and Augmented Reality Adjunct (ISMAR-Adjunct), pp. 132–137 (2018). https://doi.org/10.1109/ISMAR-Adjunct.2018.00051

10. Jiang, H., Weng, D., Zhang, Z., Chen, F.: HiFinger: one-handed text entry technique for virtual environments based on touches between fingers. Sensors **19**(14), 3063 (2019)

11. Lu, X., Yu, D., Liang, H.N., Goncalves, J.: iText: hands-free text entry on an imaginary keyboard for augmented reality systems. In: The 34th Annual ACM Symposium on User Interface Software and Technology, pp. 815–825 (2021)

12. Lu, X., et al.: Exploration of hands-free text entry techniques for virtual reality. In: 2020 IEEE International Symposium on Mixed and Augmented Reality (ISMAR), pp. 344–349. IEEE (2020)

13. MacKenzie, I.S.: A note on calculating text entry speed. Unpublished work (2002). http://www.yorku.ca/mack/RN-TextEntrySpeed.html

14. MacKenzie, I.S., Soukoreff, R.W.: Phrase sets for evaluating text entry techniques. In: CHI 2003 Extended Abstracts on Human Factors in Computing Systems, pp. 754–755 (2003)

15. Mott, M.E., Williams, S., Wobbrock, J.O., Morris, M.R.: Improving dwell-based gaze typing with dynamic, cascading dwell times. In: Proceedings of the 2017 CHI Conference on Human Factors in Computing Systems, pp. 2558–2570 (2017)

16. Pham, D.M., Stuerzlinger, W.: HawKEY: efficient and versatile text entry for virtual reality. In: 25th ACM Symposium on Virtual Reality Software and Technology, pp. 1–11 (2019)

17. Ruan, S., Wobbrock, J.O., Liou, K., Ng, A., Landay, J.A.: Comparing speech and keyboard text entry for short messages in two languages on touchscreen phones. Proc. ACM Interact. Mob. Wearable Ubiquit. Technol. **1**(4), 1–23 (2018)

18. Shneiderman, B.: The limits of speech recognition. Commun. ACM **43**(9), 63–65 (2000)

19. Soukoreff, R.W., MacKenzie, I.S.: Metrics for text entry research: an evaluation of MSD and KSPC, and a new unified error metric. In: Proceedings of the SIGCHI Conference on Human Factors in Computing Systems, pp. 113–120 (2003)

20. Vertanen, K.: Efficient correction interfaces for speech recognition. Ph.D. thesis, Citeseer (2009)

21. Whitmire, E., et al.: DigiTouch: reconfigurable thumb-to-finger input and text entry on head-mounted displays. Proc. ACM Interact. Mob. Wearable Ubiquit. Technol. **1**(3), 1–21 (2017)

22. Wikipedia contributors: International phonetic alphabet—Wikipedia, the free encyclopedia (2022). https://en.wikipedia.org/w/index.php?title=International_Phonetic_Alphabet&oldid=1087464357. Accessed 14 May 2022

23. Xu, W., Liang, H.N., Zhao, Y., Zhang, T., Yu, D., Monteiro, D.: RingText: dwell-free and hands-free text entry for mobile head-mounted displays using head motions. IEEE Trans. Visual Comput. Graphics **25**(5), 1991–2001 (2019). https://doi.org/10.1109/TVCG.2019.2898736

24. Xu, Z., et al.: BiTipText: bimanual eyes-free text entry on a fingertip keyboard. In: Proceedings of the 2020 CHI Conference on Human Factors in Computing Systems, pp. 1–13 (2020)

25. Yu, C., Gu, Y., Yang, Z., Yi, X., Luo, H., Shi, Y.: Tap, dwell or gesture? Exploring head-based text entry techniques for HMDs. In: Proceedings of the 2017 CHI Conference on Human Factors in Computing Systems, pp. 4479–4488 (2017)
26. Yu, D., Fan, K., Zhang, H., Monteiro, D., Xu, W., Liang, H.N.: PizzaText: text entry for virtual reality systems using dual thumbsticks. IEEE Trans. Visual Comput. Graphics **24**(11), 2927–2935 (2018). https://doi.org/10.1109/TVCG.2018.2868581

Subthreshold Depression Recognition and Correlation Study from Pulse Condition via Stacking Ensemble Algorithm

Han Jiang[1,2(✉)], Ming Li[1,2], Yang Gao[1,2], and Peiru Li[2]

[1] State Key Laboratory of Virtual Reality Technology and Systems, Beihang University, Beijing, China
{09324,minglee,gaoyangvr}@buaa.edu.cn
[2] School of Computer Science and Engineering, Beihang University, Beijing, China
22371237@buaa.edu.cn

Abstract. Subthreshold depression, a transition state to depression, seriously hinders the early diagnosis of depression. Current studies mostly use heterogeneous definitions of subthreshold depression, making the results of such meta-analyses questionable. Therefore, it is of vital significance to develop an objective method for the diagnosis of subthreshold depression based on objective criteria. In traditional Chinese medicine (TCM), symptoms similar to subthreshold depression have been extensively explored. However, diagnostic methods in TCM still depend heavily on the experience of doctors and lack integration with modern diagnostic techniques, which makes it challenging to explain the pathogenesis of subthreshold depression. Consequently, we propose an explainable framework, based on a stacking ensemble algorithm, for subthreshold depression recognition from biomarkers in the pulse waveform and concepts of pulse in TCM. In this method, Naive Bayes, Random Forest, Extremely Randomized Trees, Categorical Boosting and Logistic Regression are chosen as basic learners, and XGBoost is selected as the meta-classifier. Based on the five-fold cross-validation method, grid search method and repetition of training, the stacking ensemble model shows superiority on most performance evaluation metrics including AUC, F1 scores, MCC, precision and sensitivity. Besides, by analyzing the Adjusted Odds Ratio of features in the pulse waveform, we obtained four features that have a high correlation with the occurrence of subthreshold depression and derived physiological changes in patients with subthreshold depression based on their physiological significance.

Keywords: Subthreshold depression · Pulse · Traditional chinese medicine · Stacking ensemble algorithm · Adjusted odds ratio

1 Introduction

Subthreshold depression(SD) refers to a condition where a patient experiences at least any 2 of the depressive symptoms without the essential features [1],

© The Author(s), under exclusive license to Springer Nature Singapore Pte Ltd. 2025
W. Song et al. (Eds.): ICXR 2024, LNCS 15461, pp. 179–194, 2025.
https://doi.org/10.1007/978-981-96-3679-2_12

including symptoms such as low mood, insomnia, mental fatigue, difficulty concentrating, and negative self-evaluation. The prevalence of subthreshold depression in the general population is 11.9% and patients have a risk of developing major depression in the future that is three times higher than healthy people. As a psychological subhealth state, subthreshold depression produces remarkable decrements in health and does not qualitatively differ from full-blown episodes of depression as currently defined, and lies on a continuum with more severe forms of depressive episodes but are distinct from normal mood changes [3].

The lack of clear objective criteria complicates the clinical assessment, often resulting in confusion with mild depression or missed diagnosis [4]. Objective physiological criteria are rarely studied and applied in the diagnosis of subthreshold depression. Psychiatrists always employ standardized scales, such as HAMD, PHQ-9, MADRS and BD [5,6] to subjectively evaluate and corroborate diagnoses based on their extensive clinical experience. This subjective assumption results in great bias in diagnostic outcomes. Therefore, it is of vital significance to develop a convincing and objective diagnostic method, harnessing physiological signals that provide comprehensive physiological information [7,8].

Common physiological signals, including functional near-infrared reflectance spectroscopy(fNIRS), electroencephalography (EEG), electrocardiography (ECG), and electromyography(EMG), perform well in the diagnosis of major depression. According to Tao Ran et al. [9], based on sleep EEG signals, it was found that the EEG signal characteristics of the delta-theta-beta wave combination during the REM stage achieved a depression recognition accuracy of 92.8% and a precision of 93.8%. Hong Song et al. [10] utilized fNIRS and achieved a satisfactory classification with an accuracy of 89.71% for total and 92.59% for patients. However, those signals are not utilized in the diagnosis of subthreshold depression. Therefore, we put forward a creative method using pulse condition, a new concept that combined pulse waveform and pulse-related concepts in Traditional Chinese Medicine(TCM) in the stacking ensemble algorithm(Stella).

As one of the most popular machine learning methods, initially put forward by Wolpert in 1992 [11], its basic idea is to train a number of different models(basic learners) and then train a single model(meta learner) that takes the output of each previously trained model as input to produce a final output. In most supervised learning tasks (regression, classification, etc.), it often achieves better performance than any basic learner.

The pulse condition, selected in our Stella model as the original input, can fully reflect the physiological condition of the body. Pulse waveform represents the rhythmic expansion and contraction of arteries due to the pumping action of the heart. As shown in Fig. 1, the pulse waveform represents the rhythmic expansion and contraction of arteries due to the pumping action of the heart. The waveform typically consists of a sharp upstroke, known as the percussion wave peak, followed by a gradual decline, which represents the percussion wave norch. Following the percussion wave, the tidal wave and dicrotic wave oscillate in a similar manner. Pulse condition signal, combining pulse waveform and TCM concepts such as pulse width, pulse body, pulse stream and pulse power, is widely utilized in disease detection [12–16]. When combined with TCM concepts, these signals can offer a comprehensive reflection of human physiological conditions. According to Muhammad N. Iqbal et al. [17], subthreshold depression has been linked to an increased risk of developing cardiovascular disease. Besides, according to the theory of TCM, emotions have an important influence on the physical condition of a person [18]. It can be speculated that the use of pulse signals to identify subthreshold depression has great feasibility.

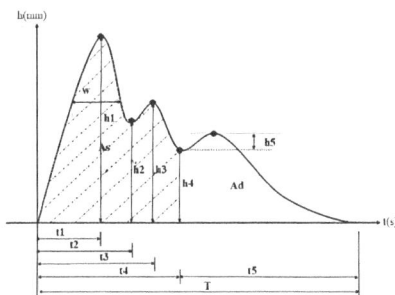

Fig. 1. Frequently used pulse wave features. h_1: Amplitude of percussion wave peak. h_2: Amplitued of percussion wave notch h_3: Amplitude of tidal wave peak. h_4: Amplitude of dicrotic notch. h_5: Amplitude difference of dicrotic wave and its norch. t_i: Arrival time of h_i. as: Integral of pulse waveform during contraction. ad: Integral of pulse waveform during diastole. w_i: The i'th wave duration of the width of a third place. t: Pulse cycle.

Current models based on pulse conditions are more inclined to use discrete data and TCM features extracted from pulse waveform data. After denoising, baseline wander removal and pulse signal quality assessment, the processed pulse signals then undergo period segmentation and normalization. Following this, a sliding window is employed to pinpoint the peak of each individual period. Subsequently, various strategies are employed to identify the split points on the left side of each peak. [19] Therefore, discrete data can be obtained by time domain and frequency domain analysis methods, such as fast fourier transform(FFT), wavelet transform (WT) and short-time fourier transform(STFT) [20–22]. In long-term experiments, researchers identify important features in the pulse waveform and frequently use them in the detection of disease.

Models based on pulse waveform have achieved promising outcomes in tasks related to cardiovascular disease, but perform poorly in the domain of mental illness. The primary rationale behind this oversight lies in the neglect of physiological information from other organs within the pulse waveform. According to existing research, mental illness exacts a toll on the body holistically [24–26]. As physicians in TCM can infer the overall health status of the human body from aspects such as the frequency, rhythm, filling degree, patency, and amplitude of fluctuation of the pulse, we consider those concepts. We summarize our contributions and the pipeline is shown in Fig. 2.

1. We propose the Stella model consisting of five basic learners using discrete features extracted from pulse waveform and pulse condition in TCM to achieve the identification of patients with subthreshold depression.
2. In the experiment, we compare the performance of our Stella model with other machine learning methods using five evaluation metrics and demonstrate its effectiveness compared with related works.
3. Using the Adjusted Odds Ratio, we obtained biomarkers that correlate to a great extent with the development of subthreshold depression in the pulse waveform.

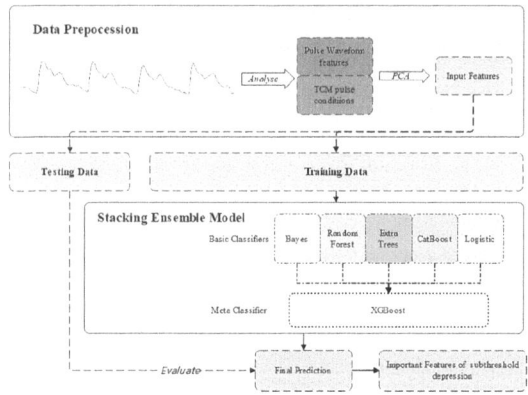

Fig. 2. Schematic overview of the workflow. After extracting two types of feature values from the waveform data, PCA is performed and then the results are used to train our Stella model. Finally, features that have a great correlation with subthreshold depression are extracted.

2   Materials and Methods

2.1   Dataset

Pulse waveform and TCM features utilized in this study are extracted from the ZM-IIIC type pulse acquisition system developed by Shanghai Yilian Medical Instrument Development Ltd, since there is no publicly available dataset with both pulse waveform and TCM features. All the data was collected from the pulse signal while the subject was in a sitting position. After 6 rounds of equidistant pressure sampling every 10 s, we select an optimal pressure set for a 45-second sampling to obtain the final waveform. Subsequently, TCM features and discrete features in the waveform are obtained through instrument analysis. The dataset includes 42 subthreshold depression patients (12 males and 30 females, aged between 18–30) and 21 healthy subjects (19 males and 2 females, aged between 18–30), with no between-group differences in age and gender. All subthreshold depressive patients met the criteria of the HAMD-17 scale, with scores ranging from 7 to 17 and experiencing two or more depressive symptoms for at least two weeks, as diagnosed by professional psychiatrists.

Even though the gender distribution is imbalanced, we investigate from a previous research [45] that there are no significant differences between the genders in terms of impaired subjective, social and occupational functioning. In case that samples came from undergraduate, graduate and doctoral students, the main factors that lead to subthreshold depression are social and occupational functioning. The imbalanced gender distribution is negligible.

2.2 Data Preprocessing

Noise and baseline wander, caused by the surrounding environment and physiological activities including slight movement of the wrist and breath [27], were reduced by the instrument. We obtain fifteen biomarkers that can be directly extracted from the pulse waveform. In order to determine whether there are strong correlations between the features in the waveform, correlation analysis is performed and the results are shown in Fig. 3.

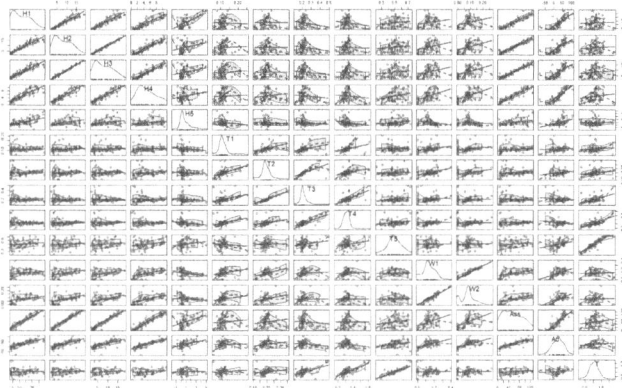

Fig. 3. the Scatter Plot Matrix of the Correlation Analysis.

Besides, multicollinearity among features is tested and it is discovered that the variance inflation factors(VIF) of h_3(144.04), h_4(30539.97), h_5(72740.31), ass(105.19) and T(125046.01) are much more than 10, which indicates that there is severe multicollinearity among those features [28] and dimension reduction is necessary. After adding other features including TCM concepts that are unrelated to each other and $h_3/h_1, h_4/h_1, h_5/h_1, t_5/t_4, w_1/T$ and w_2/T which can reflect the coefficient of tension, elasticity and residence of peripheral artery [29], the data dimension before dimension reduction ultimately reached 35. Therefore, Principal Component Analysis(PCA) is performed to reduce the dimensionality of the dataset while preserving most of its variability [30]. The dimension of 35 feature values was reduced to 18 and the scatter plot(two principle components for visualization) is shown in Fig. 4.

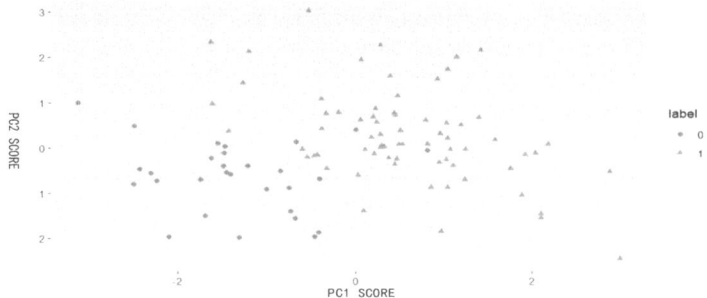

Fig. 4. PCA Scatter Plot. Label 1 means patients with subthreshold depression and label 0 means healthy people.

2.3　Stacking Ensemble Algorithm Model

The stacking ensemble algorithm, as one of the most popular ensemble algorithms, stands out for its multilevel framework. It usually adopts a two-tier architecture, where the initial layer comprises multiple basic learners, while the subsequent layer houses a meta-learner. It typically employs strategies such as weighted averaging or voting to combine the predictions of multiple basic models. These strategies involve weighting based on the performance of each model or voting based on the prediction probabilities of basic learners, resulting in the final prediction outcome. Due to their excellent generalization ability and robustness, ensemble learning models can reduce model variance and improve the overall performance of the model. In practical applications, ensemble learning offers the flexibility to select suitable ensemble learning algorithms based on specific problems and data characteristics and to fine-tune the base learners and ensemble strategies to achieve better predictive performance.

Given the high degree of dispersion in our features and the utilization of a small-scale dataset, we have opted for tree-based and linear-based basic learners. These basic learners are less constrained by sample size limitations, which can avoid overfitting problems whenever possible. In this study, Gaussian Naive Bayes (Bayes) [31], Random Forest (RF) [32], Extra Trees (ET) [33], Categorical Boosting (clf) [34] and Logistic regression (lg) [35] were chosen as basic learners, and XGBoost (xg) [36] was selected as the meta classifier, based on the idea of reducing the sensitivity of the model to noise and discrete data. Our idea of selecting base learners is based on the stacking idea of increasing diversity regarding algorithmic principles, strengths, and weaknesses.

1. Gaussian Naive Bayes is a simple probabilistic model based on Bayes' theorem and assumes feature independence. It performs well on small datasets and for problems where the independence assumption approximately holds.
2. Random Forest is effective in handling datasets with higher dimensionality and is less sensitive to noisy data, making it a solid choice for stacking due to its robustness.

3. ET makes it less prone to overfitting and faster to train. It adds additional diversity to the ensemble by introducing randomness, which complements the base learners well.
4. Logistic Regression is a simple, linear model that performs well for binary classification. Its inclusion adds a linear perspective to the ensemble, which helps balance the more complex models.
5. CatBoost is a gradient-boosting algorithm that excels at handling categorical data. It helps improve the ensemble's ability to capture complex, non-linear relationships in the data.

Besides, the GridSearchCV method was used for adjusting model parameters and 5-fold cross-validation was utilized to evaluate the performance of basic learners. GridSearchCV is quite well-suited for small datasets. This approach utilizes enumeration to achieve automatic parameter tuning, aiming to obtain the optimal results and parameters. Through stacking, basic learners' distinctive characteristics and strengths can be fully leveraged, therefore better utilizing the features and enhancing the overall performance. Our Stella architecture is shown in Fig. 5.

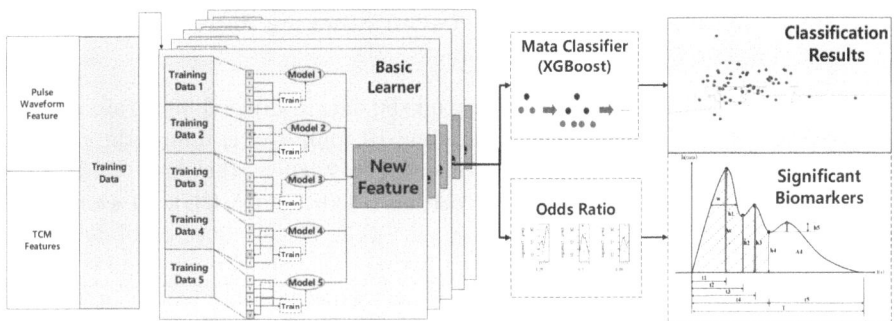

Fig. 5. The Architecture of Our Stella Model.

2.4 Correlation Study Method

To obtain the strength of association between the subthreshold depression and pulse features, Odds Ratio(OR) was introduced. In binary classification tasks, it is usually defined as the ratio of the probability of an event occurring between two groups. If the event occurs with probability $P1$ and $P2$, then OR can be defined as follows:

$$\text{Odds Ratio} = \frac{P_1/(1 - P_1)}{P_2/(1 - P_2)} \tag{1}$$

OR is often used in research to investigate the difference between two treatments, two treatments, or two influencing factors, and to assess the impact of a factor on the occurrence of an event. It can provide a deeper understanding and help researchers make more accurate inferences and decisions. Therefore, in this study, considering the multi-factor influence, we refer to the adjusted Odds Ratio(adj. OR) to analyze features that have a significant correlation with the occurrence of subthreshold depression.

Using logistic regression model [37], we can calculate the adjusted odds ratio (adj. OR) to analyze features significantly correlated with the occurrence of subthreshold depression while considering multiple influencing factors. For example, if β_1 is the coefficient of feature X_1, the adj. OR for X_1 would be e^{β_1}. This provides a measure of the relative impact of each feature on the odds of subthreshold depression, adjusting for the effects of other variables in the model.

The significance of the adj. OR can be assessed using confidence intervals and hypothesis testing. A 95% confidence interval that does not include 1 indicates that the odds ratio is statistically significant at the 0.05 level, suggesting a significant association between the feature and the occurrence of subthreshold depression. Using the adj. OR, we can obtain features that have a high correlation with the occurrence of subthreshold depression.

3   Experiments and Results

3.1   Performance Comparison Between Stacking and Basic Models on the Testing Datasets

Performing Stratified Random Sampling on the data is divided into training and testing sets in a 13:7 ratio. After undergoing 10 rounds of training, the metrics are averaged to derive the final outcome. In this study, the Area Under the ROC Curve(AUC), the Matthews Correlation Coefficient (MCC), F1 score(F1), accuracy and sensitivity are employed to assess the performance of models. The outcomes of the performance comparison between our Stella model and its basic models on the AUC, F1, MCC, precision and sensitivity are shown in Table 1 and Fig. 6.

Table 1. Comparison of the performance of models

Index	Bayes	Random Forest	Extra Trees	Categorical Boosting	Logistic	Stella
AUC	**0.9286**	0.8095	0.7143	0.6429	0.4524	0.8810
F1	0.72 ± 0.01	0.61 ± 0.072	0.67 ± 0.12	0.69 ± 0.03	0.54 ± 0.05	$\mathbf{0.89 \pm 0.05}$
MCC	$0.54 \pm 6e^{-3}$	$0.65 \pm 9e^{-3}$	$0.51 \pm 1e^{-3}$	$0.49 \pm 1e^{-3}$	$0.36 \pm 1e^{-3}$	$\mathbf{0.74 \pm 6e^{-3}}$
Precision	$0.83 \pm 2e^{-4}$	$0.79 \pm 4e^{-4}$	$0.81 \pm 4e^{-4}$	$0.825me^{-4}$	$0.74 \pm 4e^{-4}$	$\mathbf{0.92 \pm 3e^{-4}}$
Sensitivity	0.5707	0.7784	0.5912	0.7500	0.6334	**0.8079**

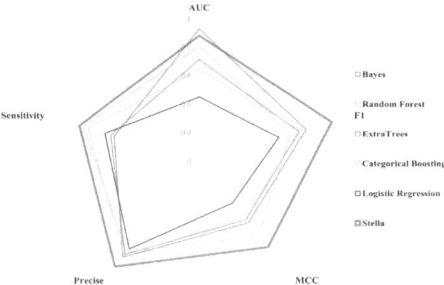

Fig. 6. the Performance of Basic Models and Our Stella Model.

As shown in Fig. 6 and Table 1, our Stella model has the highest F1 score, MCC, precise and sensitivity. The model's performance metrics (such as accuracy, recall, F1 score, AUC-ROC area under the curve, etc.) meet the expected standards and demonstrate good performance across different evaluation metrics. The comparative outcomes suggest that the Stella model can capture more features in the dataset and perform well in the diagnosis of subthreshold depression, which enables our model to capture general patterns in the data rather than memorizing specific instances from the training data. As for AUC, our Stella model did not show its superiority. This may be because if the number of samples in one class of the training data is much larger than that of the other classes, the Stella model may tend to optimize the dominant class, resulting in poorer classification performance for the smaller classes [38].

Besides, we show the ACC results in the Table 2. The results indicate that our Stella model can achieve a high accuracy rate while maintaining stable variance. To evaluate and compare the goodness of fit, we use the metric, Akaike Information Criterion(AIC) is defined as follows:

$$AIC = 2k - 2ln(L) \tag{2}$$

Here, k is the number of parameters and L is the likelihood function. AIC can evaluate the complexity of the estimated model and the goodness of fit. Upon most occasions, using the same dataset, models with lower AIC value have better goodness of fit and lower risk of overfitting [39].

Table 2. ACC Results

Model Name	ACC Results
Stella	**90.40 ± 1.47**
Bayes	83.03 ± 4.64
Random Forest	82.19 ± 4.97
ExtraTrees	80.46 ± 1.90
Categorical Boosting	81.18 ± 2.81
Logistic	70.43 ± 4.45

However, when calculating the Akaike Information Criterion(AIC) to evaluate the goodness of fit of models, we find that the AIC of the Stella model is much more higher than its basic learners. Detailed AIC values are shown in the Table 3.

Table 3. AIC of Stella and its Basic Learners

Model Name	Akaike Information Criterion
Stella	**232.8067**
Bayes	27.4588
Random Forest	46.2631
ExtraTrees	38.0000
Categorical Boosting	21.7153
Logistic	57.6371

The AIC of the Stella model is several times higher than its basic learners, which may indicate the Stella model is ineffective. However, considering the aforementioned metrics, the Stella model can still perform well in the diagnosis of subthreshold depression. Our stacking approach resulted in a significant increase in the number of parameters, and therefore increased the value of k; We attribute this sharp increase in AIC values to the fact that the stacking ensemble method combines several machine learning methods and therefore increases the complexity of the Stella model, which sharply increases AIC.

In Fig. 7, we analyze the Pearson correlation results of the basic models utilized within the Stella model framework.

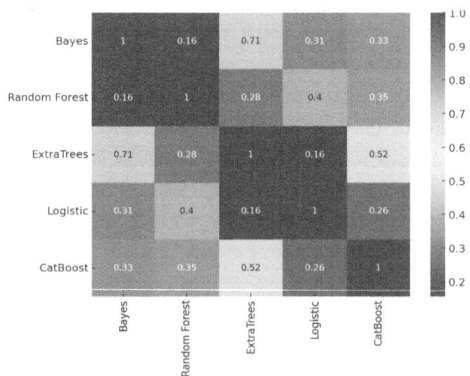

Fig. 7. Results of Basic Model Correlation Studies

These results reflect the appropriateness of our model selection, demonstrating strong correlations between predicted outcomes and actual results. The high correlation coefficients suggest that the chosen basic models effectively capture the underlying patterns in the data, thereby validating the rationality of leveraging them in the Stella model.

In conclusion, the Stella model is more stable, robust and accurate than its basic learners. Even though the stacking ensemble learning method has increased the complexity of the Stella model, it performs well in many metrics. Besides, the classification result of our Stella model is shown in Fig. 8. The boundary in the picture shows that in the small-size dataset, the Stella model can still perform well in this classification task.

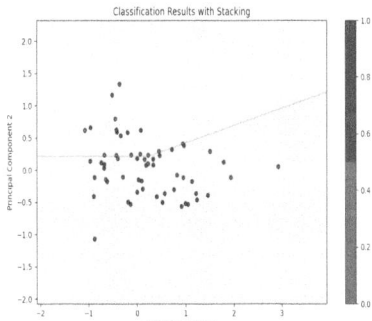

Fig. 8. Classification Result of the Stella Model. Blue lable means patients with subthreshold depression and red means healthy people. (Color figure online)

3.2   Comparision with Related Studies

Compared to other studies employing various biomarkers and AI techniques, our model has exhibited superior diagnostic accuracy for subthreshold depression.

In the research conducted by Yao et al. [40], serum levels of histone deacetylase-3 (HDAC3) and brain-derived neurotrophic factor (BDNF) were utilized for diagnosing subthreshold depression. The area under the curve (AUC) values for diagnosing subthreshold depression in adolescents based on serum HDAC3 and BDNF levels, both individually and in combination, were found to be 0.815, 0.777, and 0.866, respectively, which are comparatively lower than ours.

Additionally, in the realm of deep learning methodologies, Yin Xiaolong et al. [41] integrated collected MRI and fMRI data into the BrainNetCNN framework and employed network fusion techniques to comprehensively analyze the two distinct modalities for detecting subthreshold depression. Regarding traditional machine learning approaches, Costafreda, Sergi G et al. [42] utilized MRI data, while Marquand, Andre F et al. and Rondina [43] employed fMRI data, consistently employing Support Vector Machine(SVM) classifiers for the recognition of subthreshold depression.

A comparative analysis of the same metrics across different studies is presented in Table 4. It indicates that our stacking ensemble model has a better integrated performance of precision and recall. The lack of sensitivity may be due to the higher complexity of CNN, and the insufficient amount of training data.

Table 4. Comparison with BrainNetCNN and SVM models

Method Name	Modality	Precision	F1	Sensitivity
BrainNetCNN	MRI+fMRI	0.7857	0.8188	**0.8714**
Costafreda SVM	MRI	0.6760	/	0.6490
Marquand SVM	fMRI	0.6800	/	0.6500
Rondina SVM	fMRI	0.7200	/	0.7700
Stella	Pulse	**0.9167**	**0.8899**	0.8079

3.3   Odds Ratio Results

When exploring the biomarkers with a high correlation with the occurrence of subthreshold depression, we select 13 features in the pulse waveform in order to get a clearer physiological meaning. The features that we select include t_1 to t_5, h_1 to h_5, $w1$, $w2$ and T. Using Logistic Regression, Curves of the corresponding adj. OR values are shown in Fig. 9.

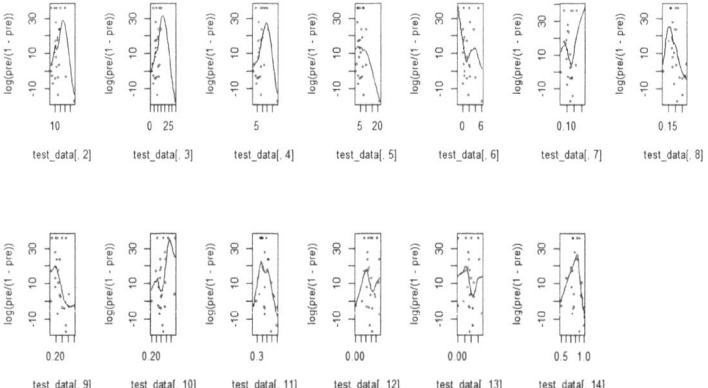

Fig. 9. Curves of adj. OR value(test data from 2 to 14 are t_i, h_i, w_1, w_2 and T).

The adj. OR values of features in the pulse waveform that have an important correlation (the absolute value of the difference from 1 is greater than 0.5) within the interval of 95% confidence level and their physiological meanings are shown in Table 5. The table shows that the increase in h_2 and h_3, and the decrease in h_1 and h_5, will promote the occurrence of subthreshold depression. According to their physiological meanings, we can infer that in patients with subthreshold depression, there is a decrease in left ventricular ejection function, arterial elasticity of large arteries, and aortic valve function, alongside an increase in peripheral arterial resistance.

Table 5. Significant features in the pulse waveform and their physiological meanings

Feature Name	adj. OR Value	physiological meaning
h_1	0.3865178	Ejection function of left ventricle, the compliance of aorta
h_2	1.8078769	Arterial elasticity, peripheral resistance status
h_3	4.1894124	the same with H_2
h_5	0.4292125	Great arterial elasticity, aortic valve function

It is noteworthy that the adj. OR value of h_3 is 4.1894124, which has a much stronger correlation with the occurrence of subthreshold depression, compared to other significant biomarkers. h_3 represents the height of the tidal wave peak, which reflects the pumping capacity of the heart, arterial elasticity, blood pressure level and peripheral resistance. This height is directly related to arterial blood pressure. If the crest height is too high, it may indicate hypertension, which is one of the major symptoms of mental illness.

3.4 Limitations

This study's limitation lies in its exclusive reliance on machine learning classifiers, neglecting the utilization of deep learning models. Deep learning models usually require large amounts of labeled data for training. If the dataset is too small, the model may struggle to learn meaningful features and is prone to overfitting. However, the available data for subthreshold depression patients and healthy people is notably limited. Besides, due to the lack of pertinent data for patients with depression, it is difficult to distinguish the pulse characteristics of patients with subthreshold depression from those with depression.

4   Conclusion

In the absence of objective diagnostic methods for subthreshold depression, this research proposes the Stella model based on the stacking ensemble algorithm in machine learning. Based on the self-collected dataset, we found that our model has shown stability and accuracy in the diagnosis of subthreshold depression when compared with related works. Besides, by introducing the Adjusted Odds Ratio into this study, we obtained significant features in pulse waveforms that have a high correlation with the occurrence of subthreshold depression.

Acknowledgments. This work was supported by the National Key R&D Program of China (2023YFC3604500), National Natural Science Foundation of China (L2324214), and CAMS Innovation Fund for Medical Sciences (CIFMS) under Grant (2019-I2M-5-016).

References

1. Judd, L.L., et al.: Subsyndromal symptomatic depression: a new mood disorder? J. Clin. Psychiatry **55**(Suppl), 18–28 (1994)
2. Zhang, R., Peng, X., Song, X., et al.: The prevalence and risk of developing major depression among individuals with subthreshold depression in the general population. Psychol. Med. **53**(8), 3611–3620 (2023)
3. Ayuso-Mateos, J.L., et al.: From depressive symptoms to depressive disorders: the relevance of thresholds. Br. J. Psychiatry: J. Ment. Sci. **196**(5), 365–371 (2010)
4. Ma, Y., et al.: What can facial movements reveal? Depression recognition and analysis based on optical flow using Bayesian networks. IEEE Trans. Neural Syst. Rehabil. Eng. **31**, 3459–3468 (2023)
5. Seemüller, F., et al.: A factor analytic comparison of three commonly used depression scales (HAMD, MADRS, BDI) in a large sample of depressed inpatients. BMC Psychiatry **23**(1), 548 (2023)
6. Kroenke, K., et al.: The PHQ-9: validity of a brief depression severity measure. J. Gen. Intern. Med. **16**(9), 606–613 (2001)
7. Liu, T., et al.: Multichannel flexible pulse perception array for intelligent disease diagnosis system. ACS Nano **17**(6), 5673–5685 (2023)
8. Mo, S.: Research of emotion recognition based on photoplethysmography (PPG). Hans J. Biomed. **11**, 75–86 (2021)
9. Tao, R., et al.: Identifying depressive disorder with sleep electroencephalogram data: a study based on deep learning. J. Sichuan Univ. (Med. Sci.) **54**(2), 287–292 (2023)
10. Lan, K.-C., et al.: Traditional Chinese medicine pulse diagnosis on a smartphone using skin impedance at acupoints: a feasibility study. Sens. (Basel Switz.) **20**(16), 4618 (2020)
11. Wolpert, D.H.: Stacked generalization. Neural Netw. **5**(2), 241–259 (1992)
12. Song, H., et al.: Automatic depression discrimination on FNIRS by using general linear model and SVM. In: 2014 7th International Conference on Biomedical Engineering and Informatics, Dalian, China, pp. 278–282 (2014)
13. Moura, N.G.R., et al.: Traditional Chinese medicine wrist pulse-taking is associated with pulse waveform analysis and hemodynamics in hypertension. J. Integr. Med. **14**(2), 100–113 (2016)
14. Chen, J., et al.: A machine learning method correlating pulse pressure wave data with pregnancy. Int. J. Numer. Methods Biomed. Eng. **36**(1), e3272 (2020)
15. Chao, W., et al.: Effect of traditional Chinese medicine combined with western medicine on blood lipid levels and inflammatory factors in patients with angina pectoris in coronary heart disease identified as intermingled phlegm and blood stasis Syndrome: A Network Meta-Analysis. J. Tradit. Chin. Med. = Chung I Tsa Chih Ying Wen Pan **43**(4), 640–649 (2023)
16. Zeng, C., et al.: Efficacy of traditional Chinese medicine, Maxingshigan-Weijing in the management of COVID-19 patients with severe acute respiratory syndrome: a structured summary of a study protocol for a randomized controlled trial. Trials **21**(1), 1029 (2020)

17. Iqbal, M.N., Iqbal, F.: Subthreshold depression and its association with cardio-vascular risk. Ann. Clin. Psychiatry: Off. J. Am. Acad. Clin. Psychiatrists **31**(2), 130–136 (2019)
18. Liu, S., et al.: The interpretation of human body in traditional Chinese medicine and its influence on the characteristics of TCM theory. Anatom. Rec. (Hoboken N.J.: 2007) **304**(11), 2559–2565 (2021)
19. Zhang, Z., et al.: A sensor-based wrist pulse signal processing and lung cancer recognition. J. Biomed. Inform. **79**, 107–116 (2018)
20. Zhang, D., et al.: Wavelet based analysis of doppler ultrasonic wrist-pulse signals. In: 2008 International Conference on BioMedical Engineering and Informatics, vol. 2, pp. 539–543 (2008)
21. Guo, Q.-L., Wang, K.-Q., Zhang, D.-Y., Li, N.-M.: A wavelet packet based pulse waveform analysis for cholecystitis and nephrotic syndrome diagnosis. In: 2008 International Conference on Wavelet Analysis and Pattern Recognition, Hong Kong, China, pp. 513–517 (2008)
22. Huang, Q., et al.: Key points recognition of pulse wave based on wavelet transform. In: 2011 4th International Conference on Biomedical Engineering and Informatics (BMEI), Shanghai, China, pp. 1753–1756 (2011)
23. Chan, K.L., et al.: Central regulation of stress-evoked peripheral immune responses. Nat. Rev. Neurosci. **24**(10), 591–604 (2023)
24. Shrestha, M., et al.: Association between subthreshold depression and self-care behaviours in adults with type 2 diabetes: a cross-sectional study. J. Clin. Nurs. **30**(17–18), 2462–2468 (2021)
25. Muldoon, M.F., Sloan, R.P.: Editorial to accompany AMGP-22-25R1. Visit-to-visit blood pressure variability and subthreshold depressive symptoms in older adults, by Sible, et al.: blood pressure variability: trash or treasure?. Am. J. Geriatr. Psychiatry: Off. J. Am. Assoc. Geriatr. Psychiatry **30**(10), 1120–1122 (2022)
26. Mokhtar, N.M., et al.: Prevalence of subthreshold depression among constipation-predominant irritable bowel syndrome patients. Front. Psychol. **11**, 1936 (2020)
27. Zschocke, J., et al.: Reconstruction of pulse wave and respiration from wrist accelerometer during sleep. IEEE Trans. Bio-Med. Eng. **69**(2), 830–839 (2022)
28. Snee, R.: Who invented the variance inflation factor? (1981). https://doi.org/10.13140/RG.2.1.3274.8562
29. Li, X., et al.: Computerized wrist pulse signal diagnosis using gradient boosting decision tree. In: 2018 IEEE International Conference on Bioinformatics and Biomedicine (BIBM), Madrid, Spain, pp. 1941–1947 (2018)
30. Pearson, K.: LIII. On lines and planes of closest fit to systems of points in space. London Edinburgh Dublin Philos. Mag. J. Sci. **2**(11), 559–572 (1901)
31. Jahromi, A.H., Taheri, M.: A non-parametric mixture of Gaussian naive Bayes classifiers based on local independent features. In: 2017 Artificial Intelligence and Signal Processing Conference (AISP), Shiraz, Iran, pp. 209–212 (2017)
32. Breiman, L.: Random forests. Mach. Learn. **45**(1), 5–32 (2001)
33. Geurts, P., Ernst, D., Wehenkel, L.: Extremely randomized trees. Mach. Learn. **63**(1), 3–42 (2006)
34. Dorogush, A.V., et al.: CatBoost: gradient boosting with categorical features support. ArXiv abs/1810.11363 (2018)
35. Komarek, P.: Logistic regression for data mining and high-dimensional classification. Carnegie Mellon University (2004)
36. Chen, T., Guestrin, C.: XGBoost: a scalable tree boosting system. In: Proceedings of the 22nd ACM SIGKDD International Conference on Knowledge Discovery and Data Mining (2016)

37. Burgess, S., CRP CHD Genetics Collaboration: Identifying the odds ratio estimated by a two-stage instrumental variable analysis with a logistic regression model. Stat. Med. **32**(27), 4726–4747 (2013)
38. Mohammed, R., Rawashdeh, J., Abdullah, M.: Machine learning with oversampling and undersampling techniques: overview study and experimental results. In: 2020 11th International Conference on Information and Communication Systems (ICICS), Irbid, Jordan, pp. 243–248 (2020)
39. Akaike, H.: A new look at the statistical model identification. IEEE Trans. Autom. Control **19**(6), 716–723 (1974)
40. Yao, Q., Kang, Y., Zhou, J., Liu, X., Xu, Q.: Subthreshold depression cognitive dysfunction histone deacetylase-3 brain-derived neurotrophic factor diagnosis in adolescents. J. Difficult Dis. **5**, 479–483 (2023)
41. Xiaolong, Y., Li Demin, T., Ya, S.B.: Identification of subthreshold depression based on deep learning and multimodal medical image fusion. J. Med. Imaging **29**(8), 1234–1245 (2020)
42. Costafreda, S., et al.: Prognostic and diagnostic potential of the structural neuroanatomy of depression. PloS One **4**, e6353 (2009)
43. Marquand, A.F., et al.: Neuroanatomy of verbal working memory as a diagnostic biomarker for depression. Neuroreport **19**(15), 1507–1511 (2008)
44. Rondina, J.M., et al.: SCoRS-a method based on stability for feature selection and mapping in neuroimaging. IEEE Trans. Med. Imaging **33**(1), 85–98 (2014)
45. Piccinelli, M., Wilkinson, G.: Gender differences in depression: critical review. Br. J. Psychiatry **177**(6), 486–492 (2000). https://doi.org/10.1192/bjp.177.6.486

SIE-DepthNet: Semantic-Guided Monocular Depth Estimation for Dynamic Environment

Zilong Song[1], Yang Gao[1], Sijia Dai[2], Shuai Li[1], Aimin Hao[1], and Shoulong Zhang[3(✉)]

[1] State Key Laboratory of Virtual Reality Technology and Systems,
Beihang University, Beijing, China
{sy2306306,gaoyangvr,lishuai,ham}@buaa.edu.cn
[2] China Nuclear Power Engineering Co., Ltd. Hebei Branch, Ningde, China
[3] Zhongguancun Laboratory, Beijing, China
zhangsl@zgclab.edu.cn

Abstract. Depth estimation is a fundamental aspect of spatial computation in virtual-real fusion contexts, wherein self-supervised monocular depth estimation presents a persistent challenge within the fields of computer vision and augmented/mixed reality (AR/XR) applications. However, existing methods face difficulties with moving objects, occlusions, and motion blur, resulting in inaccurate estimates, particularly in dynamic regions. Previous solutions either omit challenging areas in the training process or employ pseudo-depth labels, which still cannot fully address the issues. In this paper, we introduce our semantically implicit and explicit depth estimation network, SIE-DepthNet, a novel approach that leverages semantic information to improve monocular depth estimation in dynamic scenes. We articulate a Depth Semantic Feature Fusion Network (DSFFNet) to provide implicit guidance, ensuring consistent depth distributions across categories. Additionally, we propose a semantic-guided ranking loss that optimizes depth accuracy by aligning estimated values with segmentation boundaries, using uncertainty-aware weighting to mitigate the impact of segmentation noise. Extensive experimental results demonstrate that SIE-DepthNet achieves accurate depth map predictions, significantly enhancing performance in dynamic and static scenarios.

Keywords: Semantic-guided self-supervised depth estimation ·
Monocular depth estimation · Attention mechanism

1 Introduction

Monocular depth estimation [13] has garnered significant attention in the computer vision community for various downstream tasks, such as salient object detection [46], 3D reconstruction [26], AR/XR scenario reconstruction [12], novel

© The Author(s), under exclusive license to Springer Nature Singapore Pte Ltd. 2025
W. Song et al. (Eds.): ICXR 2024, LNCS 15461, pp. 195–210, 2025.
https://doi.org/10.1007/978-981-96-3679-2_13

view synthesis [1], and visual odometry [3,42]. Although several deep learning-based approaches have achieved impressive results in depth estimation in static scenes, it is crucial to consider additional difficulties, such as moving objects, occlusions, and motion blur, that commonly arise when using monocular depth estimation in AR/XR-related applications.

Visual depth estimation methods are hindered by their inability to precisely estimate camera pose, especially in occluded areas (e.g., object boundaries) and dynamic objects, which contradict the assumptions of consistent photometric [47] and geometric properties [3] employed by these methods. Numerous previous studies [3,29,47] have chosen to identify these challenging regions and omit them from the training. Consequently, this leads to poor results for dynamic regions during inference, as these areas are not sufficiently regularized during training. Other methods [35,43] employ pseudo-depth labels to initialize pre-calculated depth for fine-grained optimization. However, the above efforts are still not fully resolved in the problem of ambiguous dynamic object regions.

An effective strategy involves utilizing additional information to improve depth prediction capabilities in challenging scenarios. Several methods [5,20,24] have proven the effectiveness of using semantic segmentation to enhance monocular depth estimation. Their underlying mechanisms can be broadly categorized into two types: 1) Semantic information provides implicit class-level guidance to mitigate the ill-posedness of monocular depth estimation. Suppose that the pixels within a region are classified as the same object during semantic segmentation. In that case, they typically exhibit similar feature distributions in the latent space, thereby providing consistent constraints for specific categories during depth estimation. Utilizing information from the semantic latent space for depth learning aids in achieving category-distinct depth distributions, thereby alleviating estimation ambiguities across different scenes. 2) Additionally, semantic information also provides explicit guidance for object depth. Generally, semantic boundaries correspond to depth boundaries, and the estimated depth within each category region tends to be smooth. Thus, semantic boundaries can serve as guiding information to avoid abrupt depth changes within object regions. Based on these observations, we offer a novel semantic-guided depth estimate approach that employs semantics both implicitly and explicitly.

In this paper, we propose SIE-DepthNet to leverage semantic information for accurate depth estimation. We provide implicit semantic guidance to the depth network during the decoding phase through a pre-trained semantic segmentation model. Given the high correlation between depth distributions and semantic categories, we introduce the Depth Semantic Feature Fusion Network (DSFFNet) framework, which enforces category-specific depth distributions by spatially modulating the fused segmentation and depth features in a multi-scale manner. Using a more advanced transformer architecture [39], we enhance the guiding capability. In addition to implicit semantic guidance, we propose a semantic-guided ranking loss to explicitly improve the quality of the estimated depth maps. We perform depth maximization/minimization operations using semantic segmentation predicted labels on point pairs sampled from cross-border and internal boundary regions. Our contributions can be summarized as follows:

1) We propose SIE-DepthNet, which utilizes semantic information for robust self-supervised learning of monocular depth in highly dynamic scenes, enabling accurate depth map predictions.
2) We propose a new Depth Semantic Feature Fusion Network (DSFFNet) module that implicitly enforces category-specific depth distributions through spatial modulation operations on semantic label priors.
3) We propose a novel semantic-guided ranking loss that explicitly applies soft constraints to the depth, aligning it with the boundaries of the segmentation predictions. Uncertainty-aware weighting is introduced to handle noisy segmentation labels.

2   Related Work

2.1   Self-supervised Monocular Depth Estimation

Self-supervised methods [17,18,31,47] transform the deep supervision problem into image-based supervision, enabling learning without the need for depth annotations. As pioneering approaches using stereo image pairs to train depth networks [15,17], Zhou et al. [47] introduced a more general pipeline to train purely image sequences. Since then, significant advances have been made in improving self-supervised frameworks, particularly in loss functions, occlusion handling, and new architectures. Yang et al. [40] and Li et al. [25] enhanced photometric loss to improve robustness against lighting variations, while Shu et al. [31] proposed a feature metric loss that improved backpropagation in low-gradient areas. To address issues of scene occlusion and object motion during depth training, several methods [3,18,47] introduced learning-based and geometrically selective masks to filter out unreliable losses. Additionally, to leverage more information for self-supervised methods, optical flow [29] and pseudo-depth [43] were incorporated for additional constraints. In terms of new architectures, Guizilini et al. [19] proposed novel packing and unpacking modules that preserve more detailed details. However, this approach demands considerable computational resources, which are often not feasible for real-world applications. Sun et al. [35] utilizes a model that is trained only once on a large-scale dataset to generate pseudo-depth labels, somewhat reducing the computational resources required. However, this method struggles to clearly identify object edges.

2.2   Semantic Guidance for Depth Estimation

Semantic segmentation has previously demonstrated its effectiveness for depth estimation. Depending on how image semantics are utilized, these methods can be categorized into two groups. The first group provides implicit semantic guidance by delivering feature-level information. Chen et al. [6] generated depth maps and semantic maps using a unified scene representation. Choi et al. [8] employed

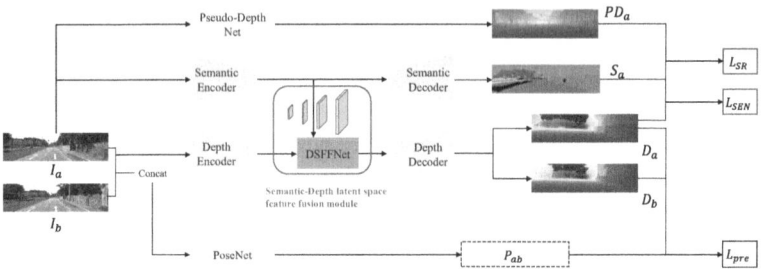

Fig. 1. Method overview. Our proposed DSFFNet fuses the multi-scale latent space feature maps, which are the intermediate outputs of the Semantic Encoder and Depth Encoder. Additionally, we provide explicit guidance to ensure that the depth is consistent with segmentation borders using the proposed losses L_{SR} and L_{SEN}.

a semantic network to provide cross-propagation and affine propagation units for features. Similarly, Guizilini et al. [20] proposed using semantic guidance to enhance depth features; however, they utilized local convolutions [34] on a pretrained segmentation network. While we employ a global cross-attention module and use explicit guidance derived from labels obtained from semantic masks, resulting in a global guidance with better fidelity, rather than relying on local latent features.

Another group of methods employs semantic segmentation to directly constrain or supervise depth networks. Ramirez et al. [28] and Chen et al. [6] used semantic maps to enforce depth smoothness. Casser et al. [5] and Klingner et al. [24] addressed the problem of dynamic objects by specifying motion areas through semantic object labels, while Wang et al. [37] proposed a divide-and-conquer strategy to learn semantically guided depth. Zhu et al. [48] introduced a dual-purpose method that generates edge-aligned depth estimates using semantic maps. However, in Zhu's approach, the generated pseudo-labels do not capture the missing latent real values of the initial depth, and the quality of the pseudo-depth is highly correlated with the provided semantic predictions. In contrast, our method proposes a ranking loss that constrains on the basis of the relative depth of pseudo-depth labels, independent of the accuracy of the pseudo-depth. Additionally, our approach distinguishes itself by introducing robust cross-border sampling and point pair weighting, which mitigate the impact of noisy segmentation labels.

3   Method

3.1   Overview

Figure 1 presents an overview of our model. Within the self-supervised learning framework, the monocular depth estimation network (DepthNet), relative 6-DoF camera pose estimation network (PoseNet), and Depth Semantic Feature

Fusion Network (DSFFNet) are jointly trained on a large dataset of monocular videos. Given a pair of consecutive images (I_a, I_b) randomly sampled from the training video, DepthNet predicts their depths (D_a, D_b) through forward propagation, while PoseNet estimates their relative 6-degree-of-freedom camera pose P_{ab}. We then use the predicted depths and poses to generate a warped optical flow between the two images and synthesize I_a' from I_b using bi-linear interpolation. Finally, we penalize the color inconsistency between I_a and I_a', and we further impose geometric consistency between D_a and D_b, which back-propagates the gradient through the network.

3.2 Semantic-Depth Latent Space Feature Fusion Module

To provide implicit semantic guidance to the depth network, a segmentation branch is proposed to conduct joint learning with the depth branch in a multi-scale scheme. To enforce category-specific depth distribution, we modulate the semantic and depth features using the semantic segmentation network (Sem-SegNet) and the depth-semantic feature fusion network (DSFFNet), utilizing external full-category semantic labels to provide global semantic guidance with higher fidelity.

SemSegNet. For the semantic segmentation task, we use SegFormer [39], a modern Transformer-based architecture that stands out as the semantic segmentation network (SemSegNet) because of its high efficiency and performance. Thus, it is particularly suitable for real-time uncertainty quantification. Seg-Former consists of two main modules: A hierarchical transformer-based encoder that generates high-resolution coarse features and low-resolution fine features and a lightweight all-MLP segmentation decoder. The latter fuses the multi-level features of the encoder to produce a final segmentation prediction, which can be formulated as:

$$p(z) = \frac{e^{z_i}}{\sum_{k=1}^{K} e^{z_k}}, \tag{1}$$

where $p(z)$ are the class probabilities of the softmax function that exponentiates each of the K elements of the input vector x, often referred to as logits, and then normalizes the results to obtain a probability distribution. Since SegFormer [39] only outputs logits at a $\frac{H}{4} \times \frac{W}{4}$ resolution given an input image of size $H \times W$, we use bi-linear interpolation before applying the softmax function on z to obtain the original resolution for the final segmentation prediction. It is worth noting that we use a pre-trained SegFormer model with frozen parameters, which does not participate in the joint training of the network.

DSFFNet. As shown in Fig. 2, during the decoding stage, we have multi-scale semantic features $F_S \in \mathbb{R}^{C \times H \times W}$ and depth features $F_D \in \mathbb{R}^{C \times H \times W}$, where C denotes the channels of the feature block. DSFFNet contains four cross-attention

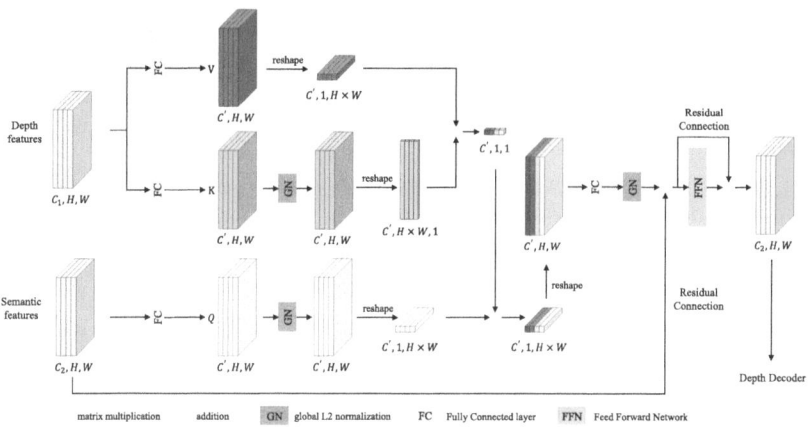

Fig. 2. Architecture of the Depth Semantic Feature Fusion Network (DSFFNet).

blocks, with each block being used to process the feature map at each corresponding scale.

In standard attention, the input features in $\mathbb{R}^{C \times H \times W}$ are projected and reshaped to produce queries Q, keys K, and values V in $\mathbb{R}^{T \times D}$. T is the number of tokens (equal to $H \times W$) and D is the number of feature dimensions. According to [4], we can reformulate the standard attention computation as follows to enhance efficiency:

$$A(Q, K, V; \phi) = \phi(Q)(\phi(K)^T V), \tag{2}$$

where $\phi(\cdot)$ is a kernel function. Thus, we first are allowed to compute $\phi(K)^T V$, which is $O(D^2 T H')$. Compared to $O(T^2 D H')$, computational cost decreases observably, since D is always much smaller than T. To further reduce computational cost, Hydra Attention [4] attempts to decrease D to 1 and increase head number H' to D. It reduces the computational cost to $O(TD)$ while maintaining a relatively high accuracy for the image classification task.

To leverage the latent space information of semantic features to guide depth features while keeping the computational cost at a low level, we design a module of cross-attention based on the main idea of Hydra attention [4]. As shown in Fig. 2, the inputs of depth features are first reshaped and projected to get K and V fully connected. Q is produced by the semantic features in the same way. We use cosine similarity as our kernel function, which means that $\phi(\cdot)$ is a $L2$ normalization. Since the feature dimension is reduced to 1, we perform $L2$ normalization to Q and K globally rather than head-wise. Q, K and V are further reshaped so as to perform matrix multiplication. After reshaping, the token number T is equal to $H \times W$ (all of the pixels), the head number is C' and the feature dimension is 1. What we are going to do next is perform two matrix multiplications on the order of Eq. 2 for every head. The results of the final matrix multiplication are reshaped and projected by feed-forward network(FFN) and layer normalization to produce the final outputs, which have the same shape as the input Q, while retaining its residual structure throughout the process. The computational cost of cross-attention block mainly comes from the fully-connected operations and matrix multiplications. The processes of two matrix multiplications are both $O(TC')$, and all the fully-connected used are $O(TC'C)$.

3.3 Semantic-Based Dynamic Region Refinement

In this section, we will introduce the refinement of dynamic region depth explicitly based on semantic information. First, we propose a semantic-guided mask ranking loss that constrains the ordinal depth (nearer/further relation) between pixels based on their semantic labels. Second, we apply edge-aware normal loss to semantic maps, which constrains the object boundaries in the predicted semantic map to align with the edges in the depth map, thereby forming a shared constraint.

Semantic-Guided Mask Ranking Loss. The key to our proposed semantic-guided mask ranking loss is based on two assumptions, including (i) that the depth values of pixels belonging to the same object should be similar; (ii) given sufficient accurate semantic segmentation, these pixels should be assigned the same semantic category. Therefore, when sampling pixel pairs for the mask ranking loss, we assign different weights to the pixel pairs, increasing the penalty for pairs where the two pixels belong to different semantic categories:

$$L_{SR} = \frac{1}{|\Omega|} \sum_{p \in \Omega} \omega \cdot \phi(p), \tag{3}$$

where $\phi(\cdot)$ was proposed in [7]:

$$\phi(p_0, p_1) = \log\left(1 + \exp\left(-\ell(p_0 - p_1)\right)\right), \tag{4}$$

and ℓ is the ground truth ordinal label, which can be induced by a ground truth depth map:

$$\ell = \begin{cases} +1, & p_0^*/p_1^* \geq 1 + \tau \\ -1, & p_0^*/p_1^* \leq \frac{1}{1+\tau} \\ 0, & \text{otherwise.} \end{cases} \tag{5}$$

Here p^* denotes pseudo-depth. whereas ω in Eq. 3 is the weight of pixel pair:

$$\omega = \begin{cases} x, & p_0 \sim p_1 \\ y, & p_0 \nsim p_1, \end{cases} \tag{6}$$

where $\sim$ means that the two points p_0 and p_1 belong to the same semantic category, while $\nsim$ indicates the opposite. Empirically, we assign $x = 1$ and $y = 10$.

Semantic Edge-Aware Normal Loss. Inspired by the performance of the Edge-aware relative normal loss proposed in [35], we propose the semantic edge-aware normal loss. Specifically, we sample point pairs around semantic mask edges and constrain the relative normal angles of sampled point pairs to be consistent with pseudo-depth. Here, we use edge-guided sampling that was proposed in [38] to construct point pairs $\langle A, B \rangle$, and we define the Semantic edge-aware normal loss as:

$$L_{\text{SEN}} = \frac{1}{N} \sum_{i=1}^{N} \left\| n_{Ai}^S \cdot n_{Bi}^S - n_{Ai}^* \cdot n_{Bi}^* \right\|_1, \tag{7}$$

where n_A^S denotes the normal of a sampled point from the predicted semantic map, and $*$ denotes pseudo-depth.

Losses. Based on the proposed two loss functions, we write the overall loss function as:

$$L = L_{pre} + \alpha L_{SR} + \beta L_{SEN}, \tag{8}$$

where L_{pre} denotes the loss function in our baseline [35] and set $\alpha = 0.1$, $\beta = 0.1$ in training based on empirical tuning.

4   Experiments

4.1   Datasets

Our proposed method focuses on enhancing self-supervised monocular depth estimation in challenging dynamic scenes. Therefore, we primarily evaluate our approach on two dynamic datasets: the DDAD driving dataset [19] and the TUM dataset [33] (*Dynamic Objects* split). DDAD consists of 150 training scenes (12,650 images) and 50 validation scenes (3,950 images), depth ranges are limited to 200 m, and images are resized to 640 × 384 for training. *Dynamic Objects* category of TUM consists of 11 sequences, the last two (1,375 images) used for testing. The remaining nine dynamic videos are reserved for training, and the images are resized to 320 × 256 for input into the networks. Note that these datasets contain fast-moving objects, making them more challenging than the widely used KITTI [16] and NYUv2 [32] datasets, which we assume to be almost static. KITTI is the most widely used for self-supervised monocular depth estimation. Following previous studies [3,18,19,47], we adopt Eigen's split [13], using 697 images for testing and the remaining sequences for training, the depth ranges are limited to 80 m, and images are resized to 832 × 256 for training. NYUv2 includes 654 static scene testing images for depth evaluation, while the remaining videos without testing images are used to train neural networks. The images are resized to 320 × 256 before input into the network. All mentioned self-supervised methods were trained separately in each dataset to ensure a fair comparison.

4.2   Depth Evaluation Metrics

Following most of the recent work, we use standard depth evaluation metrics, including mean absolute relative error (AbsRel), root mean squared error (RMS), root mean squared log error (RMSlog), and the accuracy under threshold ($\delta_i < 1.25^i, i = 1, 2, 3$). The detailed definition of these depth metrics can be found in [13]. In addition, following previous work [3,47], we multiply the predicted depth maps by a scalar that matches the median with that of the ground truth for evaluation, i.e., $s = median(D_{gt})/median(D_{pred})$, since self-supervised methods cannot recover the metric scale. We use the semantic segmentation mask of testing images provided by [35]. In driving datasets (i.e., KITTI and DDAD), all vehicle and pedestrian segments are regarded as dynamic objects, and other regions are regarded as static backgrounds. In indoor datasets (i.e., TUM), we consider all human segments as dynamic regions. Note that we align the global scale to the ground-truth depth first and then individually evaluate depth accuracy on static regions, dynamic regions, and full images, individually.

4.3   Implementation Details

Our pose network is the same as in previous work [3], where we use the ResNet-18 [21] backbone for both depth and pose estimation networks. As in [35], the depth network is a U-Net structure [30] with a DispNet [47] as the decoder, while the inputs are changed to depth-semantic fusion feature maps. Our semantic network is trained on Cityscapes [10] and ADE20K [44]. The pretrained model is provided by MMSegmentation [9]. The pose network accepts two RGB frames as input and outputs the 6D relative pose. For DSFFN, we set $C' = 256$. The DSFFN is used on four scales (1, 2, 3, 4) of decoder, in which the scale of 4 has the lowest resolution.

We implement the proposed method using the PyTorch library [27]. Following [29,36,47], we use a snippet of three sequential video frames as a training sample. The images are augmented with random scaling, cropping, and horizontal flips during training. We use the Adam [23] optimizer and set the learning rate to 10^{-4}. We initialize the encoder using the pre-trained model on ImageNet [11]. We train our networks in $100k$ iterations on each dataset.

4.4   Evaluation Results

Results on Dynamic Datasets. We use two dynamic datasets mentioned above to evaluate the proposed method, and the quantitative results of depth estimation are reported in Table 1 and 2, respectively. We show the results of the qualitative comparison in Fig. 3. A more detailed analysis is conducted below.

We report the depth estimation results on the DDAD dataset in the Table 1, comparing our method with previous state-of-the-art approaches, including Monodepth2 [18], PackNet [19], and SC-DepthV3 [35]. The results indicate that our method significantly outperforms previous methods, particularly in dynamic areas. Notably, our method surpasses PackNet [19], although the latter employs a much larger backbone network. This highlights our main contribution in this

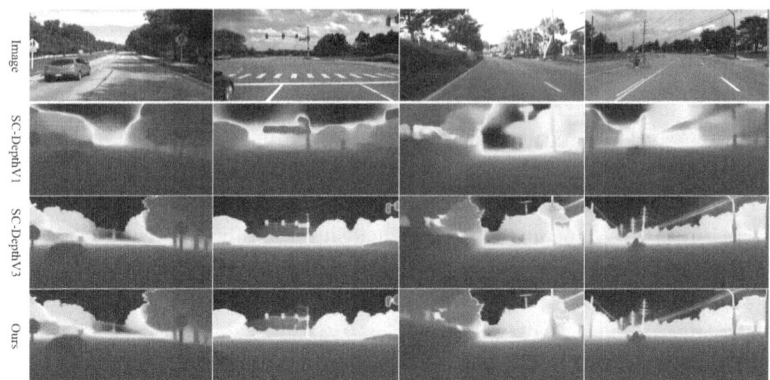

Fig. 3. Qualitative monocular depth estimation results on DDAD datasets. Our proposed method predicts sharper and more accurate depth at object boundaries than existing methods.

Table 1. Self-supervised monocular depth estimation results on the DDAD driving dataset. We segment vehicles and pedestrians as dynamic objects and consider the rest of the areas as static backgrounds. This dataset is more challenging than KITTI because the scenes are more complex, there are fewer parked vehicles, and the depth range is longer (200 m vs 80 m). The best results are in **bold**. Note that DynamicDepth uses two frames for depth estimation, and PackNet uses a large backbone, while other methods including ours use the ResNet-18 encoder.

Methods	Full Image							Dynamic		Static	
	AbsRel↓	SqRel↓	RMS↓	RMSlog↓	δ_1 ↑	δ_2 ↑	δ_3 ↑	AbsRel↓	δ_1 ↑	AbsRel↓	δ_1 ↑
Monodepth2 [18]	0.239	12.547	18.392	0.316	0.752	0.899	0.949	0.747	0.432	0.188	0.771
PackNet [19]	0.182	7.945	**15.021**	0.259	**0.828**	**0.925**	0.961	0.564	0.520	**0.137**	**0.843**
SGDepth [24]	0.200	7.944	17.149	0.289	0.769	0.911	0.957	0.619	0.446	0.170	0.786
DynamicDepth [14]	0.156	3.305	15.612	0.258	0.785	0.914	0.962	0.258	0.612	0.149	0.792
SC-Depth [3]	0.169	3.877	16.290	0.280	0.773	0.905	0.951	0.345	0.546	0.155	0.783
SC-DepthV3 [35]	**0.142**	3.031	15.868	0.248	0.813	0.922	0.963	0.199	0.697	0.140	0.813
Ours	**0.142**	**2.963**	15.506	**0.245**	0.806	0.924	**0.966**	**0.194**	**0.706**	0.143	0.808

paper: robust learning of monocular depth in dynamic driving scenes. Here, our baseline method is a modified version of SC-Depth that integrates the advantages of Monodepth2. The results demonstrate that the performance of these models is significantly lower than that of our complete model, validating the effectiveness of our proposed losses.

We report the depth estimation results on the TUM dataset in Table 2. This indoor dataset poses greater challenges than driving datasets like DDAD, as the proportion of dynamic areas to the complete image is significantly higher. Consequently, previous methods such as Monodepth2 [18] and SC-Depth [3] exhibit lower accuracy on the TUM dataset. In contrast, our method demonstrates markedly better results, attributed to our proposed loss function, which enables robust depth estimation from dynamic videos.

Table 2. Self-supervised monocular depth estimation results on the TUM dataset. We use videos under the category of "Dynamic Objects" for training and testing, where the moving objects occupy a significant proportion of pixels in each image.

Methods	Full Image					Dynamic		Static	
	AbsRel↓	RMS↓	δ_1 ↑	δ_2 ↑	δ_3 ↑	AbsRel↓	δ_1 ↑	AbsRel↓	δ_1 ↑
Monodepth2 [18]	0.312	1.408	0.474	0.793	0.905	0.431	0.348	0.262	0.526
SC-Depth [3]	0.257	-	0.616	0.814	0.909	0.512	0.274	0.176	0.715
SC-DepthV2 [2]	0.223	-	0.643	0.862	0.932	0.283	0.494	0.206	0.686
SC-DepthV3 [35]	0.163	1.327	**0.797**	0.882	0.937	**0.165**	**0.796**	0.171	**0.780**
Ours	**0.158**	**1.158**	0.773	**0.900**	**0.969**	0.202	0.713	**0.153**	**0.780**

Fig. 4. Qualitative monocular depth estimation results on NYUv2 datasets. Our method predicts sharper and more accurate depth at object boundaries than existing methods, effectively mitigating the influence of planar patterns on object surfaces in depth estimation.

Results on Static Datasets. Our method also performs well in nearly static scenes, with results reported on the widely used KITTI driving dataset and the NYUv2 indoor dataset. The depth estimation results for KITTI, presented in Table 3, indicate that our method demonstrates significantly better performance, with the most notable improvements observed across all datasets.

The depth results on the NYUv2 dataset are reported in Table 4, where we compare our method with previous state-of-the-art approaches, such as SC-DepthV3 [35] and MonoIndoor [22]. The results indicate that our method significantly outperforms the earlier methods. This improvement is primarily due to the NYUv2 dataset being composed of entirely static indoor scenes, allowing us to utilize a semantic segmentation model trained on a similar ADE20K [44] dataset, resulting in better generalization performance. We also show the qualitative comparison results in Fig. 4.

Table 3. Self-supervised monocular depth estimation results on KITTI. Note that PackNet uses a large backbone, while other methods including ours use the ResNet-18 encoder.

Methods	Full Image							Dynamic		Static	
	AbsRel↓	SqRel↓	RMS↓	RMSlog↓	δ_1 ↑	δ_2 ↑	δ_3 ↑	AbsRel↓	δ_1 ↑	AbsRel↓	δ_1 ↑
Monodepth2 [18]	0.114	0.848	4.986	0.198	0.869	0.956	0.980	**0.187**	0.731	0.104	0.884
PackNet [19]	0.109	0.839	4.696	0.188	0.884	0.961	0.981	0.208	**0.737**	0.099	**0.901**
SGDepth [24]	0.111	0.857	4.739	0.189	0.884	0.962	0.982	0.209	0.728	0.101	0.899
SC-Depth [3]	0.118	0.870	4.997	0.196	0.860	0.956	0.981	0.242	0.698	0.108	0.878
SC-DepthV3 [35]	0.118	0.756	4.709	0.188	0.864	0.960	0.984	0.205	0.703	0.108	0.881
Ours	**0.111**	**0.688**	**4.466**	**0.181**	**0.880**	**0.965**	**0.985**	0.183	**0.750**	0.102	**0.895**

Table 4. Monocular depth estimation results on the NYUv2 dataset. Our method outperforms all the self-supervised methods.

Methods	Error ↓		Accuracy ↑		
	AbsRel	RMS	δ_1	δ_2	δ_3
Zhou et al. [45]	0.208	0.712	0.674	0.900	0.968
Zhao et al. [43]	0.189	0.686	0.701	0.912	0.978
Monodepth2 [18]	0.169	0.614	0.745	0.946	0.987
SC-Depth [3]	0.159	0.608	0.772	0.939	0.982
P2Net [41]	0.150	0.561	0.796	0.948	0.986
SC-DepthV2 [2]	0.138	0.532	0.820	0.956	0.989
MonoIndoor [22]	0.134	0.526	0.823	0.958	0.989
SC-DepthV3 [35]	0.123	0.486	0.848	0.963	**0.991**
Ours	**0.120**	**0.479**	**0.852**	**0.965**	**0.991**

4.5 Ablation Studies

In this section, we will demonstrate the effectiveness of the proposed method and discuss the reasons for our method's performance on the BONN dataset.

As shown in the Table 5, incorporating our semantic segmentation network, SemSegNet, into the baseline leads to a noticeable performance improvement. At this stage, the semantic features are introduced into the Depth Decoder through a simple concatenation method. Following the introduction of DSFFNet, there is further enhancement in performance; however, this improvement is not significant in the absence of our proposed loss functions, SRL and SEL. Additionally, under the same settings, we compared the impact of the Encoder's network size on performance.

Table 5. We present the ablation experiment results on the KITTI dataset. "DSFFN/SRL/SEL" respectively represent the proposed Depth Semantic Feature Fusion Network, Semantic-guided Ranking Loss, and Semantic Edge-aware normal Loss.

Methods	Full Image							Dynamic		Static	
	AbsRel↓	SqRel↓	RMS↓	RMSlog↓	δ_1 ↑	δ_2 ↑	δ_3 ↑	AbsRel↓	δ_1 ↑	AbsRel↓	δ_1 ↑
baseline	0.118	0.756	4.709	0.188	0.864	0.960	0.984	0.205	0.703	0.108	0.881
baseline + SemSegNet	0.114	0.744	4.676	0.186	0.870	0.962	0.984	0.197	0.722	0.106	0.883
DSFFN w/o (SRL, SEL)	0.115	0.736	4.542	0.184	0.873	0.964	0.985	0.195	0.724	0.106	0.887
DSFFN w/o SRL	0.113	0.714	4.682	0.183	0.871	0.962	0.985	0.187	0.731	0.105	0.884
DSFFN w/o SEL	**0.111**	**0.678**	4.530	0.182	0.877	0.964	0.985	0.187	0.731	0.104	0.890
Ours	**0.111**	0.688	**4.466**	**0.181**	**0.880**	**0.965**	0.985	**0.183**	**0.750**	**0.102**	**0.895**

5 Conclusion

In this paper, we enhance self-supervised depth estimation by leveraging both implicit and explicit semantic guidance. We introduce a semantic-guided spatial feature fusion attention module, which implicitly modulates the depth distribution through semantic class-level information. Additionally, we propose a semantic-guided ranking loss that explicitly constrains the depth map to align with the segmentation boundaries. Extensive experiments demonstrate the superiority of our approach, showing the potential of dynamic depth estimation applicable to CV and VR related applications. However, during network inference, our method still relies on precomputed pseudo-semantic labels.

For future work, we plan to explore self-supervised semantic co-training strategies within the self-training process of the depth network, using self-learned labels to further boost depth estimation performance. Moreover, semantic and depth information could be refined iteratively to produce even better results.

Declaration of Conflicts of Interest. The authors state that there are no known financial conflicts of interest or personal relationships that could have influenced the work presented in this paper.

References

1. Bian, J.W., Zhan, H., Reid, I.: NVSS: high-quality novel view selfie synthesis. In: 2021 International Conference on 3D Vision (3DV), pp. 1085–1094 (2021)
2. Bian, J.W., Zhan, H., Wang, N., Chin, T.J., Shen, C., Reid, I.: Auto-rectify network for unsupervised indoor depth estimation. IEEE Trans. Pattern Anal. Mach. Intell. 9802–9813 (2022)
3. Bian, J.W., et al.: Unsupervised scale-consistent depth learning from video. In: IJCV 2021 (2021)
4. Bolya, D., Fu, C., Dai, X., Zhang, P., Hoffman, J.: Hydra attention: efficient attention with many heads. In: Computer Vision - ECCV 2022 Workshops - Tel Aviv, Israel, October 23-27, 2022, Proceedings, Part VII. Springer (2022)

5. Casser, V., Pirk, S., Mahjourian, R., Angelova, A.: Depth prediction without the sensors: leveraging structure for unsupervised learning from monocular videos. In: Proceedings of the AAAI Conference on Artificial Intelligence, pp. 8001–8008 (2019)
6. Chen, P.Y., Liu, A.H., Liu, Y.C., Wang, Y.C.F.: Towards scene understanding: unsupervised monocular depth estimation with semantic-aware representation. In: 2019 IEEE/CVF Conference on Computer Vision and Pattern Recognition (CVPR) (2019)
7. Chen, W., Zhao, F., Yang, D., Deng, J.: Single-image depth perception in the wild. Cornell University - arXiv, Cornell University - arXiv (2016)
8. Choi, J., Jung, D., Lee, D.H., Kim, C.: Safenet: self-supervised monocular depth estimation with semantic-aware feature extraction. Cornell University - arXiv, Cornell University - arXiv (2020)
9. Contributors, M.: MMSegmentation: Openmmlab semantic segmentation toolbox and benchmark (2020). https://github.com/open-mmlab/mmsegmentation
10. Cordts, M., et al.: The cityscapes dataset for semantic urban scene understanding. In: Proceedings of the IEEE Conference on Computer Vision and Pattern Recognition (CVPR) (2016)
11. Deng, J., Dong, W., Socher, R., Li, L.J., Li, K., Fei-Fei, L.: Imagenet: a large-scale hierarchical image database. In: 2009 IEEE Conference on Computer Vision and Pattern Recognition (2009)
12. Dickson, A., Knott, A., Zollmann, S.: Benchmarking monocular depth estimation models for VR content creation from a user perspective. In: 2021 36th International Conference on Image and Vision Computing New Zealand (IVCNZ), pp. 1–6 (2021)
13. Eigen, D., Puhrsch, C., Fergus, R.: Depth map prediction from a single image using a multi-scale deep network. Cornell University - arXiv, Cornell University - arXiv (2014)
14. Feng, Z., Yang, L., Jing, L., Wang, H., Tian, Y., Li, B.: Disentangling object motion and occlusion for unsupervised multi-frame monocular depth. In: Computer Vision - ECCV 2022 - 17th European Conference, Tel Aviv, Israel, October 23-27, 2022, Proceedings, Part XXXII, pp. 228–244. Springer (2022)
15. Garg, R., B.G., V.K., Carneiro, G., Reid, I.: Unsupervised CNN for single view depth estimation: geometry to the rescue, pp. 740–756 (2016)
16. Geiger, A., Lenz, P., Stiller, C., Urtasun, R.: Vision meets robotics: the kitti dataset. Int. J. Robot. Res. 1231–1237 (2013)
17. Godard, C., Aodha, O.M., Brostow, G.J.: Unsupervised monocular depth estimation with left-right consistency. In: 2017 IEEE Conference on Computer Vision and Pattern Recognition (CVPR) (2017)
18. Godard, C., Aodha, O.M., Firman, M., Brostow, G.: Digging into self-supervised monocular depth estimation. In: 2019 IEEE/CVF International Conference on Computer Vision (ICCV) (2019)
19. Guizilini, V., Ambrus, R., Pillai, S., Raventos, A., Gaidon, A.: 3D packing for self-supervised monocular depth estimation. In: 2020 IEEE/CVF Conference on Computer Vision and Pattern Recognition (CVPR) (2020)
20. Guizilini, V., Hou, R., Li, J., Ambrus, R., Gaidon, A.: Semantically-guided representation learning for self-supervised monocular depth. In: International Conference on Learning Representations (2020)
21. He, K., Zhang, X., Ren, S., Sun, J.: Deep residual learning for image recognition. In: 2016 IEEE Conference on Computer Vision and Pattern Recognition (CVPR) (2016)

22. Ji, P., Li, R., Bhanu, B., Xu, Y.: Monoindoor: towards good practice of self-supervised monocular depth estimation for indoor environments. In: 2021 IEEE/CVF International Conference on Computer Vision (ICCV) (2021)

23. Kingma, D., Ba, J.: Adam: a method for stochastic optimization. arXiv: Learning,arXiv: Learning (2014)

24. Klingner, M., Termöhlen, J.A., Mikolajczyk, J., Fingscheidt, T.: Self-supervised monocular depth estimation: solving the dynamic object problem by semantic guidance, pp. 582–600 (2020)

25. Li, R., He, X., Zhu, Y., Li, X., Sun, J., Zhang, Y.: Enhancing self-supervised monocular depth estimation via incorporating robust constraints. In: Proceedings of the 28th ACM International Conference on Multimedia, vol. 1, pp. 3108–3117 (2020)

26. Newcombe, R.A., et al.: Kinectfusion: real-time dense surface mapping and tracking. In: 2011 10th IEEE International Symposium on Mixed and Augmented Reality (2011)

27. Paszke, A., et al.: Automatic differentiation in pytorch (2017)

28. Ramirez, P., Poggi, M., Tosi, F., Mattoccia, S., Stefano, L.: Geometry meets semantics for semi-supervised monocular depth estimation. arXiv: Computer Vision and Pattern Recognition,arXiv: Computer Vision and Pattern Recognition (2018)

29. Ranjan, A., et al.: Competitive collaboration: joint unsupervised learning of depth, camera motion, optical flow and motion segmentation. In: 2019 IEEE/CVF Conference on Computer Vision and Pattern Recognition (CVPR) (2019)

30. Ronneberger, O., Fischer, P., Brox, T.: U-Net: convolutional networks for biomedical image segmentation, pp. 234–241 (2015)

31. Shu, C., Yu, K., Duan, Z., Yang, K.: Feature-metric loss for self-supervised learning of depth and egomotion, pp. 572–588 (2020)

32. Silberman, N., Hoiem, D., Kohli, P., Fergus, R.: Indoor segmentation and support inference from RGBD images, pp. 746–760 (2012)

33. Sturm, J., Engelhard, N., Endres, F., Burgard, W., Cremers, D.: A benchmark for the evaluation of RGB-D slam systems. In: 2012 IEEE/RSJ International Conference on Intelligent Robots and Systems (2012)

34. Su, H., Jampani, V., Sun, D., Gallo, O., Learned-Miller, E., Kautz, J.: Pixel-adaptive convolutional neural networks. In: 2019 IEEE/CVF Conference on Computer Vision and Pattern Recognition (CVPR) (2019)

35. Sun, L., Bian, J.W., Zhan, H., Yin, W., Reid, I., Shen, C.: SC-DepthV3: robust self-supervised monocular depth estimation for dynamic scenes. IEEE Trans. Pattern Anal. Mach. Intell. (TPAMI) (2023)

36. Wang, C., Buenaposada, J.M., Zhu, R., Lucey, S.: Learning depth from monocular videos using direct methods. In: 2018 IEEE/CVF Conference on Computer Vision and Pattern Recognition (2018)

37. Wang, L., Zhang, J., Wang, O., Lin, Z., Lu, H.: SDC-depth: semantic divide-and-conquer network for monocular depth estimation. In: 2020 IEEE/CVF Conference on Computer Vision and Pattern Recognition (CVPR) (2020)

38. Xian, K., Zhang, J., Wang, O., Mai, L., Lin, Z., Cao, Z.: Structure-guided ranking loss for single image depth prediction. In: 2020 IEEE/CVF Conference on Computer Vision and Pattern Recognition (CVPR) (2020)

39. Xie, E., Wang, W., Yu, Z., Anandkumar, A., Alvarez, J.M., Luo, P.: Segformer: simple and efficient design for semantic segmentation with transformers. arXiv preprint arXiv:2105.15203 (2021)

40. Yang, N., von Stumberg, L., Wang, R., Cremers, D.: D3vo: deep depth, deep pose and deep uncertainty for monocular visual odometry. In: 2020 IEEE/CVF Conference on Computer Vision and Pattern Recognition (CVPR) (2020)

41. Yu, Z., Jin, L., Gao, S.: P^2Net: patch-match and plane-regularization for unsupervised indoor depth estimation, pp. 206–222 (2020)

42. Zhan, H., Weerasekera, C.S., Bian, J.W., Reid, I.: Visual odometry revisited: what should be learnt? In: 2020 IEEE International Conference on Robotics and Automation (ICRA) (2020)

43. Zhao, W., Liu, S., Shu, Y., Liu, Y.J.: Towards better generalization: joint depth-pose learning without PoseNet. In: 2020 IEEE/CVF Conference on Computer Vision and Pattern Recognition (CVPR) (2020)

44. Zhou, B., Zhao, H., Puig, X., Fidler, S., Barriuso, A., Torralba, A.: Scene parsing through ADE20K dataset. In: 2017 IEEE Conference on Computer Vision and Pattern Recognition (CVPR) (2017)

45. Zhou, J., Wang, Y., Qin, K., Zeng, W.: Moving indoor: unsupervised video depth learning in challenging environments. In: 2019 IEEE/CVF International Conference on Computer Vision (ICCV) (2019)

46. Zhou, T., Fan, D.P., Cheng, M.M., Shen, J., Shao, L.: RGB-D salient object detection: a survey. Comput. Vis. Media 37–69 (2021)

47. Zhou, T., Brown, M., Snavely, N., Lowe, D.G.: Unsupervised learning of depth and ego-motion from video. In: 2017 IEEE Conference on Computer Vision and Pattern Recognition (CVPR) (2017)

48. Zhu, S., Brazil, G., Liu, X.: The edge of depth: explicit constraints between segmentation and depth. In: 2020 IEEE/CVF Conference on Computer Vision and Pattern Recognition (CVPR) (2020)

Application of Three-Dimensional Interactive Virtual Conference in Special Education

Yikun Huang[1,2] ⓘ, Jing Liao[1(✉)], Xi Huang[1], Shenghui Chen[1], and Gang Fu[3]

[1] Concord University College, Fujian Normal University, Fuzhou, China
fjnuhyk@163.com
[2] School of Future Technology, Fujian Agriculture and Forestry University, Fuzhou, China
[3] Fuzhou Vocational and Technical College, Fuzhou, China

Abstract. In special education, the social skills and learning needs of deaf and mute students have always been a focus of attention. With the advancement of educational reforms, many learning tasks and communication activities are conducted through conference systems. However, traditional 2D conference systems are not friendly to special students, as their physiological challenges often lead to feelings of inferiority in communication, affecting participation effectiveness. To address this issue, we propose a Three-Dimensional Interactive Virtual Conference System (3DIVCS), which not only provides video, voice communication, and speech recognition features, but also enables users to interact and engage on stage as 3D virtual characters. To validate the effectiveness of 3DIVCS for deaf and mute individuals, researchers developed a set of 3DIVCS applications and conducted real-world experiences, surveys, interviews, and analyses using independent t-tests with 20 deaf and mute students. The results indicate that 3DIVCS significantly improved their learning outcomes in conferences, enhanced their confidence, and ultimately elevated their sense of participation and communication quality.

Keywords: Three-Dimensional Interactive Virtual Conference System · Special Education · Deaf and Mute Students

1 Introduction

In the field of special education, the social skills and learning needs of deaf and mute students have always been a focal point for educators. With the continuous advancement of educational reforms, an increasing number of learning tasks and communication activities are being conducted through online conferencing systems [1]. However, traditional two-dimensional conferencing systems are not user-friendly for special groups, particularly for deaf and mute students. Due to their physiological challenges, these students often feel inferior when communicating, which negatively impacts their participation and learning efficiency [2]. How to enhance their learning engagement and social confidence in virtual environments has become an urgent issue in the current process of digitalizing special education.

© The Author(s), under exclusive license to Springer Nature Singapore Pte Ltd. 2025
W. Song et al. (Eds.): ICXR 2024, LNCS 15461, pp. 211–222, 2025.
https://doi.org/10.1007/978-981-96-3679-2_14

For many years, conferencing systems have been used to address the issue of not being able to hold meetings in the same physical space. Many work meetings, academic conferences, or online courses often use conferencing systems as communication tools. The development of internet technology has accelerated the adoption of conferencing systems, making them a tool for communication among students, employees, and friends. Some scholars conducted a survey on students' willingness to continue using conferencing systems for course learning after the pandemic, and the results showed that even after the pandemic, users still expressed a positive attitude towards the use of virtual conferencing systems [3].

According to the World Federation of the Deaf (WFD), more than 5% of the world's population (about 430 million people) suffer from disabling hearing loss, including 432 million adults and 34 million children [4]. Although some scholars are dedicated to sign language research, communication difficulties arise due to the fact that most people have trouble understanding the semantic information of sign language [5]. Deaf-mutes are prone to communication and emotional problems, making them prone to become introverted and resistant to social and face-to-face socializing. Because deaf-mutes cannot communicate with ordinary people normally, they also suffer from low self-esteem [6]. As a special group of people, deaf-mutes have the same needs of study, work and communication as normal people. As a result of the influence of physical defects, the social ability and expression ability differ from the ordinary people.

In the field of special education, the social skills and learning needs of deaf and mute students have always been a major concern for educators. With the ongoing advancement of educational reforms, an increasing number of learning tasks and communication activities are conducted through online conferencing systems. However, traditional two-dimensional conferencing systems are not user-friendly for special groups, especially deaf and mute students. Due to their physiological challenges, these students often feel inferior when participating in communication, which negatively impacts their participation and learning efficiency [7]. Enhancing these students' engagement and social confidence in virtual environments has become an urgent issue in the current process of digitalizing special education.

Traditional two-dimensional conferencing systems primarily rely on screen sharing, camera footage, and audio transmission, which may be sufficient for regular users. However, for the deaf and mute community, merely relying on visual elements and limited text information falls far short of meeting their communication needs [8]. Since they are unable to interact with others through speech, deaf and mute students often remain passive observers in these conferencing systems, lacking a sense of participation and interactivity [9]. This not only reduces their engagement in learning but also exacerbates their feelings of inferiority and social barriers.

In the 2D conference system, deaf-mute users can participate in the meeting as ordinary users, but in many cases, it is difficult for all participants to interact effectively and they can only act as an audience. With the development of 3D technology, 3D technology is also applied to virtual conference system. After the meeting system is transformed from 2D space to 3D space, users can exist as virtual characters in 3D space. Users can interact with the scene and view different angles of the 3D space freely. When the meeting is at rest, each virtual role can roam and interact in the 3D space, which enhances the immersive effect of the meeting and effectively alleviates users' participation fatigue. Some scholars used the virtual world as a conference environment to enable users to have immersive meetings and conduct high-quality media interaction, and recorded user experience by means of questionnaires and interviews. The experimental results show that participants tend to cooperate and communicate in the three-dimensional virtual environment [8]. In the past research of conference system, many scholars pay attention to the research of network communication and function of conference system. On the research of whether virtual conference system is suitable for deaf-mutes, few scholars have put forward effective research results. In order to enable the deaf-mutes to communicate with ordinary people, experts have opened intelligent apps to help them communicate with each other. Alkadhi et al. [10] developed mobile applications for deaf-mums to help them communicate with dentists. In the survey, it was also found that deaf-mums were not excluded from communicating with others with the help of smart phones, tablets and computers, and could achieve good communication effects.

In order to improve the teaching effect and learning enthusiasm of special students, virtual reality (VR) and three-dimensional interactive technologies offer us innovative solutions. The introduction of the Three-Dimensional Interactive Virtual Conference System (3DIVCS) not only enables users to communicate via video and audio but also enables them to interact as three-dimensional virtual characters. In this virtual environment, users can move freely, choose different perspectives to observe and interact, greatly enhancing the immersion and interactivity of the conference. For deaf and mute students, the representation of these three-dimensional virtual characters can conceal their physical limitations in real life, helping them engage in social interactions in an equal virtual environment, thus boosting their confidence and sense of participation. The design of the 3DIVCS system not only includes basic conference functions such as video communication, voice dialogue, screen sharing, and speech recognition, but also enables users to interact within virtual scenes through virtual characters. This approach not only breaks the passive limitations of users in traditional two-dimensional conferencing systems but also enhances users' focus and engagement through immersive experiences. Moreover, the speech recognition function provides real-time captions for deaf and mute students, helping them better understand the conference content and actively participate in discussions.

2   Related Work

In recent years, the rapid development of computer networks and virtual reality technology has led to significant advancements in virtual conference systems. These systems use virtual reality technology to combine images, sounds, and text, allowing people to communicate face-to-face regardless of their physical location. Virtual conference systems have been widely used to address meeting, learning, and communication problems, as well as to promote physical activity and health campaigns. Research has shown that digital platforms can be key in supporting physical activity participation, especially during stay-at-home restrictions such as those imposed during the COVID-19 pandemic [11]. Numerous research institutions and enterprises both domestically and abroad have conducted in-depth research on virtual conference systems. Microsoft's MSN and Tencent's QQ offer group chat with a 2D interface, while Tencent and Zoom have developed

2D virtual conference systems that allow for screen and camera sharing, as well as voice transmission. Researchers have focused on a range of communication technology issues in virtual conference systems, with many studying network communication and conference information security. For example, Isobe et al. [12] analyzed and evaluated encryption protocols in virtual conference systems to protect dialogue information, while C. Jang et al. [13] proposed a distributed conference operating system structure to relieve network loads for multiple users in virtual conference systems.

Several researchers have investigated the participation and attentiveness of users in virtual conference systems. For example, Erickson et al. conducted a three-day conference in a virtual environment and evaluated different forms of virtual conferences, leading to discussions about their potential [14]. The conventional 2D virtual conference system often fails to keep users focused during usage. To address this issue, Kamel et al. [15] developed a 2D virtual conference system that tracks users' engagement and enables them to indicate their involvement in the meeting with a single virtual swipe. Moreover, researchers have explored various ways to enhance the social communication of deaf individuals [16, 17]. Savvas et al. [18] studied an interactive tool that leverages computer vision, speech recognition, and tactile sign language analysis to aid deaf users in using computers for gaming, thereby enhancing their social interaction. Similarly, Yousaf K et al. [19] developed a mobile application that improves communication for both deaf individuals and the general population, which uses Meir frequency cepstral coefficients for feature extraction, a hidden Markov model toolkit for speech recognition, and 3D virtual characters for visualization. This intervention has helped to enhance face-to-face social interactions for deaf individuals with the aid of mobile technology.

Creative teams are increasingly developing portable VR glasses for 3D virtual space, with the proposed display system offering advantages such as ease of use, low production cost, high portability and mobility. This technology is expected to be widely used in the future for 3D virtual space [20]. Additionally, Ruofei Du et al. [21] have constructed an interactive mixed reality social media platform that includes a geotagged virtual world for users to chat and collaborate. The study found that the platform has strong interactivity and creativity, which is conducive to the development of social activities. As such, it is anticipated that users will eventually move from traditional text and 2D media to 3D media. Ibanez et al. [22] suggest that while the learning process of the traditional learning management system has been widely studied, research literature on user learning in 3D virtual worlds is relatively limited. However, the 3D virtual world is a promising environment that enables users to immerse themselves as virtual characters and improve their concentration.

The social abilities of deaf-mutes can be severely impacted by their introverted nature in social situations and their difficulty using traditional communication methods like voice-based virtual conference software. To address this issue, researchers have explored the application of gesture recognition technology to convert gestures into words and assist with communication [19]. Another approach involves using mobile applications to convert spoken language into sign language through 3D virtual characters, as suggested by J. P. Bigham et al. [23]. However, converting spoken language into sign language can result in information omission and hinder understanding for deaf-mutes who are already able to recognize written language. To improve the user experience and enthusiasm of deaf-mutes in virtual conference systems, this study proposes a 3D interactive virtual conference system based on the 2D virtual conference system. This new system aims to facilitate smoother communication and interaction for deaf-mutes in virtual conference environments.

3 Proposed Methodology

3.1 Enhancing Functionality of the 3D Interactive Virtual Conference System

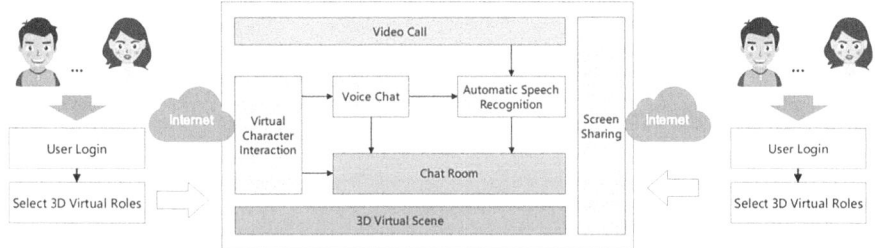

Fig. 1. Function module structure of 3D interactive virtual conference system.

This study developed an interactive virtual conferencing system based on a three-dimensional virtual environment, with the system architecture illustrated in Fig. 1. Unity3D 2022.2.1 was employed as the development engine, and coding was conducted in Visual Studio 2019, with MySQL utilized for data storage. Three-dimensional scenes and character models were edited and UVW-mapped in 3ds Max 2019, after which the models were imported into the Unity engine for further texture mapping and animation development. Functionalities were implemented within Unity, encompassing a user login module, 3D virtual character selection module, conference room connection module, 3D scene module, screen sharing, video calling, voice communication, speech-to-text module, virtual character interaction and dialogue module (e.g., exchanging business cards), and a text communication module.

Figure 1 illustrates the process of using the 3D Interactive Virtual Conference System (3DIVCS). Firstly, users are required to log in to the system with their username and select their 3D virtual character model. This character will represent the user in the system and participate in the meeting. Once logged in, users are assigned a seat in the 3D virtual meeting scene. During the meeting, the user's screen displays the 3D virtual environment, which can be freely navigated during breaks. At the beginning of the meeting, users are allocated a seat in the virtual conference room, which consists of three screens. The main screen is used for screen sharing, while the two secondary screens display camera images and subtitles generated from voice-to-text conversion. In particular, the secondary screens serve as an important tool for deaf-mute users who cannot hear the audio content. Figure 2 demonstrates the use of the secondary screen for accessing conference content. During breaks and after the meeting, users are free to roam around the 3D virtual environment and interact with other 3D virtual characters through collision detection. Users can also exchange personal business cards via text or voice, subject to the consent of the other party.

3.2   Enhancing User Participation in Virtual Conferences Through the 3D Interactive Virtual Conference System

Fig. 2. An user perspective interface of 3D virtual conference system.

The effect of user participation in virtual conference systems has been a topic of interest for many researchers. The 3D Interactive Virtual Conference System (3DIVCS) incorporates three screens, with the main screen used for displaying users' PPTs or screen sharing, while the other two display camera footage and subtitles generated by speech recognition. By placing speech recognition as a primary feature in the scene, the 3DIVCS enables deaf-mute users to access conference communication content via the subtitle screen. This feature is highly beneficial for deaf-mute users, as it enables them to see the conference screen and follow the speech content. Moreover, during long meetings, users can adjust their perspective to view other users around them, which facilitates alleviate the fatigue associated with prolonged viewing of a static image.

3.3   The Benefits of Using 3D Virtual Characters in the 3DIVCS for Deaf-Mute Users

Incorporating 3D virtual characters as users in the 3D Interactive Virtual Conference System (3DIVCS) provides several advantages, especially for deaf-mute users. Research by Halbreich et al. [24] suggests that deaf-mutes often experience communication barriers due to congenital reasons, which can result in a lack of confidence and inferiority, and severe communication problems with others. Using 3D virtual characters equalizes all users and facilitates deaf-mute users conceal their limitations. In the 3DIVCS, users are

Fig. 3. A dialog interface between two user avatars in a 3d virtual conference system.

randomly assigned seats in the 3D virtual scene. Before the meeting starts or during a break, users can move around freely and initiate conversations with other virtual characters through collision detection, as shown in Fig. 3. When two characters are close, they can exchange personal business cards and chat applications, which can be followed by video, voice or text conversations. Using virtual characters can help deaf-mute users feel more expressive and confident, enabling them to better participate in the conference.

4 Experimental Results and Discussions

4.1 Participants

This study examines the efficacy of 3DIVCS for deaf-mute users. The research randomly selected 20 deaf-mute students (10 in grade 2 and 10 in grade 3) from the Special Education College of Fuzhou Vocational and Technical College of China. Participants were informed that they could withdraw from the study at any time if they felt uncomfortable. The students were randomly divided into two groups, each with the same prior knowledge. Two virtual conference systems were used in the experiment: the TENCENT Conference system, a 2D system without 3D virtual scenes or roles, and the 3D Interactive Virtual Conference System (3DIVCS) developed by the research team. The 3DIVCS incorporates 3D virtual roles and voice-to-text functionality, whereas the TENCENT Conference system is moderated and referred to as 2DVMS.

4.2 Experimental Procedure

The main focus of this study was to investigate the effectiveness of a 70-min virtual meeting, moderated by a teacher, in facilitating learning and communication related to professional knowledge. The meeting included a 10-min break every 30 min. The meeting was presided over by the teacher. The first group conducted the experiment in a 2D virtual conference system, the first group was the reference group and the second group was the experimental group, and the experiment was conducted in a 3D interactive virtual conference system. The members of Group one and group two are all using the conference system in different places. In order to better understand the participation effect of deaf-mute users using 3D interactive virtual conference system, we adopted the five-point quantification table of cognitive load proposed by Hwang et al. [25] for development. This post-test usefulness sets The questionnaire in terms of Perceived usefulness and Perceived ease of use of The virtual meeting system. Among them, the perceived usefulness evaluation of virtual reality conference system has 6 questions in the questionnaire, and the perceived ease of use evaluation of virtual reality conference system has 7 questions in the questionnaire. The maximum score for each answer is 5 points, with a minimum of 1 point.

Each group was led by a professional teacher who spent 15 min at the start of the experiment introducing the main features of the virtual conference system. During the 60-min professional learning activity, each group used either the 2D virtual conference system (group one) or the 3D interactive virtual conference system (group two) and then filled out usability questionnaires at the end of the meeting. During the break, the participants in group two were encouraged to interact with each other using avatars. The primary differences between the two groups were the virtual meeting systems they used and the methods they used to communicate with other group members. Following the experiment, the moderator conducted interviews with and summarized the experiences of the two groups of deaf students.

4.3   Results

After conducting the questionnaire survey, we utilized an independent t-test to analyze the data samples. An independent sample t-test is suitable for testing the difference in data obtained from two groups of unrelated samples. In this study, we used two different groups to conduct experiments on the 2D virtual conference system and 3D virtual conference system, respectively. As these groups met the conditions for the use of independent t-test, we adopted this method for statistical analysis. Table 1 presents the experimental results, with the mean representing the average value of the experimental data and SD reflecting the degree of dispersion among individuals in the group. The t-test was utilized to compare the differences between the two conference systems, analyzing the relationship between categorical and quantitative data.

An independent sample t-test was conducted to compare the post-test results of the two groups. The results showed a significant difference ($t = 5.635$, $P < 0.05$), indicating that the 3D interactive virtual conference system effectively facilitates communication for deaf-mute users. However, in terms of human-computer interaction, the post-test did not reach a significant level ($t = 0.000$, $P > 0.05$), indicating that the 3DIVCS and 2D virtual conference system have similar ease of human-computer interaction. Regarding the perceived usefulness, the post-test of the two groups was significantly different ($t = 7.019$, $P < 0.05$), with a mean value of 4.53, indicating that the 3DIVCS was more useful than the 2D virtual conference system. However, in terms of perceived ease of use, the post-test results did not show a significant difference ($t = 0.397$, $P > 0.05$), suggesting that 3DIVCS and 2D virtual conference system have similar ease of use, and

Table 1. Independent sample t-test the congnitive loads between the two groups.

	Group	N	Mean	SD	t
Help with communication	3DIVCM	10	4.70	0.483	5.635**
	2DVCM	10	2.60	1.07	
Human Computer Interaction	3DIVCM	10	4.90	0.316	0.000
	2DVCM	10	4.90	0.316	
Perceived usefulness	3DIVCM	10	4.53	0.204	7.019**
	2DVCM	10	3.48	0.426	
Perceived ease of use	3DIVCM	10	4.80	0.204	0.397
	2DVCM	10	4.77	0.099	
Total	3DIVCM	10	4.67	0.113	7.494**
	2DVCM	10	4.17	0.177	

** $p < 0.05$

deaf-mute users do not encounter operational difficulties. Overall, the results indicate that 3DIVCS is beneficial for deaf-mutes to communicate with other users online, and the perceived usefulness of the 3DIVCS system is higher than that of the 2D virtual conference system. In terms of human-computer interaction and perceived ease of use, 3DIVCS is similar to 2D virtual conference system, which is relatively easy to operate.

4.4 Interview

An additional interview section was included in the experiment, following the interview method developed by Hwang et al.[26]. The interview consisted of four questions designed to assess the impact of the 3D interactive virtual conferencing system on deaf-mute users. The interview questions included: "What are the differences between the 3D interactive virtual conferencing system and the 2D conferencing system you have used before?", "Did this meeting system help you to participate in online meetings? If so, how?", "Overall, what are the advantages of the 3DIVCM system?", and "What kind of support did you receive through this system?" To gain a comprehensive understanding of the impact of the 3D interactive virtual conferencing system on deaf-mute students, five participants were randomly selected from each group to participate in the interview, resulting in a total of 10 participants. The comparison of the frequency of mentions for 3DIVCM and 2DVCM across interviews on different topics and content is shown in Table 2.

During the interview, U01 from the 3DIVCM group expressed that the communication mode of 3D characters is similar to that of games, which makes communication feel more relaxed and enjoyable. U02 appreciated the simplicity of the 3DIVCM operation, which allowed him to communicate with ease and without pressure. In contrast, U06 from the 2DVCM group did not feel pressured to interact, but also had limited contact and communication with others in the system. U09 mentioned that the 2DVCM display screen being controlled by the host can be tiring over time. Overall, the 3DIVCM appears to be more helpful in facilitating communication and providing a more relaxed communication experience for deaf-mute users. Additionally, the 3DIVCM system shows better man-machine operation performance and enables deaf-mutes to participate more actively in meetings. The operation difficulty of the 3DIVCM system did not pose any significant challenges for deaf-mute users, who found the system to be easy to use.

Table 2. The analysis results of the interviews.

Theme	Main content	The number of times mentioned	
		3DIVCM	2DVCM
Improve frequency of communication	Initiate communication with others	2	1
	Relaxing	2	1
	Ask for Help	2	0
Improve motivation to attend virtual meetings	I'll spend more time operating the conference system	2	0
	Always focus on the conference system	3	0
	Love the meeting format	1	1
The operation difficulty of the system	Can pick it up quickly	3	3
	Not hard	3	3
	Receivability	3	3
Acceptence	Better than the past Conference system	4	1
	Hope taking all Conference will be this	3	2
	Try again in the future	2	2

3DIVCM and *2DVCM* represent users of different systems, respectively.

5   Conclusion

With the rapid development of internet technology, online meeting systems and online classrooms have gradually been recommended for special education reform efforts. However, traditional online meeting systems have not considered the needs of deaf-mute users, resulting in a poor participation experience for them. To address this issue, we developed a 3D Interactive Virtual Conference System (3DIVCS) that takes into account the learning styles and individual characteristics of deaf-mute users. In addition to providing multi-user video communication, voice communication, and speech recognition functionalities, the system enables users to communicate and interact within a virtual scene through 3D avatars. To evaluate the effectiveness of the 3D Interactive Virtual

Conference System (3DIVCS), we conducted a user experience experiment with deaf-mute participants and compared it with a 2D Virtual Conference System (2DVCS) using questionnaires and interviews. Our findings show that 3DIVCS outperformed 2DVCS in terms of "facilitating communication" and "perceived usefulness," while there was no significant difference in human-computer interaction and perceived ease of use. During the interview phase, 3DIVCS users reported feeling more motivated to communicate and interact when using virtual avatars, which is consistent with previous research on gamification and learning motivation. Participants also found no significant difference between 3DIVCS and 2DVCS in terms of system operation difficulty and ease of use. We believe that the 3D Interactive Virtual Conference System can significantly improve the participation experience for deaf-mute users and could bring benefits to all users in the future. We plan to conduct more experimental tests with other user groups. In the future, we will expand the research group and conduct further research work on the social interaction of deaf-mute people with the aid of metaverse technology.

Funding Statement. This work is supported by the Natural Science Foundation of Fujian Province (No. 2022J01644), The Higher Education Scientific Research Planning Project(No. ZD202309). Fujian Province young and middle-aged teachers education research project (No. JAT210651 and No.JAT210653).

Data Availability. We provided the information about the research purpose, possible risk, discomfort, human rights, and choices during the research implementation to the teachers and students who voluntarily participated in this research. They knew that their participation was voluntary and they could withdraw from the study at any time. The data can be obtained by sending a request e-mail to the corresponding author.

Disclosure of Interest. The author declares that there are no conflicts of interest.

References

1. Sharabi, L.L.: The enduring effect of internet dating: meeting online and the road to marriage. Commun. Res. **51**, 259–284 (2024)
2. Du, X., Huang, T., Wang, X., Wu, S., Chen, X., Jiang, J., et al.: Difficulties in implicit emotion regulation of the deaf college students: an ERP study. Heliyon **10**, e34451 (2024)
3. Yi, Y., Moon, R.H.: Sustained use of virtual meeting platforms for classes in the post-coronavirus era: the mediating effects of technology readiness and social presence. Sustainability **13**(15), 8203 (2021)
4. WHO. Deafness and hearing loss (2023)
5. Aziz, M., Othman, A.: Evolution and trends in sign language avatar systems: unveiling a 40-year journey via systematic review. Multimodal Technol. Interact. **7**, 97 (2023)
6. Vostanis, P., Hayes, M., Du, M.: Detection of behavioural and emotional problems in deaf children and adolescents: comparison of two rating scales. Child Care Health Dev. **23**(3), 233–246 (1997)
7. Educational Programs for Deaf Students. aad, 169, 117–66 (2024)
8. Fraser, S., Mancl, D.: Virtual and the future of conferences. Commun. ACM **67**, 32–34 (2024)
9. Verstraete, P., Romeiras Amado, M., Manique, C.: Paedagogica Historica themed issue: gaining momentum - new cultural histories of education and disability. Paedagog. Hist. **60**, 587–591 (2024)

10. Alkadhi, O.H., Abdulrahman, B.I., Alhawas, S.A., Almanie, L.A., Alsalmi, H.E., Aljumah, A.A.: The need for a smart phone application to facilitate communication between deaf-mute and hearing-impaired patients and dentists. J. Fam. Med. Primary care. **10**, 2928 (2021)

11. Parker, K., Uddin, R., Ridgers, N.D., Brown, H., Veitch, J., Salmon, J., et al.: The use of digital platforms for adults' and adolescents' physical activity during the COVID-19 pandemic (our life at home): survey study. J. Med. Internet Res. **23**, e23389 (2021)

12. Isobe, T., Ito, R.: Security analysis of end-to-end encryption for zoom meetings. IEEE Access **9**, 90677–90689 (2021)

13. Jang, C.: A multiple servers conference service system by media control channel/distributed conference manipulation architecture. J. Korea Inst. Inf. Electron. Commun. Technol. **12**, 224–230 (2019)

14. Erickson, T., Shami, N.S., Kellogg, W.A., Levine, D.W.: Synchronous interaction among hundreds In: An Evaluation of a Conference in an Avatar-Based Virtual Environment, pp. 503–512 (2011)

15. Kamel, P., Brookmeyer, C., Tang, H., Solnes, L., Lin, C.T.: Conference attendance tracking and evaluation in the era of virtual conferences. Acad. Radiol. **29**, S76-81 (2022)

16. Atasoy, M., Şılbır, L., Erümit, S.F., Bahçekapılı, E., Yıldız, A., Karal, H.: Visual appearance features of sign language avatars. Kastamonu Educ. J. **31**, 386–403 (2023)

17. Hartman, M.C., Smolen, E.R., Powell, B.: Curriculum and instruction for deaf and hard of hearing students: evidence from the past—considerations for the future. Educ. Sci. **13**, 533 (2023)

18. Argyropoulos, S., Moustakas, K., Karpov, A.A., Aran, O., Tzovaras, D., Tsakiris, T., et al.: Multimodal user interface for the communication of the disabled. J. Multimodal User Interfaces **2**, 105–116 (2008)

19. Yousaf, K., Mehmood, Z., Saba, T., Rehman, A., Rashid, M., Altaf, M., et al.: A novel technique for speech recognition and visualization based mobile application to support two-way communication between deaf-mute and normal peoples. Wireless Commun. Mob. Comput. **2018**(1), 1013234 (2018)

20. Hsu, C.-H., Wu, Y.-L., Cheng, W.-H., Chen, Y.-J., Hua, K.-L.: HoloTube: a low-cost portable 360-degree interactive autostereoscopic display. Multimedia Tools Appl. **76**, 9099–9132 (2017)

21. Du, R., Li, D., Varshney, A.: Geollery: a mixed reality social media platform, pp. 1–13 (2019)

22. Ibanez, M.B., Crespo, R.M., Kloos C.D.: Assessment of knowledge and competencies in 3D virtual worlds: A proposal. Springer, pp. 165–76 (2010)

23. Bigham, J.P., Kushalnagar, R., Huang, T.H.K, Flores, J.P., Savage, S.: On how deaf people might use speech to control devices, pp. 383–384 (2017)

24. Halbreich, U.: Influence of deaf-mute parents on the character of their offspring. Acta Psychiatr. Scand. **59**, 129–138 (1979)

25. Hwang, G.-J., Yang, L.-H., Wang, S.-Y.: A concept map-embedded educational computer game for improving students' learning performance in natural science courses. Comput. Educ. **69**, 121–130 (2013)

26. Hwang, G.-J., Yang, T.-C., Tsai, C.-C., Yang, S.J.: A context-aware ubiquitous learning environment for conducting complex science experiments. Comput. Educ. **53**, 402–413 (2009)

Visual Street Localization Refinement Method Using Differentiable Rendering

Jiannan Ye[1], Xiaoting Miao[2], and Xubo Yang[1(✉)]

[1] Shanghai Jiao Tong University, Shanghai, China
{wsyhdyjn,yangxubo}@sjtu.edu.cn
[2] Z-ONE Technology Co., Ltd., Shanghai, China

Abstract. Estimating the accurate location and pose of the camera on a vehicle is important for AR driving applications. In this work, we use a single image input and GIS map information to refine the raw geo-location and orientation from sensors on urban streets. We parse the urban scene in the image and obtain semantic and depth cues of buildings in the image using state-of-the-art deep learning methods. A 2.5D map is used as a reference to render the corresponding virtual semantic and depth maps given the initial sensor input. A camera pose optimization is performed by taking advantage of differentiable rendering to achieve maximal matching between the real image and the rendering. The results show that our method performs well on the Cityscapes dataset.

Keywords: Mixed/augmented reality · Image processing · Outdoor localization

1 Introduction

Knowing accurate geo-location and viewing pose is an important task for many outdoor Augmented Reality (AR) applications, including AR driving applications on urban streets. In AR driving applications, geo-location is first used to retrieve nearby digital map content and then the precise viewing pose including translation and rotation is used to project and superimpose the virtual content such as guidance, advertisements, and information about buildings and roads on images captured by the camera or on the real world with AR head up display. Since consumer-level Low-end GPS (Global Positioning System) sensors, heading sensors and dashcams are widely available and are installed in most cars nowadays, these AR driving applications enriching the surroundings hold great promise for improving the driving and riding experience and achieving business success. However, the accuracy of location and car heading from the sensors is limited. The GPS signal error can go up to 12.5 m [30] due to multipath effect or in cluttered environments. Because of this error, the initial AR effect is unsatisfactory. For example, we find that the car locations and headings of Cityscapes Dataset [12] are not accurate enough to generate convincing visual augmentations when blended with the real-world view (Fig. 1). For accurate AR

© The Author(s), under exclusive license to Springer Nature Singapore Pte Ltd. 2025
W. Song et al. (Eds.): ICXR 2024, LNCS 15461, pp. 223–235, 2025.
https://doi.org/10.1007/978-981-96-3679-2_15

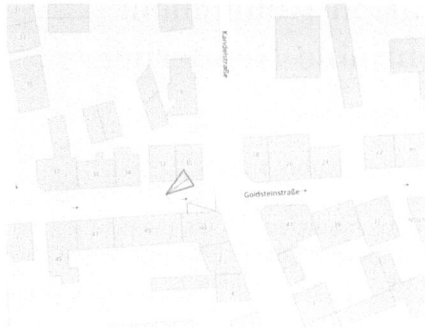

(a) Raw Camera location and orientation before and after refinement.

(b) 2.5D map rendering before and after refinement.

(c) Augmented image with virtual content

Fig. 1. The purpose of this paper is as follows: (a) The initial camera geo-location and orientation provided by sensors are shown as a red icon. The proposed method refines the initial location and orientation, enabling the buildings on 2.5D maps to be rendered correctly, as shown in (b) bottom compared with the initial rendering on the top. (c) Using the refined pose of the camera, we can augment the urban surroundings by superimposing virtual content on the captured image. (Color figure online)

experience, we need to refine the location and orientation initially provided by the sensors.

The images captured by the camera can be used to extract visual cues of the scene and determine the accurate geo-location of the visual acquisition system based on a geo-reference and possibly a prior location. Generally, this kind of problem is called visual-based localization [25] and has been a focus of the Computer Vision community for a long time. Depending on the data type of the geo-reference, research can be divided into many categories, with the two most common being geo-tagged image dataset-based methods and 3D structure-based methods. However, the prior knowledge they typically require, such as registered images [1,14,18,29] or a detailed 3D model (point clouds built by structure-from-motion methods [15,27], LiDAR data [10], detailed digital elevation models [5,6], etc.), is cumbersome to acquire and maintain. Compared with detailed 3D structures, digital maps such as Google Maps and OpenStreetMap[1] are very common resources and are already widely available. Many studies have shown the potential of using a digital map as a lightweight geo-reference for visual-based localization in both a 2D planar form [7,11,23] or an untextured 2.5D model form built based on the outlines of buildings and approximate heights [2–4,20,24,28]. In this paper, we also follow this route to fully leverage the advantages of 2.5D models built using OpenStreetMap.

Having the image input and the surrounding 2.5D map, the localization of the camera is achieved through aligning the image features with their equivalents in the 2.5D map. Existing work parses the input image and extracts geometric features like building vertical edges [2–4,11,28], rooflines [5,31], corners [31], building facades [2,23,28], and depth [24], etc. However, some of these features are difficult to extract reliably [4,31] or have specific constraints on the image [11], making the image-to-map matching error-prone. In this paper, we novelly combine the idea of semantic area matching from [6] and extend the column-wise 1D depth sequence matching [24] to a 2D depth map. We use building segments and the depth map as higher-level semantic and geometric features from the input image to achieve robustness in complex driving scenarios.

For camera pose optimization, some existing work define a likelihood function and sample over a grid to get the pose with the maximal likelihood value [4,23,24] or iteratively perform a linear search in a certain direction given by a neural predictor [3], which are slow. Other methods build different specialized minimal solvers [2,11], which, however, are difficult to generalize.

In this paper, we adopt the idea of render-and-compare [19] which is widely applied in differentiable rendering [16,21,26]. They build a differentiable rendering pipeline to optimize parameters in 3D space such as vertex positions of a mesh model, lighting parameters, and camera pose by back-propagating the loss gradient computed using the rendered image and the ground truth 2d image. In our case, given a camera pose, a virtual image can be generated by rendering the 2.5D model to the camera (Fig. 1) and various geometric information can be projected and rendered on the image such as buildings' semantic mask, depth, normal etc. The best camera pose produces the maximal consistency between the real image and the rendered image, in other words, has the minimal reprojection error. The loss functions can be defined to describe the inconsistency between the two images and using differentiable rendering, we manage to build a general optimization scheme to directly regress the camera pose by backpropagating the loss gradient from image space to camera parameters.

Briefly speaking, in this paper, we propose a method, that takes a coarse GPS location and heading as the initial parameters, together with the image

---

[1] OpenStreetMap: https://www.openstreetmap.org/.

captured by the camera as input, to refine the camera pose. Our method takes full advantage of the availability of digital map, the deep learning capability of parsing single images and the differentiable nature of differentiable rendering to do optimization. The refined location and heading can be used to accurately blend virtual and real worlds, initialize Simultaneous Localization And Mapping (SLAM) system and recover the AR system when it loses tracking. Note that the cost of our solution is very low. The monocular camera can be replaced with a binocular camera to get a more accurate depth map. And the method can be integrated seamlessly into a continuous AR system and the refinement can be performed asynchronously from time to time.

The contributions of this paper are summarized below.

– We propose a method to improve the vehicle-camera pose by matching the depth map and semantic map estimated from the image and the semantic mask and depth information rendered from surrounding buildings in the digital map.
– We propose a novel differentiable rendering-based optimization scheme to effectively refine the geo-location.
– We conduct experiments using images from the Cityscapes dataset, and demonstrate that the geo-locations are accurately refined.

2   Related Work

Two major groups of visual-based localization methods are image set based methods and structure based methods.

2.1   Image Set Based Method

Image set based methods share many similarities with image retrieval methods while the images are often registered with geo-tags, and the pose of the query image is the final target. Im2gps [14] leveraged a dataset of over 6 million GPS-tagged images from Internet and built features for each of the images. The system then found the nearest neighbors of the query image in feature space and computed the distribution of the query across the world. Zamir et al. [29] leveraged a dataset of about 100,000 Google Street View images as the reference images. They indexed the SIFT descriptors of reference images in a tree and queried the tree when given a query image. They used GPS-tags to remove less reliable descriptors and each descriptor voted for the nearest neighbor. NetVLAD [1] showed great power of learning image descriptors and performed well in visual place recognition under varying visual conditions. [17, 18] trained a CNN to predict a 6 DoF camera pose directly from an input image. It requires massive images for a certain area and does not scale well spatially.

2.2   Structure Based Method

Image set based methods are considered as 2D-to-2D matching to align the query image to a reference. Given a detailed 3D structure, matching between 3D and 2D is performed in structure based localization. A large-scale 3D model built by SfM is the geo-reference for [15,27]. They found the correspondences between feature points on the image and those in the reconstructed point cloud using synthetic visual documents [15], Vocabulary-based Prioritized Search [27]. SfM points naturally contain feature while other 3D structures such as LiDAR [10] and digital elevation maps [5] contains reliable skylines to effectively align the image to pre-acquired models.

Our work here is most related to existing work uses 2.5D maps (2D maps with height information) to calibrate camera locations. Among these work, Chu et al. [11] took an image of a single urban building and extracted the building corner edges to generate location-orientation hypotheses on a map to refine the initial signals. However they only solved the simplest situations and can not be applied to more complex scenarios. Arth et al. [4] estimated the camera rotation from straight line segments and translation aligning the 2.5D map with the semantic segmentation of the image. They used this method to initialize and extend a SLAM map to global coordinate system. Liu et al. [20] initialized a SLAM system leveraging the point-facade depth association. Armagan et al. [3] trained segmentation neural network to segment the input image into building edges and facades and also trained a convolutional neural network (CNN) to predict which direction the camera should move and rotate to get a better semantic region matching between rendered image and real image. Their method iteratively optimized the camera pose and is slow until it converges. Later, the authors [2] improved it by minimal solvers.

2.3   Differentiable Rendering

To relate changes in rendered images to changes in parameters in 3D space, and backpropagate the gradient from image space to 3D space, recent papers have described differentiable rendering. OpenDR [22] managed to generate approximate derivatives from pixel to parameters and is now widely used in human body reconstruction. [16] approximated the gradient with a handcraft function and [9,21] made the rendering pipeline differentiable using weighted aggregation operators. Differentiable rendering makes it possible to optimize parameters by minimizing the reprojection error. It has shown strengths in reconstructing 3D models, estimating lighting and appearance parameters using only 2D supervision. And it is also promising to estimate camera pose and making it a good fit for this context.

3   Proposed Method

3.1   Coordinate System and Problem Statement

The purpose of this work is to find a refined transformation matrix $g \in SE(3)$ for a camera based on the rough initial camera pose and the corresponding image.

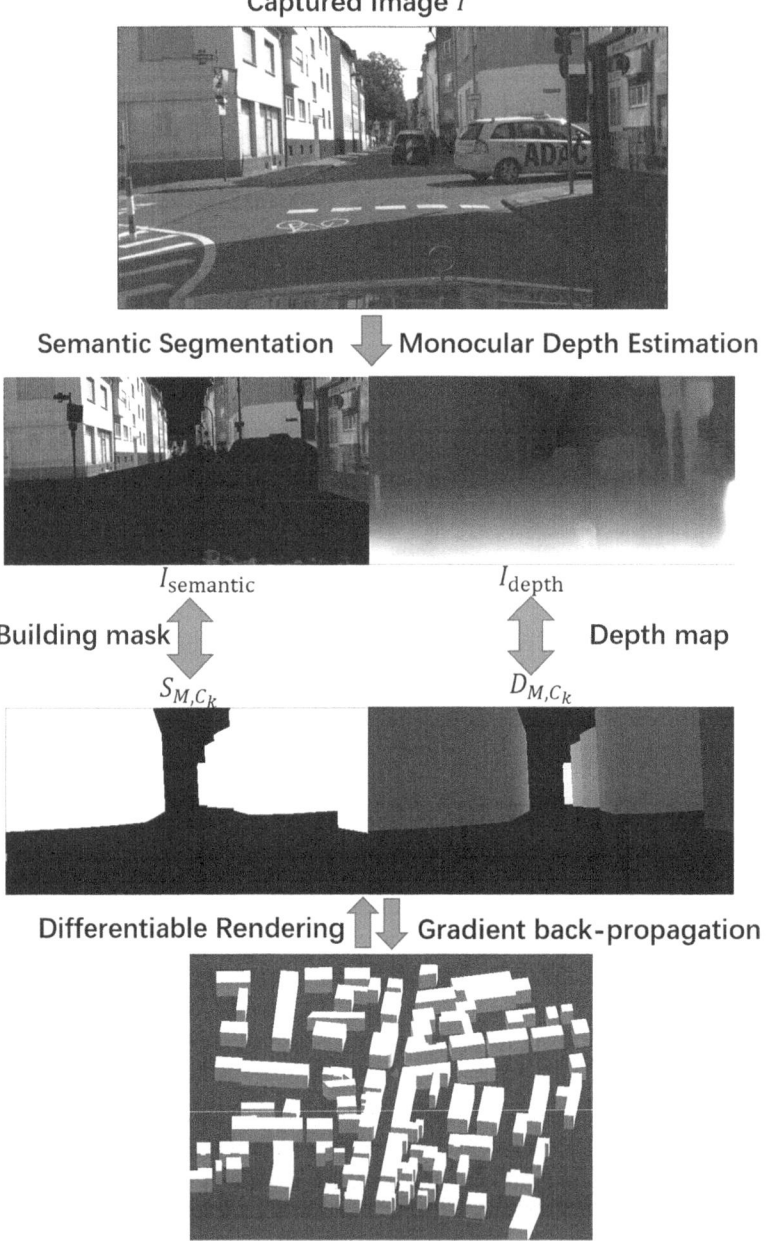

Fig. 2. Overview of the proposed method. Building mask and depth map are estimated from the captured image and are compared with the rendered ones using differentiable rendering and the gradient of loss is backpropagated to optimize the camera parameters.

In this paper, we only consider the equipment setup of Cityscapes Dataset [12] where a monocular camera is rigidly installed in a car, and the intrinsic matrix of the camera as well as the extrinsic matrix of the camera with respect to the coordinate system of the GPS and heading sensor are known in advance. We assume that the pitch, roll, and altitude of the vehicle camera are fixed. Therefore, we focus on estimating the accurate 2D geo-location, including the 2D position on the ground plane and the yaw orientation of the vehicle camera.

Given the initial GPS location (lon_i, lat_i), we use OpenStreetMap API to query the $200\,\mathrm{m} \times 200\,\mathrm{m}$ square map tile centered at (lon_i, lat_i) which serves as the origin of the world coordinate system. The 2D map tile provides the GPS coordinates of each point on the outlines of the nearby buildings. For simplicity, we set the heights of buildings to $10\,\mathrm{m}$. As the most common longitude-latitude based WGS84 system is not in metric units, we convert the GPS footprints to metric coordinates and build simple mesh models M (see Fig. 2) for the buildings based on outlines and heights in the world coordinate system. Using the extrinsic matrix we can obtain the initial 6-DoF camera pose in the world coordinate system. With height, pitch, roll fixed, we define the initial camera parameters as a vector $\mathbf{C}_i = [x_i, z_i, yaw_i]$. A modification vector $\Delta\mathbf{C} = [\Delta x, \Delta z, \Delta yaw]$ is what we aim to estimate the refine $\mathbf{C}$ by simply adding $\Delta\mathbf{C}$. Initially, $\Delta\mathbf{C}_i = [0, 0, 0]$.

From the input image I, we will obtain the mask for building semantic segments $I_{semantic}$ and inverse depth map for the building region I_{depth}. The details are described in Sect. 3.2. Given a camera pose $\mathbf{C}_k = \mathbf{C}_i + \Delta\mathbf{C}_k$, we can get the rendered image of building silhouette S_{M,C_k} and depth map D_{M,C_k} using a differentiable silhouette renderer and a differentiable depth renderer respectively (Sect. 3.3). We will define a loss functions consist silhouette loss $L_{sil}(S_{M,C_k}, I_{semantic})$ and depth loss $L_{depth}(D_{M,C_k}, I_{depth})$ and we aim to estimate the $\Delta\hat{\mathbf{C}}$ that minimizes the loss function.

$$\Delta\hat{\mathbf{C}} = \arg\min_{\Delta\mathbf{C}_k}(L_{sil}(S_{M,C_k}, I_{semantic}) + \lambda L_{depth}(D_{M,C_k}, I_{depth}) \qquad (1)$$

3.2   De-Rendering: Semantic Segmentation and Depth Estimation

Given an input image I, our system is designed to work with any pre-trained network that can generate dense segmentation labels on the input image. In our work, we use DeepLab v3+ [8] trained on the Cityscapes dataset [12] for the semantic segmentation because of its superior accuracy from our experiments. The DeepLab v3+ architecture is an encoder-decoder network, and attains a test set performance of 82.1% without any post-processing. It labels each pixel of the input image with a semantic class and here we only focus on the building class. We apply the pretrained model to infer semantic region covered by buildings and create a mask $I_{semantic}$ by labeling pixels of the building as 1 and the others as 0 as shown in Fig. 2.

To generate the inverse depth map for building region I_{depth}, we take full advantage of the power of deep learning on monocular depth estimation and also adopt a state-of-the-art learning method - Monodepth2 [13] to estimate the depth map of the input image I. The model infers the disparity map and we inverse it and multiply it with a scale factor to get the metric depth map. Then we pixel-wise multiply the depth map with the building mask and inverse it to produce an inverse depth map for only the building region.

$$I'_{depth} = c_{scale\,factor}/I_{disparity} \otimes I_{semantic} \tag{2}$$

$$I_{depth} = I'_{depth}/max(I'_{depth}) \tag{3}$$

The $I_{semantic}$ and I_{depth} we get are considered as a reference or target image for rendered image to match as much as possible to get a minimal loss.

3.3 Differentiable Rendering

For differentiable rendering, we use modified PyTorch3D library [26] which implements the soft rasterization method from [21]. Here, we briefly introduce the core idea of this method. Many steps in the traditional rendering pipeline are naturally differentiable such as transformation, projection and color computation except for rasterization and z-buffering. Rasterization is a discrete step determining the covering primitive for each pixel based on the relative positions between the pixels and triangles. Z-buffering calculates the depth of each pixel from the pixel to the corresponding primitive according the rasterization and is also non-differentiable. [21] uses 2D probability maps $\{P_j\}$ to model the probability of each pixel staying inside the triangle j using a sigmoid function based the signed distance between pixel and the projected triangle in image plane. Then use a aggregate function to fuse all probability maps based on probability value and pixel-to-triangle depth. This modifications makes it possible for camera to receive gradient from the image.

Here we define two renderers, namely soft silhouette renderer and soft depth renderer to differentiably generate silhouette mask and depth map given the camera parameters $\mathbf{C}$ and 2.5D model $\mathbf{M}$. For silhouette, for each pixel i we cumulatively multiply $1 - P_j^i$ and get the alpha channel value for each pixel (P_j^i stands for the probability of pixel i staying inside triangle j). S_{M,C_k} is generated accordingly as shown in Fig. 2.

$$S_{M,C_k}(i) = 1 - \prod_j (1 - P_j^i) \tag{4}$$

For soft depth map D_{M,C_k}, for each pixel i, the view dependent depth vector d_j^i for each triangle j can be obtained by projection and interpolation (if triangle j doesn't cover pixel i, $d_j^i = 0$). This vector is provided directly by PyTorch3D. Then for each pixel, we need to get the minimal value in d_j^i to be the depth value of pixel i. Directly selecting the minimal value is non-differentiable so here we adopt a log-sum-exp as a smooth min function.

$$D_{M,C_k}(i) = -\gamma \log \frac{1}{N} \sum_{j=1}^{N} exp(-\frac{d_j^i}{\gamma}) \tag{5}$$

where N is the number of triangles we take in account for each pixel i and $\gamma \to 0^+$. Finally, we apply the same masking and normalization as in I_{depth}. We carefully control the parameters that influence transparency and blurriness to ensure that the minor differences between the soft depth map and the real depth map, as well as those between the soft silhouette map and the real silhouette map, are negligible.

3.4 Optimization

In order to get the best camera pose, we design a loss function to measure the inconsistency between the rendered image and the input image.

In order to utilize both semantic cues and geometric depth cues, we define silhouette loss as the buildings' semantic region Intersection over Union (IoU) loss.

$$L_{sil}(S_{M,C_k}, I_{semantic}) = 1 - \frac{\|I_{semantic} \otimes S_{M,C_k}\|_1}{\|I_{semantic} \oplus S_{M,C_k} - I_{semantic} \otimes S_{M,C_k}\|_1} \quad (6)$$

where $\otimes$, $\oplus$ are the element-wise product and sum operators respectively.

The depth loss is defined as the L1 norm between two masked inverse depth maps.

$$L_{depth}(D_{M,C_k}, I_{depth}) = \|I_{depth} - D_{M,C_k}\|_1 \quad (7)$$

Since the differentiable rendering is implemented within a deep learning framework, we can directly use Adam optimizer to minimize the loss function without any modifications. It shows the power of solving camera pose and other 3D parameters with a differentiable rendering framework allowing one to leverage powerful optimizers from the deep learning community and can easily extend the loss function and incorporate more 2D features from the image.

4 Evaluation

In this experiment, we select 70 images which contain considerable building regions and cover different scenarios from 7 European cities in CityScapes dataset and use OpenStreetMap as 2D maps. The initial geo-location and camera pose is also provided by the dataset. The images are resize to 256×512. The experiments were conducted on an RTX 3090, using the software frameworks PyTorch3D 0.7.1 and PyTorch 1.12.1.

Figure 3 shows the qualitative results of our method. In different scenes a car may encounter, such as buildings on each side of the images, crossings and urban valley, the proposed method refines the rough camera poses with visually significant errors and reproduce rendering results with satisfying overlapping of the reprojected building models and the real building regions.

For quantitative evaluations, first we measure of IoU improvement comparing the initial average IoU of building regions before refinement and the IoU after refinement. Since there is no exact ground truth for the geo-locations and orientations in CityScapes dataset, we manually adjust the camera poses by which the

Fig. 3. Qualitative Refinement Results. Left column: rendering of the 2.5D map using the initial GPS and heading signals. Right column: rendering results after geo-location and orientation refinement. Red edges indicate the outlines of the buildings. (Color figure online)

projection results of maps match the captured images well considering building edges, building identities and overlapping. And we calculate the average position and orientation errors before and after refinement. The results are shown in Table 1. The IoU increases significantly as it is the target of optimization but the IoU does not approach 1 since the height of building is not accurate and real buildings are occluded by trees, pedestrians, and cars. The orientation error decreases significantly while position error doesn't seem to decrease since the manually calibrated positions are also ambiguous and error-prone. Additionally, the depth estimation is not accurate enough, and some scale errors persist.

Table 1. Quantitative evaluation of the proposed refinement method

Method	IoU (%)	Position error (m)	Orientation error (degree)
Initial	46.05	6.02	34.59
Ours	70.47	5.44	10.46

5   Conclusion and Future Work

In this paper, we present a novel visual-based localization refinement method built in the recently developed differentiable rendering framework. We extract the semantic segmentation and depth cues from the real images and compare them with the corresponding ones rendered from the 2.5D map and the camera pose. Loss functions are designed for the semantic and depth channels, and the camera pose is optimized by backpropagating the gradient.

This optimization framework is promising because it is scalable: other features such as building edges, corners, and normals can be introduced by just defining the differentiable renderer and designing the loss function in image space and which we plan to explore in the future. The real world is highly dynamic, and only static parts like buildings and roads are useful for refinement. However, since static parts are often occluded, removing the influence of occlusion is also of great importance. We also need to do more solid quantitative evaluations and integrate the proposed method into an AR system in the future.

Acknowledgments. This work was supported by SAIC Motor Corporation Limited.

Disclosure of Interests. All authors disclosed no relevant relationships.

References

1. Arandjelovic, R., Gronat, P., Torii, A., Pajdla, T., Sivic, J.: NetVLAD: CNN architecture for weakly supervised place recognition. In: Proceedings of the IEEE Conference on Computer Vision and Pattern Recognition, pp. 5297–5307 (2016)
2. Armagan, A., Hirzer, M., Roth, P.M., Lepetit, V.: Accurate camera registration in urban environments using high-level feature matching. In: BMVC (2017)
3. Armagan, A., Hirzer, M., Roth, P.M., Lepetit, V.: Learning to align semantic segmentation and 2.5 d maps for geolocalization. In: Proceedings of the IEEE Conference on Computer Vision and Pattern Recognition, pp. 3425–3432 (2017)
4. Arth, C., Pirchheim, C., Ventura, J., Schmalstieg, D., Lepetit, V.: Instant outdoor localization and slam initialization from 2.5 d maps. IEEE Trans. Vis. Comput. Graph. **21**(11), 1309–1318 (2015)
5. Bansal, M., Daniilidis, K.: Geometric urban geo-localization. In: Proceedings of the IEEE Conference on Computer Vision and Pattern Recognition, pp. 3978–3985 (2014)
6. Brejcha, J., Cadík, M.: Camera orientation estimation in natural scenes using semantic cues. In: 2018 International Conference on 3D Vision (3DV), pp. 208–217. IEEE (2018)

7. Cham, T.J., Ciptadi, A., Tan, W.C., Pham, M.T., Chia, L.T.: Estimating camera pose from a single urban ground-view omnidirectional image and a 2d building outline map. In: 2010 IEEE Computer Society Conference on Computer Vision and Pattern Recognition, pp. 366–373. IEEE (2010)
8. Chen, L.C., Zhu, Y., Papandreou, G., Schroff, F., Adam, H.: Encoder-decoder with atrous separable convolution for semantic image segmentation. In: Proceedings of the European Conference on Computer Vision (ECCV), pp. 801–818 (2018)
9. Chen, W., Ling, H., Gao, J., Smith, E., Lehtinen, J., Jacobson, A., Fidler, S.: Learning to predict 3d objects with an interpolation-based differentiable renderer. In: Advances in Neural Information Processing Systems, pp. 9605–9616 (2019)
10. Chiu, H.P., Murali, V., Villamil, R., Kessler, G.D., Samarasekera, S., Kumar, R.: Augmented reality driving using semantic geo-registration. In: 2018 IEEE Conference on Virtual Reality and 3D User Interfaces (VR), pp. 423–430. IEEE (2018)
11. Chu, H., Gallagher, A., Chen, T.: GPS refinement and camera orientation estimation from a single image and a 2d map. In: 2014 IEEE Conference on Computer Vision and Pattern Recognition Workshops, pp. 171–178. IEEE (2014)
12. Cordts, M., et al.: The cityscapes dataset for semantic urban scene understanding. In: Proceedings of the IEEE Conference on Computer Vision and Pattern Recognition (CVPR) (2016)
13. Godard, C., Mac Aodha, O., Firman, M., Brostow, G.J.: Digging into self-supervised monocular depth prediction (2019)
14. Hays, J., Efros, A.A.: Im2gps: estimating geographic information from a single image. In: 2008 IEEE Conference on Computer Vision and Pattern Recognition, pp. 1–8. IEEE (2008)
15. Irschara, A., Zach, C., Frahm, J.M., Bischof, H.: From structure-from-motion point clouds to fast location recognition. In: 2009 IEEE Conference on Computer Vision and Pattern Recognition, pp. 2599–2606. IEEE (2009)
16. Kato, H., Ushiku, Y., Harada, T.: Neural 3d mesh renderer. In: Proceedings of the IEEE Conference on Computer Vision and Pattern Recognition, pp. 3907–3916 (2018)
17. Kendall, A., Cipolla, R.: Geometric loss functions for camera pose regression with deep learning. In: Proceedings of the IEEE Conference on Computer Vision and Pattern Recognition, pp. 5974–5983 (2017)
18. Kendall, A., Grimes, M., Cipolla, R.: Posenet: a convolutional network for real-time 6-dof camera relocalization. In: Proceedings of the IEEE International Conference on Computer Vision, pp. 2938–2946 (2015)
19. Kundu, A., Li, Y., Rehg, J.M.: 3D-RCNN: instance-level 3d object reconstruction via render-and-compare. In: Proceedings of the IEEE Conference on Computer Vision and Pattern Recognition, pp. 3559–3568 (2018)
20. Liu, R., Zhang, J., Chen, S., Arth, C.: Towards slam-based outdoor localization using poor GPS and 2.5 d building models. In: 2019 IEEE International Symposium on Mixed and Augmented Reality (ISMAR), pp. 1–7. IEEE (2019)
21. Liu, S., Li, T., Chen, W., Li, H.: Soft rasterizer: a differentiable renderer for image-based 3d reasoning. In: Proceedings of the IEEE International Conference on Computer Vision, pp. 7708–7717 (2019)
22. Loper, M.M., Black, M.J.: Opendr: an approximate differentiable renderer. In: European Conference on Computer Vision, pp. 154–169. Springer (2014)
23. Mousavian, A., Kosecka, J.: Semantic image based geolocation given a map. arXiv preprint arXiv:1609.00278 (2016)

24. Ogawa, M., Aizawa, K.: Identification of buildings in street images using map information. In: 2019 IEEE International Conference on Image Processing (ICIP), pp. 984–988. IEEE (2019)
25. Piasco, N., Sidibé, D., Demonceaux, C., Gouet-Brunet, V.: A survey on visual-based localization: on the benefit of heterogeneous data. Pattern Recogn. **74**, 90–109 (2018)
26. Ravi, N., et al.: Pytorch3d (2020). https://github.com/facebookresearch/pytorch3d
27. Sattler, T., Leibe, B., Kobbelt, L.: Fast image-based localization using direct 2d-to-3d matching. In: 2011 International Conference on Computer Vision, pp. 667–674. IEEE (2011)
28. Yuan, J., Cheriyadat, A.M.: Combining maps and street level images for building height and facade estimation. In: Proceedings of the 2nd ACM SIGSPATIAL Workshop on Smart Cities and Urban Analytics, pp. 1–8 (2016)
29. Zamir, A.R., Shah, M.: Accurate image localization based on google maps street view. In: European Conference on Computer Vision, pp. 255–268. Springer (2010)
30. Zandbergen, P.A., Barbeau, S.J.: Positional accuracy of assisted GPS data from high-sensitivity GPS-enabled mobile phones. J. Navig. **64**(3), 381–399 (2011)
31. Zhao, Y., Qi, J., Zhang, R.: CBHE: corner-based building height estimation for complex street scene images. In: The World Wide Web Conference, pp. 2436–2447. ACM (2019)

A Survey of Smart Wearable Devices For Motion Capture

Xiao Jiang[1] , Shihui Guo[1] , Caihua Huang[2] , and Jing Zheng[2(✉)]

[1] School of Informatics, Xiamen University, Xiamen, China
[2] Xiamen University of Technology, Xiamen, China
zhengjing@xmut.edu.cn

Abstract. As the demand of motion capture in long time and unlimited environment grows, smart wearable devices have become a popular technology in motion capture. These devices are designed to track and analyze human movement with increasing accuracy, while ensures the comfort of wearing and removes the restrictions of the environment. They are expected to continuously monitor, collect, and process motion data and enhancing applications in sports, healthcare, and entertainment. This paper begins with a comprehensive overview of motion capture techniques and the evolution of wearable devices in this domain. We then classify the types of wearables for motion capture and examine the key sensors utilized. Following this, we introduce the algorithms that facilitate the predication of human motion, and discuss the limitations and challenges of current systems. Finally, we explore future trends in wearable motion capture technology and innovations that promise to enhance user experience and broaden the applications of these devices.

Keywords: Smart Wearable · Wearable Devices · Motion Capture

1 Introduction

In recent years, the rapid development of sensor technology and artificial intelligence has significantly driven the advancement and widespread use of smart wearable devices. These devices have found diverse applications, particularly in areas such as health monitoring [8], human-computer interaction [20], and entertainment [14], where they enhance daily life through real-time data collection and analysis. These smart wearables, by integrating advanced sensor technology and sophisticated data processing algorithms, offer users a variety of functionalities, from tracking physical activity to controlling digital environments.

At the same time, motion capture technology, once confined to specialized fields, is becoming more embedded in everyday life, it is now extensively used in filmmaking, gaming, animation, and robotics control [9]. However, motion capture has traditionally depended on expensive optical systems and limited environments, which prevented its use in outdoor settings and by individuals. Smart wearable devices has played a critical role in making motion capture

© The Author(s), under exclusive license to Springer Nature Singapore Pte Ltd. 2025
W. Song et al. (Eds.): ICXR 2024, LNCS 15461, pp. 236–250, 2025.
https://doi.org/10.1007/978-981-96-3679-2_16

more accessible and versatile, which has led to increasing research attention as shown in Fig. 1. The continued advancement of these technologies has not only expanded the scope of motion capture but also made it practical and affordable for a broader range of applications, from professional settings to personal use.

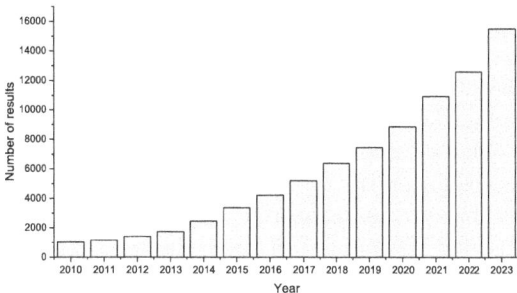

Fig. 1. Google Scholar search results for "Smart wearable motion capture" keywords from 2010 to 2023.

In contrast to traditional optical systems, these wearables offer a flexible solution that can be used in any environment, whether in gym, homes, or hospital. In healthcare, for example, wearable motion capture systems are being used to monitor patient progress during rehabilitation [5], and even help in diagnosing movement disorders such as Parkinson's disease [15]. These devices provide a non-invasive, continuous method of capturing movement data, offering healthcare professionals valuable insights into patient mobility over time. Similarly, in sports and fitness, wearables are helping athletes optimize their performance by analyzing their biomechanics, detecting inefficient movement patterns, and providing personalized training feedback. In the entertainment industry, wearable motion capture technology has revolutionized the way animations and visual effects are created. Instead of relying on expensive, fixed camera setups, actors can wear sensor-based suits that capture their movements in real-time, even in dynamic outdoor environments. This flexibility opens up new creative possibilities for filmmakers and game developers, allowing for more natural and immersive character animations. Moreover, in the gaming and virtual reality (VR) sectors, wearable devices enable players to experience a new level of interaction, where their physical movements are mirrored in the digital world, enhancing immersion and realism [14].

Despite the clear advantages of wearable motion capture technology, there are still several challenges that need to be addressed. Sensor accuracy can be affected by factors such as drift, signal interference, and environmental conditions. Moreover, ensuring comfort, battery life, and real-time data processing remains a significant challenge, especially for prolonged use. These limitations highlight the need for continuous advancements in both hardware and software to fully realize the potential of wearable motion capture systems.

As smart wearable technology continues to evolve, future trends point towards even more integrated and seamless solutions. Emerging technologies such as flexible electronics, stretchable sensors, and energy-harvesting materials will likely play a crucial role in making wearables more comfortable, efficient, and versatile. Furthermore, advancements in artificial intelligence and machine learning are expected to enhance the accuracy and efficiency of motion capture systems, enabling more precise tracking and real-time feedback in complex and dynamic environments. With the integration of 5G and edge computing, wearable devices will be able to process large amounts of data locally, minimizing latency and improving the responsiveness of motion capture applications.

This paper provides a comprehensive survey of smart wearable devices used for motion capture, exploring the types of wearables, the sensors they integrate, and the algorithms that process captured senor data. It will also introduce the various applications and advantages of these devices, expound the limitations and challenges they face, and discuss the emerging trends shaping the future of wearable motion capture technology.

2   Background

2.1   Motion Capture

Motion capture technology, often abbreviated as MoCap, refers to the process of recording the movement of objects or individuals, which is subsequently translated into digital data [9]. Its applications are broad, spanning industries such as filmmaking, animation, sports, healthcare, and robotics. By accurately capturing the dynamics of human motion, MoCap technology provides detailed data that can be used for creating realistic animations, analyzing athletic performance, improving rehabilitation processes, and even controlling robotic systems.

Traditionally, motion capture has been dominated by optical systems. These systems often rely on markers attached to key points on the subject's body. Multiple cameras are set up in a controlled environment to track these markers as the subject moves. The data collected from the cameras is then processed to calculate the position and movement of the body in three-dimensional space. This method, known as marker-based optical motion capture, is highly accurate but comes with several limitations: it requires expensive equipment, careful setup in controlled environments, and the markers can sometimes shift or fall off during movement, leading to data inconsistencies. In contrast, markerless optical motion capture uses computer vision techniques to track the body without requiring markers [11]. This system eliminates the need for physical markers by detecting body landmarks directly from video footage using advanced algorithms. While this approach reduces the complexity of setup and is less intrusive, it still requires multiple cameras and a controlled environment to maintain accuracy. Additionally, both marker-based and markerless optical systems are limited by occlusion problems, where parts of the body are blocked from the camera's view, leading to incomplete or inaccurate data capture.

As an alternative to optical systems, motion capture based on inertial measurement units (IMU) has gained significant popularity in recent years. IMU-based systems, such as Xsens and Noitom, measure the orientation, velocity, and position of body segments with small, lightweight sensors that combine accelerometers, gyroscopes, and magnetometers. These sensors are attached to various joints across the body. By tracking the movement of each sensor, the system can reconstruct the subject's full-body motion in real-time, without the need for cameras or a controlled environment. This method offers more flexibility and portability compared to optical systems, making it suitable for use in dynamic environments, such as sports fields or outdoor settings. However, a high number of IMUs to accurately track every joint are required, which can be cumbersome and expensive.

To address the limitations of using numerous IMUs, recent research has focused on reducing the number of sensors required for accurate motion capture. Advances in deep learning have enabled the development of algorithms that can infer full-body motion using only a few strategically placed IMUs. For example, systems that use sparse IMUs (typically 6 IMUs) placed on key body parts can now achieve motion tracking with a high degree of accuracy. This reduction in sensor count is achieved by training machine learning models on large datasets of motion capture data, allowing the system to predict the movement of other joints based on the information from the sparse IMU placement. This approach significantly improves the practicality and comfort of IMU-based motion capture systems, making them more user-friendly and less obtrusive.

Beyond IMUs, researchers are also exploring the use of other types of sensors for wearable motion capture systems. For instance, stretch sensors [4] can be embedded in fabrics to measure the deformation of the material as the body moves, providing another means of capturing motion data. These non-invasive, textile-based sensors are increasingly being integrated into smart clothing, offering an alternative to traditional IMU-based systems. This emerging approach further enhances the flexibility and comfort of wearable motion capture technology, potentially leading to new applications in healthcare, sports, and everyday use.

2.2 Smart Wearable Devices

A smart wearable device is an electronic device that can be worn on the body, equipped with sensors to collect data, process it, and communicate with other devices or applications for various purposes, such as health monitoring and human-computer interaction. A key advantage of smart wearable devices is their portability and ease of use, this makes them can be used in various environments, whether during a workout, in clinical settings, or even in outdoor sports activities. Additionally, smart wearables are designed to be comfortable and unobtrusive, allowing users to wear them for extended periods without interference.

Another important feature of smart wearable devices is their ability to process data in real-time. Equipped with powerful processors and machine learning algorithms—in local or remote—modern wearables can analyze captured data on the fly and deliver immediate feedback to the user. This real-time capability is crucial in applications such as sports and fitness, where athletes and coaches rely on instant feedback to adjust performance. It is equally valuable in healthcare, where continuous monitoring can provide early warnings of potential health issues.

In conclusion, smart wearable devices have changed the way people interact with computers and brought more possibilities to people's daily lives. By integrating multiple sensors and leveraging real-time data processing, these devices provide many applications. As the technology continues to advance, they are expected to become even more integral to fields such as healthcare, sports, and entertainment.

3   Wearables Types

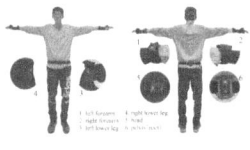

(a) Motion capture system that attaches sparse IMU to the human body through straps [18].

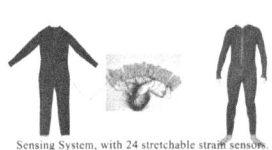

(b) An design of tight-fitting clothes for MoCap [16].

(c) An Prototype demonstration of the loose-fitting clothes for MoCap. [22].

Fig. 2. Three types of smart MoCap wearables: straps, tight-fitting clothes and loose-fitting clothes.

3.1   Straps

Attaching sensors to body with straps is one of the most common wearable solutions for motion capture, this method typically involves securing small devices, such as IMUs, cameras or other sensors, to joints using adjustable straps. The primary advantage of strap-based systems is their portability and adaptability, allowing for motion capture in various environments without the need for extensive setups or specialized equipment.

In the commercial market, several motion capture systems rely on strap-based setups to provide accurate and real-time motion tracking. One of the most well-known examples is the Xsens system. Xsens uses a series of straps embedded with IMUs that are placed on key joints and body parts. These IMUs capture detailed motion data, which is then processed by proprietary software to generate a full-body kinematic model. The system can be used in a wide range of environments, including sports fields, outdoor settings, and laboratories, making it a popular choice in industries such as film production, sports analysis, and biomechanics research. However, these systems typically use a larger number of sensors—usually 17 or more—to capture the full range of motion for each joint in the body. While this results in high accuracy, wearing numerous sensors can be cumbersome for the user, especially during extended motion capture sessions.

To address the limitations of wearing multiple sensors, researchers have introduced sparse motion capture solutions using fewer IMUs while still maintaining accuracy [6,17–19]. For example, this solutions often rely on just six sensors attached to critical locations such as the head, hips, arms, and legs, as shown in Fig. 2a. Sparse motion capture systems provide several advantages over traditional multi-sensor setups. They are less intrusive and more comfortable, making them ideal for long-term use. Additionally, fewer sensors reduce both the cost and complexity of the system, making it more accessible to a broader range of users.

3.2   Tight-Fitting Clothes

Tight-fitting clothing is another innovative approach to wearable motion capture. These garments are embedded with various sensors, such as IMUs, stretch sensors, or electromyography (EMG) sensors, allowing for seamless and accurate tracking of body movement. By integrating sensors directly into the fabric, these systems provide a comfortable and non-intrusive solution for capturing human motion, making them ideal for a wide range of applications, from sports performance analysis to rehabilitation and healthcare.

Ancans et al. [1] designed a tight-fitting garment integrated with multiple IMUs for motion capture. The sensor placement was selected, taking the anatomical properties of the human body and physical exercises chosen for experiments mentioned above into account. Additionally, researchers have focused on the integration of stretch sensors into tight-fitting clothes [7]. Stretch sensors, embedded along the fabric of the clothing, measure the deformation of the fabric as the body moves, providing detailed information about joint angles and body posture [4]. Figure 2b shows an design of tight-fitting clothes for MoCap, where the wiring layout is designed to minimize the intervention to human motion [16].

The primary advantage of tight-fitting clothes for motion capture is their comfort and ease of use, reduce the difficulty of sensor setting. Unlike systems that rely on multiple external sensors or straps, smart garments provide a more natural and seamless user experience. The sensors are directly integrated into the fabric, eliminating the need for cumbersome setups or devices that may interfere with the user's movement.

3.3   Loose-Fitting Clothes

Loose-fitting clothes equipped with sensors offer a more relaxed and comfortable alternative to tight-fitting garments for motion capture [22]. Figure 2c shows the prototype demonstration of the loose-fitting clothes for motion capture designed by Zuo et al. [22]. These clothes typically have textile-based sensors, such as

IMUs, embedded into the fabric to detect body movements. The loose fit provides greater flexibility and comfort, making it suitable for applications where a tight fit might be restrictive or uncomfortable, such as in casual settings or for prolonged use.

One of the main challenges with loose-fitting garments is that the relaxed fit can lead to huge motion artifacts in sensor data, where the movement of the fabric itself interferes with accurate measurements. Current research focuses on developing algorithms and data processing techniques to mitigate these affects. By using advanced filtering methods and machine learning algorithms, researchers can distinguish between actual body movements and those caused by the garment's motion, ensuring more reliable data capture.

The primary advantages of loose-fitting clothes include enhanced comfort and breathability, making them ideal for long-term wear. These garments provide a non-intrusive way to monitor motion without restricting natural movements, which is particularly beneficial for applications in daily activities, rehabilitation, or elderly care.

4   Related Sensors

4.1   IMUs

IMUs are one of the most widely used sensors in wearable motion capture systems. An 9-axis IMU consists of three main components: accelerometers for acceleration, gyroscopes for angular velocity, magnetometers for magnetic field. These sensors work together to provide comprehensive data on an object's motion and orientation in space.

IMUs are highly versatile and can be embedded into wearable devices such as smart clothing, wristbands, or shoes, making them suitable for a wide range of motion capture applications. They are capable of tracking rapid, dynamic movements as well as subtle changes in posture.

4.2   Stretch Sensor

Stretch sensors are flexible, wearable components that detect deformation in the fabric or material they are embedded in. These sensors measure the elongation or contraction of the fabric as the body moves, providing detailed data about joint angles, muscle movement, and body posture [4,7]. Stretch sensors are often integrated into smart garments for applications such as rehabilitation, sports training, and biomechanics research. For example, when a joint bends or a muscle contracts, the stretch sensor embedded in the clothing measures the extent of the deformation and translates that into meaningful motion data.

One of the main benefits of stretch sensors is their ability to conform to the body's natural shape and movements. They are lightweight, flexible, and do not hinder movement, offering continuous monitoring without discomfort. Additionally, their integration into clothing makes them a discreet and comfortable option for long-term monitoring.

5   Algorithm

In traditional wearable full-body motion capture systems where an IMU is attached to each joint, algorithms primarily focus on sensor fusion and kinematic modeling to combine the data from multiple IMUs. Each IMU provides raw data on acceleration and rotation, which must be processed to calculate the precise orientation and position of each body part. This often involves Kalman filtering or complementary filtering techniques to reduce sensor noise and drift, producing accurate real-time tracking of body motion. These methods require complex computations to integrate the data from many sensors and ensure that the motion is tracked consistently across all joints.

Emerging smart wearable motion capture solutions, which use sparse IMUs or a combination of other sensors, rely more on data-driven approaches to reconstruct full-body motion [6,7,17,19,22]. Given the sequential nature of motion data, time-series models such as Recurrent Neural Networks (RNN), Long Short-Term Memory (LSTM) networks, and Transformer models are commonly used to process the sensor data. These models are trained on large datasets of human motion, allowing them to infer missing joint movements and predict the full-body pose over time by capturing temporal dependencies in the movement patterns based on the input from a few key sensors. RNN excel at modeling sequential dependencies but struggle with long-term memory due to vanishing gradient problems. LSTM address this limitation with a gating mechanism, making them more effective for capturing long-range dependencies in complex motion sequences. In contrast, Transformer rely on self-attention mechanisms, allowing them to capture global relationships across the entire sequence in parallel, making them highly efficient for long-term, sparse data like IMU-based pose estimation. These machine learning algorithms help reduce the need for extensive sensor setups, making motion capture more accessible and practical for real-world applications.

In addition to model architectures, researchers have explored various methods to further optimize motion prediction in wearable systems. Transformer Inertial Poser (TIP) [6] leverages a Transformer model to predict joint angles while compensating for sensor drift over time. TIP is also capable of generating realistic terrain data in real-time, making it ideal for AR/VR applications. Another approach, Physical Inertial Poser (PIP) [17], improves prediction accuracy by combining a neural kinematics estimator with a physics-aware motion optimizer. The kinematics module first regresses the motion status as a reference, and then the physics module refines the motion to satisfy the physical constraints, for more realistic results.

Since these models typically require large amounts of training data, generating training data through simulation has become a widely adopted approach by researchers. However, due to the differences between simulated and real-world data, much attention is focused on eliminating these discrepancies or making simulated data more closely resemble real data in order to achieve better human pose prediction results. In sparse IMUs motion capture area, the Physical Non-inertial Poser (PNP) [19] introduces the concept of non-inertial effects by using a physics-based autoregressive estimator to model these effects (e.g., virtual forces). This method allows for more precise handling of IMU measurements related to forces, such as acceleration, enabling the system to more accurately capture motion that involves dynamic forces and external interactions. For tight-fitting clothes, data distributional shifts caused by displacements of flexible sensors are a huge challenge. Fang et al. [3] proposed a novel Sim2Real MoCap solution based on domain adaptation, eliminating the need for labeled data yet achieving comparable accuracy to supervised learning. Zuo et al. [21] proposes a novel self-adaptive motion tracking network to solve this problem. They remap shifted data distributions to match the training set efficiently by an Affine Transformation layer, captures richer frequency components by a Fourier-encoded LSTM network, and adjusts Affine Transformation parameters unsupervised by a Sequence Discrepancy loss with auxiliary regressors. This method can effectively adapt to unknown displacements of flexible sensors worn at different positions. In loose-fitting clothes, motion artifacts in sensor data are further amplified, prompting researchers to explore new methods to address this issue. Loose Inertial Poser (LIP) [22] integrates 4 IMUs into a loose-wear jacket, proposing a Secondary Motion AutoEncoder, which synthesizes the effects of secondary motion between skin and loose clothing on IMU data, creating synthetic training datasets to significantly enhance pose estimation accuracy, even with sparse loose-wear data. Figure 3 shows the real-time upper-body motion capture result of LIP.

Fig. 3. The real-time upper-body motion capture through a loose-wear jacket equipped with 4 IMUs achieved by LIP [22].

These techniques demonstrate the growing sophistication of motion capture algorithms, as they not only refine movement predictions but also address sensor limitations and environmental factors, paving the way for more accurate and robust motion tracking solutions.

6 Applications and Advantages

6.1 Sports and Fitness

In sports and fitness, smart wearable devices for motion capture have become essential tools for performance analysis [13]. By using IMUs, stretch sensors, and other integrated technologies, athletes can track their movements in real-time, gaining insights into their posture, speed, acceleration, and body alignment. This data helps athletes optimize their technique, improve overall performance.

For example, in sports like running, wearable devices can analyze stride length, ground contact time, and joint angles, providing feedback to runners on how to adjust their movements for better efficiency. In weightlifting, smart garments embedded with sensors monitor muscle engagement and body posture, ensuring that athletes maintain proper form throughout their workouts, reducing the likelihood of strains or overuse injuries.

Additionally, motion capture wearables can track progress over time, enabling athletes and coaches to develop more personalized training programs based on the specific needs of the individual. This continuous monitoring can also be used for rehabilitation purposes, allowing injured athletes to safely return to training while minimizing the risk of re-injury.

In conclusion, the wearable motion capture technology offers significant advantages in sports and fitness by providing athletes with detailed, real-time feedback, enhancing both performance and safety.

6.2 Healthcare

In healthcare, wearable motion capture devices play a crucial role in monitoring patient movements and assisting in rehabilitation [5,15]. By using IMUs, stretch sensors, and other embedded technologies, these devices can track a patient's body movements with high precision, providing valuable data for doctors and physical therapists to assess mobility, joint function, and muscle coordination. This data-driven approach allows for personalized treatment plans and more accurate tracking of recovery progress.

Wearable devices are especially beneficial in physical therapy and post-surgery rehabilitation. Patients recovering from injuries or surgeries can wear smart garments that monitor their movements during prescribed exercises. These devices ensure that the patient is performing the exercises correctly, reducing the risk of improper movement that could lead to complications. Real-time feedback helps adjust exercises on the go, enhancing recovery outcomes.

For patients with chronic conditions like Parkinson's disease or arthritis, motion capture wearables offer continuous monitoring, tracking changes in gait, balance, and movement patterns over time. This allows healthcare providers to detect early signs of deterioration or improvement, enabling timely interventions and adjustments in treatment.

6.3   Entertainment and Gaming

In the fields of entertainment and gaming, wearable motion capture devices have revolutionized how human movement is integrated into digital environments [14]. These devices are widely used in animation, film production, and virtual reality (VR) gaming to capture realistic body movements and translate them into digital avatars or characters.

In film and animation, wearable motion capture suits embedded with IMUs and other sensors allow actors to perform scenes while their movements are recorded in real-time. This data is then used to animate characters with a high degree of realism, making it a crucial tool for creating lifelike animations in movies, TV shows, and video games.

In gaming, particularly with the rise of VR and augmented reality (AR) platforms, wearables provide players with an immersive experience by tracking their full-body movements. Players can interact with virtual worlds more naturally, with their movements being reflected accurately in-game. This enhances the sense of immersion and allows for more interactive, physically engaging gaming.

7   Limitations and Challenges

7.1   Sensor Drift and Motion Artifact

One of the major limitations in wearable motion capture systems is sensor drift. Sensor drift refers to the gradual deviation or shift in the sensor's output readings from the true or expected value over time. This phenomenon occurs due to factors like environmental changes, sensor aging, or inherent imperfections in the sensor. Algorithms like Kalman filters are often employed to mitigate drift, but they can't completely eliminate the issue.

Another challenge is the relative displacement of sensors on the body. In wearable systems, especially when using loose-fitting garments or poorly secured sensors, the sensors can shift from their intended positions during motion. This sensor misalignment can lead to motion artifacts, where the sensor records not just the body's movement but also the independent motion of the sensor itself [10]. Therefore, when a sensor moves relative to the skin, the data might inaccurately reflect body motion, reducing the accuracy of the tracking.

Addressing both sensor drift and motion artifacts is one of the key of ongoing research. Solutions include developing algorithms to compensate for drift, improving sensor placement and attachment methods, and using data from multiple sensors to correct for relative displacement.

7.2   Comfort and Difficulty of Wearing

Another challenge with wearable motion capture devices is ensuring comfort and ease of use. Tight-fitting garments or multiple sensors attached to the body can feel restrictive, uncomfortable, or cumbersome, especially during long periods of wear. Devices that rely on straps or multiple IMUs can be difficult to put on and adjust, leading to improper sensor placement, which can affect data accuracy.

To address these issues, research is focusing on developing lightweight, flexible materials, and more user-friendly designs that are easy to wear while maintaining accurate sensor alignment. Achieving a balance between comfort and performance is essential for broader adoption in both casual and professional applications.

7.3   Battery Life

Battery life is a significant limitation in wearable motion capture devices. Many sensors, such as IMUs and stretch sensors, require continuous power to collect and transmit data in real-time. For applications like sports training or healthcare monitoring, where devices need to operate for extended periods, limited battery life can be a major constraint. Frequent charging or battery replacement disrupts the user experience and reduces the practicality of long-term monitoring.

Efforts to improve battery life include optimizing power-efficient sensors, implementing low-power communication protocols, and developing energy-harvesting technologies. However, balancing longer battery life with maintaining accurate and responsive motion capture remains an ongoing challenge.

7.4   Real-Time Processing

Real-time processing is another challenge in wearable motion capture systems. The vast amount of data generated by multiple sensors, such as IMUs or stretch sensors, must be processed instantly to provide timely feedback. This requires powerful processing capabilities, especially in applications like sports training or gaming, where immediate response is critical.

The complexity of motion data, combined with the need for filtering, sensor fusion, and sometimes machine learning algorithms, can introduce latency. Additionally, some solutions need to upload data to a smartphone or utilize remote servers for computation can further delay the feedback. Ensuring real-time performance while maintaining accuracy is difficult, particularly in low-power, portable devices. Ongoing research focuses on optimizing algorithms to reduce computational load, enhancing on-device processing, and leveraging edge computing to meet the demands of real-time applications.

8   Future Trends

The future of wearable motion capture technology is promising, driven by advancements in sensor technology, machine learning, and user experience design. Several key trends are emerging in this field:

Improved Machine Learning Algorithms. As machine learning techniques continue to evolve, we can expect more sophisticated algorithms capable of processing complex motion data in real-time. Techniques like deep learning and reinforcement learning may enhance the accuracy of motion prediction and analysis, making wearable devices more effective in various applications.

Enhanced User Experience. The design of wearable devices will prioritize comfort and usability, with innovations in materials, form factors, and user interfaces. Expect to see lighter, more flexible garments that integrate seamlessly into daily life, as well as intuitive apps for users to easily access and interpret their motion data.

Augmented and Virtual Reality Applications. As AR and VR technologies advance, wearable motion capture systems will become integral to creating immersive experiences in gaming, training simulations, and interactive entertainment. Enhanced motion tracking will enable more realistic interactions within virtual environments.

Data Privacy and Security. With the increasing use of wearables to collect personal data, there will be a growing emphasis on ensuring data privacy and security. Developers will need to implement robust encryption and data protection measures to safeguard user information.

In summary, the future of wearable motion capture technology will be characterized by more integrated and intelligent systems that enhance user experience, broaden applications, and prioritize data security. These advancements will pave the way for innovative solutions in sports, healthcare, entertainment, and beyond.

9   Conclusion

In this paper, we provided a comprehensive overview of smart wearable devices for motion capture, outlined the rapid advancements in sensor technology and artificial intelligence that have propelled the growth of these devices and explored the fundamentals of motion capture, including traditional and emerging techniques. We categorized wearable devices for motion capture into straps, tight-fitting clothes, and loose-fitting clothes, each type offering distinct advantages for motion tracking. We further discussed related sensors, focusing on IMUs and stretch sensors. We introduced algorithm used for processing motion data, emphasizing the shift towards data-driven approaches. We also detailed the applications and advantages of wearable motion capture in sports, healthcare, entertainment and gaming, demonstrating their potential to improve performance and user experience. In limitations and challenges, we highlighted issues such as sensor drift, comfort, battery life, and real-time processing that need to be overcome. Lastly, we explored future trends that promise to enhance the capabilities of wearable motion capture technologies, paving the way for more innovative and user-friendly solutions.

References

1. Ancans, A., Greitans, M., Cacurs, R., Banga, B., Rozentals, A.: Wearable sensor clothing for body movement measurement during physical activities in healthcare. Sensors **21**(6), 2068 (2021)
2. Chen, X., et al.: Dispad: Flexible on-body displacement of fabric sensors for robust joint-motion tracking. In: Proceedings of the ACM on Interactive, Mobile, Wearable and Ubiquitous Technologies, vol. 7, no. 1, pp. 1–27 (2023)
3. Fang, J., et al.: SuDA: support-based domain adaptation for sim2real motion capture with flexible sensors. arXiv preprint arXiv:2405.16152 (2024)
4. Glauser, O., Wu, S., Panozzo, D., Hilliges, O., Sorkine-Hornung, O.: Interactive hand pose estimation using a stretch-sensing soft glove. ACM Trans. Graph. (ToG) **38**(4), 1–15 (2019)
5. He, Z., Liu, T., Yi, J.: A wearable sensing and training system: towards gait rehabilitation for elderly patients with knee osteoarthritis. IEEE Sens. J. **19**(14), 5936–5945 (2019)
6. Jiang, Y., Ye, Y., Gopinath, D., Won, J., Winkler, A.W., Liu, C.K.: Transformer inertial poser: real-time human motion reconstruction from sparse IMUs with simultaneous terrain generation. In: SIGGRAPH Asia 2022 Conference Papers, pp. 1–9 (2022)
7. Kim, D., Kwon, J., Han, S., Park, Y.L., Jo, S.: Deep full-body motion network for a soft wearable motion sensing suit. IEEE/ASME Trans. Mechatron. **24**(1), 56–66 (2018)
8. Li, J., Ma, Q., Chan, A.H., Man, S.: Health monitoring through wearable technologies for older adults: Smart wearables acceptance model. Appl. Ergon. **75**, 162–169 (2019)
9. Menolotto, M., Komaris, D.S., Tedesco, S., O'Flynn, B., Walsh, M.: Motion capture technology in industrial applications: a systematic review. Sensors **20**(19), 5687 (2020)
10. Michael, B., Howard, M.: Gait reconstruction from motion artefact corrupted fabric-embedded sensors. IEEE Robot. Autom. Lett. **3**(3), 1918–1924 (2018)
11. Nakano, N., et al.: Evaluation of 3d markerless motion capture accuracy using openpose with multiple video cameras. Front. Sports Active Living **2**, 50 (2020)
12. Ponton, J.L., Yun, H., Aristidou, A., Andujar, C., Pelechano, N.: Sparseposer: teal-time full-body motion reconstruction from sparse data. ACM Trans. Graph. (2023)
13. Rana, M., Mittal, V.: Wearable sensors for real-time kinematics analysis in sports: a review. IEEE Sens. J. **21**(2), 1187–1207 (2020)
14. Rostami, S., Maier, M.: The metaverse and beyond: implementing advanced multiverse realms with smart wearables. IEEE Access **10**, 110796–110806 (2022)

15. Schlachetzki, J.C., et al.: Wearable sensors objectively measure gait parameters in Parkinson's disease. PLoS ONE **12**(10), e0183989 (2017)
16. Wang, K., et al.: Computational design of wiring layout on tight suits with minimal motion resistance. In: SIGGRAPH Asia 2023 Conference Papers, pp. 1–12 (2023)
17. Yi, X., et al.: Physical inertial poser (pip): physics-aware real-time human motion tracking from sparse inertial sensors. In: Proceedings of the IEEE/CVF Conference on Computer Vision and Pattern Recognition, pp. 13167–13178 (2022)
18. Yi, X., Zhou, Y., Xu, F.: Transpose: real-time 3D human translation and pose estimation with six inertial sensors. ACM Trans. Graph. (TOG) **40**(4), 1–13 (2021)
19. Yi, X., Zhou, Y., Xu, F.: Physical non-inertial poser (PNP): modeling non-inertial effects in sparse-inertial human motion capture. In: SIGGRAPH 2024 Conference Papers (2024)
20. Yin, R., Wang, D., Zhao, S., Lou, Z., Shen, G.: Wearable sensors-enabled human-machine interaction systems: from design to application. Adv. Func. Mater. **31**(11), 2008936 (2021)
21. Zuo, C., Jiawei, F., Guo, S., Qin, Y.: Self-adaptive motion tracking against on-body displacement of flexible sensors. In: Advances in Neural Information Processing Systems, vol. 36 (2024)
22. Zuo, C., et al.: Loose inertial poser: Motion capture with IMU-attached loose-wear jacket. In: Proceedings of the IEEE/CVF Conference on Computer Vision and Pattern Recognition (CVPR), pp. 2209–2219 (2024)

Fish Detection and Quantity Estimation Based on Sonar Images

Wenxiang Du[1,2], Shuai Yan[2], and Yue Qi[1,2(✉)]

[1] State Key Laboratory of Virtual Reality Technology and Systems, Beihang University,
Beijing 100191, China
{dwxiang,qy}@buaa.edu.cn
[2] Qingdao Research Institute of Beihang University, Qingdao 266100, China
ys469716378@sdust.edu.cn

Abstract. Due to the complex underwater environment and dense targets, it is difficult to quickly and accurately calculate the location and quantity of fish targets in marine ranching. We have developed an underwater target detection and counting algorithm based on sonar images, which includes four parts: image preprocessing, background subtraction, contour detection, and target counting. Firstly, we design a sliding-window-based gain algorithm based on the uneven grayscale value of sonar images, which amplifies the effective signal while smoothing the grayscale of the image. Secondly, background subtraction is used to separate the foreground and background of the sonar image, which can remove background noise and filter the target using a filtering algorithm to generate a binary image with clear targets. Then, target detection is combined with morphological processing techniques and contour detection algorithms. Finally, we use image erosion technology to separate overlapping targets, calculate the contour position of the targets, and count the quantity. A large number of results indicate that our algorithm can quickly and accurately detect the position of fish in sonar images while also counting the number of fishes.

Keywords: Fish detection · Image processing · Sonar image · Target counting

1 Introduction

As an environmentally friendly new form of marine industry, ocean ranching represents the development trend of ecological fisheries and is an essential carrier for developing modern fisheries and building a fishing power. Sonar, as an important underwater exploration tool, has been widely used in modern intelligent ocean ranches. In recent years, target detection based on sonar images has become one of the research hotspots. On the one hand, due to the complex and ever-changing underwater environments, sonar is not only affected by environmental noise but also faces interference such as sound wave absorption and scattering. The quality issue of sonar images has increased the difficulty of underwater target detection. On the other hand, in practical applications, factors such as dense targets, overlapping, and occlusion are not conducive to inferring the position and counting the number of fishes.

© The Author(s), under exclusive license to Springer Nature Singapore Pte Ltd. 2025
W. Song et al. (Eds.): ICXR 2024, LNCS 15461, pp. 251–263, 2025.
https://doi.org/10.1007/978-981-96-3679-2_17

To address the issue of low sonar image quality, target detection tasks typically combine multiple image enhancement and filtering techniques. For example, algorithms such as median filtering and wavelet transform can be used to remove sonar noise, and the visual effect of sonar images can be improved through methods such as enhancing image contrast and bilinear interpolation. This type of image processing method has improved the quality of sonar images to a certain extent, but due to the limitations of the algorithm, the obtained sonar images still have problems such as image blur and uneven grayscale. Image preprocessing, as the foundation of sonar target detection, is crucial for improving detection performance. Analyzing the imaging characteristics of sonar images and integrating multiple image processing techniques is the key to improving the quality of sonar images. A grayscale gain algorithm is proposed to address the issue of uneven grayscale in sonar images. The brightness of the target at a distance is improved by adjusting the grayscale values of the image through a sliding window. However, there are still some issues with the low brightness of the target, which can lead to missed detections. The detection of dense small targets has always been a challenge in the field of object detection. In optical images, researchers often use deep-learning-based object detection algorithms. With the development of deep learning and hardware devices, although training neural networks for object detection has become increasingly convenient, due to the scarcity of sonar data and the difficulty of annotating dense targets, deep learning algorithms are difficult to apply to acoustic images. In acoustic images, most object detection algorithms find it difficult to accurately detect target positions and calculate the number of targets from low signal-to-noise ratio and dense target scenes.

This article proposes a new sonar target detection algorithm. Firstly, a sliding window gain algorithm was designed to enhance target brightness and suppress background noise while smoothing image grayscale. Secondly, the background subtraction method is used to extract foreground information, and the median filtering algorithm is used to filter the target. Then, the target contour is detected using contour detection algorithms, and overlapping targets are separated using morphological processing methods. Finally, the number of targets was counted, and the effectiveness of the algorithm was demonstrated through experimental results. The main contributions of this article include:

1. A complete underwater target detection system. This system combines various image processing techniques such as image preprocessing, background removal, and contour detection to perform real-time fish swarm monitoring and statistics.
2. Improved preprocessing method of sonar images. Design an image preprocessing algorithm that can smooth the grayscale of the image while amplifying the image signal.
3. Fish target tracking. Implementing target tracking in complex and dense scenes to assist the system in counting.

2   Related Work

In current research, various image processing techniques are usually combined for target detection in sonar images [1, 2].

Sonar images are susceptible to noise interference, which greatly reduces image quality and makes target detection in sonar images very difficult. Sonar images are susceptible to noise interference, which greatly reduces image quality and makes target detection in sonar images very difficult. Based on spatial domain algorithms, various filtering techniques are directly applied to sonar images. This type of algorithm has the advantages of simple calculation and fast speed, which can smooth the target image and reduce noise. By combining with other denoising algorithms, good results have been achieved in many studies. Li et al. [3] combined the improved wavelet threshold with non-local-mean-filtering to preserve the detailed information of the denoised image and alleviate image blur. The filtering algorithm based on the transform domain usually uses the Fourier transform algorithm [4] and wavelet thresholding algorithm [5, 6]. By transforming the image from the spatial domain to other domains and analyzing its transformation domain characteristics, effective signals, and interference signals are separated. Liu et al. [7] proposed a new wavelet threshold denoising method to address the issue of edge information loss. This algorithm protects the edge wavelet coefficients and avoids the loss of high-frequency information. Algorithms based on deep learning often have better denoising effects [8, 9]. This type of algorithm improves denoising performance by designing models with stronger performance and optimizing training strategies. Kashvolayat et al. [10] proposed a hybrid deep neural network model that combines preprocessing techniques with LSTM networks to improve denoising performance. However, this algorithm requires a large amount of training data and has higher requirements for computing resources.

The removal of background mainly includes the frame difference method, background subtraction algorithm, etc. Among them, the frame difference algorithm is simple and has good real-time performance, but it is very sensitive to environmental noise and has certain requirements for threshold selection [11]. Recently, Pang et al. [12] proposed a small object detection algorithm based on the frame difference method and an improved quadratic image segmentation algorithm. However, the multiple segmentation of the image increases the computational complexity of the algorithm, and the underwater environment is more complex, making it challenging to ensure robustness in low signal-to-noise ratio sonar images. Sharma et al. [13] proposed a new foreground extraction algorithm to address the issue of background changes in videos. This algorithm combines front and back frames to model the background, effectively reducing vulnerability issues in dynamic background updates. Tang et al. [14] addressed the issue of slow speed in Gaussian mixture model algorithms and proposed new methods for shadow detection and noise removal, which demonstrated good accuracy.

Edge detection algorithms [15] or contour detection algorithms [16] can quickly obtain object edges and calculate target positions. Zitnick et al. [17] proposed an algorithm for object detection using bounding boxes. This algorithm achieves a high detection rate through a simple detection strategy, but it cannot distinguish the content in the bounding box and is prone to more errors in complex acoustic images. Chi et al. [18] proposed an image sequence detection method based on active contours. This method first uses a background subtraction algorithm to remove static background, then uses an improved contour detection algorithm to extract the target contour, and finally tracks the active contour in each frame of the image. CFAR (constant false alarm rate) was initially used for target detection in radar images [19]. When dealing with noise and clutter interference, using a fixed threshold for filtering can lead to false alarm problems and affect radar monitoring performance. Multiple studies have applied this algorithm to sonar target detection [20] [21]. Acosta et al. [21] extended the CA-CFAR technique to sonar images, which segments sonar images into acoustic bright spots and seabed reverberation areas, greatly optimizing computation speed and parameters. FCM (Fuzzy C-Means) can also achieve good detection results. Zhang et al. [22] developed a new FCM algorithm that can more accurately and directly segment images while classifying detection targets, backgrounds, and even noise. However, this type of method requires continuous iteration to gradually improve the segmentation effect, which is too computationally intensive.

3   Method

In order to quickly complete target detection and counting from sonar data, we divided the entire process into four parts: image preprocessing module, background subtraction module, contour detection module, and target counting module. The algorithm process is as follows (Fig. 1):

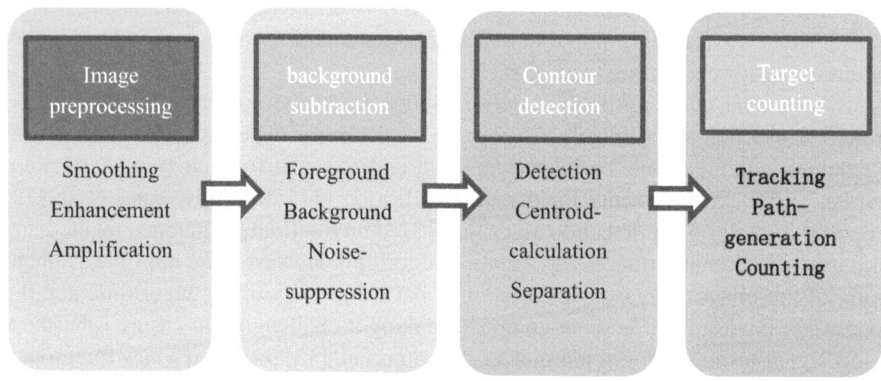

Fig. 1. Diagram of algorithm process.

In the image preprocessing module, a sliding window gain algorithm is designed according to the characteristics of the sonar image. Its purpose is to smooth the image brightness, amplify the effective signal, and suppress part of the background noise. In the second module, the background subtraction and post-processing module can eliminate the interference caused by static objects and large-area noise. At the same time, the processing results are median filtered to filter the speckle noise and obtain the binary image. In the part of contour detection, the accurate position of each contour in the image is obtained by the contour detection algorithm, and morphological operation is carried out for the contour with too large area to separate overlapping targets. Finally, the centroid position of the contour is calculated, and the number of targets is counted.

3.1   Image Preprocessing

In the process of sending, reflecting, and receiving sound waves, due to the influence of propagation loss and absorption, the problem of reducing the intensity of sound waves will occur. This problem leads to uneven brightness in sonar images, and the image brightness of close pixels is much higher than that of long-distance pixels, causing interference to target detection, counting, and other algorithms. In order to solve the problem caused by sonar transmission loss, the usual solution is image gray gain. Given the window size and step size, the algorithm adjusts the average brightness in the window according to the average brightness in the image and smoothing the gray value between windows. The formula is as follows:

$$P_n = \frac{M}{M_w} \times P_n \tag{1}$$

where P_n is the gray value of pixels in the sliding window, M_w is the average gray value in the current sliding window, and M is the average gray value of the whole image. If the average gray level in the current sliding window is lower than the average gray level, the gray value in the current area will be enlarged, and vice versa. Through this algorithm, the gray changes between regions are smoothed effectively. The smaller the height of the sliding window, the better the smoothing effect is.

There are still targets with weak echoes in sonar images, and there will be missed detection when using a contour detection algorithm for target detection. In order to highlight the targets in the sonar image and improve the detection effect, the signal with gray value higher than the surrounding pixels is further amplified while sliding the window for brightness gain, and the signal with gray value lower than the surrounding pixels is suppressed. While amplifying the effective sonar signal, the background noise is reduced. The formula is as follows:

$$P_n = \begin{cases} P_n \times A, P_n >= M_w \\ P_n \times B, P_n < M_w \end{cases} \tag{2}$$

where A is the coefficient of amplified sonar signal and B is the coefficient of suppressed sonar signal. The gray value in the sliding window area is modified according to the average gray value in the window so that the pixels with higher echo intensity have higher brightness. The algorithm can dynamically process each window, which is helpful in distinguishing the foreground and background.

3.2 Background Subtraction

The foreground and background separation method is to accurately detect the target in sonar images. On the one hand, the extraction of the foreground eliminates the interference of the static objects in the sonar image to the detection target. On the other hand, the segmentation of the background removes a large amount of noise in the sonar image, which can effectively improve the robustness of the detection algorithm and improve the detection effect.

Background subtraction is one of the key algorithms of traditional moving target detection, and its performance depends on the modeling method of the background model. Due to the complex underwater environment, there are environmental interference and noise in sonar images, so background modeling for sonar images is challenging. We have tried a variety of background modeling methods, including the FCM method.

The traditional methods cannot effectively and accurately detect the foreground and background. FCM and MFCM filtering algorithms can model the foreground and background. This method clusters and segments the image pixels in an iterative way. It can segment fish in a far range, but it performs poorly in the close range with large noise and requires a lot of iteration when processing sonar images in each frame. The calculation process is too redundant to be used for fish detection and calculation in marine ranches. This paper implements and optimizes the foreground and background separation method based on background differences. Sonar is unstable, and sonar images usually contain a part of noise with large gray value. This type of noise is often detected as a "moving" foreground by the background subtraction algorithm, resulting in a large number of target detection errors. For such errors, median filtering can effectively filter this part of noise from the results of background subtraction (Fig. 2).

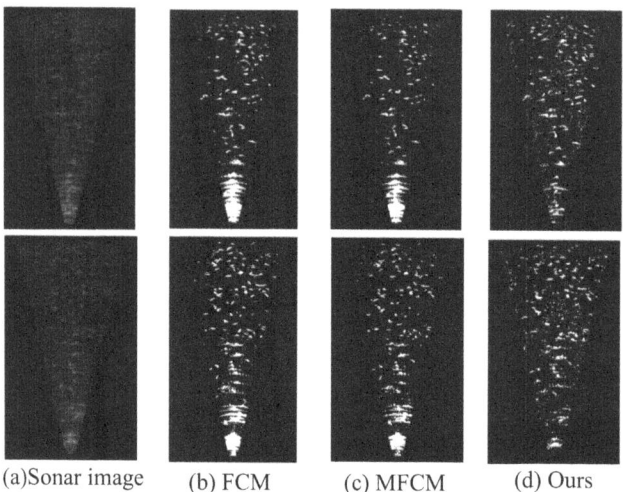

(a)Sonar image   (b) FCM   (c) MFCM   (d) Ours

Fig. 2. Comparison with FCM algorithm.

3.3 Contour Detection

The purpose of contour detection is to extract closed regions from sonar images. In the actual detection, multiple overlapping targets lead to the contour detection to obtain the contour with too large area, which can't reflect the correct target position and number. In order to solve this problem, the area statistics are carried out after obtaining the contour, and the contour whose contour area is much larger than the average area is corroded to separate the overlapping multiple targets. Considering that the number of overlapping targets may be large, an iterative method is used to corrode the contour area. When the number of contours in the region changes and the size of each area is close to the average area, the iteration is stopped, and the number of contours is updated. The algorithm flow is shown in the following figure (Fig. 3).

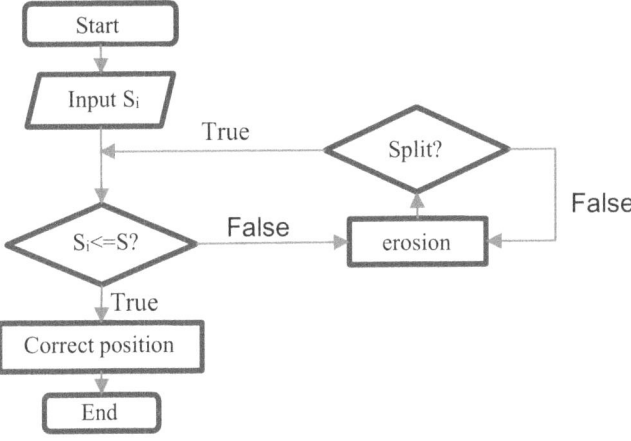

Fig. 3. Erosion separation algorithm flowchart.

Where S is the average area of all contours, and S_i is the current contour area. By detecting the contour of the binary image and extracting the closed graph, the more accurate target position and number can be obtained. However, the overlapping phenomenon often occurs in high-density fish schools, and the contour detection cannot distinguish the overlapping targets, resulting in inaccurate quantity statistics. The overlapping parts can be separated by image etching technology, which effectively improves the detection effect. For the targets with different overlapping degrees, repeat the corrosion operation in the same iterative way until the separation is successful (Fig. 4).

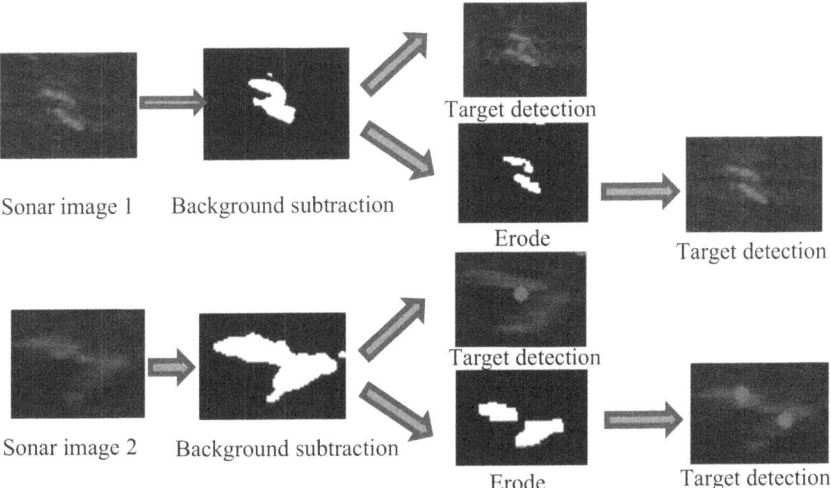

Fig. 4. Erosion separation algorithm.

3.4 Target Counting

In order to visualize the results of target detection, the centroid positions of all contours are calculated. Due to the dense targets in the application scene, only the centroid position is marked. The number of all centroids in the current sonar image is the total number of fish.

In the process of counting, there are still some noises that affect the accuracy of statistics. To further improve the effect of fish detection and distinguish between noise and target, the most effective way is to track fish. Continuously track the moving target, count the number of stable tracks, and eliminate the occasional noise interference. This task can be regarded as a multi-target tracking task for a large number of points in the image. Considering the calculation speed and prediction quality, the Kalman filter algorithm is selected to predict the motion of fish. Kalman filtering algorithm can model the motion, predict the target position in the current frame by using the target position information in the previous frame, and calculate the cost matrix. The target position in the previous and subsequent frames is matched by the Hungarian algorithm to update the motion trajectory. Finally, combined with the sonar frame order, the number of fish and motion trajectory, statistics, and analysis of the number of fish changes and extreme values, through the form of statistical line chart and data pie chart to reflect the number of fish changes and movement mode, improve the monitoring ability of underwater environment (Fig. 5).

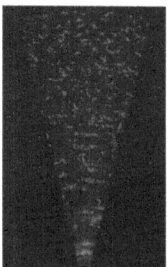 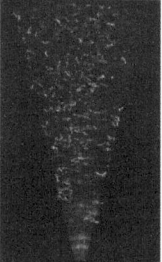

(a) The historical location of fish   (b)The track of fish movement

Fig. 5. Fish tracking results.

4   Experimental Result

4.1   Analysis of Test Results

The algorithm in this paper is used to detect and count fish from sonar data. Due to the uneven gray level and low signal-to-noise ratio of the sonar raw data, the sonar gray level is smoothed, and the effective signal is amplified by the image preprocessing module. The sliding window height is set to 1/3 of the sonar image height, the amplification threshold is set to 1.2, and the reduction threshold is set to 0.8. The image processing results are shown in the figure. The brightness of the sonar image is more uniform, part of the background noise is eliminated, and the brightness of the detection target is significantly improved. The sonar image obtained by pretreatment can effectively improve the effect of the background subtraction module and contour detection module and obtain more accurate target counting.

The essence of the sliding window gain algorithm is to adjust the brightness by threshold. Although it has certain adaptability, it can't eliminate the large area of background noise. Generally, target detection using the background subtraction method after directly extracting the foreground performs well in the optical image, but the signal is unstable due to acoustic scattering, reflection, crosstalk, and other phenomena. In the sonar image, the noise flickers continuously and is distributed in spots in the image, which makes it difficult for background subtraction and target recognition. Background subtraction will recognize the "moving" noise as the foreground, resulting in a large number of speckle noise in the extracted results. To solve this problem, the median filtering algorithm is used to process the image. Finally, the binary image containing only moving targets is obtained.

The erosion separation algorithm is used to better distinguish the overlapping targets. During the processing of the algorithm, the moving targets with contour areas higher than a certain threshold are regarded as overlapping targets and are separated by the erosion separation algorithm. In the experiment, the threshold was set to 1.4 times the

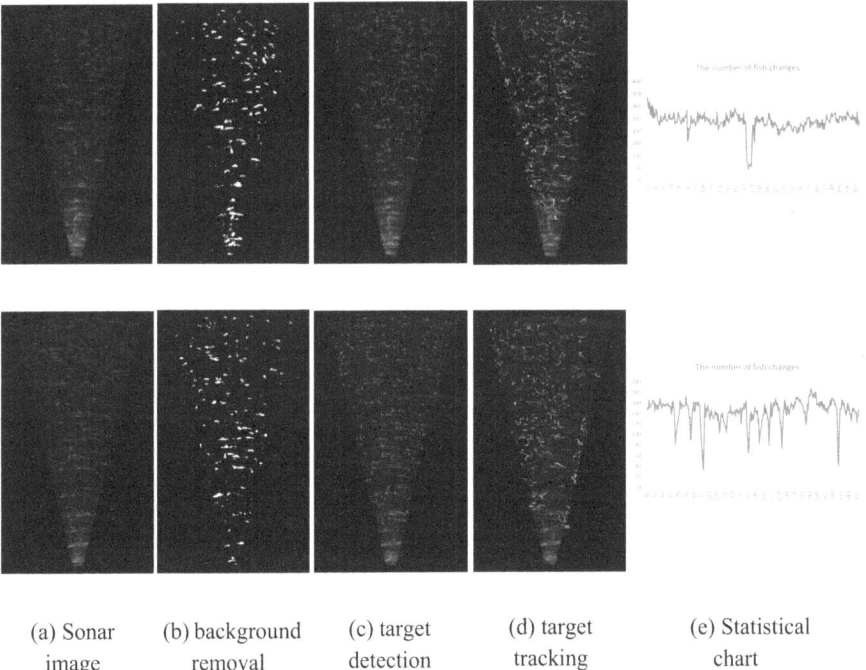

| (a) Sonar image | (b) background removal | (c) target detection | (d) target tracking | (e) Statistical chart |

Fig. 6. The entire process of sonar image processing. The figure shows the results generated by sonar images during each processing step, and after processing, the changes in the number of fish schools are statistically analyzed in the form of a line graph.

average contour area. Finally, the number of fish in the whole sonar is counted to get the line graph (Fig. 6).

4.2 Comparative Experiment

Echoview is the world's best underwater acoustic data processing software with powerful functions and flexible applications. After years of development, it has been used by global fishery and environmental scientists as one of the important means to study fishery resources and marine and freshwater ecological environment. This paper compares it with the algorithm in Echoview. Echoview is an underwater acoustic data processing software which can monitor the underwater environment. In Echoview, the process of target detection mainly includes three parts: background removal, median filtering, and target detection. The background removal process includes noise reduction, filtering, and other processing. The experiments were carried out for target detection in two scenarios: sparse fish school and dense fish school. The experimental results are shown in the following figure (Fig. 7).

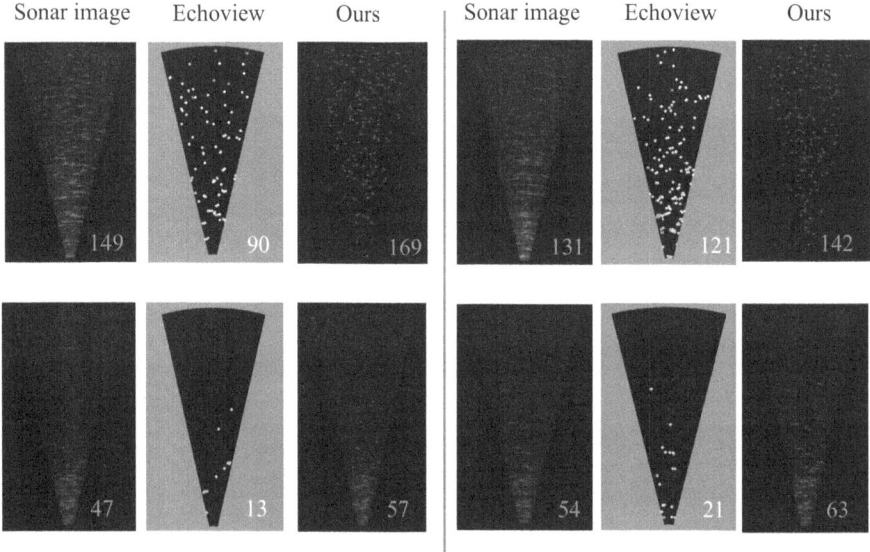

Fig. 7. Compared with Echoview. The number in the image represents the total number of fish schools in the current frame.

It can be seen from the figure that it is difficult to detect all the targets in the scene with dense fish swarm using the Echoview algorithm. There are a lot of missed detection problems for targets with low gray values in sonar images. In contrast, the number of targets counted by this method is closer to the real value, and the detection results can correctly reflect the distribution of fish in sonar images. For the scene with the sparse fish swarm, the median filter in the algorithm used by Echoview filters out most of the smaller targets, which seriously affects the statistical quantity. The method in this paper accurately detects the moving small target, and the detection result is more accurate.

4.3 Ablation Experiment

To investigate the impact of the two critical modules proposed in this article on counting effect, ablation experiments were conducted on the sliding window gain algorithm and corrosion separation algorithm proposed in this article, and the results were compared with those of Echoview again. Three hundred fifty frames of sonar data were extracted for comparison in the experiment, and different methods were used to estimate the quantity, which was then compared with the results obtained through manual statistics. Among them, the average number of fish schools obtained through manual statistics is 170.87, and the comparison results are shown in Table 1. It can be seen that when using both the sliding window gain algorithm and erosion separation algorithm simultaneously, the accuracy of target counting reaches the highest value. The sliding window gain algorithm greatly improves the accuracy of counting, and a more uniform grayscale distribution and higher contrast effectively alleviate the problem of missed detections. Meanwhile, the erosion separation algorithm has brought some improvements to the accurate counting of fish schools. Although the numerical improvement compared to the sliding window gain algorithm is not significant, it is beneficial in analyzing the habits and movement patterns of local fish schools. Due to its iterative algorithm concept, this algorithm will cause significant performance loss, making it more suitable for more detailed analysis of fish schools.

It's important to note that even without the erosion separation algorithm, the pipeline effect proposed in this paper still outperforms Echoview by 13.27%. While we were unable to obtain the accurate calculation time of Echoview due to its software limitations, the methods proposed in this article demonstrate the potential to meet the real-time requirements of sonar equipment. This research provides valuable insights that can inform the development of more efficient and accurate fish school counting algorithms.

Table 1. The influence of different modules on experimental results. (✓ indicates that the function module is enabled, while ✗ indicates the opposite)

Sliding window gain	Erosion separation	Echoview	Average quantity	Accuracy /%
✓	✗	✗	142.66	83.49
✗	✓	✗	125.95	73.71
✗	✗	✗	115.95	67.86
✗	✗	✓	93.27	54.59
✓	✓	✗	158.21	92.59

5   Conclusion

Aiming at the problems of dense targets and inaccurate quantity calculation in sonar target detection tasks, this paper proposes a fish swarm detection and quantity estimation algorithm based on sonar images. The algorithm can detect and count the number of fish through four modules: image preprocessing, background subtraction, contour detection, and target counting. In order to improve the quality of sonar images, a new sonar image gain algorithm is designed. By sliding the window, gray smoothing and signal amplification are carried out at the same time, which effectively improves the image signal-to-noise ratio and visual effect. Aiming at the overlapping phenomenon of dense fish swarm, an iterative separation method based on image erosion is designed to alleviate the counting error caused by the overlapping problem of targets.

Acknowledgments. This work was supported by the Laboratory construction funds of Qingdao LaoShan District and National Natural Science Foundation of China (No. 62072020).

Disclosure of Interests. The authors have no competing interests to declare that are relevant to the content of this article.

References

1. Steiniger, Y., Kraus, D., Meisen, T.: Survey on deep learning based computer vision for sonar imagery. Eng. Appl. Artif. Intell. **114**, 18 (2022)
2. Tian, Y., Lan, L., Sun, L.: A review of sonar image segmentation for underwater small targets. In Proceedings of the 2020 International Conference on Pattern Recognition and Intelligent Systems, vol. 2, pp. 1–4 (2020)
3. Feng, L., Wang, J.: Research on image denoising algorithm based on improved wavelet threshold and non-local mean filtering. In: 2021 IEEE 6th International Conference on Signal and Image Processing, pp. 493–497 (2021)
4. Zhang, X., Jiang, S.: Application of Fourier transform and butterworth filter in signal denoising. In: 2021 6th International Conference on Intelligent Computing and Signal Processing, pp. 1277–1281 (2021)
5. Sadeghipour, Z., Babaie-Zadeh, M., Jutten, C.: An adaptive thresholding approach for image denoising using redundant representations. In: 2009 IEEE International Workshop on Machine Learning for Signal Processing, pp. 1–6 (2009)
6. Du, X., Leng, X., Rao, S., Feng, L.: Debris flow infrasound denoising based on improved wavelet threshold algorithm. In: 2022 5th International Conference on Pattern Recognition and Artificial Intelligence, pp. 810–816 (2022)
7. Liu, W., Ma, Z.: Wavelet image threshold denoising based on edge detection. In: The Proceedings of the Multiconference on "Computational Engineering in Systems Applications, pp. 72–78 (2006)
8. Terai, S., Ahmed, S.S., Messali, Z.: Comparative study of Video/Image denoising algorithms based on Convolutional neural network CNN. In: 2022 2nd International Conference on Advanced Electrical Engineering, pp. 1–6 (2022)
9. Jiang, Z., Li, C., Chang, X., Chen, L., Zhu, J., Yang, Y.: Dynamic slimmable denoising network. IEEE Trans. Image Process. **32**, 1583–1598 (2023)
10. Kashfolayat, S., Shiri, H., Baniasadi, A.: Denoising task-based functional magnetic resonance imaging data using hybrid deep neural network model. In: 2023 International Conference on Intelligent Computing, Communication, Networking and Services, pp. 34–37 (2023)
11. Lu, D., Zhou, N., Huang, G.: Research on an improved visual background extraction algorithm. In: 2017 12th International Conference on Intelligent Systems and Knowledge Engineering, pp. 1–4 (2017)

12. Pang, X., Peng, X., Lou, Q., Feng, X., Li, Z.: Moving small object detection algorithm based on three-frame difference and improved twice image segmentations in HSV space. In: 2024 43rd Chinese Control Conference. pp. 7369–7374 (2024)
13. Sharma, R.D., Agrwal, S.L., Gupta, S.K., Prajapati, A.: Optimized dynamic background subtraction technique for moving object detection and tracking. In: 2017 2nd International Conference on Telecommunication and Networks, pp. 1–3 (2017)
14. Tang, Z., Miao, Z. Fast background subtraction and shadow elimination using improved gaussian mixture model. In: 2007 IEEE International Workshop on Haptic, Audio and Visual Environments and Games, pp. 38–41 (2007)
15. Hallman, S., Fowlkes, C.C: Oriented edge forests for boundary detection. In: 2015 IEEE Conference on Computer Vision and Pattern Recognition, pp. 1732–1740 (2015)
16. Yun, J., Li, P., Wen, Y.: Contour segmentation using an improved GAC model. In: 2011 International Conference on Multimedia Technology, pp. 508–511 (2011)
17. Zitnick, C.L., Dollar, P.: Edge boxes: locating object proposals from edges. In: European Conference on Computer Vision (2014)
18. Chihaoui, M., Elkefi, A., Bellil, W., Amar, C.B.: Detection and tracking of the moving objects in a video sequence by geodesic active contour. In: 2016 13th International Conference on Computer Graphics, Imaging and Visualization, pp. 212–215 (2016)
19. Xu, C., Wang, F., Zhang, Y., Xu, L., Ai, M., Yan, G. Two-level CFAR algorithm for target detection in MmWave radar. In: 2021 International Conference on Computer Engineering and Application, pp. 240–243 (2021)
20. Lu, S., Sun, X., Ding, F., Li, R.: Robust distributed sonar CFAR detection based on modified VI-CFAR detector. In: 2019 International Conference on Control, Automation and Information Sciences, Chengdu, China, pp. 1–6 (2019)
21. Acosta, G.G., Villar, S.A.: Accumulated CA–CFAR process in 2-D for online object detection from sidescan sonar data. IEEE J. Oceanic Eng. **40**(3), 558–569 (2015)
22. Zhang, X., Pan, W., Wu, Z., Chen, J., Mao, Y., Wu, R.: Robust image segmentation using fuzzy c-means clustering with spatial information based on total generalized variation. IEEE Access **8**, 95681–95697 (2020)

Predicting User Intention as Next Direction in Redirected Walking

Er-Xia Luo⬤, Qiang Tong(✉)⬤, Ling-Long Zou⬤, and Xiao-Tong Liu⬤

Beijing Information Science and Technology University, Chang Ping, Beijing, China
{er-xia_luo,tongq85,liuxiaotong}@bistu.edu.cn

Abstract. How to freely explore virtual space in a limited physical space is a technical challenge in virtual reality technology. In this paper, a new Redirected Walking (RDW) technique based on user intention prediction is proposed. By collecting the walking data of real users, the short-term future walking intention is inferred by utilizing the user's motion characteristics. Then physical trajectory planning is performed based on the user's intention to guide the user's walking. Simulation experiments show that the method can effectively reduce the number of user resets due to collisions with physical obstacles. Based on user experiments with 20 real users, it is shown that the method significantly reduces the number of collision resets while effectively avoiding the strong discomfort of the user in the Virtual Reality (VR) task.

Keywords: Virtual reality · Redirected walking · Interaction techniques · Intention prediction

1 Introduction

With the breakthrough of hardware and software technology, Virtual Reality (VR) technology has been developed rapidly, which gradually changes the way of human-computer interaction and makes VR technology widely used in the fields of socialization, education, and medical treatment. In all kinds of VR tasks, movement is the most basic and common interaction method. Since the virtual space is generally much larger than the physical space, it is difficult to map the user's movement in the physical space to the virtual space in a 1:1 ratio. In order to enable users to walk freely in virtual space, many mobility techniques for VR have emerged, such as invisible teleportation, walking-in-place [9,20,28], omnidirectional treadmill [18], and Redirected Walking (RDW) [23,25]. Among them, RDW is a virtual space roaming technique based on the natural walking of human beings, which mainly utilizes the user's uncertainty of perception to perform subtle manipulation of the virtual camera to change the mapping of the user's movement between the virtual space and the physical space without the user being able to notice it, with the aim of enabling the user to roam the virtual space as infinitely as possible in the limited physical space.

© The Author(s), under exclusive license to Springer Nature Singapore Pte Ltd. 2025
W. Song et al. (Eds.): ICXR 2024, LNCS 15461, pp. 264–280, 2025.
https://doi.org/10.1007/978-981-96-3679-2_18

When applying the RDW algorithm to guide the user's walking, the user's physical trajectory becomes uncertain by the effect of the perceptual gain, which leads to the user's collision with physical obstacles becoming uncontrollable. Some studies analyze the physical place by using Artificial Potential Filed (APF) [27], or by precomputing the reachable poses (position and orientation) in the physical space, and then using the idea of trajectory planning to guide the user to avoid collisions [33]. In order to realize trajectory planning, a virtual target point needs to be introduced to align with the actual physical target point for subsequent trajectory planning steps. The use of intention prediction to calculate the user's future virtual position and thus achieve reliable trajectory planning is a more effective means.

The prediction class RDW algorithm [13] dynamically adjusts the perceptual gain by predicting the user's future virtual pose or walking trajectory to avoid collisions with obstacles in the physical space. The user's future virtual pose is determined by the user's intention, which is affected by the virtual environment in which the user is located. Due to the variability of the virtual environment, if the environment data is directly utilized to assist in determining the user's intention, the model needs to be retrained every time the virtual scene is changed. Some studies have attempted to improve the prediction accuracy by directly utilizing the user's intention, such as judging the user's intention through the user's eye movement data [24,35], and combining the historical trajectory data to predict the user's future position [5]. However, such methods require the use of specific hardware devices, which increases the cost and the difficulty of data collection in practical applications. In this paper, we design a redirected walking method based on user's intention prediction, which predicts the short-term future walking intention by utilizing the user's motion characteristics, and then calculates the user's virtual position, matches this virtual position with the physical position, and realizes the planning of the user's future trajectory to be used for redirected walking. The method uses an ordinary VR headset to collect the user's walking data, which significantly reduces the requirements for hardware devices.

In summary, the contribution points of this paper can be summarized as:

1 A user intention prediction method that can be used in ordinary VR headsets is designed, which improves the applicability of prediction-based RDW algorithms.
2 We proposed an intention prediction-based RDW algorithm, which is able to speculate the user's future virtual position according to the user's intention, and then align with the standard physical position for trajectory planning to guide the user's walking, which solves the problem of the uncertainty of the user's collision with physical obstacles.
3 The algorithm effectively reduces the number of resets generated by the user's collision with physical obstacles, and at the same time effectively avoids the user's strong discomfort in the VR task.

2 Related Work

The concept of redirected walking algorithms [23] was first introduced in 2001 by Razzaque et al. Redirection-aware gain is the basic way to realize redirected walking, where inconsistencies between the user's virtual and physical motion states are achieved through subtle manipulations. Existing research works mainly classify the gains into three categories, including translation gain, rotation gain, and curvature gain [21], and these redirection gains realize the redirection control of the user by changing the user's moving speed, body rotation, and moving direction. By using different redirection gains in reasonable combinations, many redirection walking methods have been proposed to realize the user's realistic walking in a wide range of virtual spaces. However, due to the limitation of the redirection-aware gain threshold, the redirection walking technique is limited in the motion deviation that can be imposed between the user's virtual and physical motions, and the user will still inevitably collide with boundaries and obstacles during roaming, and at the same time, due to the use of gains, the collision has a great deal of uncertainty, and at present, the following types of algorithms are able to ameliorate this problem to some extent.

2.1 RDW Algorithm Based on Physical Environment Analysis

Since heuristic strategies in the past were fixed, they usually could not solve the problem of complex distribution of obstacles in physical space well. Thomas et al. generated a potential field for the whole physical environment in virtual space based on the idea of APF and assumed that places with obstacles have repulsive force on the user, pushing the user to the open space to avoid collision [27]. Later there are some approaches based on reinforcement learning that use neural networks to generate suitable physical goals for the user to guide the user to walk. Chen et al. proposed two greedy strategies, steer-to-farthest and trapezoidal roadmap, which enable the RDW algorithm to adapt to irregular physical environments [4]. Some subsequent algorithms guide the user to a specific physical location and enhance the user-environment interaction through passive tactile feedback or visual cues [14,17,38]. Later Xu et al. used predefined arcs to plan physical paths by analyzing the physical environment [31], but this algorithm lacks some flexibility and is prone to collide with obstacles. Based on this they proposed a new method to navigate the user to a specific physical location using curvature gain [33], but this method only generates a path and does not completely avoid obstacles, and changing the direction of the curvature gain several times increases the user's sense of vertigo, and at the same time, the above algorithm does not take into account the influence of the virtual environment when calculating a specific physical target point. By adding the consideration of virtual targets and making each reset as far away from the virtual target as possible, they succeeded in reducing the number of resets generated by the user's collision with physical obstacles [32].

2.2   Prediction-Based RDW Algorithm

The effectiveness of redirection algorithms based on path prediction can be significantly improved when the accuracy of the user's future virtual path prediction is high. Such algorithms applying predicted path outcomes can be categorized into two groups, short-distance path prediction and long-distance path prediction [22]. Nitzsche et al. first used the user's head-tracking data to obtain the user's expected walking direction, which can provide reliable path prediction within the next few seconds [19]. However, since the user's exploration in virtual space is irrational, in order to solve this problem, previous approaches restricted the layout of the virtual environment to narrow passages to ensure the accuracy of the predicted trajectories obtained. Hirt et al. proposed a new RDW technique for short-term prediction to address this problem [10], which introduces a teardrop shaped trajectory prediction algorithm using Bernoulli bi-nuclei representation to enable it to be application to empty virtual environments. In contrast long-term prediction requires the use of the user's virtual goal information to aid in prediction, i.e., it needs to utilize information from the virtual environment. Zank proposed a skeleton graph search algorithm for redirection planning and potential goal path point prediction [36], which is able to apply previous prediction-type algorithms to large-scale virtual environments. A 2016 study by Gandrud and Interrante found that a user's future directional intention can be obtained from head movements and eye gaze data during motion, providing a theoretical basis for subsequent user trajectory prediction using eye movement data [7]. Subsequent works have introduced neural networks and recurrent networks to improve the prediction of user trajectories by using eye-movement information as auxiliary information [2,24]. Jeon proposed a new algorithm that uses an LSTM model with a combination of the user's spatial information and eye-movement tracking data, to predict the user's future position in virtual space without any assumptions about the preconditions, and to apply these predictions are applied to existing RDW methods [13], a mechanism that significantly reduces the number of resets and increases the distance between resets, improving the effectiveness of existing RDW algorithms.

2.3   Intention Prediction Method Based on Pedestrian Posture

Currently, research related to modeling pedestrian intentions is mainly in the field of autonomous driving. Recent studies have shown that the pedestrian's movements (waving, gazing, etc.) before crossing the road are related to the person's walking intention (whether to cross the road or not). Pedestrian's pose is highly correlated with his/her gait and associated with other data such as pedestrian's head orientation and body orientation. Earlier approaches were mostly based on Convolutional Neural Networks (CNN) [34] and LongShort Term Memory (LSTM) [8] using human skeleton features for action recognition and trajectory prediction, e.g., FangZ et al. proposed monocular vision-based human pose estimation method [6] to predict the intention of pedestrians and cyclists. Zhang S et al. found that using geometric relationship features based on the distance between joints and selected lines outperforms other features [37] and provided a simple general spatial modeling method perpendicular to RNN model enhancement, which further improves the model performance. Recent studies have started to introduce graph structures in human pose estimation tasks, for example, Cadena P et al. developed a 2D pedestrian graph structure and a pedestrian graph network to predict whether a pedestrian is going to cross the road or not [3]. Huynh M et al. proposed the GPRAR model [12], which is based on a graph convolutional network for human pose reconstruction and action recognition, and the model consists of a feature aggregator, the feature aggregation The model includes a feature aggregator, which aggregates learned features such as human pose, action, and position in a channelized manner, and uses an encoder-decoder based convolutional neural network to predict future positions.

Although these methods can predict the intention of pedestrians crossing the road more accurately, the data used for training and prediction are the human skeleton feature data or the image data of a person while walking, which makes the network more demanding on computer arithmetic and more redundant information, and it is not suitable for application on VR headsets. In addition, in the RDW scenario, the user's walking intention is not only whether to cross the road or not, but also contains more complex situations such as turning and stopping. Therefore, this paper attempts to predict more complex user intentions by collecting and analyzing motion data such as user's head direction and walking speed while walking based on the existing algorithms.

3   Methods

3.1   Idea Validation

Data Collection. This paper uses Unity 2021.3.25f to build a 10 m*15 m simulation scene. The simulation scene is a simple painting exhibition with six paintings and two resting benches. In order to collect enough user motion data, seven target positions are set according to the arrangement of the paintings and the positions of the resting benches, and the user needs to follow the prompts to walk to these target positions in a certain order to complete seven kinds of actions: walk straight, turn left/right, pause, turn head to right/left and turn around.

The specific layout of the painting exhibition and the user's walking order are shown in Fig. 1, in which the blue rounded squares represent "paintings", the gray rounded squares represent "resting benches", i.e., obstacles, the red circle represents the target location, and the numbers in the circle are the order in which they appear. The red circles represent the target locations, and the numbers in the circles indicate the order in which they appear. Users will be prompted to "walk towards the red circle" before the start of each mission. When the user reaches the position corresponding to a red circle, the circle turns green and the user is prompted to walk to the next red circle. The red path in the image corresponds to the user's straight forward behavior, the blue path corresponds to the user's turning behavior, and walking to the red circle but not reaching the center of the circle corresponds to the user's stopping behavior. When the user

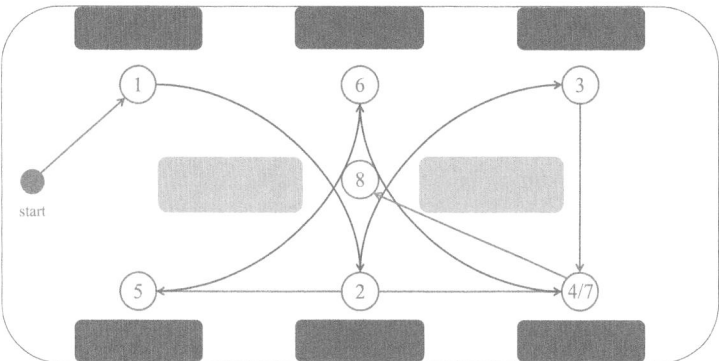

Fig. 1. The layout of the painting exhibition and the user's walking sequence. In the diagram, blue squares represent the "paintings," yellow squares represent the "resting benches," and red circles indicate the target locations, with numbers showing the order in which they appear. At the start of each task, users are prompted to "walk toward the red circle." Once they reach a target circle, the circle turns green, and users are then prompted to walk to the next red circle. The red paths on the diagram indicate straight walking behavior, while the blue paths represent turning movements. Upon reaching the final target circle (circle 8), users are asked to look at a randomly highlighted painting, which triggers head-turning behavior. (Color figure online)

walks to the final target circle (i.e., circle 8 in the figure), he/she needs to look at a randomly highlighted painting, which corresponds to the user's head-turning behavior. If the highlighted painting is located behind the user, it corresponds to the user's turning behavior. The process data of various types of user behaviors are recorded and labeled.

Real motion characterization data were collected using the Oculus Quest 2 from 10 users, 5 males and 5 females, with an age distribution between 22–25, 9 with myopia, and 5 who had used a VR headset. Each user took an average of 2 min to complete a full task, and user motion data were collected at a frequency of 20 Hz.

The data collected had a total of 6 observations, which were the coordinates of the user's position in the virtual space, the rotation angle of the user's head, and the need to standardize the user's positional coordinates in order to reduce the influence of a specific scenario on the data. The user's relative position in the whole scene is obtained as the final positional feature data by dividing the user's positional coordinates collected at each time by the length and width of the virtual scene, respectively.

The user's walking speed, acceleration, rotational angular velocity, the change in position coordinates between every two acquisition time points, and the change in rotation angle were additionally computed using six observations and an acquisition time interval (0.05 s). These nine computed values, together with the six observations, form a 15-dim vector that serves as the user motion characterization data.

Problem Modeling. In this paper, a network model containing three fully connected layers is constructed for extracting the relationship between motion data and user intention. The first two fully-connected layers of the network use the relu activation function with a cross-entropy loss function and Adam optimizer with a learning rate of 0.001, a total of 20 rounds of training, and a batch size of 128. Considering that the walking speed of a real user while wearing the headset is about 1 m/s, the model predicts the results for user intentions after 3 s. Since turning and stopping behaviors do not cause collisions with physical obstacles, the model predicts only the remaining five intentions.

Data Processing. The collected behavioral data of 10 users are divided into training set, validation set and test set in the ratio of 3:1:1. The metrics used for evaluation are precision, recall, and F1-score, where precision is the proportion of samples predicted by the model to be positive cases that are actually positive cases, which measures the accuracy of the model in the samples predicted to be positive cases. Recall is the proportion of samples correctly predicted as positive by the model to the actual number of positive samples, which measures the model's detection rate of positive samples. F1-score is the harmonic mean of precision and recall, which combines the model's accuracy and detection rate. F1-score is a commonly used composite performance indicator, especially for unbalanced category distributions.

Table 1. Prediction effect

State	Precision	Recall	F1-Score
Straight forward	0.9349	0.9497	0.9422
Turn head to left	0.8069	0.7857	0.7962
Turn head to right	0.6768	0.6537	0.6650
Turn left	0.8805	0.8995	0.8899
Turn right	0.9346	0.9340	0.9343

Data Analysis. Table 1 shows the model's prediction effect on five kinds of user walking intentions after 3 s. From the table, it can be seen that the prediction effect of walking straight, turning left and turning right is better, and the accuracy is basically above 0.85. It is worth noting that the accuracy of turning left and turning right is not high. By analyzing the collected data and observing the user's behavior during collection, it can be found that users have a certain preference for turning their heads when looking for highlighted paintings, in which there are more users who turn their heads to the left first to find paintings, so there is a certain chance that the user's behavior of turning their heads in both directions occurs at the same time during the collection of the data, which leads to the confusion of the two behaviors.

3.2 Applications of Intentional Prediction

Calculation of Virtual Postures. After getting the user's future intention, it is necessary to use it for the calculation of virtual bit position. Assuming that the user's current position is (x_s, y_s, z_s), the user's direction is θ_s, the user's future position coordinates are (x_e, y_e, z_e), and the future direction is θ_e, then the user's future bit position can be expressed by Eq. 1.

$$
\begin{aligned}
x_e &= x_s + d * \cos(\theta_s) \\
y_e &= y_s \\
z_e &= z_s + d * \sin(\theta_s) \\
\theta_e &= \theta_s + (d * c)
\end{aligned}
\tag{1}
$$

which d represents the distance traveled by the user. c denotes the curvature of the circular trajectory that the user walks, and these two are assigned values according to different situations. When the user's future intention is to walk straight, there is:

$$
\begin{aligned}
d &= v * \Delta t \\
\theta_e &= \theta_s \\
c &= 0
\end{aligned}
\tag{2}
$$

which v represents the speed at which the user is walking. When the user's future intention is to turn left or right, there:

$$
\begin{aligned}
d &= v * \Delta t \\
\theta_e &= d * c \\
c &= \tfrac{1}{7.5}
\end{aligned}
\tag{3}
$$

This c comes from the commonly used curvature gain threshold of 7.5 m, which is represented by the fact that a user walking along a straight line in virtual space can at most walk along a circular arc with a radius of 7.5 m in physical space without being aware of it.

Aligning Virtual Pose with Physical Pose. After obtaining the virtual pose, it needs to be mapped into the physical space. Firstly, the distance between the virtual pose and the user's current position is calculated, and after obtaining the distance, it is converted to a feasible distance in the physical space using the translation gain. The commonly used translation gain interval ranges from 0.86 to 1.26, which means that when the virtual distance is 1 m, the user's walking distance in the physical space can be within the range of 0.86 m to 1.26 m.

Referring to Xu et al.'s method of discretely dividing the physical space into position points [33], the physical space is sampled at equal intervals every 0.5 m to get the standard positions, and at the same time, each position is decomposed into 12 standard directions at equal intervals of 30°, and finally, the uniformly distributed reachable position points in the physical space are obtained, as shown in Fig. 2a. After that, according to the physical distance obtained from the conversion and the target direction, we find the physical position point with suitable distance and small direction deviation as the target point.

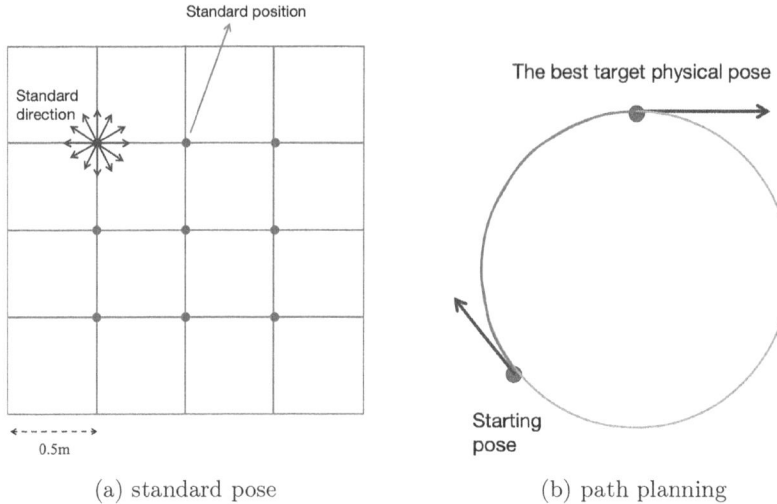

(a) standard pose   (b) path planning

Fig. 2. Schematic diagram of standard pose and path planning. As shown in (a) we sampled the physical space at 0.5-m intervals to establish standard positions. Each of these positions was further divided into 12 directions at 30° intervals. In (b), the blue dot represents the pose point, the green circle shows the path circle with a radius of at least 7.5 m, and the red line indicates the planned path. (Color figure online)

When converting, the distance from the user's current position to the virtual target position is firstly calculated, and two values are obtained after converting using the translation gain, which are the maximum and minimum distances that the user can walk in the physical space, respectively. After that, the nearest physical location corresponding to the user's current location is found, the Euclidean distance between the current physical location and all standard physical locations is calculated, and the standard location with the smallest difference between the distance value and the maximum distance or minimum distance is selected. If more than one standard location point meets the requirements, the one with the farthest distance from the physical location corresponding to the user's current location is selected. After the target location is selected, the target direction needs to be determined. Similar to the previous section, the direction with the smallest difference from the standard direction is selected as the target direction. A complete physical position point for trajectory planning can be obtained by the above steps.

Finally, an arc with a radius of 7.5 m is used to connect the user's start point to the goal point [32] as the user's planning path.

As shown in Fig. 2b, the blue points are the position points, the green circle is the trajectory circle with a radius of not less than 7.5 m, and the red color is the selected planning path. According to the radius of the trajectory circle, the trajectory curvature is calculated and converted into curvature gain, which is used to guide the user in the walking process.

4   Simulation Experiment

4.1   Additional Experimental Details

Similar to many previous approaches [1,15,27,30], in this paper, the speed of the avatar in the virtual space is set to 1 m per second and the rotation rate is set to $\pi/2$ radians per second simulate the motion of a real user in the virtual space. Each path point used to guide the virtualized avatar to walk has a random angle in the virtual space ranging from $-\pi$ to π, and the distance between each path point is in the range of 2 m–8 m.

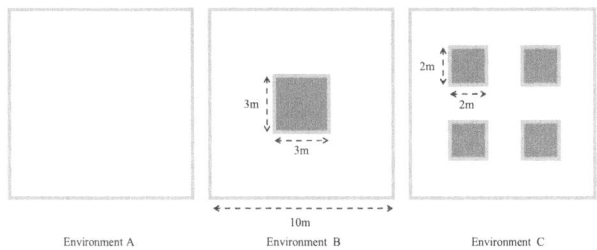

Fig. 3. Schematic diagram of path planning

The physical environments in the simulation experiments use three representative physical environments in the RDW algorithm, which are called environments A, B, and C. As shown in Fig. 3, the three environments are all squares with a side length of 10 m, in which there is no obstacle in environment A, there is an obstacle with a square with a side length of 3 m in the center of environment B, and there are four obstacles in environment C with a square with a side length of 2 m uniformly distributed in the space. At the same time, a reset buffer with a width of 0.5 m was set at all obstacles and the environment boundary.

The virtual environment was set as an open area without any objects. 100 random paths were generated in the whole area, each with 100 path points. Various comparison algorithms use the same 100 paths to exclude confounding factors in the experiment. The avatar needs to walk along each path until it touches all the path points.

The main evaluation metrics are the number of resets and the walking distance between two resets. The fewer the number of resets, the better the redirection controller, because fewer resets means fewer interruptions to the user's task, which is more conducive to safeguarding the user's immersion. The longer the distance between two resets, the better, the longer this distance represents the longer the distance the user can walk completely, also more conducive to safeguarding the user's sense of immersion.

In this paper, OpenRDW [16] is used to conduct simulation experiments, and the comparison algorithms include S2C [11], S2O [11], SRL [26], ThomasAPF [27], Zigzag [23], and a control group without algorithm interference. In case

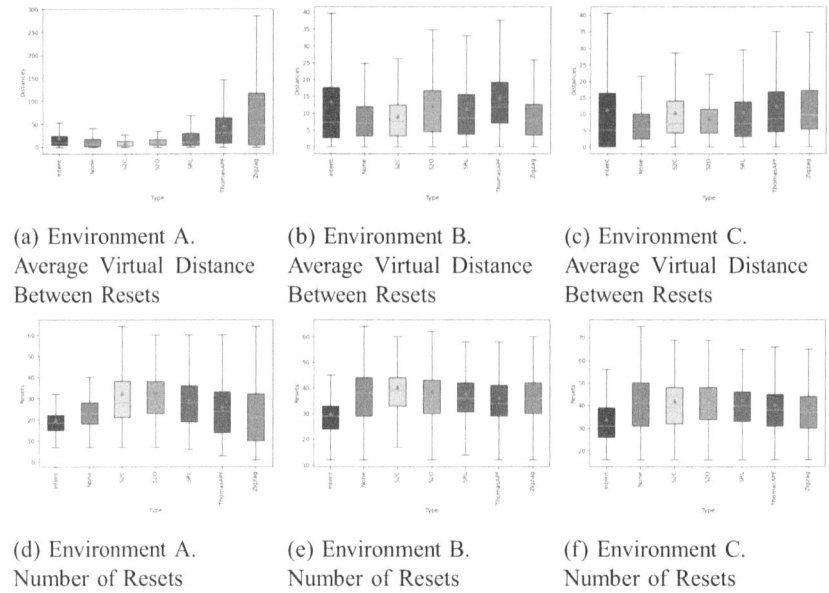

(a) Environment A.
Average Virtual Distance
Between Resets

(b) Environment B.
Average Virtual Distance
Between Resets

(c) Environment C.
Average Virtual Distance
Between Resets

(d) Environment A.
Number of Resets

(e) Environment B.
Number of Resets

(f) Environment C.
Number of Resets

Fig. 4. The box plots of the results of experiments with random paths

the user collides with a boundary or an obstacle, a reset is performed using the 2:1-turn method [29].

4.2   Experimental Results and Discussion

The distribution of the number of resets and the walking distance between every two resets for all the methods in different environment configurations are shown in Fig. 4. It can be observed that the methods in this paper show a relatively significant improvement in effectiveness compared to the existing algorithms in all three simulation experiment scenarios.

In simulation environment A, Intent presents a better effect, and its reset times are significantly reduced compared to None, S2C, S2O and SRL, and compared to ThomasAPF and Zigzag, although the effect is not much different, it is still less than these two algorithms, so Intent shows a clear advantage in the number of resets. Observing the distance between resets, it can be found that the Intent method proposed in this paper exceeds None, S2C and S2O, and is slightly worse than SRL, but there is no significant difference between Intent and SRL algorithms after analysis of variance ($P > 0.05$), and it can be assumed that the effects of both Intent and SRL are comparable. ThomasAPF is more effective in terms of the number of reset times than Intent based on the number of reset times, because it will push the user to the empty area constantly, compared with Intent based on the number of reset times. area, ThomasAPF is more adaptive than Intent in planning according to a specific location, and thus achieves better results.

For simulation environment B, from the analysis of the index of the number of resets, the only method with an average number of resets smaller than that of Intent is ThomasAPF, with an average number of resets of 27.74, which is found to have a low degree of significance after ANOVA analysis ($P > 0.05$), whereas for the other algorithms, Intent shows a clear advantage. From the metric of distance between two resets, for the rest of the algorithms except Thomas-APF, the distance between two resets is less than the Intent method. From the P-value obtained from the ANOVA, the difference between ThomasAPF and Intent is not highly significant ($P = 0.06$), and it can be assumed that Intent and ThomasAPF are equally effective. Therefore, in the simulation experiments in environment B, the Intent method is significantly better than the classical responsive algorithm and has comparable effects with the APF-based algorithm.

For simulation environment C, the overall distribution of the data shows that the number of resets goes up and the distance between resets goes down compared to the other two simulation environments. The reason for this is that the number of obstacles in the scene increases, leading to easier triggering of resets. In terms of the number of resets, the Intent method shows significant improvement compared to all types of existing methods. Analyzing the distance between resets, the Intent method is slightly less effective compared to the ThomasAPF algorithm, but the difference is not high ($P > 0.05$), and it can be considered as having a similar distance between resets. Compared with None method and classical responsive algorithm, there is a more significant improvement ($P < 0.05$).

5   User Study

Experimental Setup. In order to further validate the effectiveness of the method proposed in this paper, 20 real users were summoned, including 12 males, 8 females, and 10 people who had previous experience of using VR. The experiment used OpenRDW to build the scene framework and Oculus Quest 2 as the user headset. The experiment created a forest virtual environment. During the experiment, users needed to keep walking towards the green ball to complete the task. A 5 m*5 m square obstacle-free space was used for the physical space. The specific virtual environment schematic and physical space layout are shown in Fig. 5, where the leftmost side is the virtual scene seen by the user, the middle is the layout of the physical space where the user is located, and the rightmost side is the scene record during the experiment.

In the user's experiment, a total of 10 target points (green balls) were set up, the random distance between neighboring target points was between 2 m–8 m, and the target was generated with a random direction angle between to. It took the user approximately 5 min to complete each set of experiments. The algorithms used for control are None, S2C, and ThomasAPF, so in addition to the experimental group Intent, each user needs to complete three sets of control experiments. In order to verify whether the method in this paper causes motion sickness in users, users are asked to fill in the Simulator Sickness Questionnaire

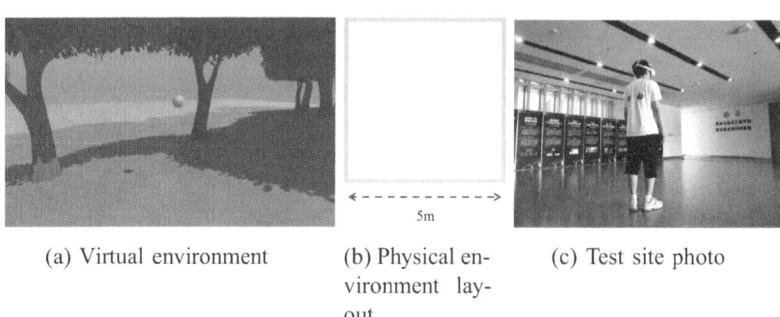

(a) Virtual environment   (b) Physical en-   (c) Test site photo
                           vironment lay-
                           out

Fig. 5. The user study.

(SSQ) in the initial stage of the experiment to record their initial state. To ensure a fair analysis of the level of discomfort caused by each algorithm, users were asked to take a 2-min break after each group of experiments and were asked to fill out the Simulator Sickness Questionnaire (SSQ) after each control and experimental group, and the effect of the group of experiments on the users was assessed by calculating the score of the questionnaire.

To assess the effect of the algorithms, the experiments recorded the number of resets and the distance between each two resets during the completion of the task and analyzed whether the users would experience discomfort during the completion of the task based on the SSQ scores.

Results and Discussion. As shown in Fig. 6, in user experiments, the Intent method proposed in this paper presents better results than other compared methods. Between two resets, the Intent method allows the user to walk a longer distance and also reduces the number of resets generated by the user's collision with the boundary. After analyzing the SSQ questionnaire scores and user interviews, it can be learned that ThomasAPF causes the strongest motion sickness reaction to the user among the methods tested, due to the fact that the algorithm continuously changes the curvature gain value during the user's action, and even flips the direction of the curvature gain several times, resulting in a strong sense of discomfort for the user. In contrast, the Intent method aligns the virtual position with the physical position by predicting the user's intention, which meets the user's expectation when guiding the user to walk, and applies the curvature gain value that is the smallest value that satisfies the current situation, so the user does not have an overly strong feeling of discomfort. As can be seen from Table 2, the Intent method has lower SSQ scores compared to ThomasAPF, which proves that the Intent method does not have a drastic effect on the user in a short period of time.

Table 2. SSQ-score. The first two columns represent the scores obtained from the SSQ questionnaires filled out by the users after completing the test group. The last two columns represent the name of the experimental group and the corresponding SSQ score, respectively.

Pre	Score	Type	Score
Test	8.27	None	7.28
		S2C	12.99
		ThomasAPF	29.14
		Intent(ours)	22.44

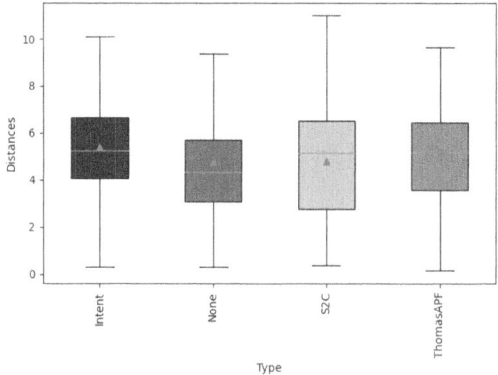

(a) Average Virtual Distance Between Resets

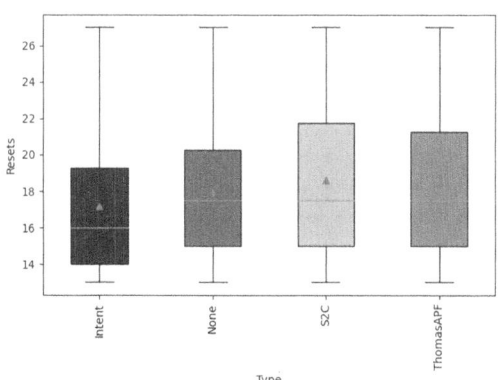

(b) Number of Resets

Fig. 6. The box plots of the results of experiments with 10 random waypoints.

6   Conclusion and Future Works

In this paper, we design a RDW algorithm based on the prediction of user's future intention, which analyzes the current user's motion data to predict the user's walking intention after 3 s, converts the user's intention into the user's possible future virtual pose points after obtaining the user's intention, and then conducts the trajectory planning by aligning it with the standard physical pose points, and finally guides the user to walk. Both simulation experiments and real user experiments show that this method can effectively reduce the number of resets generated by the user's collision with boundaries or obstacles, while not bringing strong discomfort to the user.

In this paper, a shallow neural network is used for user intention prediction, and its performance is constrained by the richness of user data. Improving the intention prediction accuracy by exploring other more complex models may yield more satisfactory results.

Acknowledgments. This study was funded by the National Key Research and Development Program of China (No. 2021YFB2600600), the Young Backbone Teacher Support Plan of Beijing Information Science & Technology University (YBT 202426), 2022 BISTU Scientific Research Fund (2022XJJ21).

References

1. Azmandian, M., Grechkin, T., Bolas, M.T., Suma, E.A.: Physical space requirements for redirected walking: how size and shape affect performance. In: ICAT-EGVE, pp. 93–100 (2015)
2. Bremer, G., Stein, N., Lappe, M.: Predicting future position from natural walking and eye movements with machine learning. In: 2021 IEEE International Conference on Artificial Intelligence and Virtual Reality (AIVR), pp. 19–28. IEEE (2021)
3. Cadena, P.R.G., Yang, M., Qian, Y., Wang, C.: Pedestrian graph: pedestrian crossing prediction based on 2d pose estimation and graph convolutional networks. In: 2019 IEEE Intelligent Transportation Systems Conference (ITSC), pp. 2000–2005. IEEE (2019)
4. Chen, H., Chen, S., Rosenberg, E.S.: Redirected walking in irregularly shaped physical environments with dynamic obstacles. In: 2018 IEEE Conference on Virtual Reality and 3D User Interfaces (VR), pp. 523–524. IEEE (2018)
5. Fan, C.W., Xu, S.Z., Yu, P., Zhang, F.L., Zhang, S.H.: Redirected walking based on historical user walking data. In: 2023 IEEE Conference Virtual Reality and 3D User Interfaces (VR), pp. 53–62. IEEE (2023)
6. Fang, Z., López, A.M.: Intention recognition of pedestrians and cyclists by 2d pose estimation. IEEE Trans. Intell. Transp. Syst. **21**(11), 4773–4783 (2019)
7. Gandrud, J., Interrante, V.: Predicting destination using head orientation and gaze direction during locomotion in vr. In: Proceedings of the ACM Symposium on Applied Perception, pp. 31–38 (2016)
8. Graves, A., Graves, A.: Long short-term memory. In: Supervised Sequence Labelling with Recurrent Neural Networks, pp. 37–45 (2012)

9. Hanson, S., Paris, R.A., Adams, H.A., Bodenheimer, B.: Improving walking in place methods with individualization and deep networks. In: 2019 IEEE Conference on Virtual Reality and 3D User Interfaces (VR), pp. 367–376. IEEE (2019)

10. Hirt, C., Zank, M., Kunz, A.: Short-term path prediction for virtual open spaces. In: 2019 IEEE Conference on Virtual Reality and 3D User Interfaces (VR), pp. 978–979. IEEE (2019)

11. Hodgson, E., Bachmann, E.: Comparing four approaches to generalized redirected walking: simulation and live user data. IEEE Trans. Visual Comput. Graph. **19**(4), 634–643 (2013)

12. Huynh, M., Alaghband, G.: Gprar: graph convolutional network based pose reconstruction and action recognition for human trajectory prediction. arXiv preprint arXiv:2103.14113 (2021)

13. Jeon, S.B., Jung, J., Park, J., Lee, I.K.: F-rdw: redirected walking with forecasting future position. IEEE Trans. Visualizat. Comput. Graph. **31**, 1970–1984 (2024)

14. Kruse, L., Langbehn, E., Steinicke, F.: I can see on my feet while walking: sensitivity to translation gains with visible feet. In: 2018 IEEE Conference on Virtual Reality and 3D User Interfaces (VR), pp. 305–312. IEEE (2018)

15. Lee, D.Y., Cho, Y.H., Lee, I.K.: Real-time optimal planning for redirected walking using deep q-learning. In: 2019 IEEE Conference on Virtual Reality and 3D User Interfaces (VR), pp. 63–71. IEEE (2019)

16. Li, Y.J., Wang, M., Steinicke, F., Zhao, Q.: Openrdw: a redirected walking library and benchmark with multi-user, learning-based functionalities and state-of-the-art algorithms. In: 2021 IEEE International Symposium on Mixed and Augmented Reality (ISMAR), pp. 21–30. IEEE (2021)

17. Luo, E.X., Tang, K.Y., Xu, S.Z., Tong, Q., Zhang, S.H.: Walking telescope: exploring the zooming effect in expanding detection threshold range for translation gain. In: International Conference on Computational Visual Media, pp. 252–273. Springer, Heidelberg (2024). https://doi.org/10.1007/978-981-97-2095-8_14

18. Madigan, R., Williams, D.: Maximum-likelihood psychometric procedures in two-alternative forced-choice: evaluation and recommendations. Percept. Psychophys. **42**, 240–249 (1987)

19. Nescher, T., Kunz, A.: Using head tracking data for robust short term path prediction of human locomotion. In: Gavrilova, M.L., Tan, C.J.K., Kuijper, A. (eds.) Transactions on Computational Science XVIII. LNCS, vol. 7848, pp. 172–191. Springer, Heidelberg (2013). https://doi.org/10.1007/978-3-642-38803-3_10

20. Nilsson, N.C., Serafin, S., Laursen, M.H., Pedersen, K.S., Sikström, E., Nordahl, R.: Tapping-in-place: increasing the naturalness of immersive walking-in-place locomotion through novel gestural input. In: 2013 IEEE Symposium on 3D User Interfaces (3DUI), pp. 31–38. IEEE (2013)

21. Nilsson, N.C., et al.: 15 years of research on redirected walking in immersive virtual environments. IEEE Comput. Graph. Appl. **38**(2), 44–56 (2018)

22. Nitzsche, N., Hanebeck, U.D., Schmidt, G.: Motion compression for telepresent walking in large target environments. Presence: Teleoperators & Virtual Environments **13**(1), 44–60 (2004)

23. Razzaque, S., Kohn, Z., Whitton, M.C.: Redirected walking (2001). https://doi.org/10.2312/egs.20011036

24. Stein, N., Bremer, G., Lappe, M.: Eye tracking-based lstm for locomotion prediction in vr. In: 2022 IEEE Conference on Virtual Reality and 3D User Interfaces (VR), pp. 493–503. IEEE (2022)

25. Steinicke, F., Bruder, G., Jerald, J., Frenz, H., Lappe, M.: Estimation of detection thresholds for redirected walking techniques. IEEE Trans. Visual Comput. Graph. **16**(1), 17–27 (2009)
26. Strauss, R.R., Ramanujan, R., Becker, A., Peck, T.C.: A steering algorithm for redirected walking using reinforcement learning. IEEE Trans. Visual Comput. Graph. **26**(5), 1955–1963 (2020)
27. Thomas, J., Rosenberg, E.S.: A general reactive algorithm for redirected walking using artificial potential functions. In: 2019 IEEE Conference on Virtual Reality and 3D User Interfaces (VR), pp. 56–62. IEEE (2019)
28. Wendt, J.D., Whitton, M.C., Brooks, F.P.: Gud wip: gait-understanding-driven walking-in-place. In: 2010 IEEE Virtual Reality Conference (VR), pp. 51–58. IEEE (2010)
29. Williams, B., et al.: Exploring large virtual environments with an hmd when physical space is limited. In: Proceedings of the 4th Symposium on Applied Perception in Graphics and Visualization, pp. 41–48 (2007)
30. Williams, N.L., Bera, A., Manocha, D.: Arc: alignment-based redirection controller for redirected walking in complex environments. IEEE Trans. Visual Comput. Graph. **27**(5), 2535–2544 (2021)
31. Xu, S.Z., Liu, J.H., Wang, M., Zhang, F.L., Zhang, S.H.: Multi-user redirected walking in separate physical spaces for online vr scenarios. IEEE Trans. Visual Comput. Graph. **30**(4), 1916–1926 (2023)
32. Xu, S.Z., Liu, T.Q., Liu, J.H., Zollmann, S., Zhang, S.H.: Making resets away from targets: poi aware redirected walking. IEEE Trans. Visual Comput. Graph. **28**(11), 3778–3787 (2022)
33. Xu, S.Z., Lv, T., He, G., Chen, C.H., Zhang, F.L., Zhang, S.H.: Optimal pose guided redirected walking with pose score precomputation. In: 2022 IEEE Conference on Virtual Reality and 3D User Interfaces (VR), pp. 655–663. IEEE (2022)
34. Yu, F., et al.: Bdd100k: a diverse driving dataset for heterogeneous multitask learning. In: Proceedings of the IEEE/CVF Conference on Computer Vision and Pattern Recognition, pp. 2636–2645 (2020)
35. Zank, M., Kunz, A.: Eye tracking for locomotion prediction in redirected walking. In: 2016 IEEE Symposium on 3D User Interfaces (3DUI). pp. 49–58. IEEE (2016)
36. Zank, M., Kunz, A.: Optimized graph extraction and locomotion prediction for redirected walking. In: 2017 IEEE Symposium on 3D User Interfaces (3DUI), pp. 120–129. IEEE (2017)
37. Zhang, S., Liu, X., Xiao, J.: On geometric features for skeleton-based action recognition using multilayer lstm networks. In: 2017 IEEE Winter Conference on Applications of Computer Vision (WACV), pp. 148–157. IEEE (2017)
38. Zmuda, M.A., Wonser, J.L., Bachmann, E.R., Hodgson, E.: Optimizing constrained-environment redirected walking instructions using search techniques. IEEE Trans. Visual Comput. Graph. **19**(11), 1872–1884 (2013)

PaintingScapeVR: Exploring Gamified Interaction in Virtual Galleries

Dongning Cai[1], Le Ren[1], Yaqi Chang[4], Xiaodan Li[1,2,3,4],
Yuxin Lin[1,2,3,4], and Junfeng Yao[1,2,3(✉)]

[1] Center for Digital Media Computing, School of Film, School of Informatics,
Xiamen University, Xiamen 361005, China
yao0010@xmu.edu.cn
[2] Institute of Artificial Intelligence, Xiamen University, Xiamen 361005, China
[3] Key Laboratory of Digital Protection and Intelligent Processing of Intangible,
Cultural Heritage of Fujian and Taiwan, Ministry of Culture and Tourism,
New Taipei City, Taiwan
[4] School of Informatics, Xiamen University, Xiamen 361005, China

Abstract. In reality, galleries usually display paintings in a protective manner, partly to delay the damage to the original artwork and ensure the long-term preservation of the artwork. On the other hand, it also hinders visitors' deep appreciation and learning of the artwork. In the face of this challenge, our research aims to provide users with immersive viewing and entertainment, as well as interactive gaming experiences with artwork, through the use of virtual reality technology. So the paper proposes PaintingScapeVR, which is based on a virtual gallery and reproduces the three-dimensional scenes corresponding to different paintings. Visitors can freely explore in this virtual environment and gain a deeper understanding of the meaning and artistic value of artworks through interaction with them. Our results indicate that the reproduction of 3D scenes and gamified interactive design can not only significantly enhance visitors' appreciation of painting art, but also leave a deeper learning impression. This immersive experience stimulates visitors' desire to appreciate and explore, prompting them to actively delve into the background and techniques of art works, thereby enhancing their artistic appreciation abilities. At the same time, this work also demonstrates its potential in enhancing visitors' understanding of painting works, allowing more people to explore the joy of painting and art.

Keywords: Three-dimensional displays · Virtual reality · Interactive gamification

1 Introduction

In the past, traditional galleries played an important role. They are not only exhibition spaces for artworks, responsible for presenting excellent works of art to the public, but also play a key role in promoting art education and cultural dissemination. However, traditional galleries have the following limitations:

© The Author(s), under exclusive license to Springer Nature Singapore Pte Ltd. 2025
W. Song et al. (Eds.): ICXR 2024, LNCS 15461, pp. 281–295, 2025.
https://doi.org/10.1007/978-981-96-3679-2_19

- Physical protection
  Traditional galleries usually adopt protective display measures for paintings, such as adding protective glass and maintaining distance. These measures clearly limit the contact and interaction between visitors and the artwork.
- Passive viewing mode
  Exhibitions are usually dominated by static paintings, which are difficult to stimulate visitors' interest and curiosity.
- Limitations on space resources
  Due to space and resource limitations, traditional galleries typically can only display a limited number of artworks.

With the continuous development of virtual reality technology, the relationship between virtual environment and art dissemination is becoming increasingly close. Virtual galleries provide a new platform for the display and dissemination of art works, enabling them to be carried in a more insightful and interactive way. Virtual environments can effectively attract audience attention and enhance engagement by providing a multi sensory experience, thereby having a positive impact on the travel experience [4,25]. Specifically, it is the use of spatial characteristics, interactive availability, and immersive VR environment with a sense of presence to enhance artistic appreciation and emotional effects [26,28,35].

Our research aims to enhance visitors' art appreciation ability of artworks by improving their interaction with paintings. Art appreciation ability usually refers to an individual's ability to understand, evaluate, and discover the meaning of artworks. The ability to appreciate art includes four dimensions-intelligence, communication, perception, and emotion [8]. Focusing on these dimensions, this study proposes PaintingScapVR on the basis of a basic virtual gallery: using modeling techniques to reproduce the paintings in the virtual gallery in three dimensions, and then organically integrating knowledge such as the meaning of the paintings, artist related information, and historical background into game design. Visitors can interact with the artwork in the game, unlocking detailed information about the artwork and the stories behind it. The interactive gamification strategy adopted in this work is treasure hunting games. Treasure hunting games can effectively stimulate positive emotions among learners [21], and many works in the field of augmented reality have also verified the key role of treasure hunting games in improving the learning experience [14,15].

The paper investigated in an exploratory manner whether there is a potential correlation between gamification of 3D painting scene interaction and users' art appreciation experience. For this purpose, this study collected multidimensional subjective indicators, including user evaluations of scene perception, intellectual game experience, and other aspects. By analyzing these data, we can gain a deeper understanding of users' immersion and art appreciation experience during the visit, and thus evaluate the effectiveness of PaintingScapVR in improving users' art appreciation ability.

Our work demonstrates the following contributions to research on virtual reality, human-computer interaction, and art learning. (1) We have found from related work that treasure hunting games based on virtual technology may contribute to the art appreciation experience of visitors in virtual galleries. (2) We have introduced a novel interactive method called PaingtingscapeVR for virtual galleries, which supports visitors to engage in deep interaction with the displayed paintings. The research results indicate that PaingtingscapeVR can provide a better appreciation experience for visitors. (3) We demonstrate that the design of PaingtingscapeVR can be used in future virtual galleries and can be transferred and expanded to other art education exhibition scenes. (4) Our research emphasizes the importance of interactive gamification in enhancing visitors' art appreciation ability, especially in the context of virtual galleries. We provide design guidelines for researchers and practitioners to explore more effective interaction solutions.

2   Related Work

In this section, we first explore the functions and limitations of traditional galleries in art appreciation. Subsequently, we analyzed the development of virtual galleries and pointed out that they rely on modern virtual reality technology to overcome many limitations of traditional galleries, providing users with richer interactive experiences and immersive art learning environments, thus achieving a wider and deeper dissemination of art works. In addition, we also explored research on gamification in art education. It has gone through a development process from early exploration to systematic application, and then to integration with virtual reality, bringing significant meaning and new opportunities to art education. These studies provide a theoretical basis for the design of this research, helping to determine how to enhance users' artistic appreciation ability and learning effectiveness through the interaction mechanism of virtual reality and gamification.

2.1   Traditional Gallery and Virtual Gallery

Traditional galleries play an important role in art appreciation, mainly reflected in art exhibitions, educational guidance, and cultural dissemination. Traditional galleries provide audiences with a physical space where they can immerse themselves in real art works [30], which is conducive to their observation [1]. In addition, traditional galleries are often equipped with guided tours and display board information, allowing visitors to obtain relevant background information [19]. From the perspective of art education, traditional galleries also play an important guiding role, promoting the cultivation of visitors' artistic literacy [12] and the dissemination of art among a wider audience [5]. However, the display mode of traditional galleries also has some limitations. Traditional galleries usually adopt isolation measures to protect their works, and static displays limit the audience's close observation and interaction, which affects the art appreciation experience [9,13].

The combination of diverse artistic appreciation experiences and advancements in virtual reality technology has led to the flourishing development of virtual galleries. Virtual galleries offer users a higher level of immersion and inter-activity in providing an art appreciation experience [10,16,27,29]. For example, Tussyadiah et al. [33] pointed out that virtual reality can effectively improve visitors' attention and satisfaction with artworks through realistic simulated environments and interactive content. In recent years, the research direction of virtual galleries has gradually shifted from a single immersive experience to enhancing interactivity and personalized experiences [18,34], greatly improving the audience's learning interest and artistic appreciation ability [6,23]. In addition, virtual galleries have become one of the main channels for global audiences to participate in art exhibitions during the pandemic, breaking the limitations of traditional galleries in terms of time and space.

2.2 Gamification of Art Education

Gamification refers to the integration of game like elements such as interactivity, goals, and feedback loops into non gaming environments to motivate and engage learners. In the context of art education, gamification aims to make the learning process more immersive and participatory, enabling students to actively interact with artistic content and historical background [20]. On the basis of gamification, serious games, as a special form of gaming, focus on achieving educational, training, or social awareness goals through gaming experiences. For example, in the context of art education, the game "Artful Escape" combines music and visual art to help students understand emotional expression in artistic creation [32].

In the early stages of research, although the concept of gamification was not yet clear, some educators began to explore introducing game elements into art teaching to enhance learners' sense of participation and motivation [17]. At the beginning of the 21st century, with the development of technology and attention to gamification concepts, game design elements began to be systematically applied in art education [11]. With the advancement of technology, such as the combination of virtual reality and art education, a more immersive art experience environment has been created for learners [7,24,36]. This immersive experience is of great significance for art education. For example, students can use virtual reality technology to enter the historical scene depicted in a famous painting, observe the details of the characters, buildings, and environment in the painting, and better understand the painter's creative intentions and the emotions conveyed by the work [22]. At the same time, this combination also brings new ways and opportunities for the dissemination and display of artistic works. In VR painting reproduction applications, users can browse works as if they were in a real gallery or museum, and gain some unique experiences [31].

However, the gamification of art education currently has certain limitations. In terms of content design, some studies have problems with single content and insufficient depth. For example, some painting learning applications only allow students to imitate the steps, lacking in-depth exploration. Moreover, most painting learning applications have limited interactive methods and lack interactive narrative experiences, making it difficult to meet personalized learning needs.

3   Design and Implementation

The overall design is based on the theoretical support of virtual reality technology and gamified learning, emphasizing the use of multi sensory stimulation and interactive mechanisms to enhance user engagement and immersion. Our goal is to significantly enhance users' engagement and memory effects in art learning by combining virtual environments with interactive experiences, thereby achieving learning outcomes similar to or even better than real-life art appreciation in virtual environments. In this work, PaintingScapeVR provides visitors with a highly immersive and valuable virtual art appreciation platform through multi-level methods such as 3D scene reproduction, free interaction, and gamified design (as shown in the Fig. 1).

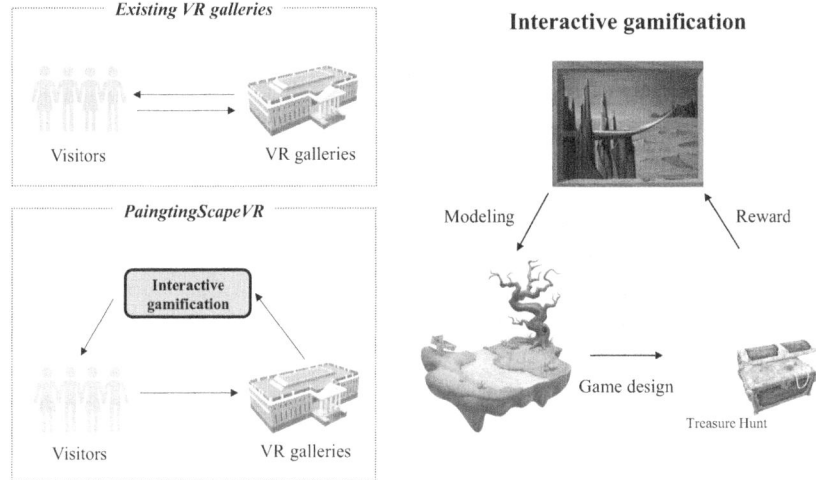

Fig. 1. The architecture of PaingtingscapeVR.

Specifically, based on the traditional gallery model, this study has set up a virtual narrator with the function of explaining painting works. Virtual narrators are free, knowledgeable, and available to serve visitors at any time. Compared to human interpreters, it would be much more convenient. When visitors are interested in a painting, they can choose to trigger entry into the corresponding scene of the painting. In traditional virtual galleries, paintings are simply displayed or scenes are simply recreated. Traditional virtual galleries often lack interactive game designs that are fun and educational. Based on the potential of treasure hunting games to stimulate learners' positive emotions, this study designed corresponding games that combine the deep meaning of painting works. This study provides visitors with a new and more attractive way of experiencing, enabling them to better understand the meaning of paintings during the game process, which is beneficial for enhancing visitors' art appreciation ability and promoting art education.

3.1   Setting of Virtual Narrators

PaintingScapeVR has set up virtual narrators whose responsibility is to provide visitors with detailed introduction about paintings. Virtual narrators have extensive knowledge and the ability to serve visitors at any time, which makes the explanation process more flexible and convenient than before. Meanwhile, virtual narrators play a crucial role in guiding visitors' interactions, greatly enhancing the accessibility and user experience of virtual galleries.

Compared to the high fidelity and more realistic MetaHuman [2], we chose to use the Ready Player Me [3] tool to create a virtual presenter image for this project(as shown in Fig. 2 and Fig. 3). The core of this choice is that this study aims to explore in depth how to enhance visitors' artistic appreciation experience through innovative interactive methods. Although MetaHuman provides extremely high realism and visual details, it also increases the corresponding computational cost. In this specific research environment, the focus is not on the realism of digital human images, but on how they effectively interact with users. In this context, the digital person created by Ready Player Me can maintain real-time interaction and efficient response while meeting basic functions.

Fig. 2. The digital humans created by MetaHuman are very similar to real humans. The expression of details such as skin texture and vivid facial expressions of digital humans is excellent. But these rich details are redundant for virtual narrators.

In this study, we constructed virtual narrators in a virtual gallery using the Ready Player Me platform (see Fig. 4). When visitors enter the display area of a certain painting, two options will be triggered. The options will appear in the form of interactive buttons. When visitors choose to learn about the painting, the virtual narrators will activate the explanation function and provide detailed textual information about the artwork. Another option is to enter the corresponding 3D scene of the painting, which will be detailed in Sect. 3.2. During this process, the virtual narrators will also incorporate certain body movements and facial expressions to make the explanation more vivid and visual, thereby enhancing the immersion and experience of visitors.

Fig. 3. Compared to the digital humans created by MetaHuman, the digital humans created by Ready Player Me shown in the picture have a more cartoonish style. This method effectively reduces computational costs and has almost no impact on the role of virtual narrators.

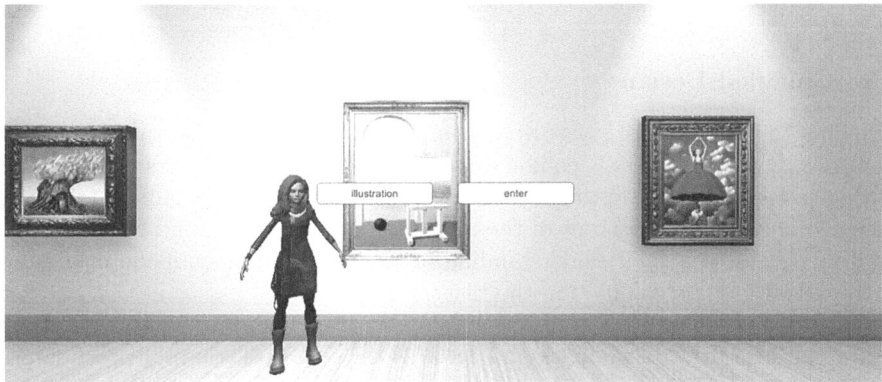

Fig. 4. When visitors walk to a painting, they will see a virtual narrators standing on one side of the painting. At the same time, two interactive buttons will be triggered, guiding visitors to learn in two ways.

3.2 Reproduction of 3D Painting Scenes

When visitors develop a strong interest in a painting, they can choose to trigger entry into the corresponding 3D virtual scene of the painting. To achieve this effect, the system used modeling techniques to pre construct the scene, ensuring a one-to-one restoration of all elements in the painting.

The reproduction of scenes is not just a simple reconstruction of images, but also includes the layout, spatial relationships, and background environmental sounds between objects, etc., to ensure that visitors can experience an atmosphere and details similar to real paintings in virtual scenes. This kind of scene reproduction helps users to have a deeper understanding of the composition and artistic expression in artistic works.

Taking the painting "The Human Condition" as an example (see Fig. 5), we have reconstructed the scene of the painting using modeling techniques in the Unity game engine. All objects in the 3D scene are directly interactive and comply with reasonable physical laws. Visitors can freely interact with all items. In order to further enhance immersion, the project also reproduces the sound of waves in the scene, allowing visitors' visual and auditory experiences to work together and achieve an immersive effect.

In the 3D scene, visitors can pick up and move objects in the scene, freely adjusting their positions and angles. Moreover, the interaction between visitors and specific items such as musical instruments, doors, windows, etc. will trigger sound effects. In addition, the light sources in the scene are constantly changing, allowing visitors to experience the scene effects under different time and lighting conditions, thus gaining a deeper understanding of the use of light and shadow and the aesthetic of composition in the work. This free interactive approach creates an immersive experience, allowing visitors not only to appreciate but also to deeply participate in the world of art.

Figure 6 and Fig. 7 respectively show the other two paintings.

3.3   Gamified Design

Based on the potential of treasure hunting games to stimulate learners' positive emotions, PaintingScapeVR combines gamification design concepts to integrate the deep meaning of painting works into game tasks. These game tasks are designed based on the content of the artwork and the background of the artist. Visitors can deepen their understanding of the themes and symbolic meanings of the artwork while completing the tasks.

Gamified design can not only stimulate visitors' interest and exploration desire, but also provide feedback and rewards through task completion, enhance learning motivation, and encourage visitors to explore art works more deeply, thereby improving their art appreciation ability and overall learning effect.

We have set up a treasure hunt game in the created 3D scene, where collecting fallen fragments based on the meaning of the painting unlocks relevant information about the author, including his life experiences and creative style. We aim to not only enhance visitors' sense of participation, but also stimulate their desire to explore through interactive games. In the paper, we will use three paintings as examples to provide detailed explanations of game design (see Table 1) and demonstrate the overall interactive process (see Fig. 8).

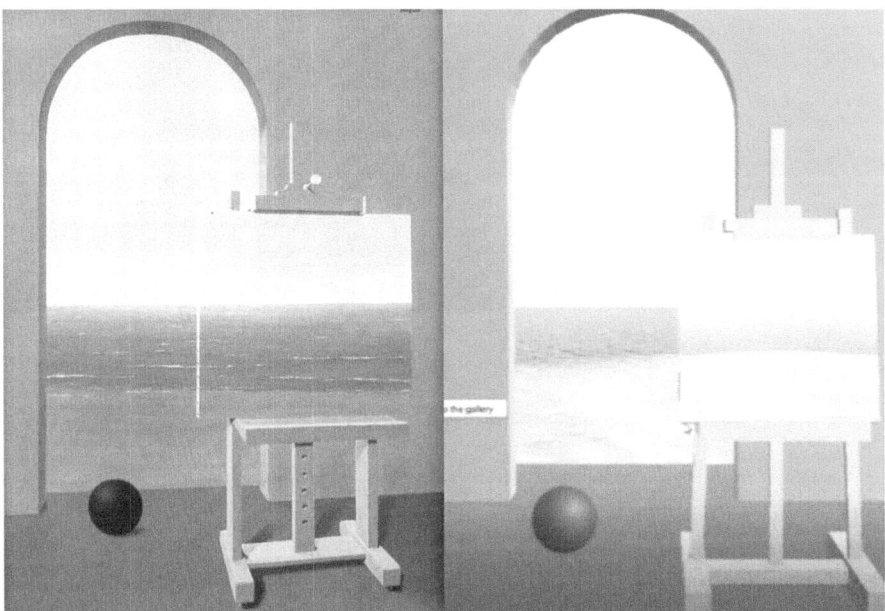

Fig. 5. Painting and scene reproduction of "The Human Condition".

Fig. 6. Painting and scene reproduction of "Listening Room".

Fig. 7. Painting and scene reproduction of "Mysterious roadblock".

Table 1. The meaning and design of the three paintings.

Painting's name	Meaning	Design
The Human Condition	Nothing in this painting is real	Correct fragments is behind the scenes
Listening Room	Hidden things are more important	Discovery of expansion space
Mysterious roadblock	Emphasize objective stimulation	Click on the seemingly abrupt tree

4   Experiment

We have designed a survey questionnaire aimed at exploring in depth whether the interactive experience brought by reproducing three-dimensional scenes of paintings and setting up treasure hunting games can effectively enhance visitors' artistic appreciation ability. The core of this study is to evaluate how gamified interactive elements affect users' sense of participation and artistic understanding ability.

In this experiment, a total of 48 participants were divided into a control group and an experimental group. Because it is common to promote painting learning through scene reproduction, and in order to explore the role of interactive gamification in art education more rigorously in this study, the control group in the experiment experienced PaintingScapVR without game design. Correspondingly, the experimental group experienced the complete PaintingScapVR, which includes interactive gamification.

The first step of the experiment is to provide participants with a detailed introduction to the experimental process, their rights, and data privacy protection. After filling out the basic information questionnaire, two groups of participants conducted different experimental contents. The experimental content of the control group is aimless free visit, that is, participants can freely browse PaintingScapeVR. Participants do not need to complete specific tasks in order to serve as a benchmark for pure scene reproduction. The participants in the

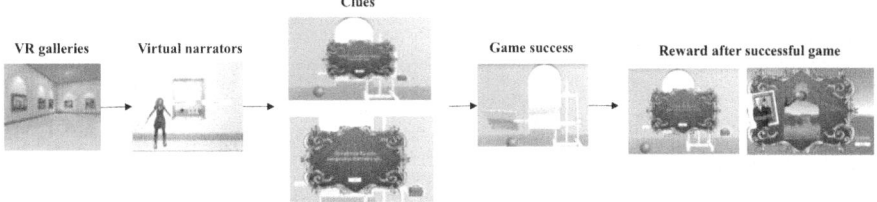

Fig. 8. Using 'The Human Condition' as an example, the process from entering a virtual gallery to winning the game is demonstrated. It showcases the specific interactive interface of PaintingScapeVR and how to provide clues to guide visitors to think.

experimental group will be informed in advance that they need to complete the game in PaintingScapeVR, but the game content is unknown. Explore the effect of interactive gamification design on enhancing user immersion, engagement, and artistic learning outcomes through data from the experimental group. After the experiment, participants will fill out an experience feedback questionnaire to evaluate their immersion, interactive experience, and artistic learning effectiveness in the virtual gallery. Table 2 presents the basic information of the participants. Meanwhile, Table 3 presents the specific content and experimental results of the feedback questionnaire.

There is a significant difference in artistic understanding and appreciation between the experimental group and the control group. The experimental group performed better than the control group in understanding the background of art works, identifying art techniques, participating in art discussions, and expressing comprehension abilities, indicating that interactive gamification design promotes art learning and communication. In addition, the experimental group has also improved in detail observation and emotional perception, which can better pay attention to the details of the work and establish stronger emotional connections. Finally, the experimental group showed the most significant improvement in artistic appreciation ability, indicating that virtual reality and interactive experience can effectively enhance the level of artistic appreciation. Overall, the interactive design of PaintingScapeVR helps enhance participants' understanding and appreciation of artworks.

Table 2. Basic Information of Participants in the Control Group and Experimental Group

Category	Option	Control Group (24)	Experimental Group (24)
Age	Under 18	1	1
	18–24	10	10
	25–34	8	7
	35–44	3	2
	45–54	2	1
	Over 55	2	1
Gender	Male	13	13
	Female	10	11
	Other	1	0
Background	Arts Background	12	11
	Non-Arts Background	12	13
VR Experience	No Experience	9	9
	Some Experience	10	10
	Very Familiar	5	5
Game Experience	No Experience	8	7
	Some Experience	12	10
	Very Familiar	4	7

Table 3. This table lists the specific questionnaire items, as well as the experimental results of the control group and the experimental group. Participants assigned scores from 5 to 1 based on their responses of strongly agree, agree, neutral, disagree, and strongly disagree, with the final average score calculated.

Question	Control Group (24)	Experimental Group (24)
Did PaintingScapeVR help you understand the artwork's context?	3.5	4.2
Could you identify the techniques used in the artwork more easily?	3.3	4.0
Did PaintingScapeVR make it easier to discuss art with others?	3.0	4.1
Did it improve your ability to express your understanding of art?	3.2	4.0
Did you notice more details in the artwork (e.g., colors, brushstrokes)?	3.4	4.3
Did you feel the emotional atmosphere of the artwork more vividly?	3.1	4.2
Did PaintingScapeVR create a stronger emotional connection with the artwork?	3.0	4.3
Do you think PaintingScapeVR enhanced your art appreciation?	3.2	4.4

5   Discussion

To develop PaintingScapeVR into a comprehensive online sharing platform, it's essential to address its current limitations and future research directions.

Firstly, the platform currently faces technological constraints. Moreover, while existing artworks have been effectively reproduced, the content library remains limited. To attract a broader audience, it's crucial to diversify the artwork available, incorporating various styles, historical periods, and cultural contexts.

Although the implementation of gamification has enhanced user experience, the current interactive features are somewhat basic. Future developments should explore more sophisticated interactive elements and personalized experiences to cater to diverse user needs. Looking ahead, cross-platform integration is a key area for research. Integrating PaintingScapeVR with social media and educational platforms can facilitate art appreciation while fostering social interactions through shared experiences and discussions. Future research should also focus on user-defined features, enabling users to create and share their own art exhibitions or gaming experiences.

In summary, by continuously improving technology, content diversity, and user experience, PaintingScapeVR can evolve into a more inclusive and open online art platform. This transformation would promote not only art appreciation but also education and cultural dissemination, ultimately enriching the user experience and fostering a deeper connection with the arts.

6   Conclusion

Through the implementation and analysis of the survey questionnaire, we have come to an important conclusion: interactive gamification design significantly enhances user experience. Participants exhibit a higher sense of participation and immersion during the game, leading to a deeper understanding and appreciation of the artwork.

Feedback shows that the interaction between treasure hunting games and 3D scenes not only enhances their artistic appreciation ability, but also stimulates their interest in exploring art. This is consistent with existing research, where many scholars have pointed out that interactive experiences can effectively increase users' learning motivation and engagement, thereby improving information retention and comprehension abilities.

In summary, this study validates the effectiveness of interactive gamification in enhancing the art appreciation experience and provides theoretical support for future applications in virtual art education and experience design. This discovery emphasizes the importance of combining technology and art, laying the foundation for designing more attractive and educational art experiences.

Acknowledgments. The paper is supported by the Natural Science Foundation of China (No. 62072388), the public technology service platform project of Xiamen City(No.3502Z20231043) and Fujian Sunshine Charity Foundation.

Disclosure of Interests. The authors have no competing interests to declare that are relevant to the content of this article.

References

1. Truner, M.: The Artful Mind: Cognitive Science and the Riddle of Human Creativity. Oxford University Press, Oxford (2006)
2. Metahuman creator (2023). https://www.unrealengine.com/zh-CN/metahuman
3. Ready player me (2023). https://readyplayer.me
4. Allcoat, D., von Mühlenen, A.: Learning in virtual reality: effects on performance, emotion and engagement. Res. Learn. Technol. **26** (2018)
5. Bedford, E.: Art, galleries and education. Aust. Art Educ. **26**(2), 12–17 (2003)
6. Carrozzino, M., Bergamasco, M.: Beyond virtual museums: experiencing immersive virtual reality in real museums. J. Cult. Herit. **11**(4), 452–458 (2010)
7. Chen, X., Gao, Y.: Application and innovation of using virtual reality in art education. In: Proceedings of the 9th International Conference on Education and Management (ICEM 2019), pp. 25–27 (2019)
8. Csikszentmihalyi, M.: The art of seeing: An interpretation of the aesthetic encounter. JP Getty Museum (1990)
9. Dean, D.: Museum Exhibition: Theory and Practice. Routledge, Abingdon (2002)
10. Dede, C.: Immersive interfaces for engagement and learning. Science **323**(5910), 66–69 (2009)
11. Deterding, S., Dixon, D., Khaled, R., et al.: From game design elements to gamefulness: defining "gamification". In: Proceedings of the 15th International Academic MindTrek Conference: Envisioning Future Media Environments. pp. 9–15 (2011)
12. Eisner, E.: The arts and the creation of mind. Lang. Arts **80**(5), 340–344 (2003)
13. Falk, J., Dierking, L.: The Museum Experience Revisited. Routledge, Abingdon (2016)
14. Farella, M., Taibi, D., Arrigo, M., et al.: An augmented reality mobile learning experience based on treasure hunt serious game. In: ECEL 2021 20th European Conference on e-Learning, pp. 148–156. Academic Conferences International Limited (2021)
15. Francese, R., Risi, M., Siani, R., et al.: Augmented treasure hunting generator for edutainment. In: 2018 22nd International Conference Information Visualisation (IV), pp. 524–529. IEEE (2018)
16. Freina, L., Ott, M.: A literature review on immersive virtual reality in education: state of the art and perspectives. In: The International Scientific Conference eLearning and Software for Education, vol. 1, pp. 10–1007 (2015)
17. Gee, J.: What video games have to teach us about learning and literacy. Comput. Entertain. (CIE) **1**(1), 20–20 (2003)
18. Giannini, T., Bowen, J.: Museums and Digital Culture: New perspectives and research (2019)
19. Hooper-Greenhill, E.: The Educational Role of the Museum. Routledge, Abingdon (1999)
20. Huaman, E.M.R., Aceituno, R.G.A., Sharhorodska, O.: Application of virtual reality and gamification in the teaching of art history. In: Zaphiris, P., Ioannou, A. (eds.) HCII 2019. LNCS, vol. 11591, pp. 220–229. Springer, Cham (2019). https://doi.org/10.1007/978-3-030-21817-1_17

21. Ihamäki, P.: The potential of treasure hunt games to generate positive emotions in learners: experiencing local geography and history using gps devices. Int. J. Technol. Enhan. Learn. **6**(1), 5–20 (2014)
22. Kuo, Y., Garcia Bravo, E., Whittinghill, D., et al.: Walking into a modern painting: the impacts of using virtual reality on student learning performance and experiences in art appreciation. Int. J. Hum.–Comput. Interact. 1–22 (2023)
23. Makransky, G., Lilleholt, L.: A structural equation modeling investigation of the emotional value of immersive virtual reality in education. Educ. Tech. Res. Dev. **66**(5), 1141–1164 (2018)
24. Nanu, A., Titieni, A., Nedelcu, M., et al.: Use of virtual reality for artistic education. In: ICERI2013 Proceedings, pp. 47–56. IATED (2013)
25. Plass, J., Homer, B., Kinzer, C.: Foundations of game-based learning. Educ. Psychol. **50**(4), 258–283 (2015)
26. Plass, J., Perlin, K., Roginska, A., et al.: Designing effective playful collaborative science learning in vr. In: Joint International Conference on Serious Games, pp. 30–35. Springer, Cham (2022). https://doi.org/10.1007/978-3-031-15325-9_3
27. Shehade, M., Stylianou-Lambert, T.: Virtual reality in museums: exploring the experiences of museum professionals. Appl. Sci. **10**(11), 4031 (2020)
28. Slater, M.: A note on presence terminology. Pres. Connect **3**(3), 1–5 (2003)
29. Slater, M., Sanchez-Vives, M.: Enhancing our lives with immersive virtual reality. Front. Rob. AI **3**, 74 (2016)
30. Smith, C.: Cultural theory: An introduction (2001)
31. Soltani, S., Harley, D.: Paintings in the age of vr reproductions: examining the design of virtual reality galleries. In: Companion Proceedings of the 2024 Annual Symposium on Computer-Human Interaction in Play, pp. 256–262 (2024)
32. Steam: The artful escape (2023). https://store.steampowered.com/app/
33. Tussyadiah, I., Wang, D., Jung, T., et al.: Virtual reality, presence, and attitude change: empirical evidence from tourism. Tour. Manag. **66**, 140–154 (2018)
34. Wee, C., Yap, K., Lim, W.: Haptic interfaces for virtual reality: challenges and research directions. IEEE Access **9**, 112145–112162 (2021)
35. Wilson, P., Foreman, N., Tlauka, M.: Transfer of spatial information from a virtual to a real environment. Hum. Fact. **39**(4), 526–531 (1997)
36. Yoon, S.: Virtual reality in art education (2010)

SmartDeco: AR for Soft Furnishing Design

Jingyuan Wang[1], Yichun Zhang[2], Ruilong Liu[2], Shiyi Chen[1], Yang Hu[1], and Junfeng Yao[2(✉)]

[1] Beijing University of Posts and Telecommunications, Haidian District, Beijing, China
wjyuan@bupt.edu.cn
[2] Center for Digital Media Computing, School of Film, School of Informatics, Xiamen University, Xiamen 361005, China
yao0010@xmu.edu.cn

Abstract. Augmented reality (AR) is increasingly being integrated into the home renovation sector, yet current AR solutions often fail to address the challenges of soft decoration design. This study introduces Smart-Deco, an AR-based application for the Chinese market, enhanced by large language models (LLMs) to improve user experiences in home decoration. Serving merchants, interior designers, and users, SmartDeco enables AR simulations of soft furnishing combinations, supports collaborative design, and utilizes LLMs to offer real-time design recommendations, addressing potential issues and improving decision-making. User testing demonstrates SmartDeco's effectiveness in enhancing usability, simplifying design processes, reducing errors, and boosting satisfaction.

Keywords: Augmented reality (AR) · Soft Furnishing Design · Large Language Model Application

1 Introduction

With the rapid advancement of Augmented Reality (AR) and its growing applications, AR is bridging the gap between the virtual and real worlds. In interior design, AR is transforming how users approach home decoration [1]. As living standards rise, so do user demands for personalization. Meeting customer expectations has become a key challenge for home decoration companies. This is especially true in China's renovation market, where aesthetics have shifted toward unique, personalized designs, creating both opportunities and challenges.

Research has introduced a domain-specific language model (DSLM), ChatHome [2], which uses large language models like GPT-4, fine-tuned for home decoration. ChatHome has proven effective in providing professional guidance during the renovation process. Building on this, we aim to create a tool that meets personalized user needs while enhancing design efficiency by analyzing current market demands.

© The Author(s), under exclusive license to Springer Nature Singapore Pte Ltd. 2025
W. Song et al. (Eds.): ICXR 2024, LNCS 15461, pp. 296–311, 2025.
https://doi.org/10.1007/978-981-96-3679-2_20

Consequently, SmartDeco utilizes AR technology to enhance the experience of soft furnishing design, allowing users to simulate various soft furnishing combinations in a real-world environment. By incorporating intelligent modes, SmartDeco guides users in making more informed design decisions. This paper first analyzes the current development status and user needs of the interior decoration industry in China, conducting a SWOT analysis to identify the strengths and weaknesses of AR-assisted design software. It then integrates an AR technology platform with large language models (LLMs) fine-tuned for specific domains to provide professional design recommendations. Following this, the Analytic Hierarchy Process (AHP) was employed to determine the task flow of core functions, and a prototype of the AR module was developed. Finally, the usability of the AR application was quantitatively evaluated using the Questionnaire for User Interaction Satisfaction (QUIS) questionnaire, identifying issues encountered by users during actual use and proposing optimization suggestions (Fig. 1).

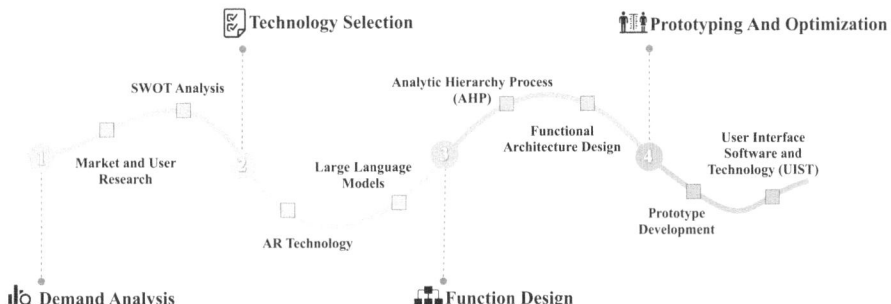

Fig. 1. Research Workflow

2   Related Work

2.1   Effects of AR on Home Renovation Experiences

With the advancement of computer technology, various auxiliary tools have facilitated designers in the home renovation process. Traditional design software, such as Auto CAD, generates detailed floor plans and elevations, enabling clear visualization of space structure and dimensions. This allows for quick and efficient design modifications, enhancing flexibility [3]. In recent years, the practical application of AR technology in home renovation design has grown [4]. AR technology refers to the process of using technology to simulate and overlay physical information that is difficult to experience within certain spatial and temporal limitations, allowing human senses to perceive it in the real world and thus providing an enhanced sensory experience [5]. Research indicates that AR can make learning experiences more engaging, facilitating the realization of ideas [6]. For instance, IKEA's IKEA Place app allows users to view virtual furniture models in real-time through their phone cameras, helping them select the right products and layouts for their spaces [7].

Thus, virtual visualization in home renovation design has become a major trend, not only enhancing user experience but also reducing the costs associated with later modifications. However, how to further simplify and smarten the use of AR technology in interior design remains an area of exploration for researchers.

2.2 Large Language Models in Home Renovation

In recent years, machine learning has been applied across various industries, including home renovation. For instance, some scholars have proposed the application of BP neural networks in modern interior design [8]. Simultaneously, the development of large language models (LLMs) such as ChatGPT [9] has revolutionized natural language processing tasks, showing impressive capabilities across numerous tasks. Some researchers have already integrated LLMs with AR technology, leveraging ChatGPT's interactive conversational abilities to effectively provide content for AR tools, yielding positive outcomes [10].

However, the renovation industry encompasses a wide range of disciplines, such as aesthetics and functionality. It is not merely about recognizing furniture or color palettes; instead, it requires a deep understanding of architectural nuances, spatial design principles, human-centered design considerations, and popular trends [11]. In prior studies, researchers have designed a language model specifically for home renovation, using a dataset of question-answer pairs based on renovation prompts to implement instruction-tuning strategies [2].

Nonetheless, research exploring the application of LLMs in home renovation is still relatively sparse, and the potential synergy between LLMs and modern renovation tools needs further exploration.

2.3 User Evaluations of Tool Products

To compare traditional home renovation design processes with those improved by AR and other intelligent technologies, a quantitative analysis of the usability and user experience of AR applications is essential [12]. The System Usability Scale (SUS) is a widely used usability assessment tool, often employed to gather feedback on the task-oriented usability of AR systems [13]. It is praised for its simplicity, ease of use, quantifiability, and standardization but lacks coverage of other important dimensions such as user satisfaction and functionality. The Software Usability Measurement Inventory (SUMI) offers a comprehensive evaluation of software usability, providing a broader perspective on user experience [14], though its length may reduce user engagement. Additionally, the Questionnaire for User Interaction Satisfaction (QUIS) is designed to assess user satisfaction with software or systems, covering multiple dimensions such as interface, functionality, and learning curve. Many studies use this method to investigate user experience and the effectiveness of tools [15].

Thus, for evaluating the application of AR technology in home renovation design and obtaining user feedback, the QUIS model combined with the Analytic Hierarchy Process (AHP) is a suitable choice.

3   Function Design

This study explores two key research questions regarding improving home decoration workflows:

RQ1: Does AR technology in soft furnishing design improve decision-making and efficiency?

We aim to allow users to preview furnishing combinations in real-world environments via smartphones, enhancing decision quality and optimizing design workflows. We assess whether AR can lead to quicker, more satisfactory design choices and reduce renovation issues.

RQ2: Does large model-based prompt interaction enhance user experience in AR design?

We examine whether large model-based interactions improve user experience in AR furnishing design, focusing on providing professional advice, preventing renovation errors, and enabling real-time communication.

This section details SmartDeco's functional design, including user needs assessment, design goals, functional hierarchy, architecture, and core task processes.

3.1   Demand Survey

Purpose of the Survey: The purpose of this survey is to gain an in-depth understanding of the current development status of the indoor decoration industry in China and to explore opportunities for leveraging AR technology within this sector. Through this research, we aim to analyze the basic knowledge and perceptions of Chinese individuals or interior designers regarding AR design assistance software, as well as to identify the specific needs of the target group for such software. Based on this analysis, we will engage in the design practice of AR-assisted decoration software and contemplate potential directions for future optimization and improvement.

Survey Content

Topics: Key factors users consider in interior decoration design. Challenges faced in the design process. User needs for AR-assisted design software.

Subjects: The survey focuses on individuals with decoration needs and interior designers.

Methods: Literature and Online Review: We review indoor decoration trends and user discussions from Chinese social media to assess the industry's status and the impact of AR technology on it. This forms the theoretical basis for AR-assisted design software.

Questionnaire Survey: Distributed online and offline, the survey gauges users' understanding and needs for AR decoration assistance software.

SWOT Analysis: This study conducts a SWOT analysis for consumer users, as detailed in the table below (see Table 1 and Table 2).

Table 1. SWOT Analysis of Consumer Users

Dimension	Description
Strengths	Saves time and cost by eliminating on-site visits. Users can preview and modify designs at home using AR, with real-time collaboration with designers
Weaknesses	AR models lack realism in lighting and colors, appearing artificial
Opportunities	Feature expansion: Add item removal and rotation functions. Collaborative design: Enable real-time collaboration between users and designers
Threats	Screen-based previews may feel less intuitive, leading to vague communication of design preferences

Table 2. SWOT Analysis of Designer Users

Dimension	Description
Strengths	Reduces time, labor, and communication costs. Collaboration mode allows joint projects with users
Weaknesses	High initial workload in scanning homes and creating models
Opportunities	Enhances communication through AR, allowing a clearer understanding of user needs
Threats	Designers may face challenges conveying intricate details via digital previews

Questionnaire Survey: The online survey collected 131 responses, with 124 considered valuable. Most participants were highly educated female users aged 18 to 45, primarily from first-tier cities in China, with an average age of 20.89 years (SD = 4.79).

Results showed that 96% of respondents value decoration design highly, and around 80% reported a moderate renovation budget (900–1100 RMB per square meter), indicating a preference for cost-effective solutions. Most respondents lived in medium-sized apartments, suitable for AR technology in decoration design. Additionally, 40% had hired professional designers, highlighting the importance of "communication and collaboration" in AR-assisted design applications.

Key challenges identified included a lack of knowledge, inability to preview effects, high design costs, and inconsistencies post-completion. Notably, 96% expressed willingness to try AR-assisted design, suggesting strong market potential.

Desired features in AR-assisted design apps included "customizable model editing" (90%) and "space scanning and modeling" (85%), indicating users' desire to take charge of soft furnishing design while collaborating with designers. Finally, summarizing the results of the needs research, five pain points can be identified: 1) the complexity of the renovation process; 2) difficulty in budget control; 3) home styles failing to meet personal preferences; 4) the quality of renovation materials being hard to control; 5) communication barriers with designers.

3.2   Design Goals

Based on survey results, this study aims to develop an AR-assisted renovation design application to enhance design efficiency and cost-effectiveness. The app will utilize AR technology to minimize time and financial costs, enabling users to conduct preliminary designs at home and view real-time effects of various styles without needing to visit stores.

The application will improve user experience with an intuitive interface, allowing users to change furniture and decoration styles easily and preview designer proposals in AR, facilitating direct modifications without relying on designer explanations.

To combat the information asymmetry stemming from users' lack of renovation knowledge, the app will integrate large language model technology to provide expert advice, helping users select suitable renovation plans and enhancing communication with designers. This collaborative approach will encourage cooperation between users and designers throughout the design process.

3.3   Functional Hierarchy Analysis

Prior to the design of the functional architecture, it is necessary to determine the priority of functions in order to support subsequent design decisions. Summarizing the requirements, the following characteristics were identified:

1. The functional system is complex and includes a multi-level decision-making framework.
2. There are no clear structural features available for direct comparison.
3. Evaluation criteria are intertwined and hierarchically structured, making simple qualitative comparisons difficult.
4. Target values are challenging to define with precision.
5. Functional characteristics are oriented towards the future, presenting a higher degree of complexity for user comprehension.

Based on these requirements, the Analytic Hierarchy Process (AHP) was selected for decision analysis to determine the priorities of our functionalities.

Firstly, a hierarchical structure was established, comprising three levels (see: Fig. 2) the Goal Level, the Criteria Level, and the Alternative Level (or Function Level).

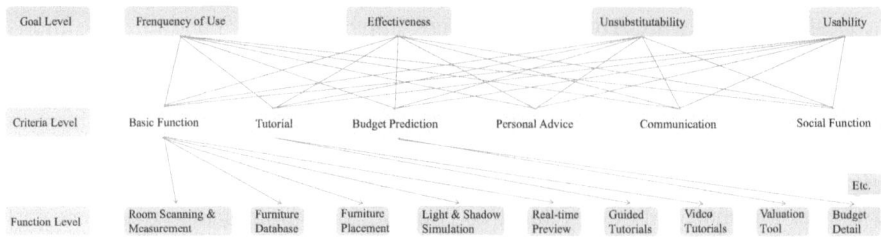

Fig. 2. Hierarchical Structure Diagram

Next, the researchers formed an expert panel consisting of 2 interior design-ers, 8 graduate students in design, and 10 consumer users with experience in interior renovation. Each expert will rate the importance of the functions based on the following criteria(see Table 3). The scoring range is 0–10, with higher scores indicating greater importance of the function. After obtaining the scores, a judgment matrix will be constructed, and the weights of each criterion will be determined by calculating the eigenvector.

Score the criteria(see Table 4) and perform a consistency check to obtain the weights of the criteria: Calculate the eigenvector by summing each column to obtain the weight vector:

Table 3. Criteria Scoring Standards

Criterion	Explanation
Frequency of Use	How frequently the function is used by users
Effectiveness	Whether the function achieves its design purpose and solves users' needs or issues
Irreplaceability	Whether the function is unique and cannot be replaced by other functions or software
Ease of Use	Whether the interface design of the function is simple and intu-itive, and easy to use

Table 4. Criterion Scores

Criterion	Frequency of Use	Effectiveness	Irreplaceability	Ease of Use
Frequency of Use	1	5	3	7
Effectiveness	1/5	1	5	3
Irreplaceability	1/3	1/5	1	7
Ease of Use	1/7	1/3	1/7	1

The weight vector is represented as:

$$\mathbf{W} = [0.4485, 0.3381, 0.1345, 0.0789] \tag{1}$$

Calculate the eigenvalues of the matrix.

$$\lambda_1 = 4.0726 \tag{2}$$

The Consistency Ratio (CR) is calculated using the following formula:

$$CR = \frac{CI}{RI} \tag{3}$$

where: CI is the Consistency Index, RI is the Random Index, which is a predetermined value based on the matrix dimensions.

For a $4x4$ matrix, $RI = 0.9$.

$$CI = \frac{1}{n-1} \sum_{i=1}^{n} \left(\frac{\lambda_i - n}{n-1} \right) = -0.0587 \tag{4}$$

$$CR = \frac{-0.0587}{1.24} \approx -0.0472 \tag{5}$$

Since the CR is less than 0.1, we consider the comparison matrix to be consistent, and the weight distribution is reliable. Therefore, the weights for usage frequency, functional effectiveness, irreplacability, and ease of use are 44.85%, 33.81%, 13.45%, and 7.89%, respectively. These weights can be used to evaluate the importance of each indicator.

Through the consistency check, we determine the results of each function under the first layer for each indicator (Table 5 present the results of each function under the irreplacability indicator):

Table 5. Criterion Scores

	Basic Functions	Teaching Guidance	Renovation Estimation	Renovation Suggestions	Contact Designer	Social Features
Basic Functions	1	3	3	5	5	7
Teaching Guidance	1/3	1	3	5	5	7
Renovation Estimation	1/3	1/3	1	3	5	7
Renovation Suggestions	1/5	1/5	1/3	1	3	5
Contact Designer	1/5	1/5	1/5	1/3	1	3
Social Features	1/7	1/7	1/7	1/5	1/3	1

Similarly, by using formulas (1), (2), and (3) to calculate the eigenvector and consistency ratio, the weights for Basic Functions, Teaching Guidance, Renovation Estimation, Renovation Suggestions, Communication with Designer, and Social Features are found to be 39.52%, 29.76%, 21.43%, 15.48%, 8.33%, and 5.48%, respectively. These weights can be used to assess the importance of various indicators.

Next, the weights of each function at the functional level under the individual indicator level and criterion level are determined through consistency testing.

Here are the weights of each function under the Basic Functions criterion level: Room Scanning and Measurement: 15.8%. Furniture Library: 26.3%. Furniture Placement: 21.1%. Lighting and Shadow Simulation: 15.8% . Real-Time Preview: 21.1%

Next, calculate the overall weight of a specific function (here we present the weight of Room Scanning and Measurement's irreplacability within the entire system).

$$A1 = 13.45\% + 13.45\% \times 39.52\% + 13.45\% \times 39.52\% \times 15.8\% = 19.61\% \quad (6)$$

Calculate the weight of a specific function within the entire system.

$$A = A1 + A2 + A3 + A4 \tag{7}$$

Calculate the weight of all functions within the entire system, and sort the results according to the weight calculation. The results are shown in the Table 6.

Table 6. Sorted Results of Function Weights

Ranking	Function	Weight	Ranking	Function	Weight
1	Guided Tutorial	6.59%	10	Material Recommendations	5.27%
2	Furniture Library	6.50%	11	Color Suggestions	5.26%
3	Furniture Placement	6.41%	12	Style Suggestions	5.15%
4	Real-Time Preview	6.41%	13	Real-Time Communication	4.83%
5	Lighting and Shadow Simulation	6.32%	14	Sharing Function	4.81%
6	Room Scanning and Measurement	6.32%	15	Messaging System	4.79%
7	Video Tutorials	5.94%	16	User Community	4.68%
8	Estimation Tool	5.73%	17	User Personal Homepage	4.65%
9	Detailed Cost Breakdown	5.73%	18	Likes and Comments	4.62%

3.4   Function Architecture

The platform is primarily divided into two main structural directions: the "Designer Side" and the "Consumer Side" (see Fig. 3). The Designer Side allows designers to upload renovation plans and communicate with users to gain a deeper understanding of their specific needs. The Consumer Side encompasses two main components: AR Renovation and Social Mode. Within AR Renovation, there are three sub-modules: Scanning and Modeling, Minimal Mode, and Intelligent Mode.

Scanning and Modeling Module: It enables users to scan their home layout and synchronize information with designers, facilitating the design process.

Minimal Mode: Users can import furniture models to quickly preview individual or complete furniture templates and communicate with designers in real-time.

Intelligent Mode: This mode integrates large model technology, which includes not only a teaching mode that offers novice tutorials through AR visuals but also a budgeting mode that intelligently generates renovation plans based on user-provided information, such as renovation area, budget, and city details, as well as a suggestion mode that provides recommendations based on the residents' body shape indices.

Specifically, the teaching mode utilizes AR visuals to offer novice tutorials, generating easy-to-understand interactive teaching content through large language models. Users can visually see demonstrations of operations within a virtual space and converse with a virtual assistant to inquire about professional knowledge related to renovation. This interactive approach allows users to better understand and grasp the basic concepts and technical details of renovation, enhancing their confidence and proficiency in actual operations(see Fig. 4).

Additionally, the budgeting mode leverages the powerful reasoning capabilities of large language models and their understanding of context to intelligently generate renovation plans that meet user requirements based on the provided renovation area, budget, and city information. The model can quickly assess reasonable renovation strategies based on the parameters provided by the user and guide them in making selections and adjustments through conversation, helping users achieve the best renovation results within their budget constraints.

The suggestion mode also takes advantage of the large language model's capabilities to provide personalized spatial design recommendations based on residents' body shape indices, such as height and weight. For example, based on the user's physical parameters, the model can automatically calculate suitable furniture heights and widths, as well as details such as the positions of doors and windows, ensuring that the design is both aesthetically pleasing and practical.

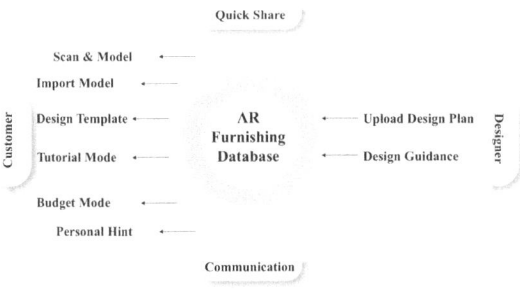

Fig. 3. Enhancing Soft Furnishing Design Experience in AR-based Renovation

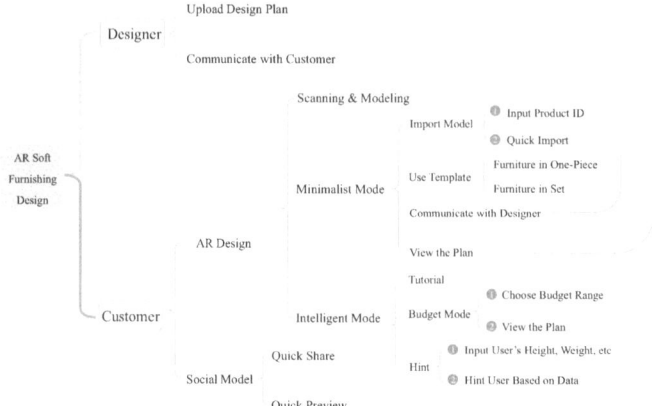

Fig. 4. Functional Architecture

4 Prototyping and Optimization

4.1 Prototype Design

Prototype design is an indispensable part of this research, as it helps to verify the feasibility and usability of the product. The primary goal of prototype design is to identify and address potential issues in the early stages, thereby reducing risks during the development process and enhancing product quality and user experience. The Fig. 5 illustrates the prototype design of the AR section within the app.

4.2 QUIS User Evaluation Questionnaire Analysis

We invited 200 users who are doing home decoration to experience SmartDeco software for free, and conducted QUIS questionnaire analysis on them, and finally recovered 196 valid questionnaires. Using the QUIS user evaluation model tailored for home decoration design, we analyzed a sample of 200 users of the SmartDeco home decoration software. The results are summarized below.

User Profiles and Types

Our analysis of 200 users revealed that 65% are aged between 25 and 45, with female users slightly outnumbering male users at 55%. Approximately 70% hold a bachelor's degree, indicating a relatively high education level. The user base is diverse, with 60% living in large cities, which informs our market positioning. We categorized users into three types based on their needs and usage:

First-time Renovators (40%): Looking for inspiration and design guidance, valuing usability.

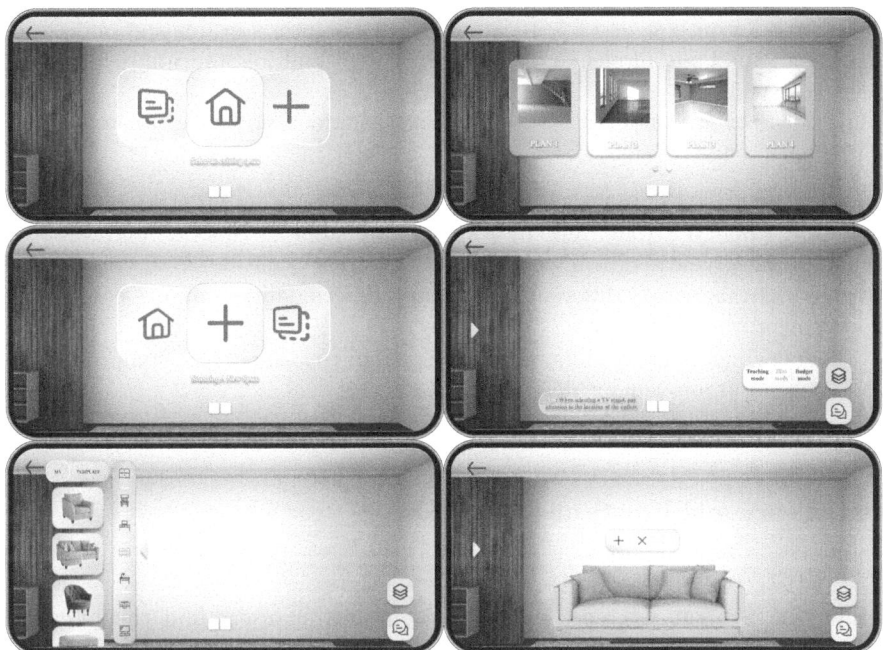

Fig. 5. Prototype Design

Renovation Users (35%): Looking to enhance existing spaces with a focus on details.

Professional Users (25%): Designers and architects needing advanced features. This classification helps us understand varied user expectations.

Dimensional Evaluation Coefficient Description

Here identified 5 key metrics for evaluation(w means weight):

1. User Experience (**UX**, $w=0.25$): Evaluate the overall feeling of users when using the software, including the aesthetics of the page design, the experience of interaction design, the fluency of operating the software, the overall emotional feeling of using the software, etc., with 2 points for each item, the range is 1–10 points.
2. Functionality (**F**, $w=0.20$): Evaluate the completeness and ease of use of various features of the software, including camera functions, design functions, etc., on a scale of 1–10, and collect user suggestions for software improvements.
3. AR Effectiveness (**ARE**, $w=0.25$): Evaluate the intuitiveness and practicability of AR technology in home improvement design on a scale of 1–10 points, and collect users' evaluation and experience of AR effect for evaluation and improvement of core technology.
4. Large Language Model Suggestion Effectiveness (**LLMSE**, $w=0.15$): Evaluate the relevance and practicability of the design suggestions provided by the

large model on a scale of 1–10, and collect the user's evaluation and experience of the large model suggestions for the evaluation and improvement of the core technology.

5. Overall Satisfaction (**OS**, w=0.15): User satisfaction rating, on a scale of 1–10.

By substituting the ratings into the formula, we can compute the comprehensive index, where a higher value indicates greater user satisfaction and software quality. These given weight index with their average scale can be used for comparative analysis across different versions or functionalities, aiding continuous improvement.

The following is the formula used in this paper to evaluate the comprehensive index of home improvement design software:

$$\textbf{Compositeindex} = w_1 \times \textbf{UE} + w_2 \times \textbf{F} + w_3 \times \textbf{ARE} + w_4 \times \textbf{LLMSE} + w_5 \times \textbf{OS} \tag{8}$$

Convenience and Practicality Analysis

Key metrics for user experience include:

1. Interface Design: Average score of 8.5, indicating users find the interface friendly.
2. AR Usability: Satisfaction score of 9.0, showing ease of use.
3. Suggestion Accuracy: Average rating of 8.7, reflecting approval of design advice.
4. Visual Effects: Score of 9.2, with users satisfied with AR display effects.
5. Overall Satisfaction: Average score of 8.8, showcasing software's innovation and practicality.

Overall, 89% believed the software met their design needs and indicated they would recommend the software, praising its innovative use of AR technology. However, about 18% noted some lag in complex scenarios, which could impact their experience. What's more, Users expressed a desire for more design templates and styles in future versions to meet their personalization needs.

Core Technology Evaluation User responses showed high satisfaction with AR technology and large language model integration. Specifically, 85% found AR technology improved visualization and decision-making efficiency, while 78% appreciated the simplification of design complexity through intelligent suggestions. Users felt more confident and satisfied in the design process, with positive feedback on convenience and practicality.

Based on user feedback, we propose the following: Improve response speed in complex scenarios (Optimize Performance); Expand design styles and templates(Diversify Templates); Foster user interactions and inspiration sharing (Enhance Community Features); Provide the latest trends and tips(Regular Updates).

Overall, users express high satisfaction with the SmartDeco software, recognizing its advantages in practicality, convenience, and innovation through AR and large models.

4.3   Optimized Design

Based on user feedback, we propose the following changes:

1. Optimize software performance: Improve response speed in complex design scenarios to enhance user experience.
2. Enrich design templates: Add diversified design styles and templates to meet the individual needs of different users.
3. Enhance community features: Encourage users to share their design examples and build a community of users to facilitate interaction and inspiration sharing.
4. Continuously update content: Regularly push the latest home improvement trends and design techniques to help users maintain sensitivity to home improvement design.

Throughout the user analysis data, users have a high degree of satisfaction with the SmartDeco home improvement design software designed by us, and believe that the home improvement design software with AR technology and large model technology has obvious advantages in practicality, convenience and innovation. Through detailed user profiles and classifications, we are able to better understand user needs, so that we can continuously optimize the product experience in future development.

5   Discussion

This paper presents "SmartDeco", a platform that leverages AR and large model technologies to enhance the soft decoration design experience. It explores the impact of AR technology in the home decoration sector, particularly how it offers a more intuitive and interactive design experience compared to traditional design tools when integrated with intelligent large model prompt systems.

During the research process, we first analyzed market and user survey results to clarify design needs and objectives. We then employed the Analytic Hierarchy Process (AHP) for a detailed weight analysis of various functions, leading to the establishment of the platform's functional architecture. Based on this, we outlined the task flow for core functions and presented the prototype design for the AR module. Finally, using the UIST scale, we measured and evaluated the platform, revealing that SmartDeco excels in enhancing design efficiency and user experience.

In summary, SmartDeco not only provides a novel solution for home decoration design but also lays a solid foundation for the digital transformation of the industry. However, the research has highlighted areas needing improvement, such as optimizing AR modeling technology to enhance model accuracy and interaction fluidity; increasing the accuracy of personalized suggestions generated by large models; and continuously improving the user interface's friendliness and usability to meet the diverse needs of different user groups. Future work will focus on addressing these issues to further enhance the overall performance and user experience of the platform.

Acknowledgments. The paper is supported by the Natural Science Foundation of China (No. 62072388), the public technology service platform project of Xiamen City(No.3502Z20231043) and Fujian Sunshine Charity Foundation.

Disclosure of Interests. The authors have no competing interests to declare that are relevant to the content of this article.

References

1. Sultana, M., Kim, I.S., Jung, S.K.: Deep matting for AR based interior design. In: Frontiers of Computer Vision: 26th International Workshop. IW-FCV 2020, Ibusuki, Kagoshima, Japan, February 20–22, 2020, Revised Selected Papers 26, pp. 31–42. Springer, Heidelberg (2020)
2. Wen, C., Sun, X., Zhao, S., Fang, X., Chen, L., Zou, W.: Chathome: development and evaluation of a domain-specific language model for home renovation. arXiv preprint arXiv:2307.15290 (2023)
3. Fang, X.: Application of computer aided design software in interior design. In: 2021 2nd International Conference on Urban Engineering and Management Science (ICUEMS), pp. 181–184. IEEE (2021)
4. Chen, X.Y., Kanaparan, G.: Arid–an augmented reality mobile application for interior design. In: Krüger, E.L., Karunathilake, H.P., Alam, T. (eds.) Resilient and Responsible Smart Cities, pp. 3–17. Springer, Cham (2023). https://doi.org/10.1007/978-3-031-20182-0_1
5. Kılıç, T.: Investigation of mobile augmented reality applications used in the interior design. Turk. Online J. Des. Art Commun. **9**(2), 303–317 (2019)
6. Omar, M., Ali, D., Mokhtar, M., Abdullah, A.: The use of virtual environment and augmented reality to support engineering education and enhance visualization skills. J. Fundam. Appl. Sci. **10**(6S), 977–988 (2018)
7. Ozturkcan, S.: Service innovation: using augmented reality in the IKEA place app. J. Inf. Technol. Teach. Cases **11**(1), 8–13 (2021)
8. Chen, X.Y., Kanaparan, G.: Arid—an augmented reality mobile application for interior design. In: Krüger, E.L., Karunathilake,H.P., Alam, T. (eds.) Resilient and Responsible Smart Cities, pp. 3–17. Springer, Cham (2023)
9. Liu, Y., et al.: Summary of chatgpt-related research and perspective towards the future of large language models. Meta-Radiology **1**, 100017 (2023)
10. Topsakal, O., Topsakal, E.: Framework for a foreign language teaching software for children utilizing AR, voicebots and chatGPT (large language models). J. Cogn. Syst. **7**(2), 33–38 (2022)
11. Huang, H.C., Perng, Y.H.: Factors influencing the success of communities of practice in the interior decoration industry. In: 2017 International Conference on Organizational Innovation (ICOI 2017), pp. 341–345. Atlantis Press (2017)
12. Lacoche, J., Villain, E., Foulonneau, A.: Evaluating usability and user experience of AR applications in VR simulation. Front. Virtual Reality **3**, 881318 (2022)
13. Brice, D., Rafferty, K., McLoone, S.: AugmenTech: the usability evaluation of an AR system for maintenance in industry. In: De Paolis, L.T., Bourdot, P. (eds.) AVR 2020. LNCS, vol. 12243, pp. 284–303. Springer, Cham (2020). https://doi.org/10.1007/978-3-030-58468-9_21

14. Kulkarni, R.,Padmanabham, P., Sagare, V., Maheshwari, V.: Usability evaluation of ps using sumi (software usability measurement inventory). In: 2013 International Conference on Advances in Computing, Communications and Informatics (ICACCI), pp. 1270–1273. IEEE (2013)
15. Hussain, J., et al.: Model-based adaptive user interface based on context and user experience evaluation. J. Multimodal User Interfaces **12**, 1–16 (2018)

Where Should a Virtual Guide Stand in a VR Museum?

Xinda Liu[1]([✉])[ID], Kun Jiang[1], Jian Wu[2], Lili Wang[2], and Guohua Geng[1]

[1] Northwest University, Shanxi 710127, China
liuxinda@nwu.edu.cn
[2] State Key Laboratory of Virtual Reality Technology and Systems,
Beihang University, Beijing 100191, China

Abstract. In VR museums, where virtual guides play a key role, optimizing their position is critical to enhancing user experience. This paper models the location relationship between relic, visitor and virtual guide through user studies, and introduces the Asymmetrical Mutual Virtual Retargeting (AMVR) method, which addresses challenges related to visual occlusion and multi-user sensory inconsistency. AMVR uses a unique virtual retargeting technique applied to both users simultaneously. The method redirects each user's gaze to the other's guide, while confusing the direction of view and body orientation, so that each user believes everyone is looking at their guide. This approach optimizes the guide's position based on the differing locations of users, resulting in asymmetrical rotational gains during retargeting. By improving the spatial interaction between users and virtual guides, AMVR ensures smoother, more comfortable navigation while maintaining consistent guide presence for all users. Two user studies conducted to evaluate the method demonstrated significant improvements in task efficiency and user satisfaction, particularly in reducing occlusion and enhancing the perception of the consistent guide. Questionnaire results showed AMVR did not increase user discomfort and provided a more intuitive experience compared to other methods. AMVR offers a promising solution for optimizing multi-user interactions in VR museums, providing a strong basis for future research in virtual human-computer interaction.

Keywords: Virtual guide · Rotational gain · Virtual retargeting

1 Introduction

Virtual Reality (VR) museums [16,17] are revolutionizing the way cultural artifacts are exhibited, utilizing 3D visualization and interactive technologies to create immersive digital spaces. These virtual institutions offer a unique platform for the curation and dissemination of cultural heritage, providing global audiences with unparalleled access to historical and artistic collections. By fostering a deeper understanding of cultural legacies, they break down physical barriers

© The Author(s), under exclusive license to Springer Nature Singapore Pte Ltd. 2025
W. Song et al. (Eds.): ICXR 2024, LNCS 15461, pp. 312–328, 2025.
https://doi.org/10.1007/978-981-96-3679-2_21

and offer innovative ways to engage with our shared heritage. Virtual museum guides, interactive digital avatars, are central to enhancing the visitor experience within these VR environments, leveraging augmented and mixed reality technologies to deliver personalized, immersive tours [8,12,15]. These guides enrich cultural exploration by offering tailored educational content and narratives, making virtual museums more accessible and inclusive, particularly in overcoming interpersonal alienation [11] and physical limitations [1]. This expanding role of virtual guides in digital display and cultural education signals a growing focus on museum informatisation and the future of heritage interpretation.

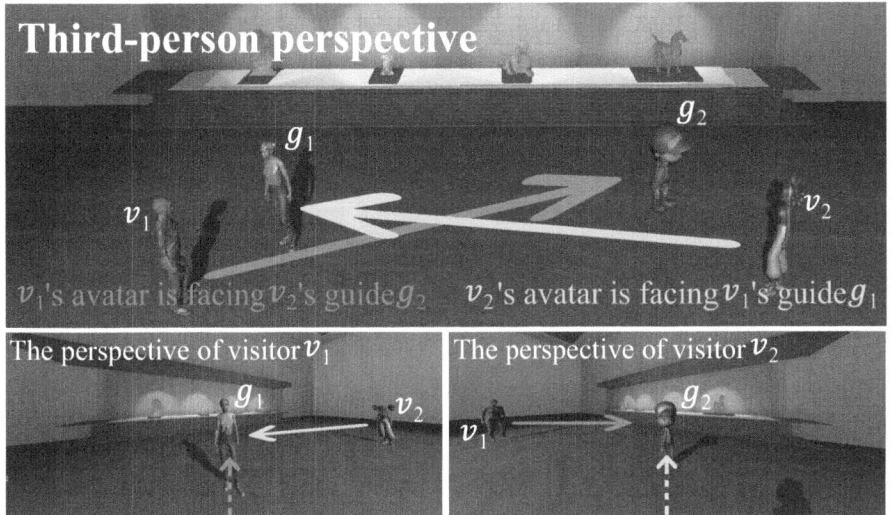

Fig. 1. A schematic representation of the inspirational concept behind the proposed method. The top panel shows the spatial arrangement of two visitors and their respective virtual guides from a third-person perspective. The bottom panels depict each visitor's view: v_1 and v_2 can only see their own guides (g_1 and g_2), preventing visual occlusion. Interestingly, from each visitor's perspective, it appears that the other visitor is looking at their own guide.

Despite advancements, there remains a significant gap in research focusing on optimizing user comfort and natural interaction in virtual museum environments [5,18]. Most current studies emphasize the technical implementation and preliminary user evaluation of virtual guides, often overlooking critical factors that affect overall user experience. For instance, Sylaiou et al. [18] explore the emotional impact of virtual avatars but devote limited attention to practical aspects such as guide positioning, pacing, or interaction tone. Similarly, De Carolis et al. [5] focus on usability, with little consideration for subtler interactions that could enhance user comfort. Ensuring that virtual guides not only deliver accurate and engaging content but do so in a manner that feels seamless and unobtrusive is key to creating an optimal user experience. This shift in focus requires deeper research into the subtleties of human-virtual guide interaction, emphasizing comfort and ease of use alongside technological advancement.

To address these gaps, this study introduces a novel method based on Asymmetrical Mutual Virtual Retargeting (AMVR), designed to improve the spatial relationship between the tour guide and the user, ensuring a more comfortable and intuitive experience. Our approach tackles the occlusion problem inherent to multi-user environments by making each visitor's tour guide visible only to them. Additionally, we address perceptual inconsistencies by implementing rotational gain, whereby each user's sightline subtly redirects its orientation toward the other guide when the user looks at their own guide (Virtual Retargeting). This mutual retargeting process is applied asymmetrically, reflecting the different positions and orientations of the users.

We formalize this problem and propose a feasible solution, evaluating our approach through two controlled user studies. The results demonstrate that our method significantly reduces occlusion, enhances the efficiency of information acquisition, and minimizes perceptual inconsistency compared to existing approaches. Figure 1 illustrates how the AMVR method operates: each visitor sees only their own guide, preventing visual occlusion, while perceiving that all other visitors are similarly engaged with their own guides. This design ensures a seamless and coherent user experience, free from informational clutter.

The contributions of this paper are summarized as follows:

– We introduce a method for generating tour guide positions that prioritize user comfort and spatial coherence, providing a reference for VR museum guide systems.
– We propose an optimized Asymmetrical Mutual Virtual Retargeting method, enhanced by rotational gain, that improves the efficiency of information retrieval and ensures cognitive consistency across multiple users.

2   Related Works

The expansion of VR technology has introduced a new paradigm in museum experiences: the virtual museum. These digital spaces utilize 3D visualization and interactive technologies to offer immersive exhibitions of cultural artifacts, granting global audiences unprecedented access to historical and artistic collections [16,19]. Within this framework, the virtual museum guide has emerged as a critical feature [3], enhancing visitor experience through personalized tours within virtual environments. These interactive avatars leverage augmented and mixed reality to deliver educational content in an immersive manner [8,15].

While research on virtual museum guides has grown, much of it remains focused on technical aspects, such as natural language processing, 3D avatar modeling, and AI integration for responsive behaviors [5,14]. Although these advancements are essential for functionality, they often neglect subtle yet crucial elements of user experience that define comfort and engagement. Current studies frequently emphasize the accuracy of information delivered by virtual guides [20], yet place less focus on how this information is presented to maintain an organic and unobtrusive visitor experience. Key areas requiring further investigation include the spatial relationship between guide and user, guide positioning and orientation, and adaptability to user preferences and behaviors. Sylaiou et al. [18], for example, explore the emotional impact of avatar personas in virtual museums, shedding light on the affective potential of virtual guides, though overlooking how positioning influences user comfort and immersion. Similarly, De Carolis et al. [5] examine virtual agents for museum navigation with an emphasis on system usability, but give limited attention to critical user-guide interactions, such as optimal positioning, distance, tone, and speed for a comfortable user experience.

These gaps are especially evident in multi-user environments, where challenges like visual occlusion and inconsistent perception of virtual guides are more pronounced. Existing technical solutions often lack consideration of broader implications for user comfort and experience quality. In light of these issues, a need exists for research prioritizing the nuanced dynamics of human-virtual guide interaction. Specifically, examining guide positioning, visibility, and behavior is essential to enhance comfort, naturalness, and user experience consistency. Addressing these factors will ensure that advancements in virtual museum guides are informed by a deep understanding of user needs and behaviors, promoting a more accessible and inclusive cultural experience.

3   Method

This section outlines the methodology employed in our research, from the initial pilot study through to the implementation of the Asymmetrical Mutual Virtual Retargeting (AMVR) method. The approach was designed to optimize the spatial positioning of virtual guides and enhance the overall user experience in multi-user virtual environments.

3.1   Pilot Study on Optimal Tour Guide Positioning

In the quest to determine the optimal positioning of virtual guides within a VR museum, we embarked on a comprehensive pilot study. The aim was to understand user preferences regarding the relative positioning of virtual guides, users, and cultural relics, ultimately modeling the spatial relationships between these entities.

Objectives and Hypotheses. The primary objective is to determine whether the virtual guide should be positioned with a focus on the user or the cultural relics. Moreover, according to Dr. Edward Hall's theory of proxemics [6,7], the social distance is delineated as ranging from 4 to 12 ft, which is approximately 1.2 to 3.7 m. This range is typically appropriate for more formal social contexts.

The interaction between a tour guide and tourists, while not always formal, often involves the conveyance of information and a degree of social interaction. Therefore, 1.2 to 3.7 m may be a reasonable distance between the virtual guide and the visitor. This distance can not only respect the personal space of tourists and make them feel at ease, but also enable tour guides to ensure the effective transmission of information and improve the interactive effect. We formulated the following hypotheses:

H0-a. Visitors are more inclined to the virtual wizard should focus on the user.

H0-b. A reasonable distance between the virtual guide and visitor is 1.2 to 3.7 m.

In order to validate these hypotheses, we designed an experimental device to systematically change the direction of the virtual tour guide and the distance from the visitor.

Experimental Setup. The virtual guide was positioned at varying angles and distances to simulate different interaction scenarios. We varied the position of the virtual guide across different angles ($0°$, $15°$, $30°$, $45°$, etc., up to $180°$) and distances (1 to 4 m) with the visitor v placed at a fixed point, as shown in Fig. 2 (a). This setup allowed us to simulate various interaction scenarios and assess user comfort and interaction dynamics with the virtual guide in relation to the cultural relic r. A total of 20 subjects participated in the pilot study. Participants were asked to interact with the virtual environment while the guide was positioned at each of the predetermined angles and distances. Their comfort level, ease of interaction, and overall experience were assessed through a combination of direct feedback and observational analysis.

Results and Analysis. In the course of the experiment, users without exception require virtual tour guides to face themselves, rather than cultural relics or other directions. They also do not pay attention to the relationship between virtual guides and cultural relics, The results support **H0-a**. The experimental results, as illustrated in Fig. 2 (b), revealed a distinct preference among users. The majority favored positions where the guide was angled at $15°$ or $30°$ relative to the user, indicating a preference for direct engagement rather than the guide's focus on the relics. Additionally, the preferred distances for the guide were found to be between 2 to 3 m, striking a balance between intimacy and personal space. This result supports **H0-b**.

Optimal Positioning Area. Based on the collective data, an optimal positioning area was identified, as depicted in Fig. 2 (c). We abstract the relationship between the cultural relics r, visitors v, and the tour guide g into three-tuple (r, v, g). This area, denoted as region A, represents the most favorable positions for the virtual guide g in relation to a single user. The corresponding axisymmetric region A', relative to the user-relics axis rv, solidifies the guide's positioning strategy for an enhanced user experience, and, being in the same situation as A, can also serve as an alternative region.

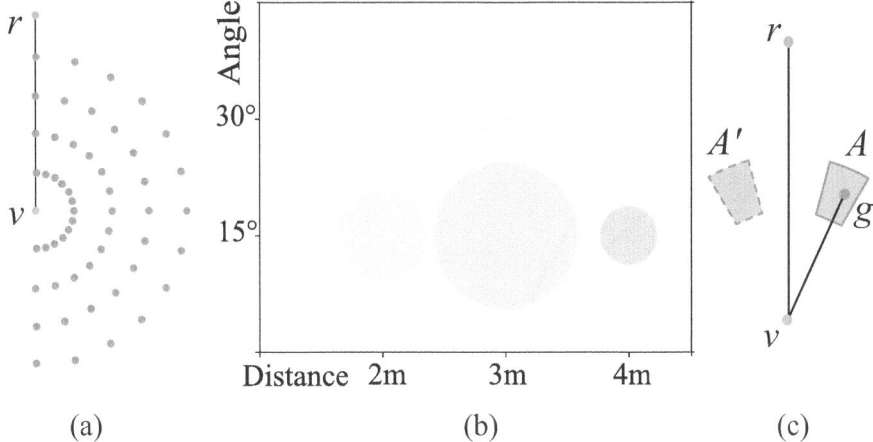

(a)   (b)   (c)

Fig. 2. (a) The experimental design, (b) The experimental results, and (c) the foundational relationship model inferred from the pilot study.

3.2   Guide Positioning and Visibility in Multi-user Environments

The intricacies of virtual tour guide positioning escalate in scenarios with multiple users and their respective guides. This section delves into the challenges and potential solutions for maintaining an effective and non-disruptive guide presence in a multi-user virtual environment. The most critical is the visibility and consistency of virtual guides when multiple users share the same space. We aimed to mitigate the risk of visual obstructions between guides and to ensure a seamless user experience. Figure 3 simulates a multi-user environment where each user is accompanied by a virtual guide. The setup involved two users, v_1 and v_2, each with their guide, g_1 and g_2, positioned in proximity to a central cultural artifact r.

A critical issue arises when the guide intended for one user obstructs the view of another user's guide, as depicted in Fig. 3 (a). Here, the line of sight from v_2 to r is obstructed by g_1, potentially disrupting the experience for v_2. One solution is to render the guide visible solely to its designated user, thus avoiding obstructions. However, this introduces a new challenge: perceptual inconsistency. As shown in Fig. 3 (b), v_2 perceives g_2 but not g_1, which is invisible. When g_1 delivers a presentation, v_2 may notice v_1 facing an empty space, causing confusion. This inconsistency is quantified by the angle γ between v_1g_1 and v_1g_2.

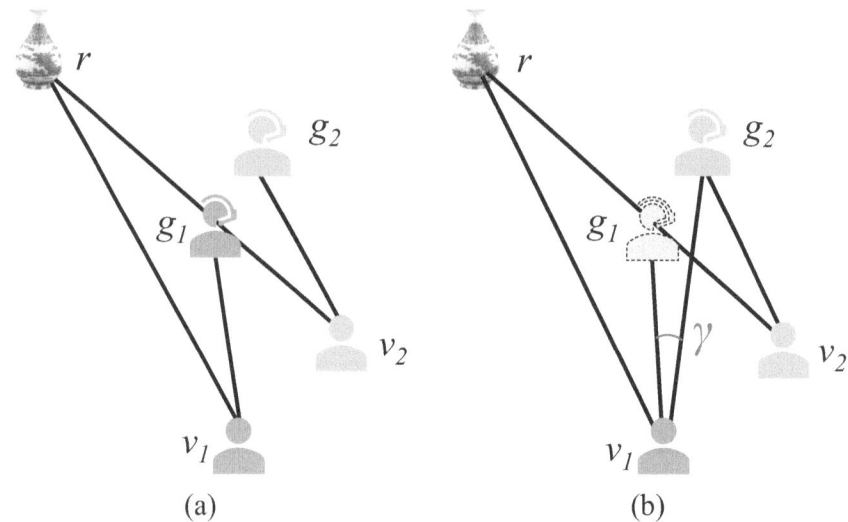

Fig. 3. (a) Demonstrates the occlusion issues that basic methods may encounter in a multi-user environment, (b) A method to reduce occlusion by concealing guides of others, which, however, may lead to cognitive inconsistencies.

3.3 Asymmetrical Mutual Virtual Retargeting for Multi-user Consistency

To address the challenges of guide visibility and user orientation in virtual environments, we introduce an innovative virtual retargeting method that employs an enhanced rotational gain. This method is designed to align the user's viewpoint with their respective guide while simultaneously aligning their body orientation towards the other user's guide, thereby creating a consistent perceptual experience for all parties involved.

Figure 4 shows the basic idea of the proposed method in a possible case. In scenarios where visitors v_1 and v_2 are positioned at fixed locations, the guides g_1 and g_2 are constrained to specific appropriate regions, typically depicted in different colors for distinction. The proposed method leverages the concept of rotational gain to adjust the user's perspective and body orientation. When the user v_1 is attracted by the explanation of the virtual guide g_1, its line of sight turns from the cultural relics r to its own guide g_1, but its body turns from the cultural relics r to g_2. Therefore, from the perspective of v_2, the user v_1 is attracted by its own guide g_2, thus maintaining consistency. Visitor v_1 sees the same way, so as to achieve the effect that both sides feel that there is only one guide, that is, their own guide. At this time, the rotation gain of user v_1 is $k_1 = \beta_1/\alpha_1$, and the rotation gain of v_2 is $k_2 = \beta_2/\alpha_2$.

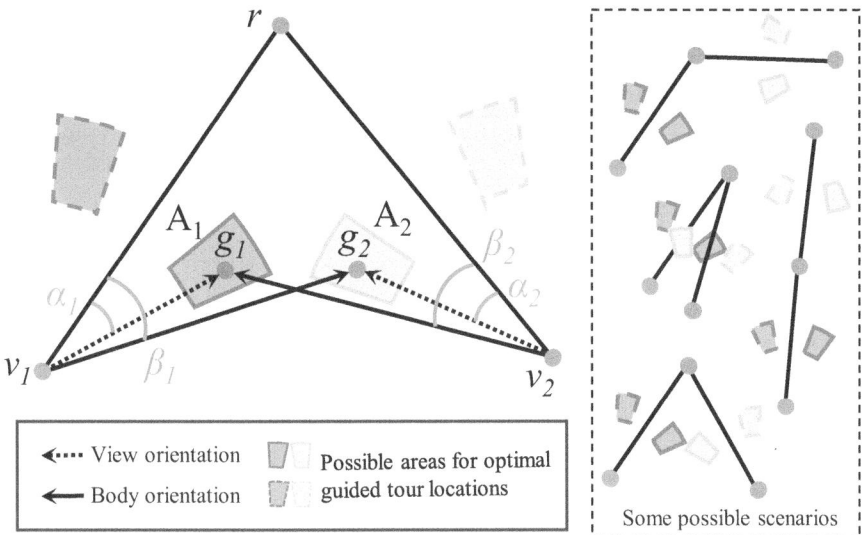

Fig. 4. A schematic diagram of the method

Although the retargeting of virtual objects can be completed by increasing the rotation gain, too large or too small gain ratio will cause the user's rotation speed to be too fast or too slow in the eyes of others, becoming unnatural and affecting the sense of immersion. Therefore, the optimal positioning of the virtual guides g_1 and g_2 is crucial to minimize the rotation gains $\|k_1 - 1\|_2$ and $\|k_2 - 1\|_2$, that is, the whole problem can be formalized as Eq. 1.

$$\begin{aligned} \text{minimize} \quad & F(g_1, g_2) = \omega_1 \times \|k_1 - 1\|_2 + \omega_2 \times \|k_2 - 1\|_2 \\ \text{subject to} \quad & g_1 \in A_1, \quad g_2 \in A_2, \end{aligned} \tag{1}$$

where ω_1 and ω_2 are weight coefficients, which are used to balance the importance of k_1 and k_2 in the overall objective function.

Indeed, there is a complexity of multiple scenarios for different users' stations and corresponding tour guide positions. According to the firstness principle, we adopt a straightforward yet effective strategy to find the optimal positions for g_1 and g_2. The goal is to make g_1 and g_2 as close as possible in their designated areas A_1 and A_2 to reduce the above angles, thereby minimizing perceptual differences.

We analyze the geometric relationships between the guides' positions by connecting the centers of their respective regions. We study the intersection of the line connecting these centers with the regional boundary and divide it into three different situations. When the line intersects two arcs in each region, the positions of g_1 and g_2 can be calculated by Algorithm 1. In cases where the line intersects two straight lines, the positions of g_1 and g_2 can be calculated by

Algorithm 2. The positions of g_1 and g_2 can be computed by the Algorithm 3 in the case where the centre line intersects one arc and one line.

Algorithm 1. Point Selection in the Case of Intersection with Two Line Segments

---

1: **Input:** Line segments SL_1 and SL_2
2: **Output:** Optimal points g_1, g_2
3:
4: Calculate the distance between the endpoints of SL_1 and SL_2.
5: Choose the two endpoints that are closer in distance.
6: Draw perpendicular lines from the two endpoints to the other line segment.
7: **if** Both perpendicular points are on the line segments **then**
8:     Choose the shorter perpendicular segment ends as g_1, g_2.
9: **else if** One perpendicular point is on the line segment **then**
10:     Choose the ends of the perpendicular segment as g_1, g_2.
11: **else**
12:     Choose the aforementioned endpoints as g_1, g_2.
13: **end if**

Algorithm 2. Point Selection in the Case of Intersection with Two Arc Segments

---

1: **Input:** Arc segments AL_1 and AL_2
2: **Output:** Optimal points g_1, g_2
3:
4: Connect the centers C_1 and C_2 of the arc segments to get the connection N.
5: **if** N intersects with both arcs **then**
6:     Calculate the two intersection points as g_1, g_2.
7: **else if** N intersects with only one arc **then**
8:     Connect the center of the intersecting arc with the vertex of the non-intersecting arc.
9:     Calculate the distance between the intersection point and the vertex.
10:     Choose the point with the smaller distance as g_1, g_2.
11: **else**
12:     Calculate the distance between the endpoints of the two arc segments.
13:     Choose the endpoint with the smallest distance as g_1, g_2.
14: **end if**

---

4   Experiences

We initially conducted simulations through automated experiments to preliminarily validate the estimations of occlusion and consistency for various methods. Subsequently, we designed a user study, which involved two tasks to confirm the advantages of the proposed approach.

Algorithm 3. Point Selection in the Case of Intersection with One Line and One Arc

---

1: **Input:** Line segment SL_1 and arc segment AL_2
2: **Output:** Optimal points g_1, g_2
3:
4: Draw a perpendicular line from the center C_2 of arc AL_2 to line SL_1.
5: **if** The perpendicular point is on the line segment **then**
6:     Calculate the intersection point between the perpendicular line and the arc.
7:     Choose the intersection point and the perpendicular point as g_1, g_2.
8: **else**
9:     Calculate the distance between the line segment endpoints and the arc endpoints.
10:     Choose the endpoint with the smallest distance as g_1, g_2.
11: **end if**

4.1 Automated Quantitative Analysis

In this study, we conduct simulation experiments to meticulously evaluate the comparative merits and demerits of various methodologies. The experimental framework is structured around two distinct control groups. The **first control group (CG1)** employs the methodology delineated in Fig. 3 as method (a), while the **second control group (CG2)** adheres to the protocol outlined in the same figure as method (b). The **experimental group (EG)** used the proposed virtual retargeting method.

Probabilistic Analysis of Occlusion in CG1. Our analysis commences with a stochastic generation of two virtual tourists and their respective tour guides within a predefined environment. We establish connections between the tourists and the cultural artifacts, and subsequently ascertain the presence of tour guides along these linkages. This process culminates in the computation of the associated probabilities, which serve as a metric for the efficacy of the masking technique. After nearly 6000 simulations, **the average occlusion probability is 29.61%**. Since users cannot see other people 's guides, there is no occlusion in the EG method.

Quantitative Assessment of Inconsistency in CG2. To assess perceptual dissonance when a visitor observes another seemingly gazing into emptiness, we define 'inconsistency' as the angular discrepancy between the expected and actual gaze directions. This discrepancy is measured when the user's gaze aligns with the two guides, offering a quantifiable index of consistency. Experimental results show an **inconsistency of** $30.87°$. In contrast, the **EG** method eliminates inconsistency due to the effect of rotational gain.

4.2 User Study Settings

Overview and Hypotheses. We designed user experiments to validate the effectiveness of the methodology, encompassing three aspects: efficiency of information access, consistency perception, and comfort. Thus, we formulate the following hypotheses:

H1. It takes less time to finish the information access task with the AMVR method.

H2. The AMVR allows the user to feel that both parties are sharing a virtual guide.

H3. The AMVR method does not reduce user comfort.

Participants and Metrics. We have recruited 35 participants, 20 male and 15 female, between 18 and 35 years old. 6 of our participants had used immersive VR applications before. Participants had normal or corrected vision, and none reported vision or balance disorders. The participants were randomly assigned to two control groups and one experimental group. Task performance is measured by the following objective metrics: (1) **Correctness Rate**, defined as the ratio of the number of tasks completed correctly to the total number of tasks; (2) **Task completion time**, measured in seconds; and (3) **On-time Completion Rate**, the ratio of the number of persons who were able to complete their tasks within the specified time to the total number of persons. We also evaluated the proposed method in this paper by two subjective indicators: (4) **Occlusion rate**, the ratio of the number of people who felt they were occluded to the total number of people, and (5) **Agreement rate**, the ratio of the number of people who felt that they and another person were guided by the same guide to the total number of people. Still, we evaluated the VR experience with three commonly used questionnaires: (6) user task load, as measured by the standard **NASA-TLX** questionnaire [9,10], (7) user perception of the usability of the proposed methodology as assessed by the **SUS** questionnaire [2], and (8) user cybersickness as measured by the standard **SSQ** questionnaire [13].

For the time metric, the EG values were compared to CG1. The comparison was performed using a Mann-Whitney U Test Calculator. In addition to the p value of the statistical test, we also use Cohen's d [4] to estimate the effect size. Cohen's d is a standardized measure of the difference between two groups, indicating the standardized mean difference. In this text, the values of Cohen's d are translated into different qualitative estimates of effect size: Huge ($d > 2.0$), Very Large ($1.2 < d \leq 2.0$), Large ($0.8 < d \leq 1.2$), Medium ($0.5 < d \leq 0.8$), Small ($0.2 < d \leq 0.5$), and Very Small ($0.01 < d \leq 0.2$).

Task Design. We designed two tasks for the user study, Counting Circles on the Wall and Sphere Matching Task, as shown in Fig. 5. In the **first task (T1)**, subjects had to count how many circles were contained in a drawing on a wall from the number of circles contained in it within a time limit, as shown in Fig. 5(a). Tests were conducted in the same environment using different methods. When the counting is complete, the user and the guide are transported to a new random location to start the next round of counting. The size of the virtual environment is 5 m × 5 m. The user is located in the centre of the virtual environment and the painting is on one of the side walls. After several rounds of counting, the task is completed. The task examines the efficiency of the user's access to the overall information under different methods.

In the **second task (T2)**, a 32 cm diameter sphere was generated around the tour guide, while five different coloured spheres of the same size were generated near the wall, and participants had to locate the same coloured sphere and use the joystick to send out rays for pointing, as shown in Fig. 5(b). Again, the task was completed after several rounds of tapping. This task simulates the scenario of finding the corresponding content at the artefacts when the user receives some instructions or information from the guide.

(a)   (b)

Fig. 5. Schematic diagrams of the two tasks: Counting Circles on the Wall and Sphere Matching.

4.3   Results and Discussion

Table 1. Correctness rate results.

Task	Condition	Avg. ± std.dev.	p	Cohen's d	Effect size
Task1	EG	100 ± 0			
	CG1	93.8 ± 12.0	0.09	0.73	Medium
	CG2	95.0 ± 8.9	0.08	0.79	Medium
Task2	EG	99.7 ± 1.1			
	CG1	97.1 ± 4.2	0.01	0.86	Large
	CG2	98.9 ± 2.7	0.09	0.38	Small

Correctness Rate. Table 1 compares Task 1 and Task 2 results across the Experimental Group (EG) and two control groups (CG1, CG2). For Task 1, which assessed visual information processing by counting circles, EG achieved perfect accuracy (100 ± 0%), while CG1 (93.8 ± 12.0%) and CG2 (95.0 ± 8.9%) had lower rates, though not significantly different (p = 0.09 and p = 0.08), respectively. Effect sizes were medium for both CGs. In Task 2, involving locating a color-matched sphere, EG excelled with a near-perfect accuracy (99.7 ± 1.1%), significantly outperforming CG1 (97.1 ± 4.2%, p = 0.01, large effect size). CG2's performance (98.9 ± 2.7%) was closer to EG but not significantly different (p = 0.09, small effect size). Overall, EG showed higher accuracy in both tasks, with Task 2 demonstrating a significant advantage for the AMVR method used by EG, highlighting its effectiveness in complex tasks.

Task Completion Time. Table 2 shows the time (in seconds) taken by different groups to complete Tasks 1 and 2. For Task 1, EG completed the task in an average of **14.4 ± 1.5 s**, significantly faster than CG1 (**25.6 ± 6.0 s**, (p < 0.001), large effect size) and CG2 (**17.7 ± 3.5 s**, (p < 0.001), very large effect size), indicating AMVR's efficiency. In Task 2, EG again showed efficiency with an average time of **29.6 ± 3.7 s**. CG1 was significantly slower (**45.5 ± 9.8 s**, (p < 0.001), huge effect size), while CG2 was closer but still significantly slower (**32.9 ± 5.3 s**, (p = 0.011), medium effect size). Overall, the AMVR method (EG) significantly improved task efficiency in both tasks, with large effect sizes compared to both control groups, highlighting its facilitation of faster interactions in the virtual environment.

Table 2. Time taken to complete tasks, in seconds.

Task	Condition	Avg. ± std.dev.	p	Cohen's d	Effect size
T1	EG	14.4 ± 1.5			
	CG1	25.6 ± 6.0	<0.001*	2.59	Huge
	CG2	17.7 ± 3.5	<0.001*	1.25	Very Large
T2	EG	29.6 ± 3.7			
	CG1	45.5 ± 9.8	<0.001*	2.15	Huge
	CG2	32.9 ± 5.3	0.011	0.72	Medium

On-Time Completion Rate. Table 3 details the on-time completion rates for Task 1. EG achieved an on-time completion rate of **98.8 ± 5.0%**, demonstrating high consistency and effectiveness of the AMVR method in meeting time constraints. CG1 had a significantly lower rate at **45.0 ± 29.7%** ((p < 0.0001), huge effect size), indicating substantial variability and inefficiency. CG2 outperformed CG1 with a rate of **88.8 ± 21.9%** ((p = 0.05), medium effect size), but still fell short of EG's performance. The AMVR method in EG ensured nearly all participants finished Task 1 on time with minimal variation, significantly out-performing CG1 and providing a measurable advantage over CG2. These results support the hypothesis (**H1**) that the AMVR method enhances task efficiency, accuracy, and adherence to time limits.

Table 3. On-time completion rate results.

Task	Condition	Avg. ± std.dev.	p	Cohen's d	Effect size
T1	EG	98.8 ± 5.0			
	CG1	45.0 ± 29.7	<0.0001*	2.53	Huge
	CG2	88.8 ± 21.9	0.05	0.63	Medium

Subjective Perception. Table 4 shows user perceptions of obstruction and guide continuity. In EG, **90.32%** of users felt unobstructed and believed both avatars had the same guide, reflecting a strong sense of continuity with the AMVR method. CG1 had **75%** of users feeling obstructed, likely due to inter-ference with information access, significantly affecting their experience. CG2, despite no obstruction reports, had only **9.09%** believe in shared guide con-tinuity, indicating that visual obstructions alone don't define user experience. Overall, EG's AMVR method enhanced unobstructed interaction and guide con-tinuity, while CG1's obstructions disrupted experience, and CG2 lacked coherent cues, supporting **H2**.

Table 4. Experimental results of users' subjective perception of being obscured and users' perception that the tour guide is the same person.

Condition	Feeling obscured	Believes both guides are the same person
EG	NOT obstructed	90.32%
CG1	75%	-
CG2	NOT obstructed	9.09%

Table 5. NASA-TLX Task Load Index data.

Task	Condition	Avg. ± std.dev.	p	Cohen's d	Effect size
Task1	EG	20.8 ± 13.3			
	CG1	20.0 ± 12.6	0.43	0.06	Very Small
	CG2	17.5 ± 27.8	0.33	0.25	Small
Task2	EG	30.9 ± 15.3			
	CG1	30.3 ± 25.0	0.36	0.03	Very Small
	CG2	30.8 ± 9.8	0.47	0.01	Very Small

NASA-TLX Task Load Index. Table 5 reveals no significant task load differences between EG and control groups across two tasks. In Task 1, EG's task load was **20.8 ± 13.3**, similar to CG1 (**20.0 ± 12.6**) and slightly higher than CG2 (**17.5 ± 27.8**), with non-significant differences (($p = 0.43$) and ($p = 0.33$)). Task 2 saw nearly identical task loads across groups (EG: **30.9 ± 15.3**, CG1: **30.3 ± 25.0**, CG2: **30.8 ± 9.8**), again with non-significant differences (($p = 0.36$) and ($p = 0.47$)). Overall, both tasks showed minimal variation in task load among groups, suggesting that while AMVR may offer benefits like reduced visual clutter, it did not significantly reduce perceived effort.

System Usability Scale Score. Table 6 shows that EG had significantly higher SUS scores for usability in Task 1 compared to both CG1 and CG2. In Task 1, EG scored **80.8 ± 5.6**, significantly higher than CG1 (**68.3 ± 14.6**, ($p = 0.06$), large effect size) and CG2 (**68.0 ± 23.3**, ($p = 0.03$), medium effect size). This indicates a substantially better user experience with the experimental method in Task 1, which involved counting circles. While Task 2 results were not detailed, they suggest that EG continued to show better usability, though with less dramatic differences. Overall, AMVR provided a significantly more user-friendly experience, particularly in simpler tasks like Task 1, and remained more usable in more complex interactions.

Table 6. SUS scores for methods in two tasks.

Task	Condition	Avg. ± std.dev.	p	Cohen's d	Effect size
Task1	EG	80.8 ± 5.6			
	CG1	68.3 ± 14.6	0.06	1.13	Very Large
	CG2	68.0 ± 23.3	0.03	0.76	Medium
Task2	EG	83 ± 6.7			
	CG1	75.4 ± 19	0.07	0.53	Medium
	CG2	70.7 ± 22.7	0.05	0.73	Medium

Simulator Sickness Questionnaire Score. Table 7 details Simulator Sickness Questionnaire (SSQ) scores, focusing on changes within each group. In Task 1, EG saw a slight, non-significant increase in sickness (from **4.5 ± 1.6** to **5.3 ± 1.8**, ($p = 0.2$)), while CG1 remained stable (**3.8 ± 1.1**, ($p = 0.5$)), and CG2 showed no further discomfort with constant scores (**7.8 ± 5.3**, ($p = 0.5$)). For Task 2, EG maintained stable sickness levels (**3.2 ± 0.4**, ($p = 0.5$)), CG1 showed a non-significant increase (**5.2 ± 3.7** to **8.2 ± 6.9**, ($p = 0.18$)), and CG2 experienced a non-significant decrease (**7.0 ± 8.4** to **5.0 ± 2.9**, ($p = 0.19$)). Overall, EG showed minimal increase in simulator sickness in both tasks, suggesting the AMVR method did not significantly add discomfort. CG1's increase in Task 2 and CG2's adaptation suggest varying impacts of traditional methods. None of these changes were statistically significant, supporting **H3**.

Table 7. Simulator Sickness Questionnaire score.

Task	Condition	PREAvg. ± PREstd.dev.	POSTAvg. ± POSTstd.dev.	p
Task1	EG	4.5 ± 1.6	5.3 ± 1.8	0.2
	CG1	3.8 ± 1.1	3.8 ± 1.1	0.5
	CG2	7.8 ± 5.3	7.8 ± 5.3	0.5
Task2	EG	3.2 ± 0.4	3.2 ± 0.4	0.5
	CG1	5.2 ± 3.7	8.2 ± 6.9	0.18
	CG2	7.0 ± 8.4	5.0 ± 2.9	0.19

5 Conclusion

The present study sought to address the pivotal yet understudied issue of determining the optimal position for virtual tour guides in VR museums, with the aim of enhancing user experience through reduced occlusion and improved multi-user sensory consistency. The development and evaluation of the Asymmetrical Mutual Virtual Retargeting (AMVR) method address key challenges related to user comfort, efficiency, and consistency, offering a promising solution for enhancing the multi-user VR museum experience. The findings of this study provide a solid foundation for further research and development aimed at refining the AMVR method and expanding its application to other domains of virtual human-computer interaction.

Acknowledgement. This work is supported by the National Natural Science Foundation of China through Project 62271393, by Technology Innovation Leading Project of Shaanxi (2024QY-SZX-11), by Science and Technology Planning Project of Xi'an (2024JH-CXSF-0014), by the Open Project Program of State Key Laboratory of Virtual Reality Technology and Systems, Beihang University (No.VRLAB2024C02).

References

1. Atienza, J.M.A., Hilario, S.M., Lopez, N.E., Pagara, J.J.T., Gamoso, R.A., et al.: The virtual tour guides on tourists' satisfaction: role of sense of presence. In: European Proceedings of Social and Behavioural Sciences (2024)
2. Brooke, J.: Sus: a quick and dirty usability scale. Usabil. Eval. Ind. **189**, 4–7 (1996)
3. Cannavò, A., Pacchiotti, S., Retta, N., Terzoli, M., Spallone, R., Lamberti, F.: Passive haptics and conversational avatars for interacting with ancient Egypt remains in high-fidelity virtual reality experiences. ACM J. Comput. Cult. Herit. **17**(2), 1–28 (2024)
4. Cohen, J.: Statistical Power Analysis for the Behavioral Sciences. Routledge, Abingdon (2013)
5. De Carolis, B., Macchiarulo, N., Valenziano, C.: Marta: a virtual guide for the national archaeological museum of taranto. In: AVI²CH (2022)
6. Hall, E.T.: A system for the notation of proxemic behavior. Am. Anthropol. **65**(5), 1003–1026 (1963)

7. Hall, E.T.: The silent language. Anchor (1973)

8. Hammady, R., Ma, M., Al-Kalha, Z., Strathearn, C.: A framework for constructing and evaluating the role of mr as a holographic virtual guide in museums. Virt. Real. **25**(4), 895–918 (2021)

9. Hart, S.G.: Nasa-task load index (nasa-tlx); 20 years later. In: Proceedings of the human Factors and Ergonomics Society Annual Meeting, vol. 50, pp. 904–908. Sage publications Sage CA, Los Angeles (2006)

10. Hart, S.: Development of nasa-tlx (task load index): Results of empirical and theoretical research. Human mental workload/Elsevier (1988)

11. Hu, Q., Liu, Q., Wang, Z.: Meaning in life as a mediator between interpersonal alienation and smartphone addiction in the context of covid-19: a three-wave longitudinal study. Comput. Hum. Behav. **127**, 107058 (2022)

12. Katsarou, E., Wild, F., Sougari, A.M., Chatzipanagiotou, P.: A systematic review of voice-based intelligent virtual agents in efl education. Int. J. Emerg. Technol. Learn. (iJET) **18**(10), 65–85 (2023)

13. Kennedy, R.S., Lane, N.E., Berbaum, K.S., Lilienthal, M.G.: Simulator sickness questionnaire: an enhanced method for quantifying simulator sickness. Int. J. Aviat. Psychol. **3**(3), 203–220 (1993)

14. Liu, S., Hao, F.: Engaging with avatar in virtual regenerative tourism. J. Travel Tour. Mark. **41**(6), 864–879 (2024)

15. Rzayev, R., Karaman, G., Henze, N., Schwind, V.: Fostering virtual guide in exhibitions. In: Proceedings of the 21st International Conference on Human-Computer Interaction with Mobile Devices and Services, pp. 1–6 (2019)

16. Shehade, M., Stylianou-Lambert, T.: Virtual reality in museums: exploring the experiences of museum professionals. Appl. Sci. **10**(11), 4031 (2020)

17. Styliani, S., Fotis, L., Kostas, K., Petros, P.: Virtual museums, a survey and some issues for consideration. J. Cult. Herit. **10**(4), 520–528 (2009)

18. Sylaiou, S., Kasapakis, V., Gavalas, D., Dzardanova, E.: Avatars as storytellers: affective narratives in virtual museums. Pers. Ubiq. Comput. **24**, 829–841 (2020)

19. Testón, A.M., Muñoz, A.: Digital avatars as humanized museum guides in the convergence of extended reality. In: Proceedings of the MW21 Conference (2021)

20. Zhang, H.: Prism xr–a curated exhibition experience in virtual reality with peer annotation features and virtual guides for art and archaeology classes. arXiv preprint arXiv:2407.09528 (2024)

Author Index

© The Editor(s) (if applicable) and The Author(s), under exclusive license
to Springer Nature Singapore Pte Ltd. 2025
W. Song et al. (Eds.): ICXR 2024, LNCS 15461, pp. 329–330, 2025.
https://doi.org/10.1007/978-981-96-3679-2

The manufacturer's authorised representative in the EU is Springer
Nature Customer Service Centre GmbH, Europaplatz 3, 69115 Heidelberg,
Germany. If you have any concerns regarding our products, please
contact ProductSafety@springernature.com

Printed and bound by CPI Group (UK) Ltd, Croydon, CR0 4YY
27/04/2026
02097586-0007